■ **droppin'
science**

■

■

■

■

■

■

in the series

critical perspectives on the past

edited by

susan porter benson

stephen brier

and roy rosenzweig

temple university press   philadelphia

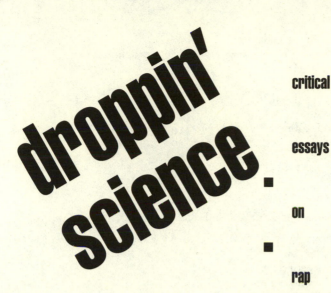

droppin' science

critical

essays

on

rap

music

and

hip hop

culture

edited

by

william

eric

perkins

Temple University Press, Philadelphia 19122
Copyright © 1996 by Temple University (except Chapter 6, copyright © Ernest Allen, Jr.).
All rights reserved
Published 1996
Printed in the United States of America

⊗ The paper used in this book meets the requirements of the American National
Standard for Information Sciences—Permanence of Paper for Printed Library Materials,
ANSI Z39.48-1984

Text design by Tracy Baldwin

Library of Congress Cataloging-in-Publication Data

Droppin' science : critical essays on rap music and hip hop culture /
    edited by William Eric Perkins.
        p.   cm.—(Critical perspectives on the past)
    Includes bibliographical references (p.   ).
    ISBN 1-56639-361-2 (cloth).—ISBN 1-56639-362-0 (pbk.)
    1. Rap (Music)—History and criticism.   2. Popular culture—United States—
History—20th century. I. Perkins, William Eric.
II. Series.
ML3531.D77   1996
782'.42164—dc20   95-1532

■ contents

■

■

■

■

■

II genres

III flavas

■ preface

■

■

■

■

■

■

■ Growing up in the South Jamaica section of Queens in New York City, my daughters, Sonya and Arianne, became big fans of rap's first wave; beginning in 1981, they frequented the playgrounds and yard parties where rap took root. They ignited my interest in rap and hip hop culture. It became evident to me that rap was based on all previous musical forms and fused the verbal and performance vernacular to an expanded rhythmic base. With my daughters and my son, Logan, I have pursued my interest in rap from its real street origins, where cassettes were eagerly anticipated and exchanged, where graffiti exploded on the subways and throughout the city's concrete jungles (this art a defiant act signaling African American and Latino youth's reclamation of public space), to the hip hop clothing style, which transformed sneakers and sweats from proletarian utility to high fashion.

This book began to take shape in 1990 at the annual meeting of the American Studies Association in New Orleans in a casual conversation with Temple University Press editor Janet Francendese. I thought that Temple would be the right publisher for a book on rap since Philadelphia was second only to New York in the early and mid-eighties among hip hop's capitals, producing at opposite ends of the rap spectrum the pop rap of the Fresh Prince as well as its virtual opposite, the violent hard-core gangsta rap of Schooly D. I also thought that hip hop had not been receiving the kind of scholarly attention it merited. In 1990, a host of mass-market books focused on hip hop, but only one serious volume, Englishman David Toop's *Rap Attack*, addressed it. Although several other serious works have recently appeared—notably those by Tricia Rose and Houston Baker, this collection of essays has a uniquely wide frame and a variety of voices.

No one has analyzed the complex interior of hip hop culture, surveyed its many genres and personalities, examined its effect on the larger white market, or acknowledged hip hop internationalization. The essayists in this book address these deficiencies and together put rap and hip hop culture into a wider framework of media and culture. They discuss the ongoing controversies about rap music within the context of contemporary debates about racial, class, and gender politics. With an acute historical vision, the contributors look at and beyond the rapidly changing trends in popular music. Their essays examine rap's significance to its makers and consumers as well as its cultural implications beyond music. Who makes this music and why? What does the making of this form of cultural expression mean in this time and place?

In Chapter 1, "The Rap Attack," I explore rap's early history, the evolution of its genres, and the expansion of its audience. Part I, "Roots," traces rap's expansive roots and recovers some of the hidden history that has eluded journalists and the mass-market side of the industry. Juan Flores locates rap within the Puerto Rican diaspora, linking Puerto Rico and New York as well as Puerto Rican and African American rap pioneers. Mandalit del Barco's imaginative essay recovers the Latin influence on the early history of hip hop, revealing the bicultural sources of New York street culture during the late 1970s and early 1980s. Nancy Guevara's essay analyzes the role of women, not only as rappers, but as writers (graffiti artists) and breakdancers as well.

The essays in Part II, "Genres," consider the political and economic environments in which the major hip hop genres took root. Robin Kelley's imaginative analysis of gangsta rap's emergence on the West Coast situates it in the context of the deindustrialization of Southern California in the 1980s. Ernest Allen's essay examines the nationalist and political trends in message rap, linking them to some of the eclectic earlier forms of African American nationalism. From their different vantage points, they also address the complex issues underlying rap's images of violence, misogyny, and social deterioration. The section closes with Armond White's exploration of the problems and contradictions inherent in the crossover formula of hip hop culture.

Part III, "Flavas," considers the performance aspects of hip hop culture. Robert Farris Thompson's essay is an original analysis of the Kongo/Angola roots of breakdancing. Katrina Hazzard-Donald explores "breakin' " within the context of the history of dance in the African diaspora. Tricia Rose focuses on hip hop's use of public space, investigating the way the state seeks to limit and contain these uses.

As students, analysts, and in some cases practitioners of the hip hop flavor, these contributors are pioneering new ways to examine African American and

Afro-Latino popular culture. We don't merely study this world, we're in it and of it, and we hope through this kind of cultural work to help mold and shape it. Few foresaw that the hip hop revolution would survive beyond the first commercial releases in 1979. Fewer still imagined that the world's youth would be so drawn to American culture, not in the form of Coca-Cola or Disney World, but the flavors and sciences of African American, Afro-Latino, and Afro–West Indian youth. In the words of Kurtis Blow, "That's the breaks."

Acknowledgments

First of all, I must thank the children and grandchildren who keep me exposed and up-to-date: Sonya, Logan, Arianne, Miles, and Julian. I am also grateful to my *palo* brothers, Daniel Dawson, Ken Dossar, and especially Carl Johnson, who spent hours with me discussing hip hop and the "tradition"; Kia-Bunseki Fu-Kiau, who sharpened my understanding of hip hop in relation to the orality of the diaspora; Marta Vega, who sees hip hop as part of the wider diaspora; Greg Tate and others of the NYC Afro-literati, who keep hip hop criticism "real"; Anu Rao and her staff at the Hospital of the University of Pennsylvania, who provided me with the comfort and support to get this done, and to Anu for introducing me to the "bhangra" music of South India; Reginald Butler, for just being my "homey"; my nephew, "Kippy," for the hip hop–house fusion and for keeping me up on the Chicago flavor; all the *raperos* in Havana and Matanzas, for their originality; the Luke crew in Miami, for keeping the "beat" in hip hop; Evan at Kansas, for giving me the opportunity to witness Native American rap; Ish and the Digable posse, for their seriousness about the music; all my Jamaican "heads," who are one fountain of this music; Todd Boyd and the Southern Cal crew, who see no borders in hip hop; and all my students over the last five years at Hunter College, Rutgers, and the University of Pennsylvania, especially Herbie "love bug," Imani Dawson, and Kameke Sweeney. Finally, my gratitude to Steve, Janet, David, and Joan is immeasurable.

William Eric Perkins

the rap attack: an introduction

william eric perkins

I was rappin' 50 years ago, my rap lyrics were a lot more dirty than those in my songs. And I did the moonwalk 50 years ago.

Cab Calloway to author, September 1991.

Hip Hop is the one music form that can change, because it thrives on other music forms.

Afro-British rappers, *Definition of Sound,* 1992

Rap music and hip hop culture's ongoing and bewildering love/hate relationship with American society requires a fresh evaluation of the role street culture plays in the continuing evolution of American popular culture. Rap music has been the subject of lawsuits and arguments before the Supreme Court, the target of hellfire-and-brimstone sermons by preachers, and even political ammunition for presidents and presidential candidates.[1] Rap has transformed American fashion with its sneakers, boots, loose-fitting clothes, and "whacked" colors and designs. Hip hop practitioners of "writing" (graffiti) have sparked a renewed interest in street art. Rap has helped fuel the African American cinema resurgence in Hollywood, while several hip hop mavens command leading roles in films and television series. When the genre first appeared in the late 1970s, culture and music critics falsely predicted a quick demise, but rap music grew and flourished, simultaneously reshaping the entire terrain of American popular culture. Even rap music's hyped commercialization cannot dampen its tough, raw, hard-core street essence. Rap music's most powerful safeguard has been its uncanny ability to reenergize itself, to remain "true to the game," in the words of one of Ice Cube's most important rhymes.

Rap music and hip hop culture have not been the subject of much serious scholarship, and a broad-based historical account is needed as the form grows more complicated in both music and style and as more and more of the old-school practitioners disappear from the scene or become victims of the twin scourges of the inner city, violent crime and cocaine. I pay particular attention to rap's pre-history and early history; its structure and culture; its genres and personalities; gender relations; and the impact of rap's commercialization.

Summoning the ancestors

Rap in general dates all the way back to the motherland, where tribes would use call-and-response chants. In the 1930s and 1940s, you had Cab Calloway pioneering his style of jazz rhyming. The sixties you had the love style of rapping, with Isaac Hayes, Barry White, and the poetry style of rapping with the Last Poets, the Watts poets and the militant style of rapping with brothers like Malcolm X and Minister Louis Farrakhan. In the 60s you also had "The Name Game," a funny rap by Shirley Ellis, and radio dj's who would rhyme and rap before a song came on.

Afrika Bambaataa, 1993

Afrika Bambaataa, one of rap music's founders, alludes to several important roots of rap music. Without doubt the African elements are part of rap's foundation. Writing of the African element in African American verbal culture, linguist David Dalby noted in 1972 that "it is at the level of interpersonal relationships and expressive behavior that the black American proletariat has preserved a large part of [its] African character: it is in this area, therefore, that we should expect the survival of African linguistic features."[2]

It is clear that rappers, like their ancestors, draw on the call-and-response form so common in ritual chanting to the gods, ancestors, or both; and the accumulated traditions of story telling are an essential element in rap music's overall structure. Taking an improvisational cue from their ancestors, rappers invent and reinvent their own vocabulary, adjusting it as the moment may require for recording, stage concerts, or the routines of everyday life. Just as Africans adapted English, French, Spanish, and Portuguese to fit the rules and formal structure of the languages they carried with them during their enslavement, rappers have adapted English to their own conventions and cultural style. When this verbal sorcery is fused with a beat, the resulting product becomes, in the words of old-school rapper Doug E. Fresh, "very African."[3] Such old-school rappers have instructed the new-school practitioners in the importance and historical significance of this verbal mastery, so that rap can claim a place alongside gospel music, work songs, jazz, and rhythm and blues in the African cultural unconscious.

Bambaataa also acknowledges Cab Calloway, the grandfather of rap music, whose vocal style borrowed the smooth elegance of scat singing (European vocal formalism joined to a distinctly African rhythm) and translated it into a street vernacular. Calloway called this style "jive scat," and it swept the country during the depression and lasted well into the 1940s. Calloway did not merely invent a new vocal style but created an entire culture around jive. *The New Cab Calloway's Hepster's Dictionary* taught the uninitiated the culture's basic vocabulary. Hepsters were resplendent in zoot suits with their long jackets and pegged pants, gold watches with long chains, and slicked-back hair (Calloway tossed his repeatedly during his stage shows). Jive scat features the improvisational style characteristic of much African music, but it also includes the call-and-response form. Calloway's signature tune, "Minnie the Moocher," is a well-formulated example of this ability to mix vocal and music styles. He recalls the tune's origins in this way:

> During one show that was broadcast over national radio in the spring of 1931, not long after we started using "Minnie the Moocher" as our theme song, I was singing and in the middle of a verse, as it happens sometimes, the damned lyrics went right out of my head. I forgot them completely. I couldn't leave a blank there as I might have done if we weren't on the air. I had to fill the space, so I just started to scat sing the first thing that came into my mind. "Hi-de-hi-de-hi-de-ho. Hi-de-hi-de-hi-de-ho. Ho-de-ho-de-ho-de-hee. Oodlee-oodlee-oldyee-oodlee-doo. Hi-de-ho-de-ho-de-hee." The crowd went crazy. Then I asked the band to follow it with me and I sang, "Dwaa-de-dwaa-de-dwaa-de-do." And the band responded. By this time, whenever the band responded some of the people in the audience were beginning to chime in as well. So I motioned the band to hold up and I asked the audience to join in. And as I sang the audience responded; they hollered back and nearly brought the roof down.[4]

Calloway's recollection illustrates the reciprocity between the band and the audience; the band leader moves and shapes the audience's participation, which then spurs the band leader and band to further improvisation. The kinetic quality of jive scat created a frenzy in the audience. Calloway's vocal improvisation would become one of the foundations of rap music's distinctive styles—"freestyle"—where rappers spontaneously engage in open verbal competitions and where the audience may be called on to respond.

Bambaataa further invokes as rap sources the lovers' raps of the late 1960s, led by soulful balladeers Isaac Hayes and Barry White. This genre used a lengthy monologue over a simple melodic line to recount the pain and peril of love. Hayes's eighteen-minute rap, "By the Time I Get to Phoenix," from his debut album, *Hot Buttered Soul,* revolutionized rhythm and blues (or soul music). The Hayes sound provided a cool, passionate, and mellow ease to the dance music that characterized the golden era of soul. Hayes's female counterpart at Stax Records, Millie Jackson, known for her x-rated raps on men, cheating, love, and sex, pioneered female lovers' rap, and her catchy duets with Hayes became legendary. Her fourth album for Stax featured her rapping to the background of Luther Ingram's smash hit, "If Loving You Is Wrong, I Don't Want to Be Right," a heated monologue on infidelity. Jackson's unique vocal style on stage combined soap-opera theatrics with musings on the entire range of love's joys and hurts, the pleasures of falling in love with married men, and the unbridled lust of sexual adventures. This style would make her the major influence on the female rappers of rap's first wave, as Roxanne Shanté has willingly acknowledged. Finally, Barry White's romantic raps of the disco era set his deep baritone against a complete orchestra complemented by French horns, violins, and cello. White's style was a disco version of the crooning balladeer—a kind of 1970s Billy Eckstine with a distinct rap style. This soulful trio made the rap genre acceptable to the black consumer market, and White's raps were one of the first to cross over into the white middle-class mainstream.

The message-oriented poetry of the Last Poets and Gil Scott-Heron laid the groundwork for the political rappers of the 1980s and 1990s. The Last Poets set lyrics to the beat of the conga drum, Gil Scott-Heron to the rhythms of a talented small band, to create a distinctive rap performance style that would have an almost infectious appeal for the masters of the old school and their successors. What characterized this version of rap was its political and social commentary, which did not spare African Americans from criticism. Coming to the fore at the end of the Civil Rights/Black Power movements, these poets invoked the most accessible form of black cultural nationalism—message word play—to reeducate and awaken the masses from the numbing sleep of the Nixon era and the emergence of "benign neglect." What makes Heron's and The Last Poets' style so important to the emergence of rap music is its orality. The poetry's effectiveness comes through only when it is spoken, just like rap. Similarly, black women poets like Sonia Sanchez, Nikki Giovanni, and others also developed a spoken style that turned words into bullets.[5]

Bambaataa also echoes the rhymes of Muhammad Ali, whose poetic couplets during the peak of his career between 1964 and 1972 provided new inspiration to inner-city youth who specialized in "signifying" or "playing the dozens." This particular form of verbal jousting continues to be quite common in African American and urban culture. Its elaborate set of rules and hidden meanings are designed to insult and ridicule opponents, thus preventing them from responding. Ethnographer Claudia Mitchell-Kernan defines *signifying* as she used it in her fieldwork during the late 1960s:

> Signifying . . . refers to a way of encoding messages or meanings which involves, in most cases, an element of indirection. This kind of signifying might best be viewed as an alternative message form, selected for its artistic merit, and may occur embedded in a variety of discourses. . . . The apparent significance of the message differs from its real significance. The apparent meaning of the sentence "signifies" its actual meaning.[6]

Mitchell-Kernan's phrase "apparent significance" is one of the key components of the rap idiom. Appearance becomes reality in the rappers' verbal art, and the extensive use of rhymed couplets (à la Ali) fuses with signifying (insulting) to create the elemental form of rap: "I float like a butterfly, sting like a bee, / There ain't no motherfucker that can rap like me" ("CC Crew Rap," CC Crew).

In addition to these various rhyming styles, the rap style also borrowed extensively from black disc jockeys who engaged in intense verbal competition to ensure and protect their market shares from the 1940s through the early 1960s. These DJs bombed the airwaves with their personal styles, in some cases becoming bigger stars than the artists they were required to play. Daddy O Daylie, Poppa Stoppa, Georgie Woods, Maurice "Hotrock" Hulbert, "Jocko" Henderson, and Herb Kent the "Cool Gent" were just a few of the radio personalities who gave the medium its identity and paved the way for today's radio personalities, from Frankie Crocker to "shock jock" Howard Stern. Central to the DJ verbal style was the elaborate rite of passage of naming, of creating an identity and personality that could not be matched. This naming ritual is another essential element in rap's structure. African American rappers adopt names that confer identity and separate them from the horde, while celebrating attributes that embody the personality the name gives. Rhyming and naming thus become a rapper's birthright, contributing to his or her image and personality.

This brief overview of the sources of the rap tradition suggests the infinite complexity and variety of rap's origins, each of which deserves major research. The rap tradition has been nurtured on the accumulated and residual forms of African and African American music, verbal art, and personal style as well as the constant process of self-innovation within each of these elements. This cultural residue is the source of much of the strength and vitality of rap and African American culture.

The first wave breaking

It is difficult to pinpoint the birth date of rap music. Although historians and critics will likely quibble over the exact time, old-school masters like Afrika Bambaataa, Grandmaster Flash, and Kool Herc generally agree that rap was born in 1974 in the South Bronx. The term *rap* came later, but Bambaataa claims he borrowed the term *hip hop* from Lovebug Starski when he began as a DJ:

> I started naming my jams, "hip-hop jams." Before scratching, there was just plain mixing. You would take a 30 second portion of a record and keep it going. Then you had breakdancing, the Hustle, deejaying, and then came rappers who just talked regularly over the music. Grandmaster Flash & the Furious Five along with Melle Mel started the rhyming. Myself and Soulsonic Force would use cliches like "Rock It, Don't Stop It," and "Shock the House." When rhyming started, that's when everybody started boasting about themselves, the flyest girls, and how many girls you could get in one

night. 1975 is when hip hop started coming into prominence throughout the Bronx, New York City, and stretching into Connecticut and New Jersey.[7]

Grandmaster Caz, another old-school master, has a different take on rap's early history. He identifies a distinct Jamaican lineage in early hip hop. Kool Herc (Clive Campbell) left Kingston in 1967 for the Bronx, bringing the "toast and boast" tradition of roots reggae, itself the product of the yard culture of West Kingston, and the food on which all of reggae superstardom was fed. Yard DJs brought huge speakers and turntables to the slums, where they rapped over the simple bass lines of the ska and reggae beats to create a style uniquely Jamaican. Artists like U Roy and Big Youth were the grandfathers of the trend that today we call dance hall, a musical genre that, like rap, prided itself on its yard cultural roots. The turntable and vinyl enabled the DJ to lyricize spontaneously about everything from love to the plight of the Jamaican masses. Caz claims that "the hip hop movement started with Kool Herc. Actual rap didn't start until later. It was deejaying and breakdancing at first. Not everybody even had a mic. It was just about your beats. Who had the baddest beats. Me too, I was deejaying."[8] The old-school masters essentially agree that the foundation of rap music is the beat. The beat is the structure around which the lyrics are developed, and samples of selected phrases from previously recorded music, jingles, solos, and so on play second fiddle. In rap vernacular, those with the "dope" beats produce the "deffest" raps.

These two takes on rap's origins cannot be minimized. The DJ ruled during hip hop's early days, and it was the DJ who established the foundations for the lyricist (the MC). The DJ's style was determined by the beats he was able to exploit from the countless riffs, solos, traps, and thousands of other snippets of sound in the audio treasure chests at his disposal. It was sound that molded the first wave of hip hop. Most popular in shaping the break-beat music of early hip hop was the percussion break popular among many groups of the 1970s like Mandrill and War, but the original source of the percussion beat has never been identified. I contend that the introduction of percussion beats in the dance music of the 1970s and in early hip hop were products of Latin music's powerful influence on New York and New Jersey popular culture. The Cuban son, Puerto Rican salsa, and Dominican (and Haitian) merengue were all driven by percussion-based bands, and many black and Puerto Rican young adults freely borrowed from this source in developing their own musical styles. One of the ironies of the African diaspora is that the musical foundations of the motherland would take such a basic element as percussion, syncretize it with European modernist elements, and create an entirely new musical form. This Latin/Jamaican lineage reveals more about the cultural continuities of the slave experience and its consequences than it does about the regional, linguistic, and cultural differences of the slaves' descendants. Afrika Bambaataa noted that DJs like Kool Herc would find one or two percussion beats/breaks and keep them going, infecting the crowd of dancers, who would boo an MC or singer. "The Beat Goes On" was the slogan of hip hop's first wave.

It is unfortunate, and another sad episode in the history of popular music, that Kool Herc and Grandmaster Caz would never enjoy the fruits of the musical form they gave birth to in the late 1970s. Left out of hip hop's early orbit, these pioneering DJs are being rediscovered today as new-school rappers delve into the sources of their own histories.

Sampling and mixing and jumping for joy

Kool Herc's place in the pantheon of hip hop's underground DJs was usurped by a young wizard, Grandmaster Flash, an expert in the electronic technology of beat creation:

> I was in the experimentation phase of trying to lock the beat together. I had to be able to hear the other turntable before I mixed it over. This is when I meet Pete DJ Jones. . . . I'm saying to myself, wow, how can he take these records and blend them on time, keep this music going without missing a beat? He told me what to do and to my amazement, wow, you can actually hear the other turntable before you play it out to the people. . . . I knew that inside the unit it was a single pole, double throw switch, meaning that when it's in the center it's off. When it's to the left you're listening to the left turntable and when it's to the right you're listening to the right turntable. I had to go to the raw parts shop downtown to find me a single pole double throw switch, some crazy glue to glue this part to my mixer, an external amplifier and a headphone. What I did when I had all this soldered together, I jumped for joy.[9]

Flash's technical skill paved the way for record sampling and helped launch the rap revolution. The crucial role of technical know-how and innovation in rap echoes in Andrew Ross's observation on the "capacity of popular music to transmit, disseminate and render visible 'black' meanings, precisely because of, and not in spite of, the industrial forms of production, distribution and consumption."[10] More than any previous form of music, hip hop represents democratized technology. Rappers have continued to reinvent the musical form by mastering the techniques of multitracking, the mixing and remixing of samples. Mark Costello and David Foster Wallace summarize this technique:

> Multi-tracking—using recorders that could capture and play back on 2 (as in stereo), 4 (as in 67's then ear-shattering, Sergeant Pepper's Lonely Hearts Club Band), 12, 16, and today 24 parallel tracks, eliminating the hiss of transference from one machine to the next. Rhythms, melodies, harmonies could all be captured on separate tracks, allowing the performer/producer to mix and listen and remix, adding vocals or lead instruments on yet another track. Rap Edisons like Kool Herc, Grandmaster Flash, and Afrika Bambaataa began as party djs, not musicians. Their wiring of twin turntables to a mixer, allowing them to "scratch" the sound of 2 different records while rapping into a mike, was a kind of crude, extemporaneous multi-tracking. . . . Digital Recording . . . is a technology that converts music to codes, or "digits." The codes are read by a computer,

one combining sophisticated sound-to-code translation hardware with a numbers crunching COS and a high-response synthesizer, at speeds of 40,000 digits per second and up. The recorded sounds, reduced to numbers, can be shaped, mangled, muffled, amplified, and even canonized. Hardware then translates the digits, as read and altered, back into sound, which itself can be re-recorded on multi-track and combined with yet more sounds. The result: hiss-free reproduction on an infinity of tracks, each of which . . . can itself be manipulated infinitely.[11]

This technological breakthrough allowed DJs to exploit an infinite number of samples from vinyl, advertising jingles, television sitcom themes, and movie sound tracks. It is sampling and mixing that gives rap music its self-renewing character. With multitracking elevated to both high art and technology, studios and producers became as essential to hip hop as DJs and MCs. Producers and DJs could now reach farther and farther into the repositories of sound for surprising samples and snippets, developing another key element in the hip hop equation— what's old is always new.

But this essential element in hip hop's evolution has been challenged by the corporate and legal gurus who control the record industry, particularly the publishing aspect. In a series of legal challenges, it has been argued that digital sampling is a violation of the legal code of fair use. Much of the legal debate revolves around the issue of "substantial similarity." Since most, if not all, samples are altered, does the use of these altered samples constitute copyright infringement? Entertainment lawyer Jason Marcus commented on the complexity generated by this issue:

> The issue of substantial similarity raises a number of questions in sound recording cases. Many of the questions were raised in the *United States v. Taxe*, wherein the defendant re-recorded music from records and tapes, adding new sounds, and changing speed, reverberation, and volume. The court used the test of substantial similarity to hold that the defendant's "piracy" had indeed infringed plaintiff's copyright. However, the court failed to explain how the substantial similarity test should be applied in the sound recording context. As such, there appears to be some degree of confusion in the courts on the issue. A digital sample is almost a per se admission of "similarity" in the sense that it is indeed the actual sound that is being appropriated. The Taxe case would probably leave the question of appropriation to the prior fact, with the instruction being to determine whether or not the defendant had indeed utilized the actual recording of the plaintiff, as pronounced in section 114(b) of the Copyright Act.[12]

The issue of substantial similarity has rocked the hip hop nation. In 1991 the Federal District Court of Manhattan found the clown prince of hip hop, Biz Markie, guilty of copyright infringement for using parts of Gilbert and Sullivan's tune "Alone Again (Naturally)" and ordered Warner Brothers to remove Markie's release "I Need a Haircut" from distribution. In another case Aaron

Fuchs of Tuff City Records filed suit against Def Jam Records, charging that the producers had illegally sampled a Tuff City drum track from a 1973 recording by the Honeydrippers, "Impeach the President," on two singles by L.L. Cool J and another by the now disbanded EPMD. If Fuchs wins this suit, recording and producing rap as we now know it would become financially impossible, given the prohibitive costs of clearing rights to use samples. This thorny business and legal issue reveals how a street form of art and culture ("straight up nigger music," as Afrika Islam calls it) has become locked in a bad marriage with corporate capitalism and the culture industry it supports. Since sampling is one of rap's multiple essences, any threat to restrict or regulate its artistic sources could put the very core of this music in jeopardy. The outcome of the sampling controversies will affect the future of rap recording and may eventually force it to return to its street and public roots. (A major victory for the artistic side of rap came in March 1994, when the Supreme Court ruled in favor of Luther Campbell's sampling of Roy Orbison's "Pretty Woman" on the grounds that parody does not jeopardize the originality of a recorded song.)

Following Flash's invention of the sampling machine, DJs came to carry weight and develop followings only to the extent that they were able to tap a huge catalogue of records (and other sounds) for sampling. Sampling was and is hip hop's ongoing link with history and tradition, including all of the African and African American musical genres; so one can say that hip hop generates its own history by recycling music and reintroducing the previous musical genres to new audiences and markets. Afrika Bambaataa recalls:

> The Bronx wasn't really into radio music no more. It was an anti-disco movement. . . . Everybody wanted the funky style that Kool Herc was playing. Myself, I was always a record collector and when I heard this DJ, I said, "Oh I got records like that." I started digging in my collection. When I came on the scene after him I built in other types of records and I started getting a name for master of records. I started playing all forms of music. Myself, I used to play the weirdest stuff at a party. . . . I'd throw on the Pink Panther theme for everybody who thought they was cool like the Pink Panther, and then I would play "Honky Tonk Woman" by the Rolling Stones and just keep that beat going. I'd play something from metal rock records like Grand Funk Railroad. "Inside Looking Out" is just the bass and drumming. . . . I'd throw on "Sergeant Pepper's Lonely Hearts Club Band"—just that drum part. . . . I'd throw on the Monkees, "Mary, Mary"—just the beat part where they'd go "Mary, Mary, where are you going?"—and they'd start going crazy.[13]

Dissin' goes commercial

Until 1979 rap was a key component of a flourishing underground culture in the Bronx and upper Manhattan, where parties went on all night in seedy nightclubs or the music was played in schoolyards and small public parks. Speakers, turntables, mixers, and the inevitable array of breakdancers nurtured rap's public roots and its reclamation of public spaces (the subject of Tricia Rose's essay in this volume). Distribution was by word of mouth or by the most democratic of technologies, the audio cassette tape, and that's how hip hop's early pioneers cultivated their personalities and followings.

Rapping then resembled some of the singing styles of 1940s and 1950s black dance music synthesized with the technology of the 1970s. The MC, as the rapper was known, developed a basic lyrical style, mixing elements of street jargon and slang, personal experience, and an occasional dose of humor to create a potpourri of simple verses that could function as both match and counterpoint to the DJ. An MC would embrace elements of Jamaican–African American "toasts and boasts," the "signifying" tradition, lovers' laments, and the tones and cadences of African American and Afro–West Indian preachers to create a personal style. MCs had to be authoritative, assertive, and hard-hitting. Dissin' (insulting or putting down) the competition became the cornerstone of early rap's style. The put-down—shooting an opponent or competitor with words, while boasting of one's own lyrical and rhyming abilities—characterized the dis as in Run DMC's example from "Sucker MCs":

> You're a five-dollar boy and I'm a million dollar man
> You're a sucker MC and you're my fan
> You try to bite lines from friends of mine,
> But you're very banal, you're just a sucker MC
> You sad-faced clown.

The dis element informs all rap styles, and MCs must be able to perform dis to gain a modicum of acceptance and respect. It has been argued that the dis element in rap reinforces the macho tendency in African American male culture.

The force and style of several personalities gave rap the allure of a new and potentially important art form, still unnoticed by the recording giants of records, television, and movies. Uptown Manhattan and the Bronx were taken over by wave after wave of young black and Latino b-boys and b-girls, blasting their boom boxes with an arsenal of cassette tapes made and distributed by hip hop's royalty—Afrika Bambaataa, Kool Herc, and Grandmaster Caz. As the disco era collapsed in its own decadence, DJs had begun to take notice of the slick instrumentation and production skills that had made disco such a dominant force. One of the genre's last gasps, Chic's "Good Times," became the guiding sample behind rap's first commercial hit, "Rappers Delight" by the Sugar Hill Gang. Rap then exploded commercially. Joe and Sylvia Robinson had recorded several hits, including 1968's "Love Is Strange" and Sylvia's solo 1972 smash, "Pillow Talk." The Robinsons founded Sugar Hill Records, named after the center of black middle-class Harlem. "Rappers Delight" reached number thirty-six on the U.S. charts and became the largest-selling twelve-inch record ever at the time. Though this was not the first rap record—the first was the disco dance group the Fatback Band's single, "King Tim 111 ((Personality Jock))"—"Rapper's Delight" was the first major rap hit and established both rap and Sugar Hill Records as forces to be reckoned with.[14]

What made the "Rappers Delight" so important in the history of hip hop was the speedy staccato word play and verbal dexterity layered over the instrumentation of Chic's "Good Times." Part of the initial fascination with the "Rappers Delight" was the novelty of the genre with its emphasis on word play and games. Lyrical manipulation would become an important part of hip hop from that moment on. "Rappers Delight" was followed by an even more ambitious lyrical melange by Grandmaster Flash and the Furious Five, "Superrappin'," which marked Flash's transition from DJ to MC in an incredible brew with true old-school flavor:

> It was a party night, everybody was breakin'
> The highs were screamin' and the bass was shakin'
> And it won't be long till everybody know when that
> Flash was on the beat box goin' that
> Flash was on the beat box goin' that
> and/ and/ and/ and
> Italian, Caucasian, Japanese, Spanish, Indian, Negro and Vietnamese
> MC's disc jockeys to all the fly kids and the young ladies
> Introducin' the crew ya got to see to believe
> We're one, two, three, four, five mc's
> I'm Melle Mel and I rock it so well
> And I'm Mr. Ness because I rock the best
> Raheim in all the ladies' dreams
> And I'm Cowboy to make you jump for joy
> I'm Creole—solid gold
> The Kid Creole playin' the role.

David Toop describes the Furious Five's innovative and influential style, in which "lines were divided up between individuals and cut in with unison ensembles and solos which highlighted the different vocal qualities and styles."[15] These hip hop trailblazers would establish the group sound of rap in which different rappers alternated, taking a verse and infusing it with their own personality and style. Grandmaster Flash and the Furious Five became rap's first successful group.

The next major rap personality was Kurtis Blow, whose 1979 hits "Christmas Rappin' " and "The Breaks" made him rap's first commercial success on a white label—Mercury. Son of a middle-class family and a City College graduate, Blow is significant in hip hop history for two reasons: he became one of the first solo performers, and his career was managed by the young Russel Simmons, soon to become the godfather of much of hip hop music and culture. Like that of a lot of early rap, Blow's lyrical style was characterized by a traditional macho posture. Bare chested and dookie chained (wearing the heavy gold chains that were a feature of rap's first male wave), Blow performed on New York City playgrounds and came to national attention when he was profiled by ABC's 20/20 in 1980. His raps have a comic aspect along with folk wisdom, "drylongso" that is an essential part of African American culture, as in this one from "The Breaks":

> If your woman steps out with another man
> (That's the breaks, that's the breaks)
> And she runs off with him to Japan
> And the IRS says they want to chat
> And you can't explain why you claimed your cat
> And Ma Bell sent you a whopping bill
> With eighteen phone calls to Brazil
> And you borrowed money from the mob
> And yesterday you lost your job
> Well, these are the breaks
> Break it up, Break it up, Break it up.

The financial success of Sugar Hill Records prodded the corporate recording industry, forever in search of novelty and new markets, to investigate this emerging genre and to sign prospective artists. The early 1980s witnessed the planting of hip hop within the large record companies and the assignment of agents to pursue this new street sound. Not only did hip hop's emergence signal a major shift in popular music, but its fashion, style, and signature art form—graffiti—were beginning to command attention as well.

Unlike his peers, Afrika Bambaataa was a charismatic Bronx gang leader who used his organizational prowess and the ritual codes of the Zulu Nation to create one of hip hop's most authentic sounds. In 1982, his smash single "Planet Rock" set the music world on fire. Borrowing samples from the German "techno-rock" group Kraftwerk's "Trans-Europe Express" and making skillful use of the TR 808 drum machine, Bambaataa gave birth to the sound he called "electro funk," a fusion of the synthesized beats of disco with the sound-system bass of early Jamaican dance hall. This new beat incorporated much of the newly emerging industrial music that was influencing rock and heavy metal. Bambaataa became one of the most important and creative DJs in rap's first years. As Melle Mel told the British rap magazine *HHC* (*Hip-Hop Connection*), "When Bambaataa made 'Planet Rock' it hurt all the other rappers. . . . They (Bambaataa) was the only ones to have this real futuristic, synthesized sound. It hurt us because it tipped everything into a different dimension." Bambaataa's innovative style depended on picking samples unfamiliar to an already sophisticated hip hop audience. As Bambaataa commented, "I was really heavy into Kraftwerk and Yellow Magic Orchestra and I wanted to be the first black group to release a record with no band, just electronic instruments."[16] His musical ideology as expressed in "Planet Rock" was really quite simple—to encourage the fun life and a "funky good time":

> You gotta rock it, pop it, 'cause it's the century
> There is such a place that creates such a melody

World's but a land of a master jam,
get up and dance
It's time to chase your dreams
Up out your seats, make your body sway
Socialize, get down, let your soul lead the way
Shake it now, go ladies, it's a living dream
Love Life Live.

Though lyrically simple, "Planet Rock" paved the way for the introduction of funk, techno, and drum synthesizers into rap music—forms of instrumentation essential to the DJ's musical arsenal. Bambaataa remarked in 1993 that electro funk gave birth to freestyle rap, the Miami bass sound, and house music. His pioneering rap style would force rap music to transform itself throughout the 1980s. Bambaataa and the Soul Sonic Force were no strangers to fashion either. The disco era's feathers, sequins, and whacky pseudoproletarian camp (the Village People) were on the wane. Bambaataa's style was an Africanized version of George Clinton's black-to-the-future Parliament Funkadelic. Carved African walking sticks, elaborate wildlife headdresses (strikingly similar to those worn by the Mardi Gras Indian tribes of New Orleans), and the infamous "Zulu" beads (a black beaded necklace featuring a black medallion carved with a figurine that resembles an African masthead with the smile face) made a bold fashion statement. Bambaataa and his crew would also, on occasion, dye their hair punk orange, purple, and pea green. He called this look the "wildstyle," and during performances, his crew's appearance mesmerized the audience as much as their music did.

The beat meets the break

These early trends in hip hop set the tone for the blossoming of rap during the Reagan years. New groups with distinctive styles and gimmicks ("props," in the current hip hop idiom); the growing domination of the hip hop attitude, style, and music on youth culture; and, perhaps most important, its lurch into the crossover market made hip hop the defining cultural expression of the eighties generation. Hip hop's identity broadened in 1983 as the breakdancing craze swept the shopping malls and inner-city playgrounds of America. The beat meets the break, and they both meet the rhyme. It is unfortunate that the Puerto Rican link to what has been categorically classified as an African American cultural form has been so ignored (though the essays by Mandalit del Barco and Juan Flores in this volume correct that omission). In 1977, Puerto Rican DJ Charlie Chase began hanging out with a group called the "Monterey Crew." They were already immersed in the b-boy style characterized by athletic sweatsuits, Kangol caps, untied designer sneakers, and a passion for the black funk music of the time—James Brown and Parliament Funkadelic. Breakin' was a set of specific dance moves done on playgrounds and club dance floors in the late 1970s and early 1980s: from twists and spins, headstands, and elaborately orchestrated footwork to the standard individual dance moves of "top rockin' and up-rockin'." Breakdancing is part classical, part popular dance, part street body language, and part performance art. South Bronx Puerto Rican young adults used St. Martin's Catholic Church as a battleground for breakdance competitions, and out of these contests came several of the best-known groups—The Disco Kids (TDK), the Apache Crew, Star Child LaRock, and the best known of breakdancing's first wave, the Rockwells. Colon, Ken Rock, Frosty Freeze, Mania, and Take became the core of the Rock Steady Crew, the first breakdancing group to merit national attention and to be featured at one of hip hop's most important clubs, the now defunct Club Negril. These appearances caused media-industry moguls to take notice, and the Rock Steady Crew appeared on a number of late-night television shows as well as being featured in hip hop's first films, *Breakin'* and *Beat Street.* The precise way in which the Rock Steady Crew executed the dance form became yet another element in expanding the use of the basic beat with the rap form; breakdancers could not break without the correct beats—thus their essential relationship to the DJ. But breakdancing did not survive corporate America's raid on hip hop culture, probably because it was truly street art. As hip hop matured, and as it continues to be shaped by the video medium, authentic breakdancers have been replaced by "video hos," fly girls, and fly boys.[17]

Catching the second wave

By the early 1980s, hip hop had attained a prominent place in American popular culture. The new personalities of the second wave—Run DMC, L.L. Cool J, and Kool Moe Dee and Big Daddy Kane—epitomized a combination of street style and musical minimalism. More than any other single group or force, Run DMC catapulted rap into the crossover mainstream. Produced by Russel Simmons (now head of the Def Jam hip hop empire) and Rick Rubin, the *wunderkind* of early rap, Run DMC's sound symbolized the merger of the black urban street sound with a slick pop overlay. The crew's lives were parlayed into a collective biography, *Tougher Than Leather,* and a feature film, *Krush Groove,* both early efforts in rap's growing command of the lucrative youth market. This is how music critics Havelock Nelson and Michael Gonzales summarized the Run DMC aura:

> Although they were products of suburbia (the neatly trimmed, upwardly mobile neighborhood of Hollis, Queens), Run DMC were raised under the influence of television and super-movie heroes like Kojak and Shaft, a part of the Black middle-class that was able to romanticize the images of distinction and chaos: nodding heroin addicts, bombed out buildings, trash-filled streets. This was, in the rushed words of rap mogul Russel Simmons, "the difference between fantasy and reality. In Queens you could hang out on the corner, but there was safety in the house, in Queens, one could be part of a gang, but it was part of a growing up process—in the ghetto it's a life-style."[18]

Decked out in black fedoras, unlaced Adidas sneakers, sweatsuits, and "dookie gold," the crew of Run DMC became hip hop's first real personalities. In harsh disses to rappers of the first wave (Afrika Bambaataa and the Soul Sonic Force, Grandmaster Flash and the Furious Five, and the Fearless Four), these middle-class upstarts proclaimed, "No leather suits and no homo boots" to their masqueraded seniors. Hence, they were "tougher than leather." Run DMC's career peaked in 1986 with the album "Raising Hell." It contained hip hop's first MTV hit, "Walk This Way," performed with the aging heavy-metal rocker group, Aerosmith, which launched hip hop into the crossover market. The album went platinum and led to widespread coverage of hip hop culture by the mainstream media.[19] But Run DMC's 1990 comeback attempt flopped, and the group reappeared in 1993 with a new look, a new album, and new "props."

L.L. Cool J, also from the black middle-class haven of Hollis, Queens, developed a new style that made him the king of the genre lovers' rap. His second album, "Bigger and Deffer," contained the amazingly successful single "I Need a Love," where he pants and whispers, elevating him to instant stardom. He carefully crafted an image of a cool and elegant ladies' man armed with raps that would make women swoon. In his 1989 release "Walking with a Panther," L.L. posed with three black women, a bottle of Moet, a cellular phone, and a black panther on a thick gold "dookie" chain. This cultivated image directly challenged the political rappers whose intimidating styles and lyrics allegedly sent rap in an anti-white direction. Political rappers castigated L.L.'s lovers' rap as a commercial sellout and labeled him a "ho." In true rap fashion, he responded with a highly successful and quotable dis, "Mama Said Knock You Out," in which he posed as a fighter in the ring ready to take on all comers.

Fat boys and b-girls

Among other surprisingly original acts in rap's second wave, the Disco 3, who became the Fat Boys, were the architects of the comic rap style. Their onstage antics earned them the nickname the "Three Stooges of Rap," and their outrageously funny lyrics reminded the mass audience that rap could maintain an innocence while being true to its roots. The core of the group was Darren "Human Beat Box" Robinson, whose uncanny vocal ability to duplicate the beats of the electronic drum machine made him the equivalent of a circus sideshow (Doug E. Fresh did the same thing, but in a far more serious vein). The group's first release, "The Fat Boys," in 1984 was a huge success, with lyrics like:

Yeah, I'm overweight
. . . Now it started off when I was very small
I devoured chocolate cakes: plates, candles and all

The Fat Boys, rap's first crossover act, starred in films—including the outrageously stereotypical *Disorderlies*—that paved the way for other comedy rappers: Biz Markie, the Afros, and Digital Underground.

In rap's first and second waves were equally charismatic crews of women who commanded the attention of male rappers and the music industry alike with a woman's point of view and, more to the point, a "sister's" point of view. I will return to these women rappers but want to note here an important recording "dis and dismiss" battle in the early 1980s essential to uncovering rap's hidden history—the Roxanne syndrome. It was important for two reasons: it elevated dis rap to new heights, and it injected a feminist current into the rap mainstream. In 1984 the male group UTFO recorded "Roxanne, Roxanne," basically the story of a black American princess who candidly rejects three male suitors. This smash single prompted numerous responses from black and Latino women, led by a fourteen-year-old b-girl from the Queensbridge projects in Long Island City, Lolita Shanté Gooden, who took the stage name Roxanne Shanté and wrote a response, "Roxanne's Revenge":

> I turned you down,
> without a frown
> Embarrassed you in front of your friends
> made you look like a clown
> And all you do is get real mad
> And you talk about me and make me look bad?!

Her rap was followed by the "The Real Roxanne," performed by a woman who called herself the Real Roxanne:

> Me, the Rox, give up the box?
> So you can brag about it for the next six blocks
> Where's the beef? You guys can't deal it
> I need a man who can make me feel it

The Roxanne cycle pitted b-boy against b-girl in the eternal battle of the sexes. Through the codes of ritualized insult, a slowly emerging feminist consciousness began to bore into rap's traditional male bravado. Women rappers were staking a claim on the traditionally male preserve of hip hop. Dissin' male suitors, in the male style, revealed women rappers' competence at rhyming; but this early feminist style also showed that rap could become a vehicle for calling attention to the problems and issues that face young inner-city women who routinely battle what the fictional Roxanne rhymes about—sexual harassment and leering by arrogant male suitors.

Rap's second wave, with its messages encoded in standard themes in African American and Latino culture—love, boasting, macho, and humor—included several new artists whose rhyming styles tapped the pulse of the inner city by documenting the pain, anguish, and social and moral crises of their generation. This school of rappers projected a style and demeanor that has helped to stigmatize rap music to the present day. Young black men are viewed as nihilistic, prone to anarchic violence, misogynistic, and greedy for the lucre associated with the trade in crack cocaine. This has made black men targets and scapegoats for both the police and "five-ohs" (street slang for narcotics officers). Rappers who promoted this style on the East Coast were led by the reclusive Schooly D of Philadelphia, whose explicit lyrics raised the ire of the music industry and state authorities alike. In his "I Don't Like Rock and Roll," he boasts: "Rock 'n Roll livin' is a thing of the past / So all you long-haired faggots can kiss my ass." Schooly D's rhymes are the musical backdrop for the films of Abel Ferrara, *King of New York,* which follows the murderous career of an idiosyncratic cocaine dealer played by Christopher Walken, and *The Bad Lieutenant,* in which Harvey Keitel plays a rogue New York City detective given to binges of booze, crack, and freak sex. Schooly D's rhymes are the lyrical equivalent of a world sunk in degeneration. His "Signifying Rapper" (with a hypnotic Led Zeppelin loop) is a tour de force, a kind of ghetto Brer Rabbit tale replete with gruesome violence, homophobia, and sexual perversion: "He say he know you Daddy, and he's a faggot / And your mother's a whore. / He says he seen you sellin' asshole / Door to door." Schooly D's twisted genius lies in his ability to paint a lyrical picture of inner-city decay. But his persona led other rappers to create equally hardened characters whose quirkiness was magnified in their lyrical and stylistic sophistication.

No one embodies these traits more than Slick Rick, whom journalist Adario Strange describes as "one half eccentric recluse, and 50% of the environment." He goes on to note, "While almost everyone has shed their gold in favor of beads, Slick seems to have increased his unmatched array of gold chains and rings. In the midst of the Afrocentric wave of rhymes, Rick has been true to the universal style of storytelling."[20] Slick Rick's twisted male bravado was articulated in his second release for Def Jam, "The Great Adventures of Slick Rick." His unique voice (which cannot be classified and may be rooted in his West Indian heritage) combined with a narrative style of rhyming made him one of the truly original favorites in rap's second wave. But his misogyny, homophobia, and sexual obsession drew the wrath of the popular music critics. In "Treat Her Like a Prostitute," he calls on black men to treat all black women as whores:

Now ya been with your girlfriend for quite awhile
Plans for the future, she's having your child
Celebrate with friends drinking cans and quarts
Telling all your friends about your family thoughts
One friend was drunk so he starts to get wild
He tells the truth about the kid
It's not your child
Acting like a jerk and on his face was a smirk
He said, "Your wife went berserk while you was hard at work
And she led him on and on and tried to please him
She didn't waste time, she didn't try to tease him"
Treat 'em like a prostitute (Do what?)
Don't treat no girlie well until you're sure of the scoop
'Cause all they do is hurt and trample.

In a 1989 interview with Armond White, Rick defended his attitudes toward women with typical male-rap bravado, boasting of his ability to get into a woman's mind: "I know how to get a male to succeed without success getting in his way. . . . In this world, if you don't know a person's mind, you'll never know if they're telling the truth or not. The best thing to do is to go for yours yourself. Make your move."[21] The "Ruler's" gangsta style doesn't end with his rhetoric. He was convicted of attempted murder in 1991 and sentenced to three and a half to ten years in prison, where he served on a work-release program until his release in late 1995.

Gangstas with attitude

Rap's second wave washed over Miami, Houston, and even Atlanta as a creative frenzy and hip hop's promise of instant fame and fortune inspired inner-city youth. Rivaling New York/New Jersey as the hip hop capital are the postindustrial metropolises of California. Gangsta rap is a product of the gang culture and street wars of South Central Los Angeles, Compton, and Long Beach and the retro-mack (the resurgence of the pimp attitude and style) culture of East Oakland. The gangsta was epitomized by the now defunct group NWA (Niggas with Attitude), which consisted of the MCs Dr. Dre, Ezy-E, Ice Cube, and MC Ren, and the still active and controversial Ice-T. This genre in rap music has given rap its criminal image and raises the whole question of authenticity.

In their 1988 hit "——— the Police," set against a sampling backdrop of droning synthesizers, NWA captured the essence of young black male rage: "A young nigger on the warpath / And when I finish, it's gonna be a bloodbath / Of cops dyin' in LA." Released during a period of intense debate about legal challenges to artistic freedom, "——— the Police" prompted an immediate reaction from police organizations all over the country and even led to an FBI investigation. Tipper Gore's organization, the Parents' Music Resource Center (PMRC), which had already been engaged in monitoring heavy-metal lyrics for allusions to satanism and other cult tendencies, now turned its attention to rap. Gore's call for parental advisory labeling on rap recordings and for industry regulation of rap artists echoes the massive reaction that greeted the arrival of rock 'n' roll as it swept small-town and suburban America during the early 1950s. This wave of reaction only strengthened gangsta rap's commercial appeal. The performance aspect of these "studio gangstas" is a complex matter that has not been carefully analyzed. Yes, there are authentic original gangsta (OG) rappers as the 1993 releases of the Bloods and Crips demonstrate, but much of gangsta rap is Hollywood hype. And that disturbs a lot of OGs (original gangstas who are actual gang members): "I'm fed up with buster [hustlers] like NWA. A lot of my homies in the neighborhood died, man, and what the niggers did was market our life and our image. All them niggers in NWA is buster! They never give back to the neighborhood."[22]

The gangsta rap craze reflects the twin maladies of deindustrialization and lumpen proletarianization, as Robin Kelley persuasively argues in this volume. It bears no resemblance to the message-oriented, political, or neonationalist genres of rap but instead celebrates hustling, street crime, women abuse, and the gun as social equalizer. Its blatant antiauthoritarianism recalls past generations of youthful rebellion, but its brutal verbal raging borders on anarchy. Instead of becoming a vehicle for a regenerative antiauthoritarianism (so necessary in an age of growing right-wing cultural fanaticism) in youth culture and black youth culture in particular, the gangsta style nurtures hysteria. The success of the gangsta-rap phenomenon can in part be attributed to the widespread press and television coverage the controversies about the genre command. Profiles have been done by all three networks, and the MTV "rockumentary" series included a thirty-minute segment showing how far into the heartland the mania has spread; from Los Angeles through the great plains of Omaha and Iowa City, the gangsta attitude sells not only records but "being real."

Ice-T's phenomenal success paralleled that of NWA. His 1987 release, "Rhyme Pays," signaled his arrival as an original gangsta with his own style, earning critical accolades from the traditionally insular East Coast rap community. Beyond recording and performing, he leads all other rappers in film and television-drama appearances, with cameos in hip hop's first two films: *Breakin'* and *Breakin' II*. In addition to making several other film appearances, he wrote the rap score for Dennis Hopper's pro-police portrayal of Los Angeles gang life, *Colors*, and he stole the stage as a rogue hip hop cop in Mario Van Peebles's brutal depiction of the life of a crack dealer, *New Jack City*. He also had a role in stimulating the retro-mack revival of the 1990s, reviving the signature tune of Gordon Parks's *Superfly*, rerecording "I'm Your Pusherman" for *Superfly II*. And BBC stations in England have broadcasted his comedy show featuring film reviews in a comedic imitation of TV's *In Living Color*. Blessed with good looks and an original style, he reminds one more of the chic cocaine dealers of Miami or New York than plaid-shirted South Central Los Angeles gangsters. In his single "High Rollers" he chimes: "They dress in diamonds and gold chains / They got the blood of Scarface runnin' through their veins." He can rap hard core or wax eloquent, as in his smash single "The Mind Is a Lethal Weapon." But Ice-T's entire persona shattered with the release of his single "Cop Killer" from his album *Home Invasion*, made with the heavy-metal rockers Body Count. The enraged police establishment refused to provide security at his concerts and called for his censorship. Other songs, such as "KKK Bitch" in which the protagonist rapes, sodomizes, and murders the daughter of a Klansman, raised such controversy that Time Warner eventually dropped Ice-T from Warner Brothers records. He defended his position, telling the *Los Angeles Weekly*, "I try to walk the edge. I'm going to tell you what you need to hear, not what you want to hear."[23]

Perhaps no gangsta-rap group embodies more of the mindless anarchy of the genre than Houston's Geto Boys. Ultraviolent, misogynistic, and creative, they reshape the sociopathic antics of Alex and his crew in their own version of *A Clockwork Orange*, which might be called a "blackwork orange." The team has taken the gangsta style to the heartland, reminding the mass audience that Houston's Fifth Ward is just as anarchic as South Central or Compton. The 1989 hit "Mind of a Lunatic" captures the Geto Boys' nihilistic rage:

Paranoid sittin' in a deep sweat
Thinkin' I got to fuck somebody before the weekend
The sight of blood excites me
Shoot you in the head, sit down and watch you bleed to death
I hear the sound of your last breath

The Geto Boys have produced an imaginative array of raps, including the 1992 single and video "Mind Playin' Tricks on Me," the story of a drug dealer tormented by violent dreams and an evil stalker (reminiscent of the Haitian loa of the cemetery, Baron Samedi). The video culminates in a violent assault on the illusory stalker, with the bloodied protagonist carried away in an ambulance. But the Geto Boys' lives seem to mirror their stage image. Bushwick Bill drank an excessive amount of white lightning and dared his girlfriend to shoot him. The gun accidentally went off, and Bill lost an eye. Bill has also earned the wrath of black feminists for his misogynistic lyrics and frequent use of the word "bitch." After releasing three albums, the group disbanded and formed again with a local Fifth Ward gangsta, Mr. Mike, replacing Willie D. But it is Mr. Scarface, the group's leader, who emerges from this chaos with a truly philosophical evaluation. In a 1993 interview he commented, "I don't do gangsta rap no more. Yeah I'll give it a new name. . . . It's gotta be something that's got to do with the end of something like Armageddon. Revelation . . . we are in the book of Revelations with our raps, cuz."[24]

But what makes gangsta rap so appealing to that upper-middle- and middle-class young white male market, especially when more and more gangsta rappers are imitating the "myth of action" (as music critic Dream Hampton labels it) so prevalent in their videos? In an age of mass overconsumption and media hype, gangsta rap no doubt represents a religion and ideology of authenticity. From gang colors to "blunts" and "forties" (hip hop vernacular for marijuana and malt liquor), from drive-by shootings to woman abuse, the idea of authenticity holds a maddening appeal for the X generation. These abstract slogans of "real niggaz," "niggaz for life," and "bein' and stayin' real" summon up romantic notions of ghetto authenticity. Oppressed by the machinery of social regulation and the police state, black and Latino youth have created a substitute social order governed by their own code and rituals of authenticity, but there is no hype to cop stops or dead homies. So as white-bread America searches for a new identity in a post-Soviet, postindustrial, globally interconnected new world order, hip hop speaks to youth's desire for identity, for a sense of self-definition and purpose, no matter how lawless or pointless. As long as youth culture is dominated by the cult of the commodity, there will be a desire for the "real."

Yo! rap with a message

Political or message rap falls into three categories: African centered, neonationalist, and Islamic (dominated by the eclectic Five Percent faction of Muslim blacks). The political rappers emerged in pointed contrast to the macho bravado and fashion excesses of hip hop's first wave. Leading the neonationalists is Long Island's (Strong Island, in the hip hop vernacular) Public Enemy, mixing the moral rage of lead rapper Chuck D with the comical shenanigans of Flavor Flav and the wicked beats of DJ Terminator X. From their 1987 release *Yo! Bum Rush the Show* to their 1994 recording, "Muse Sick—N Our Mess Age" (though disappointing), Public Enemy's lyrical style is the standard by which all political rap should be judged. The group has redefined the political terrain of rap music, helping to fuel the Malcolm X revival and political fashion while speaking out against the moral and economic decay of the inner city. Although Public Enemy's career has been shaped and nurtured by controversy, not only do they continue to thrive but their music continues to strengthen the neonationalist current in rap music and hip hop culture, forcing all practitioners of the genre to take notice.[25] In a 1992 interview, Chuck D was asked how Public Enemy developed its style:

> We wanted to be different from other artists so we would stand out. Everybody in rap at that time was talking about gold chains and being stupid, and [producer Hank Shocklee] and I wanted to find a new direction. What always gave rap a leg up on other music was the anger in it, but the anger was always directed at other rappers—"I'm better than you" and so forth. When we came along, we decided to direct our anger at something real . . . the government and people who were responsible for what was happening in society. If you look at our first record, the subtitle is "The Government Is Responsible."[26]

In their hit single from *Yo! Bum Rush the Show*, "Miuzi Weighs a Ton," they define their own personality:

> I'm a Public Enemy but I don't rob no banks
> I don't shoot bullets and I don't shoot blanks
> My style is supreme—number one is my rank
> And I got more power than the New York Yanks
>
> . . . .
>
> It's unreal they call the law
> And claimed I started the war
> It was war they wanted and war they got
> But they wilted in the heat when miuzi got hot.

As the rap establishment's leading public intellectual, Chuck D has used rap music and the public space it has opened to promote a nineties version of racial politics tinted by neonationalist rage. For example, in his quest to use his public persona to heal the physical, moral, and spiritual sickness in Afro-America, his ranting diatribes and lawsuit against the malt-liquor industry has earned him the wrath of industry executives. Chuck D even warned partner Flavor Flav against accepting an offer to do a malt liquor commercial, threatening, "I'll cut you off publicly so fuckin' bad."[27] Not only the malt-liquor industry has felt this rage. In their single and video from *Apocalypse '91*, "Shut 'Em Down," Public Enemy launches a no-holds-barred attack on corporate capitalism's irresponsibility in inner-city communities throughout the country:

> I like Nike but wait a minute
> My neighborhood supports them so put some money in it
> Corporations owe
> Dey gotta give up the dough
> to my crew or my town
> or else we gonna shut 'em down.

The video combines a historical montage of capitalism's exploitation of African Americans with a brew of cartoons, newsreels, and graphics, creating a work of art with a powerful political message. PE's 1990 single and video "Burn, Hollywood, Burn" also makes use of this style, visually documenting the negative stereotypes that film has created of African Americans, from the maids and mammies to the endless parade of big-eyed, big-lipped "coons" and "Toms." Their most controversial single and video, "By the Time I Get to Arizona," depicts a series of fictional assassinations of Arizona politicians who refused to support a law making Martin Luther King, Jr.'s birthday a state holiday.[28] Its striking political message is made even more graphic by the image of young masked guerilla warriors preparing to carry out the assassinations. The video is narrated by PE protégé Sister Souljah, herself no stranger to controversy. Lyrically Chuck D warns: "Call me the trigger man / Lookin' lookin' for the governor / I'm on the one mission / To get a politician." Public Enemy has not released an album since 1994, and only one single, a track for the movie score of Forrest Whittaker's powerful portrait of the gun culture in Brooklyn (Crooklyn, in the rap vernacular), *Strapped*. But Chuck D continues to be a powerful voice for African Americans, promoting black self-sufficiency, rappers' economic control of their music, and the moral and spiritual healing of the inner city. In a 1991 interview, he remarked:

> If I could make two requests of every black person that reads this, they would be, one, pick up as much education and information as you possibly can about surviving in the system. Surviving, as opposed to "prospering" or "overcoming" or "taking part." Yes, because surviving is basically what you're going to do. If you "prosper" that means you ain't sharing your shit around. The other one is before you criticize, do. . . . Now this is what you can do: Breakdown motherfuckin' capitalism and Marxism to a motherfucker that just wanna know how to get paid. My whole thing is that a whole lot of black people, and especially these white liberals, they get so fuckin' booked, they don't know how to bring it down to practicality.[29]

Public Enemy did not introduce message-oriented or political rap, however. As early as 1983, two singles appeared that would forever change rap. Brother D's 1983 underground hit, "How We Gonna Make the Black Nation Rise," echoed political rap's godfathers, The Last Poets and Gil Scott-Heron:

The Ku Klux Klan is on the loose,
Trainin' their kids in machine gun use
The story might give you stomach cramps.
Like America's got concentration camps.
While you're partying on on on and on,
The other may be hot by the break of dawn
The party may end one day soon
When they're roundin' niggers up in the afternoon.

This single inspired Keith LeBlanc's late 1983 release, "No Sell Out," in which snippets of Malcolm X's speeches were set to a mix of heavy beats. The release was officially endorsed by Betty Shabazz, Malcolm's widow and the guardian of his image and memory.

The Islamic rap styles of political or message rap are represented by Lakim Shabazz, the Poor Righteous Teachers, Rakim, Pete Rock and C. L. Smooth, Brand Nubian, Two Kings in a Cypher, and women rappers Star & Crescent. In 1991 *The Source* magazine initiated what Harry Allen, PE's publicist and a leading critic of mainstream coverage of rap, called an Islamic summit for the rap community in which members of the Five Percent faction of Islam laid out the ideological parameters of Islamic influence on the rap world. This summit, via Lord Jamal of Brand Nubian and Rakim, identified the first Islamic rap record in which Five Percenter science and numerology were "dropped," the mideighties release "World Famous" by the Supreme Team. This recording was followed by Unique and 3 MCs' "Fresh."[30] Islamic rappers bring to hip hop a powerful sense of recovering and reinventing history, packaging it as "science" for the visual generation. Invoking much of the eclectic and popular science of the Nation of Islam, its various factions, and the resurgence led by Minister Louis Farrakhan, they represent a submerged voice of the black rap underground. Ernest Allen's essay in this volume analyzes Islam's sophisticated ideology and its influence and impact on rap music and rappers.

XCLAN and the XCLAN posse, led by Professor X (Lumumba Carson, son of the well-known Brooklyn activist and black nationalist Sonny Carson), represent the epitome of the Africa-centered genre of political rap. They mix African garb, pop Egyptology, and a retro pink cadillac to create a visually stunning image. When asked how he entered the genre, Professor X responded:

Along with a brother like Grand Verbalizer, we found that coming back to the drum was the most important move that a black man could make. . . . The drum connects our African genes whether we are conscious of our connection or not. It is natural [from] our history, or the history that they let us know, that we talk to the drum. So what is not heard through the written word could be attached or completed by the drum. That's what our intentions are.[31]

Grounded in the cultural nationalist revival of the early 1990s, XCLAN emerged on the rap/video scene with their handcrafted staffs, their trademark leather crowns (caps), and a startling array of custom-made African clothing, and their release *To the East Blackwards*, with two platinum singles, "Heed the Word of the Brother" and "Funkin' Lesson." Using samples from Parliament Funkadelic with that pop Egyptology, "Funkin' Lesson" celebrates the metaphysical integrity of African Americans:

> Born in a cosmos where no time and space exist
> mortals label me as illogical, mythological
> They couldn't comprehend me when I brought the word
> a street called verb, a black steel nerve
> teaching those actors and actresses
> who write a coupla lines of what black is

XCLAN's freedom-or-death, unite-or-perish philosophy, along with their African garb, invokes a nostalgia for the cultural nationalism of the 1960s, while hip hop props (such as the pink Cadillac used in so many of their videos) launch the group into visual overdrive in the media-hyped 1990s. They are more than actors, however, being instrumental in organizing the Brooklyn-based Blackwatch Movement (an organization devoted to dealing with the problems of African American youth in Brooklyn, particularly the crack epidemic, violent crime, and the black male crisis). In late 1993 they released the single and video "Close the Crack House" with cameos by a number of rappers. One of the most powerful rap videos ever produced, it confronts the crack problem by highlighting the drug's devastating effects on the African American moral and social order.

Booty rap and retro-mack

Yet another school of rap has prompted the harshest reaction from the fundamentalist right and fed the call for censorship. 2 Live Crew, led by the savvy Luther Campbell, pioneered the style that has been called "booty rap." It is characterized by an obsession with sex and perverted eroticism, visually backed by scantily clothed women mimicking sex and sometimes actually performing it on stage. Their first release, *As Nasty As They Want to Be* with its signature single "Me So Horny," was an immediate hit. 2 Live Crew's Miami-based sound revolved around what Campbell called a "steady beat throughout the entire song," a strong bass beat initially backed by extensive lyrics, which have diminished as the "Miami sound" flourished. The heavy bass beat of that sound swept the South, creating a dance music that produced three smash hits in 1993: Duice's "Daisy Duks," Tag Team's "Whoop, There It Is!" and 95 South's "Whoomp, There It Is!" All three of these singles reflect the Miami-initiated obsession with "booty" and having women expose their buttocks. The latter two raps have become part of the national vernacular, chanted at sports events and repeated by newscasters.

2 Live Crew's smash single "Me So Horny" makes even the sexually explicit lyrics of the godmother of female rap, Millie Jackson, look like lessons from vacation Bible school:

I'll play with your heart just like it's a game
I'll be blowin' your mind while you're blowin' my brain
I'm just like that man they call Georgie Puddin' Pie
I fuck all the girls and I make make 'em cry
I'm like a dog in heat, a freak without warning
I have an appetite for sex 'cause me so horny.

This single along with three others ("Put Her in the Back," "Two Live Crew," and "The Fuck Shop") led Miami antipornography lawyer Jack Thompson to decide to take the group to court. Paul Hetrick, vice-president of Focus on the Family, remarked that *Nasty* includes "87 descriptions of oral sex, 116 mentions of male and female genitalia, and other lyrical passages referring to male ejaculation."[32] *As Nasty As They Want to Be* was banned from Broward County, Florida, record shops in 1990.

The sex/party foundation of the Miami sound, which frequently borders on obscenity and pornography, has unleashed a tide of black-feminist protest and radio and television censorship that continues to this day.[33] At the trial, the Crew summoned Professor Henry Louis Gates, Jr., as an expert witness after reading his defense of the group in an op-ed piece in the *New York Times*, "2 Live Crew Decoded."[34] In his testimony, Gates gave an academic defense of the lyrical content of *Nasty*, arguing that "what we saw was not what we got. . . . There was a meaning hiding beneath the surface of the obvious meaning of the lyrics." He testified that the recordings exaggerate "the worst stereotypes of black men, primarily, but also black women." Black men in classic Western culture have been represented as "oversexed and hypersexed individuals in an unhealthy way." His testimony concludes:

> Well they represent the stereotype over and over again, in such a graphic way, namely to exploit it. You can have no reaction but to bust out laughing. You realize how ridiculous this all is. That's why we all laugh when we hear the performance. I thought one of the healthy things, listening to it, as I said, was hearing the reaction of the audience. There is no cult of violence here. . . . [These songs] are being written and sung by young virile black men. Everybody understands what is going on. Even if they don't understand it as a literary critic, they understand it on a subliminal level. Their response is to bust out laughing, to view it as a joke, a parody.[35]

Gates's testimony, mired in a world of academic make-believe, was rebutted by *Village Voice* columnist Lisa Jones:

> Something Gates said stuck in my head all night long. "There is no cult of violence. There is no danger at all that these words are being sung." I wonder if he's seen 2 Live Crew in concert, as I have, and watched them push women to the floor, pour water on them and chant, "Summer's Eve, Massengil, bitch wash your stinky pussy."[36]

While we cannot eliminate the libidinal element in African American popular culture (it has always been there and always will be), for a critic to lend support to a genre and individuals that promote rape, sodomy, and the abuse of women in general, and black women in particular, is morally and culturally bankrupt. If one needs more evidence of Campbell and his posse's brutal misogyny, the following journalistic account of his 1992 Japan tour should be persuasive:

> After the first dance routine is over, Luke comes out. His Bacardi consumed, he yells: "We gonna have group sex in this motherfucker!" The crowd explodes in loud cheers. Luke's ladies continue performing dance moves patterned after some featured in Miami strip clubs like the Rolex. "We need a fuckin' interpreter up here," Luke yells. "How the fuck you say 'suckin' pussy' in Japan?" The crowd roars an answer. "Bank-O?" Alright. Mo' Bank-O, Mo' Bank-O, Mo' Bank-O!!! Three lucky Japanese kids are called up to the stage, where they get their faces sat on, and simulate fucking the girls while sitting in a chair. One of the trio really gets into the act. Luke walks over to him, while the kid is in a 69 with Luke's dancer, Desire. "Motherfuckin' BANK-O!!!," he yells to the crowd's delight.[37]

The 2 Live Crew style of booty rap has produced several female counterparts, the New York–based Bytches with Problems (BWP) and Los Angeles's Hoez with Attitude (HWA). BWP has released two albums with singles like "Fuck a Man" and "Is the Pussy Still Good?" When an interviewer asked what prompted them to take this approach in their lyrical style, BWP's Michele and Lyndah responded that "anger at woman's roles and a desire to poke fun at double standards" forced them to become "bytches" on record. Asked about this double standard and the ways in which society conditions men and women to express their thoughts about sex, they responded:

> It's okay for NWA to say "Suck my dick, bitch." But when we say, "Eat my Pussy," people go, "Oh my god, How can they say that?" Here's another example: I could go outside my house right now and there would be some guy on the corner holding his crotch. Now if a girl stood on the corner holding her crotch, you know what people would say? There's no way women are allowed to do that. But it's accepted for men.[38]

The biggest single from BWP's 1991 recording was "Two Minute Brother," as sexually explicit as a rhyme can be. The video rivals those of 2 Live Crew:

> Is this all I get?
> Is this supposed to be good dick?
> Damn! You said you was a good lover
> But you're a two minute brother
> Nigga—I ain't even bust a sweat
> Not to mention, I ain't came yet

Despite the feminism of its cultural politics, BWP has been ostracized from hip hop's mainstream. In a heated debate among female rappers on *Donahue*, even the usually cool host sweated at BWP's controversial defense of their style and persona as "bytches." BWP chided Black Entertainment Television for excluding their videos from its popular programs (the programming at BET is overwhelmingly musical with a smattering of news, current events, and specials), including "Wanted," which incorporated footage of the Rodney King beating to document the crisis of black males. BWP and HWA use the booty style as a gimmick to create raps with a message for sisters, as in the rarely played "NO Means NO," a blistering rap on date rape. HWA has also started on the comeback trail with a 1994 release, *Azz Much Ass As You Want*, with lyrics even more explicit than on their previous singles. In "True Hoez," they proclaim: "I'm not the average type of trick / Muthaphuck a nick nack / Give a hoe a dick." In "Hoe I Am," HWA chants: "I'ma jiggahigh, I'ma jiggahoe / I'ma jigga my nigga and work him low. . . . First I ride it until he work it / Since it's all up in his face / I let him slurp it." Luke and the boys, beware. In a 1994 interview with *VIBE* magazine, BWP and HWA defended such sexually explicit lyrics and the cultural politics of "being bitches and hoes":

> A woman who's in a love affair—basically she's fuckin' every night. She loves her man or her husband, okay? But now the next woman doing the same thing, she might get money from it. Basically, you're still fucking. Know what I'm saying? The woman gets what she wants out of it. . . . This is what I'm saying. As a rule, we as women growing up in the inner city have very few options to get out. The school route is cool, but it's not for everybody. So we're saying, "Use what you have." Look at that Trump lady! She might not have used her sexuality to get to the point where she is, but if that what happened, then, honey—you got there.[39]

The final element in the booty-rap style is rap's revival of "mackin'." Etymologically derived from the French word for pimp, *maquereau*, this style was pioneered and is still carried on by East Oakland's Too Short, rumored to be the largest-selling rap artist ever, and has even infiltrated "popsicle" rappers like Kris-Kros, who call themselves Mack Daddy and Daddy Mack. The mack style owes much to the wave of blaxploitation films of the 1970s, particularly *Superfly*, but more important Max Julien's wicked portrayal of the Oakland pimp Goldie in *The Mack*. As Goldie remarked, "Pimpin's big business, and it's been going on since the beginning of time. And it's gonna continue—straight ahead, until somebody up there turns the light out on the planet." In a 1992 interview, Too Short philosophized on the meaning of *The Mack* for his character and style:

> The reason we talk about it so much and it turns up in our music is because it had a real strong pimpin' message. It was about some hard-core pimpin'. It was based on a pimp from Oakland. It was filmed in Oakland, so it's legendary in Oakland. When it was filmed I didn't live out here, but you damn near had to be a nobody if your cousin or your auntie or your brother

or your sister wasn't in *The Mack*. So in this town, I won't speak on any other town, for generations to come the youngsters have to live up to the pimpin'. You don't necessarily have to go out and get a Black woman or a white woman and make her sell her pussy for you, but you have to have that pimp attitude. To me, it's positive, it's not really about degrading women, it's about the black man. It's almost like Muslims. Being a Muslim is like keeping your mind straight. The mack thing is about keepin' your mind correct. It's a self-esteem thing if you ask me.[40]

To compare Muslim and mack is sheer folly and would certainly trigger a scathing reaction from the Nation of Islam. But the Too Short style reinforces the misogyny that has become part of black male youth culture. Too Short's image is one of an everyman, neither handsome nor charismatic; he compensates with the "pimpin' attitude," a strong-willed aggressiveness, a disdain for women, and an array of props like gold jewelry and the pimp's driving machine, the customized Cadillac.

In a unique rap style that combines a vocal monotone with conversational lyrics (mackin'), Too Short is seen as the mythical reincarnation of Goldie. His lyrics are shaped by sexual conquest and control, as in "Pimp the Ho":

> But the cute red tender in the tight red dress
> She has a soft booty and a real big chest
> She said I love ya', said it again
> At the motel freaked her and her friends
> Like Too Short rappin' everybody knows
> Like the mack said, homie, pimp the ho.

The mack style is yet another version of ghetto authenticity, a way of promoting pimping as a legitimate way of life for black men. Too Short sells the reality of his East Oakland turf, while celebrating a way of life that demands both criticism and some form of internal self-regulation. Women rappers, black feminists, and the morally conservative black middle class condemn this genre of rap music as demeaning and degrading to black women, and some male rappers have even joined the chorus, as evidenced in Tupac (contemporarily revised to 2Pac) Shakur's 1993 single "Keep Your Head Up."

Ladies first: flipping the side

Hip hop's culture and its attitude of male centeredness has been challenged internally from the beginning. The b-girl, homegirl attitude borrows widely from the male style, but as Jill Pearlman notes, by turning women from object into subject.[41] Not only can women rappers "be true to the game"; they can excel at the business side of the music as well.

Identifying the first feminist rap on vinyl has raised some controversy. Nancy Guevara's early essay on female and hip hop culture's first wave, included in this volume, is an essential reference and documents these early women writers, breakers, and rappers. Most commentators acknowledge Lady B's 1979 "To the Beat Y'all" ("I've got 18 years of experience / I've got a style that all my own / You've Got Lady B on the Microphone") as one of the feminist-rap forerunners.[42] Lady B's sassy rhymes were followed by the first female crew, Sequence: Angie B, Cheryle the Pearl, and Blondie. Their 1981 underground hit, "Funk You Up," signaled the erotic tease that would become one element in the b-girl style: "I've got heavy eyes / and heavy lips to make your nature rise." This was followed by their single "Simon Says," which castigated men for engaging in premarital sex without accepting responsibility for the children. This single was an indication of the emerging sexuality of rap.

The most important rap in the origin of the female style was the Roxanne syndrome alluded to earlier, the series of response raps that made the dis technique a cornerstone of the hip hop attitude both in music and style. The two Roxannes, Roxanne Shanté and the Real Roxanne, mirror rap's early years. The episode of rap history in which they starred deserves a separate essay, for it ran a long and tortuous course.[43] The controversy extended into the 1980s, when Roxanne Shanté and Sparky D (who also issued a response in the debate) brought each other to tears in a North Carolina concert. They decided to market their rivalry, which led to t-shirts and a national tour. From the beginning, young Roxanne Shanté

> was out to define a respectable place for women in hip hop, and her pointed rhymes cut through all the misogyny and sexism associated with the art form. Not just another b-girl honey, Shante cold-cocked all the skeezoids, and on rap's battleground, she became a force to be reckoned with. She moreover blazed a trail for a new breed of female mc s, including Salt, Pepa, MC Lyte, and Antoinette.[44]

Shanté's trailblazing raps were followed by the female new wave, led by Salt-N-Pepa, hip hop's first truly commercial act. These two MCs from Queens, Cheryl "Salt" James and Sandy "Pepa" Denton, along with their DJ, DeDe "Spinderella" Roper, set the rap world on fire with their platinum record *Hot, Cool, and Vicious* and its single "I'll Take Your Man." Their rap style combined a pop sensibility with a we-can-do-anything feminist attitude that propelled them to the top of the pop charts. "I'll Take Your Man" prompted jealousy and rage among female rappers.

> Salt-N-Pepa's back and we came out to rap you
> So get out of my face before I smack you, ho
> Don't you know, can't you understand
> If you mess with me, I'll take your man
>
> . . . .

> You know what's up, I ain't no poop out
> 'Cause Pepa kicks butts off dumb young pups
> Like you and the rest of your crew
> If mom wants status, I'll did her too
> So scram, you know who I am, damn, chick
> Don't play with me close 'cause I'll take your man.

Ms. Melodie from the Boogie Down Productions (BDP) crew considered issuing a dis rap in response, "I'll Kick Your Ass," and Roxanne Shanté remarked that Salt-N-Pepa were not rappers but "pop artists." This provoked an angry response from Salt: "I'm not gonna name names, but a lot of these people who criticize us so much, they're trying to sneak in this pop stuff. Either they'll make a record with a singer or they'll use some new-Jack Teddy Riley stuff. They turn around and tell us we're not hard-core."[45]

What are the ingredients in Salt-N-Pepa's popularity? First, they acknowledge their influences musically and lyrically, particularly those already mentioned, especially Lady B and the two Roxannes. Second, they have translated the style, bravado, and lyrical rhythm of male rappers and cast them into the female idiom. Not only has this formula proved popular with a wide audience, but the street reality of a hit like "I'll Take Your Man" allows them also to maintain a legitimacy with inner-city sisters. During the early nineties they took a hiatus only to return in the fall of 1993 with two smash singles and videos, "Shoop" and "What a Man" done with En Vogue, from their album *Very Necessary*. "Shoop" has brought Salt-N-Pepa full circle to their origins with its masterful parody of women seeking men: "Here I go, Here I go, Here I go Again / What's My Weakness, Men." The enthusiastic response to Salt-N-Pepa's comeback has sparked a new debate on their appropriation of the male gaze in their videos for "Shoop" and "What a Man," drawing charges of reverse sexism from feminists. In the "Shoop" video all three women are scantily clad in pursuit of muscular young bucks on the beach at Coney Island. With this particular shift, the group matches bell hooks's description of other black women singers "who have cultivated an image which suggests that they are sexually available and licentious." And their current persona continues to fuel debate over whether provocative sexuality, no matter how theatric, is one cause of the ongoing violence against African American women.[46]

MC Lyte's (Lana Moore) 1988 release *Lyte As a Rock* continued the dis style inaugurated by the Roxanne syndrome. Her single "10% Dis" was directed at Antoinette. With Lyte's bass voice and distinctive story-telling style (reminiscent of Slick Rick), "10% Dis" literally neutralized Antoinette with this verse: "Beat biter / Dope style taker / Tell you to you face / You ain't nothin' but a faker." In "Please Understand," the originality of Lyte's lyrics shines through:

> This little player must have thought I was a fool
> He took me out to lunch and offered me a ride home
> When we got there, he asked me could he use my telephone

I said yeah sure flipped him to the floor 'cause
he said what's up and tried to feel my butt
I kicked him down the stairs and said what you provin'
Rolled him to the car and said get movin'.

A series of disastrous releases in the early nineties, including *Act Like You*, gave way to a "deffer" Lyte than ever in the 1993 release *Ain't No Other*, containing the smash single "Ruffneck," which is, as Lyte says, "raw and uncensored," a return to old-school hard core. Lyte adopted a gangsta attitude that has allowed her to reenter the pantheon of rap stars. With her lyrical wit and unique voice, she promises to lead the reinvention of feminist rap.[47]

The little-known recordings of Shazzy (Sherry Marsh from Queens) combine message rap, feminism, and the street life. In her 1990 release *Attitude: A Hip-Hop Rhapsody*, she plays the sexual game in "Heartbreakin' " and raps of a ho's lament in "Giggahoe." But it is her powerful and neglected "The Way It Is" that should command attention:

He was only 11, a mother shouts in despair
A body bag used to be her son in the school's care
And one little suspect sits in the police car
Cryin' cause he stole his brother's gun from the money jar
He was only 14, livin' a big man's dream—gangster
Rock shot him 'cause he stepped on his ice cream
Now, ol' Mrs. Smith the nicest woman in town
Comin' home from work she got robbed and beat down
It's a shame how the younger overlook and neglect
Doesn't this age have any kind of respect?
But if it isn't life the way it is, it's deadly as cancer.

A message rap that could stand some heavy rotation.

Steppin' strong: queen latifah

Heading the women's charge into rap is Queen Latifah, who has taken the genre to another level. Rapper; star of her own television show; performer in several hip hop films (as the manager of a club in *Juice* and as a college activist in *House Party II*); and CEO of her own management company, The Flavor Unit (which manages some of the leading rap acts in the country, including Naughty by Nature and Apache), the Queen has translated the street style of her Irvington/East Orange, New Jersey, roots into a mini–business empire, a "hip-hopreneur" in control of her musical and financial destiny. The Queen burst on the scene in 1990, putting Newark on the hip hop map. *All Hail the Queen* with Afro-British rapper Monie Love heralded the dawn of an Afro-feminist sensibility in hip hop music and culture. The single "Ladies First" became both a battle cry and an anthem for a new sisterhood:

The ladies will kick it, the rhyme it is wicked
Those who don't know how to be pros get evicted
A woman can bear you, break you, take you
Now it's time to rhyme, Can you relate to
A sister dope enough to make you holler and scream
Believe me when I say being a woman is great you see
I know all the fellas out there will agree with me
Not for being one but for being with one
'Cause when it's time for lovin' it's the woman that gives some
Strong steppin' struttin' movin' on
Rhymin' cuttin' but not forgettin'
We are the one to give birth
To a new generation of prophets
'Cause it's ladies first

In the video, Latifah dons a wide range of African clothing and Egyptian- or Cleopatra-inspired garb. The video is interspersed with a panorama of black women activists, including Harriet Tubman, Sojourner Truth, Angela Davis, and Winnie Mandela. With news footage of South Africa rolling, Latifah mocks a chess game of the ongoing struggle for Azanian self-determination. Skillfully produced and orchestrated by the Tommy Boy production team, the video made effective use of both a fashion statement and the Queen's version of "edutainment" (KRS One's term for his style of rap).

This debut was a tough act to follow, and, when subsequent releases failed to live up to the "Ladies First" standard, the Queen turned her talents to management, acting, and producing. She began with Naughty by Nature, whose 1991 single "OPP" was hailed as a turning point in rap, mixing a bit of the new-jack R & B beat with a catchy set of lyrics and the unforgettable lead line, "Down with OPP." In 1993 she produced a controversial single by Apache, "Gangsta' Bitch." Indeed the Flavor Unit posse is home to some of the most innovative and exciting acts in the rap orbit: Nikki D, whose smash 1991 single "Daddy's Little Girl" included the almost simultaneous sampling of Suzanne Vega's 1991 hit "Tom's Diner"; and the Fu-Schnickens, notable for their nursery-rhyme style of rap and their association with the National Basketball Association's junior attraction (Michael Jordan being the senior attraction), Shaquille "Shaq Attack" O'Neal.

Latifah's success as producer, manager, and actor has not changed her down-home style. In response to her critics, Latifah told interviewer Deborah Gregory, "I had to break people out of expecting me to wear crowns all the time, like I couldn't be Queen Latifah without them." As one of hip hop's most articulate and sincere spokespersons, Latifah embodies rap's capacity for self-innovation and self-critique. In commenting on the developing debate in the nineties on rap's hard-core lyrics, including Apache's "Gangsta' Bitch," she pleaded for "people to leave rappers alone. . . . We aren't the problem. We simply reflect what is going on in our society. Plus, if I believe in an artist and sign them, then I don't feel it's my place to tell them how to make their music."[48]

Gangsta-flavored females

West Coast feminist rappers, though few in number, have been strongly influenced by the gangsta flavor. Yo-Yo (Yolanda Whitaker), introduced to the industry by Ice Cube in his 1990 single "It's a Man's World," exploded on the scene in 1991 with her own album, *Make Way for the Motherlode*. She went on to develop her own style and persona; "My name is Yo-Yo / and I ain't no ho, ho!" became her calling card. She has founded a social/political organization, the Intelligent Black Women's Coalition, devoted to community causes and women's issues, particularly physical abuse. In a 1992 interview Yo-Yo commented on this aspect of developing black women's self-awareness: "A lot of women feel it's cool for me to hit on them, because when you were growing up, your mom would tell you she loves you, and that's why she whips you. It's just a mind thing."[49] But Yo-Yo's gangsta-influenced style and her attempt to speak for black women has led other women rappers to question her intentions. Finesse and Synquis comment:

> I think Yo-Yo is confused. Yo-Yo's cool and a dope rapper and I love all that about her, but she started this IBWC movement and in her song she talks about smoking blunts and drinking 40's. What kind of brand new intelligent woman is she? What kind of woman sings about beating up other girls, taking their men, and sending their men back home to beat them up. She contradicts herself and I don't think she realizes that she's contradicting herself because of the (gang) environment that she is in over in LA. She's allowed to smoke blunts and drink whatever she wants to drink, but they don't be talkin' about respect me and this and that.[50]

The Boss and female gangstas like Leshaun, Hurricane Gloria, and Choice have upstaged Yo-Yo's mild gangsta style with a tempting brew of "carnal knowledge, gangsta philosophy and a touch of rouge," according to a recent assessment by Omoronke Idowu. Led by the Detroit-born, Los Angeles–based rapper Boss, these are real gangsta' bitches ready to slice, dice, cut, and shoot. These women have taken the male-dominated genre and turned it inside out. Boss's first release, *Born Gangstaz*—with titles like "Recipe for a Ho"; "Progress of Elimination"; her first hit, "Deeper"; and "Diary of a Mad Bitch"—signals another wave of murderous rhymes. When Idowu asked two young black women at Washington Irving High School in New York what they thought of the female gangsta style, they commented that it was about girls "who wanted to be acknowledged by guys. . . . They try to be down with the way he talks, where he goes. They smoke weed and do what guys do. It's about respect. They want to be respected, like males."[51] Gangsta feminism, though a mirror of street reality, is also a commentary on the stunted maturity of young black adults and fuels ongoing calls for censorship and industry self-regulation.

In contrast to the nihilism of the female version of the gangsta attitude, TLC (for Tionne "T-Boz" Watkins, Lisa "Left Eye" Lopes, and Rozanda "Chili" Thomas) brought to the rap scene in 1992 a uniquely nineties style and message. The women wear outrageous colors, loose-fitting shorts and overalls, and over-sized hats, all festooned with condoms. Their message is safe sex for young men and women, as T-Boz explains: "Our thing is, if you're having sex, you should have safe sex. We show Condoms because we're trying to make it hip; people are having sex without condoms because they're embarrassed or ashamed. Girls especially, they're like, 'TLC is bold. Shoot, if they can wear them on their clothes, I can buy them.' "[52] Through fashionable clothes and feminist attitudes towards sex, TLC has neutralized the image of the "video ho." According to a 1986 study by the Annenberg School of Communications at the University of Pennsylvania, the women in videos often appeared as "predatory females," and the sex scenes were "long on titillation and physical activity but devoid of emotional involvement." By openly promoting a feminist vision and attitude in their singles and video "Ain't 2 Proud to Beg" and "Baby, Baby, Baby," TLC has served notice to male rappers like Sir Mix-A-Lot, 2 Live Crew, and others that "rumpshakin' " and "ho baitin' " are no longer acceptable. Although the TLC attitude shows a marked maturing of women rappers, the group's stage image has been badly tarnished by the ongoing spat between Lisa "Left Eye" Lopes and her boyfriend, Atlanta Falcons wide receiver Andre Rison, whom she was alleged to have shot in an Atlanta shopping mall in 1993; in June of 1994 she pleaded guilty to burning down Rison's $2 million mansion. This is another example of how the fantasy of "rapatude" seldom crosses over to reality.[53]

360 degrees of souljah

Of all the personalities to have emerged from the female side of hip hop, none has inspired more wrath in the ruling establishment than Sister Souljah. Raised in Englewood, New Jersey, in a housing project and on public assistance, she attended Rutgers University and moved to Harlem in 1986, where she became a member of the Public Enemy posse. She has appeared in numerous PE videos as the interviewer for the PE network. She does not call herself a rapper but a "raptivist," using the rap medium to promote the causes of the African world while healing its wounds and scars. She made national headlines in 1992 when her comments on the Los Angeles rebellion in a *Washington Post* interview prompted then presidential candidate Bill Clinton to chide her and other rappers. The incendiary comments were these:

> I mean, if black people kill black people every day, why not have a week
> and kill white people? You understand what I'm saying? In other words,
> white people, the government and the mayor were well aware that black
> people were dying every day in Los Angeles under gang violence. So if
> you're a gang member and you would normally be killing somebody,
> why not kill a white person? Do you know that somebody thinks that

white people are better, or are above dying, when they would kill their own kind.[54]

This angry response to the interviewer recalls the 1960s advocates of "retaliatory violence," of an eye for an eye. Souljah has immersed herself in the philosophy and literature of the period, and her current posture suggests a reincarnation of the Black Panther feminists Kathleen Cleaver and Elaine Brown, who argued with Huey Newton and Bobby Seale that the lumpenproletariat—today's marginal underclass—were the foundations of a new revolutionary movement. Candidate Clinton labeled her a racist "with a lot of influence on young people." But Souljah did not budge, boldly claiming that she "was used as a vehicle, like Willie Horton and other victims of racism." Souljah's only release to date, *360 Degrees of Power,* had one video, "The Final Solution: Slavery's Back in Effect," a mixture of fictionalized history and sci-fi futurism that depicted the reenslavement of blacks. Souljah was banned on MTV, which only increased her popularity and the demand for her as a public speaker, along with a call of "Sister Souljah for president." In defense of her politics and abrasive style, she wrote:

> Having grown up on hip hop, I always considered the drum and beats and bass to be strong and moving. It captured the feeling of the energy of our experience in white America and reestablished Black masculinity, rebellion, self-instruction and information distribution. I believe that Chuck D and Hank Shocklee asked me to be a member of Public Enemy because my life represented what they were rhyming about. Not only had I lived it, I challenged it, rebelled against it, organized and created solutions, and stayed rooted and humble in my blackness.[55]

The great white hoax

Taking its cue from the rhythm-and-blues phenomenon known as "blue-eyed soul," white rappers have struggled to earn the acceptance and respect of their African American and Latino counterparts.[56] Armond White, who has contributed an essay on this phenomenon to this volume, commented that "the white siege of rap is nothing new, after all, Al Jolson singing 'Mammy' in blackface counts as the first Beastie Boy."[57] One of *The Source*'s music critics, Reginald Dennis, labeled white rap "The Great White Hoax." What lies behind these attacks on white rap and its cousin, the crossover into the mainstream of artists like M.C. Hammer? Within the daily street reality of urban culture, black and Latino youth practice the value system of being "true to the game." Being "real" and "true" revolve around the concept of authenticity, not fakery. Public Enemy's rap "Don't Believe the Hype" celebrates the essence of being "real": "The book of the New School rap game / Writers treat me like Coltrane insane / Yes to them, but to me I'm a different kind / We're brothers of the same mind / unblind." Many white rappers cannot meet this standard, and the Hammer style might be compared to painting by numbers—a how-to formula lacking creativity, originality, and spontaneity. But in the wider arena of the culture industry, a white rapper becomes one of thousands of commodities to be consumed by an ever expanding chorus of small town and suburban consumers. The 1980s baby boomers' pimping of black style is nothing new to American popular culture, and rap's absorption by wannabe middle-class white kids desiring a "real" aesthetic is but one more chapter in the cultural exploitation of black style. As Sam Phillips of Sun Records is said to have proclaimed in the early 1950s, "If I could find a white man who had the Negro sound and the Negro feel, I could make a billion dollars." That white man became Elvis Presley.

Indeed, some authentic white rappers exist, and one group that earned the acceptance and praise of black rappers, now defunct, is 3rd Bass, composed of two Brooklyn kids, MC Serch and Prime Minister Pete Nice, who staked a claim to the black urban male style. One project resident described how Serch earned his name:

> Yeah we used to call him Serch 'cause he was always hangin' with the brothers. You don't find that many white boys chillin' with blacks, 'cause most of them are scared or they're afraid of what their moms might say. Yo, even when they was tryin' to fly that head, Serch would still come back to the hood. It wasn't like Serch was tryin' to be black, he was being himself. He was accepted, ya see. And bein' accepted in the 'hood meant a lot to him.[58]

Unlike the Beastie Boys, whose style might be dubbed "Valley white bread," 3rd Bass has been accepted as "real." The usually contrary Playthell Benjamin places the group among those

> white musicians who've wanted to perform in the black idiom. Some sought to improve it: Paul Whiteman's "symphonic jazz" or Dave Brubeck's "third stream." Others were basically parodists, from white blackface minstrels through the original Dixieland jazz band to the Beastie Boys. But others have immersed themselves in the culture, sincerely endeavoring to observe the performance values promulgated by black musicians themselves; among the most musically successful of these acolytes are the New Orleans Rhythm Kings, Benny Goodman, Eric Clapton, and 3rd Bass.[59]

3rd Bass's attitude and rap style were shaped and nurtured by the cultural codes of black masculinity. Brash and speedy, rap was their way out, as they recall in "Product of the Environment":

> In the heart of the city, you was born and bred
> You grew up smart or you wound up dead
> And your savior was a rhyme and a beat in a rap group
> A modern day production of the city street

The group's commitment to the "game" was even more thoroughly reflected in their vicious dis of Vanilla Ice, "Pop Goes the Weasel," an attack on Ice's "Do the White Thing" style of rap. In the video's finale, PM Pete Nice is shown chasing a frightened Ice with a baseball bat: "Pop goes the weasel / and the weasel goes pop."

Vanilla Ice's short-lived ascendancy in the rap world not only illustrates the market's ability to weed out those who cannot meet consumer demand but also reflects the pitfalls of imitation. Labeled the "Elvis of Rap," falsely claiming to have acquired his street authenticity in Miami, he rode to the top of the pop charts with his 1990 single "Ice Ice Baby." His album *To the Extreme* sold seven million copies, making it the biggest-selling rap album in history and alienating him from the rap mainstream. Remarking on his success, he said, "Being white helps me I guess, but I wish it didn't. . . . My being white had something to do with it, but not as much as they say it does. It depends on the contract you sign with the record company. They can make you, you know, if they push you enough."[60] The "Iceman" did enjoy his fifteen minutes of fame only to disappear in less than two years on the scene. In response to "Ice" mania, Ice Cube's cousin, Del Tha Funkee Homosapien, penned this verse from his dis "Pissin' on Your Steps": "Ice is cool, but I can't stand vanilla / Because he takes a style and tries to mock it / Ain't nuthin' personal, G / But I'm kinda into chocolate."

The "hoax" marches on with Marky Mark (famous Times Square poster boy for Jockey underwear and perpetrator of a series of heinous hate crimes) and the Funky Bunch, who engage in this parody of white rappers in "So What Chu Sayin' ":

All right, All right
What an odd sight
Here's another mc whose skin is white
A white kid, a white boy
With a white voice
Just like the Beastie Boys and 3rd Bass
Hmm. This looks like a topic for discussion
To Build racial tension
For fussin' and cussin'.

Then there are the Young Black Teenagers, whose very name (keeping in mind that naming confers identity) is the ultimate in blackface parody. White rappers and pop acts who expropriate the black vernacular frequently have black producers and managers (a producer in the case of YBT, Hank Shocklee of Public Enemy fame, and manager Maurice Starr for New Kids on the Block) who coach these acts in the black sensibility. But the black male experience cannot be duplicated, imitated, or relived, and as MC Serch said of Vanilla Ice: "Elvis, Elvis, baby, too bold, too bold / Ice Ice Baby, no soul, no soul."

Two white rap groups emerged in 1992 and 1993 that may prove to be harbingers of a trend. House of Pain's 1992 single and video "Jump Around" mixes

a bass-driven dance lyric with a "When Irish Eyes Are Smiling" sensitivity. Produced by Cypress Hill's DJ Muggs, House proclaims, "We just happen to be Irish
Americans. We're just lettin' people know where we're from. We're not tryin' to
front like anything but what we are." The celebration and incorporation of Irish
American ethnicity suggests this is one way white rap might solve its identity crisis. This was followed in late 1993 by Blood of Abraham, whose first single and
video, "Scaffold on the Chapel," was filmed on location in Jerusalem with an informed sense of Jewish/Israeli reality. Produced by the late gangsta rapper Ezy-E,
Blood promises to root their segment of rap in their reality, not a mythology.[61]

The rap revolution has come full circle—from its bawdy African American
and Latino street roots to the aesthetic voyeurism of white-bread suburbia—yet
it still commands debate on the politics of popular culture. Presidential candidates have attacked rappers from Sister Souljah to the Geto boys, yet the music,
the culture, the style still dominate, testimony to hip hop's longevity as it goes
into its second generation.

Notes

1. These facts are documented at the end of this essay, which details the controversies
   that surfaced in hip hop during 1993 and early 1994. The court cases are documented
   in the segments on sampling and the censorship cases initiated against Luther Campbell and 2 Live Crew.
2. David Dalby, "The African Element in American English," in *Rappin' and Stylin' Out:
   Communication in Urban Black America*, ed. Thomas Kochman (Urbana: University
   of Illinois Press, 1972), 174. This anthology is an essential reference for understanding the foundations of African American communicative behavior: Dalby was a pioneering scholar in the study of "black English" along with J. L. Dillard, William
   Labov, and Geneva Smitherman during the early 1970s, but the research has not
   moved beyond their initial work. In addition, my understanding of African American speech behavior, within the context of a cohesive African American cultural
   structure, has been informed by the work of University of Pennsylvania ethnographer
   William Labov, particularly his brilliant attack on the deficit theorists of African
   American culture, "Academic Ignorance and Black Intelligence," unpublished paper;
   Geneva Smitherman, "What Go Round Come Round: King in Perspective," *Harvard
   Educational Review* 1 (February 1981): 40–56; Jaquelyn Mitchell, "Reflections of a
   Black Social Scientist: Some Struggles, Some Doubts, Some Hopes," *Harvard Educa-
   tional Review* 11 (February 1982): 27–44. J. L. Dillard, *Black English: Its History and
   Usage in the United States* (New York: Random House, 1972), remains the standard
   work. Even in the 1980s and 1990s, the debate on the African American English vernacular continues. In 1985 William Labov noted, "In the black vernacular words are
   taking on new meanings and being combined in new ways to produce idioms not
   found in any white dialect or in standard English" (William K. Stevens, "Study Finds
   Blacks' English Increasingly Different," *New York Times*, March 15, 1985). These linguistic permutations are the very foundation of the improvisational style of rap. See
   also Felicia Lee, "Grappling with How to Teach Young Speakers of Black Dialect,"

New York Times, January 5, 1994, D1, 22; Lee's lengthy article charts the problems the New York City public schools are facing in dealing with "black English" speakers. The history of academic discussions of "black English" is contained in Geneva Smitherman-Donaldson, "Discriminatory Discourse on Afro-American Speech," in *Discourse and Discrimination*, ed. Geneva Smitherman-Donaldson and Teun A. Van Dijk (Detroit: Wayne State University, 1988), 144–175. The wedding of rap and the black vernacular was the source of a curious experiment in 1989; see "Prof: Must Bridge Gap between English and Rap," *Philadelphia Tribune*, July 21, 1989, 1, 5C.

3. Doug E. Fresh, in *Nation Conscious Rap*, ed. Joseph D. Eure and James G. Spady (New York: PC International Press, 1991), 5. Fresh weaves a rich analysis of this verbal magic.
4. Cab Calloway, with Bryant Rollins, *Of Minnie the Moocher & Me* (New York: Crowell, 1976), 112.
5. The essential source on the poetry of the black arts movement remains LeRoi Jones and Larry Neal, eds., *Black Fire: An Anthology of Afro-American Writing* (New York: Morrow, 1968). Much of the poetry of the period can only be comprehended as performance art, and it was this style, borrowed from the Beats, that elevated the spoken word to new heights in African American culture. This dimension is skillfully covered in Stephen Henderson, *Understanding the New Black Poetry: Black Speech and Black Music as Poetic References* (New York: Morrow 1973). The revival of performance poetry in the 1990s and rap's influence on it is covered in Ed Morales, "A Nuyorican State of Mind," *Village Voice Literary Supplement*, April 1994, 27.
6. Claudia Mitchell-Kernan, "Signifying, Loud-Talking, and Marking," in Kochman, *Rappin'*, 315, 326; one of the most important early works analyzing the *dozens* (another term for signifying) remains John Dollard's pioneering psychoanalytical treatment, "The Dozens: Dialectic of Insult," *American Imago* 1 (November 1939): 1–25. Particularly relevant for understanding the role of ritual insult in rap is his observation: "The Dozens is a pattern of interactive insult which is used by some American Negroes. . . . It is guided by well recognized rules which at once permit and govern the emotion. It is evidently played by boys and girls and by adolescents and adults. Adolescents frequently make use of rhymes to express forbidden notions" (3). The works of linguist Roger Abrahams are also essential, particularly *Positively Black* (Englewood Cliffs, N.J.: Prentice-Hall, 1969) and *Deep Down in the Jungle* (Englewood Cliffs, N.J.: Prentice-Hall, 1970), for his pioneering analyses of signifying.
7. Afrika Bambaataa, "To Know Your Future Is to Know Your Past," *Rap Sheet*, June 1993, 010.
8. "Grandmaster Caz and Hiphopography of the Bronx," in Eure and Spady, *Nation Conscious Rap*, xvii; Daisann McLane, "The Forgotten Caribbean Connection" (*New York Times*, August 23, 1992, Arts & Leisure section, 22) pinpoints the Antillean connection to hip hop.
9. This episode is recounted in David Toop, *Rap Attack 2: African Rap to Global Hip Hop* (London: Serpent's Tail, 1991), 63.
10. Andrew Ross, "Hip, and the Long Front of Color," in *No Respect: Intellectuals and Popular Culture* (New York: Routledge, 1989), 71. Hip hop's democratization and demystification of communications' and recording technologies' full impact has yet to be explored. Perhaps when this is accomplished, new strategies might be implemented in the public schools to initiate lower-class African American, Afro–West Indian, and Latino youth into these future technologies. Computer games are also a

source of this democratization and demystification. A brilliant analysis of video games is Julian Stallabrass, "Just Gaming: Allegory and Economy in Computer Games," *New Left Review* 198 (March–April 1993): 83–106.

11. Mark Costello and David Foster Wallace, *Signifying Rappers: Rap and Race in the Urban Present* (New York: Ecco, 1990), 55–56. Houston Baker has evaluated this technology in his essay "Hybridity: The Rap Race, and Pedagogy for the 1990s," in *Technoculture*, ed. Constance Penley and Andrew Ross (Minneapolis: University of Minnesota Press, 1991), 197–210, especially p. 201, where he notes that rap's "technics is the verb and reverb of the human voice pushed straight out, or emulated by synthesizers, or emulating drums and falsettoes, rhyming, chiming sound that is a mnemonic for black urbanity."

12. Jason H. Marcus, "Don't Stop That Funky Beat: The Essentiality of Digital Sampling to Rap Music," *Hastings Communications/Entertainment Law Journal* 13 (1991): 776. This is an absolutely essential reference. See also Sheila Rule, "Record Companies Are Challenging 'Sampling' in Rap," *New York Times*, April 21, 1992, C13, 18.

13. Toop, *Rap Attack 2*, 65.

14. On "King Tim 111," ibid., 82.

15. Ibid., 90.

16. Alex Constantinides and Shaun Ressner, "Return to 'Planet Rock,' " *Hip-Hop Connection* (UK), August 1992, 21.

17. Katrina Hazzard-Donald and Robert Farris Thompson analyze the intricacies of break-dancing in this volume. Other essential sources include the magnificent "how-to" poster produced by the New York City Breakers, widely circulated in 1984. This poster contains step-by-step directions on electric boogie/body poppin', moonwalking, top-rocking, footwork, and the headspin. Also Curtis Marlow, *Breakdancing* (Cresskill, N.J.: Sharon Publications, 1984); Nelson George, Sally Banes, Susan Flinker, and Patty Romanowski, *Fresh: Hip Hop Don't Stop* (New York: Random House, 1985)—Sally Banes's essay "Breaking" contains a number of now rare photographs of early Bronx breakers—and Steven Hager, *Hip Hop: The Illustrated History of Break Dancing, Rap Music, and Graffiti* (New York: St. Martin's, 1984).

18. Havelock Nelson and Michael Gonzales, *Bring the Noise: A Guide to Rap Music and Hip-Hope Culture* (New York: Crown, 1991), 203. The authors' observations on the distinctly lower-middle-class roots of Run DMC and on the role of Queens and Long Island in the genesis of rap's second wave deserve more extensive investigation. This parody of the lumpen-proletarian street culture by these lower-middle-class wannabes is another indication of art imitating life.

19. See, for example, Robert Palmer, "Street-Smart Rapping Is Innovative Art Form," *New York Times*, February 4, 1985; Robert Palmer, "Rap Music, Despite Adult Fire, Broadens Its Teen-Age Base," ibid., September 21, 1986, Arts & Leisure section, 23–24 (which documents Run DMC's breakthrough to the crossover market); and Glen Collins, "Now Rap Is 'Bum-Rushing' the Mainstream," *New York Times*, August 29, 1988, 13, 15. Collins interviewed Robert Farris Thompson, who informed him that "The style of rap boasts in which badness is turned inside out derives from the metaphoric characteristics of the Mande-kan." Curiously, the hip hop vernacular has produced its own dictionary, compiled by (canceled TV series) Yo! MTV Raps videojockey and retired writer (graffiti artist) Fab 5 Freddie, *Fresh Fly Flavor: Words and Phrases of the Hip-Hop Generation* (Stamford, Conn.: Longmeadow, 1992). Un-

fortunately, this volume is already out of date, and the self-innovative energy of the hip hop vocabulary makes obsolete even its most colloquial words and phrases.

20. Adario Strange, "Not a Children's Story Anymore," *The Source*, July 1991, 52.

21. Armond White, "Slick Rick Talks Back," *City Sun*, May 3–9, 1989, 16.

22. This comment reflects the current sentiment between Dr. Dre and Ezy-E, who refers to Dre as a "studio gangsta." The comment is from the OG Tweedy Bud Loc, quoted in Akwanza, "Hype from the Hood," *RapPages*, April 1993, 16. It also reflects the Michel Foucault notion of "passive violence," "a calm vigor, a strength no disorder can mobilize, since from the start it will be subject to the course of natural law. More than the image of vivacity and vigor, it is one of robustness that prevails, enveloping the theme in a new resistance, a young elasticity, but subjugated and already domesticated." *Madness and Civilization*, trans. Richard Howard (New York: Pantheon, 1967), 133. It is the corporate cooptation of gangsta rap that has it "subjugated and already domesticated." Finally, it would be wise to heed Sanyika Shakur's (Kody Scott) warning, "There are no other gang experts except participants," in understanding the gangsta-rap phenomenon. *Monster: The Autobiography of an L.A. Gang Member*, (New York: Atlantic Monthly Press, 1993), xiii. A useful summary of the impact of deindustrialization is Barry Bluestone, "Deindustrialization and Unemployment in America," *Review of Black Political Economy*, 17 (Fall 1988): 29–44. One can easily draw comparisons between the zoot-suit "hep cats" and "jive talkers," subjects of state repression in the 1940s, and the "studio gangstas" of the 1990s; see Bruce Tyler, "Black Jive and White Repression," *Journal of Ethnic Studies* 16 (Winter 1989): 31–66. Another indication of the attack on the youth lumpenproletariat by a former white radical activist is Mark Naison, "Outlaw Culture and Black Neighborhoods," *Reconstruction* 1 (1992): 128–132. This is an especially surprising piece since Naison had supported the lumpen-based culture of the Black Panther Party during the late sixties and early seventies. Instead of identifying the material roots of "lumpenization," Naison falls into the classic trap of middle-class moralizing about the cultural deficits of African Americans in the inner city.

23. Two informative but contrasting profiles of the rapper Ice-T are Donna Britt, "Ice-T, Warming Up," *Washington Post*, July 17, 1991, C1, 2, and Armond White, "America's Least Wanted Eleven: Ice-T Goes Buck Wild," *City Sun*, August 26–September 1, 1992, 25, 32.

24. When the Geto Boys' first major release, *Geto Boys*, was withdrawn from distribution in 1990 by Geffen records because of controversial lyrics, MC Bushwick Bill said, "We were just expressing stuff that happens in the ghetto, just being like reporters. We want to make everybody mad enough to look at the ghetto right in their own state, not just to look at the middle-class and the rich areas." Jon Pareles, "Distributor Withdraws Rap Album over Lyrics," *New York Times*, August 28, 1990, C11. Seldom is this kind of sociopolitical analysis accorded serious attention by the bourgeois press. Mr. Scarface's reflections on what might be called "apocalyptic rap" are from an extraordinary interview with Allan Gordon, "In the Face of Fire," *The Source*, October 1993, 43.

25. I have covered the Griff incident in the wider context of PE's adoption of Nation of Islam rhetoric in their lyrics. William Eric Perkins, "Nation of Islam Rhetoric in the Rap of Public Enemy," *Black Sacred Music* 5 (Spring 1991): 41–50. See also Armond White's explosive analysis, "Fear of Language: American Media and Public Enemy," *City Sun*, December 12–18, 1990, 25, 32–36, and the stunning interview, Robert

Christagau and Greg Tate, "Chuck D All Over the Map," *Village Voice*, Rock & Roll Quarterly (Fall 1991): 12–18. Griff, who ran Public Enemy's security team, called Security of the First World, was accused of blatant antisemitism in 1989. This caused PE founder Chuck D to dismiss Griff from the group, which led to a temporary hiatus that the media described as a breakup.
26. Robert Hilburn, "Checking in with Chuck D," *Los Angeles Times*, Calendar section, November 8, 1992, 65.
27. Christagau and Tate, "Chuck D All Over," 14.
28. See Seth Mydans, "For Nonviolent Legacy, a Violent Rap Message," *New York Times*, January 11, 1992, 6.
29. Harry Allen and Chuck D, "Black 11 Black," *SPIN* 6 (October 1990): 68.
30. Harry Allen, "An Islamic Summit," *The Source*, March–April 1991, 52.
31. Eure and Spady, *Nation Conscious Rap*, 191.
32. James LeMoyne, "The Men Who Took Aim at Rap Groups," *New York Times*, June 12, 1990.
33. For example, see Kimberle Crenshaw, "Beyond Racism and Misogyny: Black Feminism and 2 Live Crew," *Boston Review*, December 1991, 6, 30–32, for an eloquent analysis of the issues involved in the 2 Live Crew case in the wider context of Afro-feminist politics. Also see Paula Ebron, "Rapping between Men: Performing Gender," *Radical America* 24 (October–December 1989): 23–27. Her point that "gender is part of structuring difference between communities" is essential in keeping African American men and women divided on the broader social, political, and economic issues confronting them.
34. Henry Louis Gates, Jr., "2 Live Crew, Decoded," *New York Times*, June 19, 1990, A31.
35. Gates's testimony is recounted in Luther Campbell and John Miller, *As Nasty As They Wanna Be* (Fort Lee, N.J.: Barricade, 1992), 153–154.
36. Lisa Jones, "The Signifying Monkees," *Village Voice*, November 6, 1990, 171.
37. Ronin Ro, "Japanese Basketball: Luther Campbell, a Big Mama and HipHop Music in Japan," *The Source*, March 1993, 62.
38. Michael Small, *Break It Down: The Inside Story from the New Leaders of Rap* (New York: Citadel, 1992), 51.
39. In an extraordinary Donahue telecast that also included MC Lyte, old-school master Jazzy Joyce, and Yo-Yo, BWP took the media to task for excluding their sexually oriented raps in favor of those of male rappers and called for equal airtime standards. Donahue transcript #3216, "Female Rappers Invade the Male Rap Industry," May 29, 1991, 8.
40. Reginald Dennis, "Pimpin' Ain't Easy," *The Source*, August 1992, 36. A whole genre of ghetto literature published and distributed by Holloway House in Los Angeles was extremely popular during the late sixties and early seventies. These pulp novels by Iceberg Slim and Donald Goines (both authentic street hustlers) invaded the cultural psyche of the black college students whose lower-middle-class backgrounds belied their quest for ghetto authenticity. The cinematic representation of this genre, particularly Gordon Parks's *Superfly* and Melvin Van Peebles's *Sweet Sweetback's Bad Ass Song* (and later Max Julien's *The Mack*), sanctified the ghetto life-style and led to scores of imitations and duplications. It is ironic that the retro-mack style of Too Short has revived ghetto fiction (you can find the novels of Donald Goines and Iceberg Slim in any African American bookstore in the country or on many street corners) and even created how-to books, led by Dallas's Rufus Shaw's *How to Be a Rich Nigger*, recently reissued along with his *Street Economics*. This entire area of African American popular culture deserves serious attention, since it is a significant force in

promoting black-on-black crime and violence, misogyny, and a distinct lumpen-proletarian cultural code of conduct.

41. Jill Pearlman, "Rap's Gender Gap," *Option* (Fall 1988), 34. I provide a brief summary of the emergence of African American female rappers, "Rap Musicians," in *Black Women in America: An Historical Encyclopedia,* ed. Darlene Clark Hine et al. (New York: Carlson, 1993) 2:964–965.

42. On these see Cheryl L. Keyes, " 'We're More Than a Novelty, Boys': Strategies of Female Rappers in the Rap Music Tradition," in *Feminist Messages: Coding in Women's Folk Culture,* ed. Joan Newlon Radner (Urbana: University of Illinois Press, 1993), 207.

43. I am currently researching the origins of this episode in hip hop history. The starting point for this history remains John Lombardi, "The True Story of the Real Roxanne," *New York Daily News Sunday Magazine,* November 2, 1986, 15–18, 50.

44. Nelson and Gonzales, *Bring the Noise,* 200–201.

45. Small, *Break It Down,* 169.

46. Ibid. Tricia Rose offers an intriguing analysis of Salt-N-Pepa's emergence in her important essay "Never Trust a Big Butt and a Smile," *Camera Obscura,* May 1991, 109–131, especially 117–122. Salt-N-Pepa's response to the charges of "reverse sexism" is covered in Leonard Pitts, Jr., "The Sexism Rap," *Philadelphia Inquirer,* June 9, 1994, D1, 5, while their comeback trail is profiled in Lynette Jones, "Salt-N-Pepa: Very Necessary, Hot and Controversial," *Rap Sheet,* June 1994, 020–021. The lengthy quotes from BWP and HWA are from an interview with Ipeleng Kgostile, "Attitude Problems: Hoez with Attitude Meet Bytches with Problems," *VIBE,* May 1994, 30, and the quote from bell hooks is from her essay "Selling Hot Pussy," in *Black Looks: Race and Representation* (Boston: South End, 1992), 65.

47. Armond White has charted MC Lyte's new direction in "Ruffneck and Brassneck," *City Sun,* June 30–July 1, 1993, 20.

48. These quotations are from Deborah Gregory, "The Queen Rules," *Essence,* October 1993, 58, 118. The Queen has literally become a cottage industry. Important articles are Kim Green, "The Naked Truth," *The Source,* November 1991, 32–36; Kim Green, "Female MCs: Sisters Stompin' in the Tradition," *YSB,* November 1991, 50–53; Gerrie Summers, "This Queen's Got Flavor," *Rap Sheet,* October 1993, 012–014; and on the Queen's hit television sitcom for Fox, Andy Meisler, "The Ever-Expanding Realm of Queen Latifah," *New York Times,* January 9, 1994, Arts & Leisure section, 29, 33.

49. Gerrie Summers, "You Still Can't Play wit' YoYo," *RapPages,* October 1992, 51.

50. "Finesse and Synquis Take on BWP," *Serious Hip-Hop,* February 1992, 35.

51. Omoronke Idowu, "Ms Gangsta," *Village Voice,* October 18, 1993, 21. The gangsta style is a repudiation of women as "gold-diggin' skeezas' " and an indication of their toughness. Boss's entire persona has been erected not only to challenge the conventional stereotype of "bitch and ho'," but also to place women on an equal footing within the performance culture of hip hop. *Rap Sheet* devoted its April 1993 issue to the use of the word *bitch,* with interviews of male and female rappers.

52. Kierna Mayo, "TLC Demanding Respect," *The Source,* June 1993, 49, 61.

53. See, for example, Lisa Jones, "Gold Digging the Skeezers," *Village Voice,* July 16, 1991, 41; Donna Britt, "The Homegirls We Don't See," *Washington Post,* July 30, 1993, B1, 6; Courtland Milloy, "No 'Hoochie Mamas' for this Video," *Washington Post,* April 14, 1993, C1, 5; Michael Gonzales, "The Evolution of Exploitation: Sex, Sisters and Hip-Hop Videos," *RapPages,* October 1992, 42–46; and Robin Roberts, "Music Videos, Performance, and Resistance: Feminist Rappers," *Journal of Popular Culture*

25 (Fall 1991): 141–152. The homophobia of some rappers (male rappers like Chuck D, Big Daddy Kane, and, of course, Schooly D), is placed within the context of male supremacy and sexism in a remarkable editorial by DJ Marius, "Homophobia: Still at Odds with the Hip-Hop Nation," *RapPages*, February 1993, 20.

54. David Miller, "Sister Souljah's Rebellion Rap," *Washington Post*, May 13, 1992, B1.

55. Sister Souljah, "S.O.S.: Souljah on Souljah," *RapPages*, October 1992, 57. There is also a stunning profile: Gordon Chambra, "Souljah's Mission," *Essence*, December 1991, 60, 106–108.

56. The starting point for the blue-eyed soul phenomenon is Norman Mailer's classic essay "The White Negro," in *Advertisements for Myself*. George Melly's *Revolt into Style* (London: Lane, 1970) documents the "soul" invasion in England, which would reverberate back to the colonies, through British rock. See Iain Chambers, "A Strategy for Living: Black Music and White Subcultures," *Working Papers in Cultural Studies*, nos. 7 and 8 (Summer 1975): 157–166, for the standard analysis of the "affective" nature of black music as a counterpoint to the "increasing rationality and mathematical logic" of Western music. Benj DeMott, "The Future Is Unwritten: Working-Class Youth Cultures in England and America," *Critical Texts* 5 (1988): 42–56, is a brilliant analysis of the emergence of rap in the inner city and the contrasting effects of rock 'n' roll in the working-class ghettos of London, Liverpool, and Birmingham. Clayton Riley, "If Aretha's Around, Who Needs Janis," *New York Times*, March 8, 1970, Arts & Leisure section, 1, 9, is a scathing analysis of what he calls the "rape" of black music. It is interesting that he cites the Rascals (led by Felix Cavalieri, and one of the significant forces of blue-eyed soul during its peak in the early seventies) as "the best thieves. . . . Beautiful cats. Swift. Doing tempo things most white groups wouldn't try." See also Michael Bane, *White Boy Singin' the Blues: The Black Roots of White Rock* (New York: Penguin, 1982), and Richard Pack, Bruce Huston, Thomas Cullen, and Doug Wright, "A–Z of Blue-Eyed Soul," *Soul Survivor* (Toronto), Winter 1987, 12–15, 20, which documents every blue-eyed soul group.

57. Armond White, "The White Albums: Is Black Music under Siege?" *City Sun*, December 5–11, 1990, 19.

58. Nelson and Gonzales, *Bring the Noise*, 244.

59. Playthell Benjamin, "Two Funky White Boys: Judging 3rd Bass by the Standards of the Street," *Village Voice*, January 8, 1990, 34; also, Carter Harris, "MC Serch, 'I Have to Earn My Wings Daily,' " *RapPages*, February 1993, 31–34.

60. James Bernard, "Why the World Is after Vanilla Ice," *New York Times*, February 3, 1991, Arts & Leisure section, 26. Also see Rob Tannebaum, "Sucker MC: Vanilla Ice," *Village Voice*, December 4, 1990, 69; John Rockwell, "Hammer and Ice, Rappers Who Rule Pop," *New York Times*, November 18, 1990, Arts & Leisure section, 30, 32; Reginald Dennis, "The Great White Hoax," *The Source*, October 1991, 52–55; Marcus Preece, "Do the White Thing," *Hip-Hop Connection*, December 1993, 16–17, offers a humorous but interesting typology of white rappers: (1) the "trash," groups like House of Pain, Young Black Teenagers, and the Stereos, who "grew up in the hood," (2) the "pinkos," rappers "who hijacked rap for political ends," with groups like UK's multiracial Rage Against the Machine and Marxman, (3) the "vanillas," for which no explanation is required, and (4) the "whitecoats," led by the now defunct 3rd Bass. Vanilla Ice resurfaced in 1994 with a new look and a new single/video, "Roll 'Em Up: Hootie Mack." A dreadlocked Vanilla Ice rolls with the flavor, in this comeback. In an extraordinary interview with *Source* editor John Shecter, he laments

his lack of acceptance by black rappers and whines over his own and his management's excesses ("Under Pressure," *The Source*, March 1994, 57–62, 76). Hammer has already dissed his previous crossover image and gone hard core with his 1994 release *Funky Headhunter*, with his smash single/video, "Pumps and a Bump." In another single, "Don't Stop," Hammer castigates the hip hop critics with the rhyme, "Now if I sung that I drop 'cuz it's pop / then it's like that and you don't stop."

61. Blood of Abraham's album, released in early 1994, is an astonishing piece of work. House of Pain's dynamic 1993 European tour is covered in Paul Rogers, "Excess All Areas," *Hip-Hop Connection*, September 1993, 6–11.

roots

part

women writin' rappin' breakin'

nancy guevara

Like Aretha Franklin says, "Who's zoomin' who?"

Roxanne Shanté

Over the past few years, a rash of Hollywood hip hop movies, together with a spate of thirty-second hip hop spots for Pepsi-Cola, Kodak, and Burger King, have spun a hype fantasy-image of South Bronx b-boys boogieing, breaking, and scratching records for a massified and mainly white viewing audience. This image of hip hop is uinflected by any hint of the socioeconomic or racial context in which its practices arose, or of the cultural antecedents of these practices: in its commercial representations hip hop simply *appears* as a faddish display of male exuberance in inner-city ghettos, a sudden inexplicable burst of color and energy in the cultural vacuum of the early 1980s.

What follows is an attempt to correct one aspect of this distorted image, by foregrounding the distinct and essential creative role of *women* in the formation and development of hip hop—and by doing so through the testimony of some black and Latina women themselves. But just as the elision of women from the hip hop image (however aided and abetted in actuality by various male partici-

Reprinted from Mike Davis, Manning Marable, Fred Pfeil, and Michael Sprinker, eds., *The Year Left II, Toward a Rainbow Socialism: Essays on Race, Ethnicity, Class and Gender* (Verso/NLB, London and New York, 1987), pp. 160–175.

pants in hip hop subculture) must be seen in the context of the overall distortion of hip hop by and in the mass commercial media, so women's involvement with and contributions to the subculture of hip hop must be understood in the context of its descent from the historical continuum of creative expression of blacks and other oppressed groups in the United States. The purpose of this introduction, then, is to sketch out some of the main threads and major conjunctures about this genealogy, before moving on to the voices of some of the women rappers, breakers, and graffiti writers in hip hop.

Each of the three forms of hip hop—rap music, subway graffiti, and breakdance—had grown out of a long history of interaction between black and Latin urban cultures, whose most recent phase began during the late 1940s, when migrants arriving from colonial Puerto Rico started to take up jobs and live in neighborhoods alongside American blacks.[1] Since that time, close social interaction between blacks and Latins and their common subordination to the dominant culture have created the conditions for the development of unique alternative modes of expression. Subway graffiti, for example, descends from the 1950s street graffiti used to proclaim a black or Latino gang's hold on its territory. During the sixties, graffiti developed into a more elaborate communications network with its own codes of behavior and aesthetics to reflect the identity and concerns of black and Latino teenagers.[2] Graffiti became even more colorful and stylized during the early seventies with the advent of subway graffiti, which introduced spray paint as the key artistic medium. While the graffiti of the fifties and sixties did not travel outside the immediate neighborhood, and thus remained unseen beyond the ghettos, subway graffiti increased the circulation of names, words, and messages, carrying this persistent search for identity and self-expression both across and uptown.[3]

The roots of rap music are more complex and varied.[4] Beyond its immediate historical antecedents within black culture (from the bragging blues of Bo Diddley to the high-energy inspiration of James Brown in cuts like "Soul Power" and "Sex Machine," from radical prison toasts to those developed by hip hop DJs like Afrika Bambaataa and Grandmaster Flash), there stretches a longer history, running back through street games of "signifying" and "the dozens" all the way to the word games embedded in Caribbean and West African cultures. The appropriation and dissemination of rap by Puerto Rican DJs like Charlie Chase were facilitated by the similarity in verbal dexterity and rhythmic use of voice prized in these black traditions to those common to such Latin musical styles as the Puerto Rican *décima* and *plena*. The result of these convergent influences is a complex and highly innovative technique not only of rapping often overtly political lines over previously recorded musical accompaniments, but of mixing, cutting, scratching, and backspinning the records themselves, thus producing a whole realm of empowering uses of record music for individual and collective expression.

Similarly, the acrobatic virtuosity of breakdancing has clear precedents in early African-rooted forms like the jitterbug and rumba. Here again, James Brown appears as a direct and hugely influential precursor. His spectacular stage performances together with his dancing song hits are recognized sources of breakdancing, along with martial arts and gymnastics. But the belligerent appearance of many breakdance steps, with their emphasis on leg- and footwork, also characterizes other black and Latino dance forms, such as the *capoeira* developed by African slaves in Brazil more than three centuries ago.[5]

Of course the ahistorical commercial presentation of hip hop is neither accidental nor new. Whenever black or Latino aesthetic innovations have been repackaged and sold to white audiences as entertainment fads, the contextual and traditional meanings of those innovations have been airbrushed out.[6] Cooptation by the dominant culture invariably involves repression; and in the case of hip hop (as with bebop and bop culture forty-odd years ago), the repression comes in both hard and soft forms. We will return to this point in closing and so for now will merely note that each year more than $9 million of the New York City budget is spent on the "graffiti war" waged by its Mass Transportation Authority, and that only a few years ago black and Latino teenagers were routinely arrested for breakdancing in shopping malls and subway stations.

Nor is the exclusion or trivialization of women's role in hip hop culture a mere oversight on the part of the image makers. The undermining, deletion, or derogatory stereotyping of women's creative role in the development of minority cultures is a routine practice that serves to impede any progressive artistic or social development by women that might threaten male hegemony in the sphere of cultural production. Just as the accomplishments of women in the blues tradition or in rock 'n' roll remain largely unrecognized, so in commercial representations of hip hop, women are typically depicted in secondary roles as cheerleaders or bystanders rather than as producers and active participants. Or, when they do receive leading roles, as in most of Hollywood's hip hop films, women come to hip hop through romantic involvement with young black or Latin breakers and rappers. In this role as exotic outsiders with whom the white audience is encouraged to effect a fantasy identification, their education in rapping and breaking functions to connect hip hop to mainstream white culture.

The political challenge that hip hop represents as an expression of oppressed groups in the United States is magnified significantly when the women involved are brought into the real picture. Through the testimony of female rappers, breakers, and graffiti writers, vital aspects of the undocumented, intricate cultural contexts and contradictions of hip hop emerge. Who are these women? What do they think is the origin or future of hip hop? How do women use this style? Is theirs different from the style men use? What do they think of the social role of hip hop? The best answers to these questions come from the women themselves. Let's hear what they have to say.

Lady pink and lady heart: "this *is* a man's world"

How did Lady Pink become involved in subway graffiti? "Like any other graffiti writer. First, you're an apprentice to a master who teaches you how to tag your name properly. Then you do pieces on paper. When you have the hang of that, you're ready to go to the [subway] yards. There is so much to know before going to the yards that only masters can get away with it." To succeed, a writer must be able to create and handle intricate graffiti forms and styles, of which tags (stylized signatures) and pieces (four or more bubble letters representing a name or word) are the simplest.[7] Lady Pink (Sandra Fabara) was a consummate graffiti writer by the fall of 1980, at age fifteen. She was a participant in the historic graffiti show at Fashion Moda in the South Bronx and was the curator of an exhibit that displayed the works of twenty well-known graffiti writers. Her popularity increased after she played a leading role in the documentary film *Wild Style* (1984).

Pink came from Ecuador at age seven. In New York, she was encouraged by her seventh-grade teacher to attend the High School of Art and Design after she was singled out as the best artist of her class. There, Pink became interested in graffiti and practiced her style in the ladies' room, with her friend Lady Heart (Gloria Williams), who was born in Corona, Queens, to a family that had come north from Alabama.

During her high school years, Heart and her brother devoted long hours to practicing their tags and pieces on the walls. Soon, a teacher wanted to know who was painting the school walls. The result, to their surprise, was that Heart and her brother were commissioned to paint several murals in school and throughout the neighborhood. Thanks to an early interest in painting, Heart was already accustomed to oils and acrylics, but she became more interested in graffiti when she met Pink and went on to learn more graffiti techniques together with her.

To Pink, graffiti is a personal challenge. Her involvement is directed, as she puts it, "against the idea that women have no brains, only emotions. That at three o'clock in the morning a girl should be sleeping." It is not hard to imagine how her family responded to this defiant attitude, but what had been the reaction in the male-dominated world of graffiti? Pink and Heart recognize the talent of male graffiti masters and are quick to acknowledge the support they have received from Doze, Case, Lee, and Seen in particular. Nevertheless, female writers are often the target of jealous males who seek to discredit them. The competition that typically exists among writers takes on a special character when applied to women, as in the constant charge of "biting" (copying someone else's style) brought against female writers by any number of males.

Moreover, the artistic prestige of girl writers within the hip hop subculture too often depends less on their ability to use or create style than on their personal (meaning, as often as not, sexual) reputation. Heart explains: "Being a girl writer you have to be brave because whether you are that kind of girl or not, they figure when a girl hangs out with all these boys [she] is this kind of girl and that. And it's up to you to handle yourself accordingly when situations like that come up." Graffiti gossip extends to four boroughs, so "who knows what kind of story is gonna end up in the Bronx when it really happened in Queens," says Heart. Female writers understand that the boys' personal attacks on their reputation aim at discouraging their participation. "The stories get so outrageous that it makes you laugh. They want graffiti for boys only. I think they figure that you say something so bad about us, it's just gonna hurt our little feelings and we're not gonna want to be bothered with graffiti. But anybody that's half way on the road to maturity knows not to let what other people say really affect them."

Yet the negative comments about Pink and Heart are known in more recent times to have discouraged other females from becoming writers, or at least from going beyond tagging. But fear also seems to keep females from going to the subway yards in large numbers. As Pink says, graffiti "is a filthy business, and then going through creepy tunnels in the South Bronx at three in the morning . . ." Heart agrees: "It takes nerve to be a graffiti writer. The yards are dark, the trains make noise. Even when a train is shut off it makes noise, and you jump and look. You gotta look under the train, and up and down the lanes. Sometimes the workers sneak up on you and they'll chase you!"

Why, then, under such unfavorable conditions, do some young women get involved in graffiti? Heart believes that "a lot of girls want to be down with graffiti even if they don't write it themselves because there is something about graffiti that just draws people to it." Pink thinks graffiti writing is the result of a need to make "your mark on a city that got to be so huge," where "you're just a little nobody from the ghetto. You have no money, no school training, what can you do?" Heart adds: "It is an artistic outlet, to develop your artistic qualities and to make your own little statements." Moreover, Heart strongly disagrees with predominant accounts claiming that graffiti developed out of the desire of writers to become famous. She thinks that being a writer "takes much more than that! It started out showing your art work, your talent."

Wall and subway graffiti of the New York style, unlike others (e.g. bathroom graffiti), serve not merely to label but to reveal, even proclaim, the author's identity, ideas, and feelings. One of Pink's graffiti pieces reads (above her signature): "War, crime, corruption, poverty, inflation, pollution, racism, injustice . . . this *is* a man's world!" Her message not only expresses how she feels about the world but attributes the actuality of these conditions to men and contrasts it with a hypothetical female world. Her more overtly political works include representations of burning bodies in El Salvador, war tanks in Nicaragua, skulls after a nuclear disaster, and murals of formidable Amazons symbolizing the power of women.

There are differences in both style and subject between female and male writers. "Men have a passion for black!" exclaims Pink. "I sometimes exclude black altogether. I work more with light colors. Things that are a little softer, more tender, sensitive." Her subjects also differ from those of the young men: "I paint women. Women in distress or very strong women." Landscape and flower scenes are other subjects favored by female writers because "girls wanna more or less decorate the trains," says Heart. "Guys talk about destroyin' it, killin' it, but they want all the space for themselves. They all wanna be city kings, their names up on every train all over the city." Pink has often used stencils to paint big lips and roses instead of writing her name. And both Pink and Heart seek to "make a statement" by painting make-up and other female properties on the sides of many trains. To them, a style that is consciously, deliberately feminine will help lead to the recognition of girl writers and will contravert the oppressive attitude of their male peers.

But the women's struggle to establish a presence within graffiti encounters other serious obstacles in addition to male prejudice. Both the sudden commercial success of the graffiti style and increased official opposition to subway graffiti have altered the course of the graffiti movement, arguably to the greater detriment of women writers than of men. While graffiti on canvas is widely popular and marketable, subway graffiti remains an illegal activity. As Heart points out: "Graffiti is more dangerous now that some yards have attack dogs and tall fences with double sets of barbed wire." Earlier on, she reminisces, "there was none of that. The yards used to be dark and there was always a way in and out." And the recent prospect of fame and financial rewards has also had a severe impact on the graffiti practice. Heart explains: "A lot of new writers have the wrong perspective about graffiti. They don't know what respect is about. They just wanna write, write, write." Disrespect among writers is manifested by crossing out (covering someone else's name with one's own): "Toys [apprentice writers] in New York developed a habit of crossing out other people's work to get famous," says Pink. "Everything is destroyed, nothing lasts. It is not worth it any more. It's a waste of paint, energy, talent, and risking your life for nothing! It is not the MTA with their dogs and fences, they haven't killed graffiti half as much as the underground battles due to jealousy." She points out that female writers are a particular target and often get their work crossed out especially quickly.

Called criminals by the authorities and artists by art dealers, facing danger in the yards and derision and hostility from their male counterparts, female graffiti writers are caught up in baffling contradictions. Lady Heart, for example, joined the U.S. Army looking for the security that life in a subway yard manifestly lacks. She did not want to risk "getting caught now that I'm no longer fifteen and will go to jail for writing." Lady Pink has got commissions to fulfill, interviews to give, gallery exhibits to set up, and thus has little time to develop a women's subway style further, or to figure out female strategies to counteract male domination.

Yet despite the serious problems that beset subway writers, Heart is optimistic about the future of graffiti. She believes that "graffiti is gonna be around. It will never disappear. The little kids will keep trying." Writers will continue to try because "their talent hasn't reached the ability where they can go on canvasses right now. So the best place to practice is on the trains, where you see it running and other people see it too and they tell you how it looked."

Us girls and the revenge of roxanne

Although there are some women DJs, they participate in greater numbers as rappers. Lisa Lee (Lisa Counts) was born in the South Bronx. Her mother is Jamaican, and her father is from Atlanta, Georgia. Lisa Lee started rapping in 1976, at age thirteen. She began by writing "rhymes" for a girlfriend rapper who later encouraged her to "get on the microphone." Around 1979, Lisa Lee met Sha Rock, a rapper from North Carolina who was the one more in the group the Funky Four. Lisa recounts: "Sha Rock was also rapping. Back then it was more like competition. Other people would always compare me to her. They wanted us to battle. She wasn't into it and I wasn't into it, cause I don't like that kind of stuff. So, we got on the mike together." Soon after, Lisa Lee and Sha Rock decided to form an all-female group. By 1984, Lisa Lee, Sha Rock, and Debbie Dee were well-known as the Us Girls. They appeared in *Beat Street* and recorded one of the movie's theme songs, "Us Girls Can Boogie Too."

Lisa Lee is an experienced rapper. She rapped in male groups before the formation of Us Girls, and one of her recordings was produced by the famous Afrika Bambaataa in 1983. Like most rappers, Lisa composes rhymes or raps, which she rehearses and memorizes for performance. As she explains, rapping involves a variety of steps and skills: "A rhyme is about a situation, like, I was on the train, or about a person. You have to get a topic and put a situation into a rhyme. A routine is more for the group. I write my own rhymes; when we do routines, we all write them." To construct a routine "we all keep bringing our different ideas. I may see something that would sound good in a rap. What nobody else has talked about. Whatever idea comes to mind, we write it down and figure out how to put it into a rap. For example, we say let's talk about what's going on in the South Bronx. The parties, or what happens when you get robbed, or how people dress at the parties." In a live show "you talk about these situations. You more or less try to get the people up to party with you, you try to involve the people." But when doing a record "you try to get a message out to the people. You stick to one specific subject." The popularity of rap music has encouraged its thematic development. Rappers are now more aware of the content of their rhymes. "Before you just wanted to get the crowd to party," Lisa says. "Now you go home and you write something that makes sense. Whenever you rap, you want to relate a message to the people. Because people are more into it now, you know that they really listen to what you're saying."

Since theirs is an oral genre, rappers are more concerned with the delivery of words than with the correctness of grammar and spelling on paper. Verbal ability and memory are emphasized over writing, and words are often altered to fit the rhythm. Lisa Lee, for example, discards the written words after she has memorized a rhyme; and Roxanne Shanté, a more recent female rapper, is known for never writing her rhymes.

But what are the rhymes about? Themes of sex, money, and power predominate in rap compositions. Strong sexual imagery is frequently used to indicate personal affirmation. Like other Afro-American musical forms, rap music is infused with sexuality. It has been said that the power of black music is an expression of black social struggle, its sexuality a form of rebellion against all forms of social and political oppression.[8] Certainly the use of straightforward sexual language in rap lyrics and the unreserved movements of their stage delivery express collective sexual emotion and work to liberate the performance and the performers from prevailing inhibitions.

But female rappers are often restricted in their performance. In this regard, rap music, otherwise an emancipating collective expression, becomes oppressive and discriminatory. Lisa Lee's experience illustrates this difference: "In a show, males do different things than we can do. When they get up there, they'll say something smart to a girl in the crowd, something nasty. They like that kind of stuff, and we can't. When they have MC conventions, and all the MCs come to compete against each other, they start taking off their shirts and their pants just to win. We can't do that, we don't really get into it, but the crowd loves that." When asked why women rappers feel they cannot do the same, Lisa Lee responds laughing: "How are we going to take off our skirts? . . . If they do it, if a male does that, the audience will say, 'Man they're crazy. I like that.' If a girls does it, they'll say, 'Oh my God! they were disgusting and nasty.' That's how they judge it. I don't know. That's how it is out there."

In the case of rap performance, the response of the audience restrains or bolsters the amount and form of sexual display in ways that reflect the dominant values and judgments of the society at large. In rap music, what a female rapper may or may not say during her performance and the ways she (physically) presents herself are much more defined than in the case of her male counterpart. "Being that we're all female, we just dress more feminine," says Lisa Lee. Miniskirts and high-heeled shoes guarantee a favorable response.

Style and subject matter in rap music also vary according to gender. Female rappers tend to be less aggressive (while remaining assertive) in their use of sexual language and imagery. Compare the following two rhymes by a female and male rapper respectively:

Sophisticated is the Lady Lisa Lee
to be the man in my life, you got to be my only.
I'll always hold you secure in my arms real tight,
squeeze you real good til you feel just right.
I have a heart of gold I wanna share with you,
and give you the type of loving, that you never been through.

I worked her body till she went insane
she started talking like Lois Lane.
She said, "Hey sir, I'm your fan
cause you did me badder than Superman."

Similarly, explicitly political themes are more often found in the lyrics of male rappers then in those of women. The titles alone of many male rap cuts—for example, "How We Gonna Make the Black Nation Rise," or "White Lines"—suggest the powerful political messages they seek to convey. Yet the same feminine image whose repressive construction and projection inhibits the expression of female rappers of their own sexuality appears to constrain their ability to develop styles in the direction of political assertiveness as well.

However, more recent female rappers have begun to question this role. The case of Roxanne Shanté is an eloquent example. Lolita Shanté Gooden is from

Jamaica, Queens. Her mother is from Alabama, her father from Antigua. At age fourteen, Roxanne Shanté recorded "Roxanne's Revenge" (1984), a female "response" to the widely popular song "Roxanne Roxanne" by UTFO (1984). The revenge of Roxanne answers UFTO's sexist remarks about a girl named Roxanne with Shanté's defiant rap. " 'Roxanne's Revenge' came off the top of my head," says Shanté. "It wasn't my major subject. It's a story. Like 'Roxanne Roxanne' is the story of a girl, 'Roxanne's Revenge' is saying that guys should stop talking about girls because it's not working anymore. It's played out! Talking about girls is fine as long as you've got something good to say about them. Why do you always gotta say girls are stuck up?"

The combination of UTFO's "Call Her a Crab (Roxanne Part 2)" and "The Real Roxanne" with "Roxanne's Revenge," "Roxanne Is a Man," "The Original Roxanne," etc., exemplifies a new development in rap music: groups or individual rappers responding to other rappers' songs. A still more recent example of sexual polemic in rap is the response by Super Nature, a female group, to the very popular and witty "LA-DI-DA-DI" (by Doug E. Fresh and MC Ricky D., 1985). This active controversing and cross-reference creates dialogue aimed at complementing or, more often, challenging the statements made by other rappers; for Shanté, rap responses are important to "put guys, or anybody else with a crazy ego, in their place."

Roxanne Shanté recorded "Run Away," "Queen of Rock," and "Shanté's Turn" among other songs in 1985. Her topics vary from the personal to the socially conscious: "Out of the kitchen and into the streets. That basically sums it all up," she says. "Men say that women are only good for cooking, cleaning, and making babies. That's changing. But now if a woman goes to work, people call her a woman of the world. When men go out to work, they're just working men. Why can't they be just working women?"

With her testimony Roxanne Shanté confirms once more that female rappers are acutely aware of the prejudice against women's work. But she disagrees with other females on how to deal with the problem. While Lisa Lee worried about high heels for a performance, Shanté now goes on stage with no makeup and everyday clothes: "The audience is not there to see how you dress but to see how you perform," Shanté says. Most of her fans are older women, but, except for a few confrontations with male rappers, Shanté finds men appreciative of her: "They congratulate me on 'Roxanne's Revenge.' I look up to Run DMC and the Fat Boys in particular because they don't let their success go to their head, and you can say that's what I'm trying to be like."

Baby love: give us a break

Daisy Castro, Baby Love, is one of the few well-known female breakdancers. Her parents came from Puerto Rico in the early 1960s and decided to settle in New York City, where Daisy was born in 1968. Daisy has practiced flamenco since she was six, and by the time she joined the now famous Rock Steady Crew, around 1981, she had some breaking experience as well. Two of the crew members, Prince Ken Swift and Doze, lived near Daisy and were longtime friends before she was asked to break with the group. At the time there were other girls learning to breakdance and forming their own groups. Daisy remembers another young woman who was involved long before she herself arrived on the scene: "That was when everything was going down in breaking [around 1976], but she stopped. Now there's a lot of girls breaking."

Of the recent female crews, Daisy thinks the Dynamic Dolls is one of the best: "It's a group of three girls. They are good. There is a lot of them that are good . . . I think every girl group that's out there is good because they've got the nerve to do it. I'm very proud of them." Actually, female breakdancers have existed all along but have never received as much recognition as males. This neglect has itself conditioned the relation of women to breakdancing. Moreover, it is often claimed that because breaking, the most athletic of the breakdancing moves, requires a lot of upper-body strength, women are less likely to try it.[9] To most commentators, breakdancing developed exclusively as competition between males and requires this macho quality to be executed.[10] But the assumption that breakdancing draws only from male-related activities ignores other possible influences. The speedy footwork and acrobatic tricks of freestyle double-Dutch, for instance, are no less impressive than those of breakdancing. Like most breaking moves, this energetic female street game depends on how well the jumper balances her body weight, the swiftness of leg and feet movements, and the gracefulness of her performance.

The widespread notion of the dangers and difficulty of breaking does tend to discourage female breakers. But breakdancing has more to do with concentration, balance, practice, and precision than with sheer physical strength. As Baby Love put it: "Breakdancing is concentration. If you concentrate you'll get it. That's the way I actually feel about breaking for girls. Plus we got strength up here too. All you need is a lot of exercise and you get your strength." Some breaking moves may indeed be uncomfortable for women: the handglide, for example, in which breakers spin on one hand, with bent legs spread far apart, involves positioning the elbow across the stomach in a way that can be painful. But Baby Love insists that however much they may prefer some moves over others, female breakers can do them all.

Nontheless, when girls to get involved in breaking, they are often patronized by boyfriends or big brothers who decide which steps are sufficiently safe or feminine for them to do. The emphasis on femininity from peers and others has direct implications on the style of female breakdancers. As Baby Love expresses it: "Girls got all kinds of styles. They got b-boy style, then they mix it with b-girl style or with lock. B-girl style is more feminine. It's basically the same, just different names. The guys do it more of a man style, a girl maybe can do a little bit of turning or a little bit of jazz, and then right there you could start breaking. That would be a feminine way." In general, slower and smoother breaking moves are considered feminine and appropriate for females.

As with graffiti writing and rapping, this conventional femininity plays a twofold role in breakdancing. On the one hand, it limits the style and form of expression. But it is also used by women for self-assertion. A feminine style is stressed by girl breakers to differentiate it, and to some extent distance it, from the style of boys. "We do a more feminine style than the guys just to show that we're not girls trying to look like guys," says Daisy. "We're not trying to take a guy's place. We try to prove to people that guys are not the only ones that can do it. Girls can, too, and they've got rights!"

The relegation of females to a cheerleading role in breakdancing contests is also closely related to repressive definitions of femininity. In most breakdance contests women do not battle men. The Rock Steady Crew often performs without Baby Love: "I'm always there. But sometimes I don't battle because the other groups don't have a girl for me to battle, and it's kind of weird a girl battling a guy, you know. I stand there and cheer them up and make sure they win the battle." Daisy realizes that the increasing popularity and acceptance of breaking have encouraged greater participation from women and a restlessness with their limited function as cheerleaders: "There are girls that are dancing as good as the guys. And they're willing to take on anyone that comes their way."

Media and commercial success, Baby Love thinks, has given "an opportunity to the kids to show what they got," but it also raises concerns about the future of breakdancing: "It's gonna last in the hearts of the kids who've been doing it for a long time. But it's not gonna be something that people will keep on paying groups to do. It's gonna go right back to the streets. I think it belongs there. It belongs in people's hearts. If it does leave, it won't leave forever. We're gonna do it in the streets. It's gonna stay here but not everybody is gonna keep on making money out of it." For Baby Love, breakdancing is more than a fad destined to disappear after its commercial potential declines; it is part of her culture, a street form in which women will continue to participate in spite of the constant marginalization of their presence in the mass media hype.

Conclusions

COLLEGE GRAD for anti-litter/graffiti efforts in NYC. $15,000.

New York Times classified, October 20, 1985

Lady Pink, Lady Heart, Lisa Lee, Roxanne Shanté, and Baby Love all attest to the presence and active participation of women in hip hop. These black and Latina daughters of immigrant working-class parents belong integrally to the social landscape in which hip hop first developed, hence their familiarity with and command of styles and techniques used in hip hop. Through them, we learn that women elaborate styles and subjects of their own that are often very different from those of the men. Furthermore, these young women express a keen understanding of both the commercial establishment's interest in hip hop and the official opposition to hip hop by the political authorities, as well as the prevalent gender discrimination manifest in the expectations of their male peers and in the omission or distorted portrayal of their role by the media.

Commercial and media representations tend to conceal the strong official opposition to hip hop of which Lady Pink and Lady Heart spoke. Subway writers have been physically abused, imprisoned, and even killed (as in the widely publicized case of Michael Stewart), while mainstream artists like Keith Haring or Kenny Scharf capitalize on their graffiti-esque painting and its exhibition in Manhattan galleries. Recent attempts to combat subway graffiti have tended to deny the common social base of hip hop forms and pit them against one another, as in McDonald's Rap against Graffiti contest and the Break against Graffiti Coalition project by We Care about New York, Inc. Let us remember, too, that breakdancing was also opposed when it was still a street form that, in the eyes of the authorities, too closely resembled stylized gang fighting. More recently, in the wake of racial violence reported at showings of the rap movie *Krush Groove*, rap music has encountered increasing antagonism. Despite rampant cooptation and romanticizing, hip hop is still largely treated by officialdom as a form of pollution and a public menace. Yet perhaps the most serious threat it represents to the established culture is its example of alternative artistic practice. Lady Heart's vision of art as a public act, exposed to mass scrutiny and utilizing forbidden spaces for execution, challenges the dominant view of art as a private, individual expression limited to art schools, galleries, and other designated areas. Art in the hands of subway writers becomes a tool of public expression in the subversion of top-down cultural programming and the hegemony of billboard icons.

In the United States, Afro-American music once helped awaken the political consciousness of slaves in the fields and the church; while more recently in Britain, the Punk and Rastafarian alliance (working-class British and Jamaican youth) and the direct connection of the East End Punks with the British Socialist Workers Party in the Rock against Racism campaign have given practical examples of how "symbolic resistance can be translated into political action."[11] So today in hip hop, black and Latino expressions have the same potential to provoke and accompany the social movements of oppressed groups—a potential whose political importance has already been noted by commentators as far away as Paris, where Sidney Duteil, host of a television and dance show called *Hip-Hop*, argues that reggae, African, English, and American music are emerging as a configuration of styles that together constitute a "powerful weapon against racism."[12]

The political significance of hip hop is extended and deepened by the presence and active participation of the women of the hip hop subculture, who must fight not only the prevailing prejudice against racially oppressed groups and working-class art, but the critical double standards applied throughout Western culture to women artists. The traditional belief that women do not have the physical capacity to engage in certain high art practices (e.g., sculpture) is mirrored in the denial of women's ability to breakdance. The jealousy of male graffiti writers shows up in hostile and belittling comments toward the work of female writers like Lady Pink, and in the attempt by the graffiti boys to discredit Pink and Heart through personal sexual aspersions. Moreover, abiding notions of female delicacy and the ideal of feminine purity crop up throughout all these women's testimony and have had noticeable impact on their styles. While some women develop alternative styles that draw on such notions, for example, the use of predominantly soft colors by Lady Pink, and the jazzy moves of Baby Love, Roxanne Shanté, as we saw, refuses to comply with demands for feminine outfits in rap performances.

Far from being submissive and accepting, the female rappers, breakers, and writers strike back; but their resistance takes on a number of complex and contradictory forms. The actual variations of style and subject chosen by most of the hip hop women to state their claims do not appear to defy stereotypes of femininity. To paint big red lips on subway trains as a statement of female independence tends to reinforce sexist ideas about women's artistic expression. Similarly, the Us Girls effort to project a feminine image by wearing miniskirts during a performance, and Baby Love's search for "delicate" breaking moves, indicate signs of confusion between expression and its stereotype. But these manifestations of distinctive female styles are initiatives undertaken by the hip hop women to counter male supremacy. They represent important acts of resistance when considered within the gender structure of hop hop practice.

Women obviously experience an even more intense opposition for their involvement in hip hop than do men. On top of official harassment come family and peer demands for composure in the name of femininity. In addition, women's struggle for recognition in hip hop is sabotaged by the tendency of the media to ignore, negate, or stereotype their participation. The testimony presented here should help to dispel the illusion, propagated by Hollywood and Madison Avenue, that girls are involved in hip hop only as cheerleaders, bystanders, and exotic outsiders. The young women's dual struggle, both with the media images and within hip hop itself, represents the movement's most radical challenge: Just as hip hop poses a menace to dominant white bourgeois culture, women's participation in its supposedly masculine rituals threatens still another haven of male hegemony.

Notes

1. For a discussion of black and Latin cultural and political interaction, in relation to hip hop, see Juan Flores, "Rappin', Writin' and Breakin': Black and Puerto Rican Street Culture in New York," *Calalloo* (1986). See also, John Storm Roberts, *The Latin Tinge: The Impact of Latin American Music in the United States* (New York: Oxford University Press, 1979), for examples of this cultural convergence.
2. An interesting account is given by Herbert Kohol and John Hinton, "Names, Graffiti and Culture," *Rappin' and Stylin' Out*, ed. Thomas Kochman (Urbana: University of Illinois Press, 1972), 109–133.

3. A more detailed description of the graffiti movement and its elaborate techniques may be found in Craig Castleman, *Getting Up: Subway Graffiti in New York* (Cambridge: MIT Press, 1982).

4. The technique of deejaying and the historical background of rap music are detailed by David Toop, *The Rap Attack: From African Jive to New York Hip-Hop* (Boston: South End, 1984), and Steven Hager, *Hip-Hop: The Illustrated History of Break Dancing, Rap Music, and Graffiti* (New York: St. Martin's, 1984).

5. The origins of *capoeira* are traced to its African predecessor, the foot-fighting traditional among the Bantu of Angola, in Jan Murray, "Capoeira," *Contact Quarterly* 5, 3/4 (1980): 29.

6. A compelling account of this "decontaminating" process is given by Alfred B. Pasteur and Ivory L. Toldson, *Roots of Soul: The Psychology of Black Expressiveness* (Garden City, N.Y.: Doubleday, 1982).

7. For vivid illustrations of graffiti forms and styles see Martha Cooper and Henry Chalfant, *Subway Art* (New York: Henry Holt, 1984).

8. Simon Frith, *Sound Effects: Youth, Leisure, and the Politics of Rock 'n' Roll* (New York: Pantheon, 1981).

9. Cathleen McGuigan et al., "Breaking Out: America Goes Dancing," *Newsweek*, July 2, 1984, 47–52; Kim Watkins, "Floormasters Break Out," *Uptown Summer 83*, Summer 1983, 3; and Hagar, *Hip-Hop*.

10. In addition to the reference in note 9 above, see Dan Cox, "Brooklyn's Furious Rockers: Break Dance Roots in a Breakneck Neighborhood," *Dancemagazine*, April 1984, 79–81.

11. See A. Janowitz, *Tabloid* 6 (1982): 50–51. Janowitz reviews Dick Hebdige, *Subculture: The Meaning of Style* (London: Methuen, 1979).

12. John Duka, "In Paris a Young Black Society," *New York Times*, April 20, 1984.

rap's latino sabor

mandalit del barco

Hispanics and Hip-Hop,
they try to play us.
Hispanics:
a name they gave us;
Time to save us.
S.O.S. stands for settin' others straight.
A brother with a mind,
no time to take the bait.
Those with doubts
will know exactly what I'm talking about.
For the '90s,
I'm out.

—Kurious Jorge

Rap by Latinos is the talk-singing widestyle of beats punctuating verbal acrobatics in English, Spanish, or Spanglish—a mix of both. Rhymes about cruising the boulevard, lowriding in the 'hood, crossing borders in the cultural *mezcla* (mix) called las Americas. Rhymes about hangin' with the barrio homeboys; rhymes about being brown and proud, about representing, about setting the record straight.

His name was not Hitler
or Saddam Hussein;
They called him Columbus,
the envoy of Spain.
They tell us in school that
he discovered this place,
though already populated by a different race.

Said the church brought their god
to save pagan souls.
But don't you be fooled,
the man had other goals.

Dulce Love

Now what you call me?
—Spic.
Now what you call me?
—Spic.
Now what you call me?
—Spic.
Yeah, that's it,
'cause you can say whatever,
'cause I don't care,
sucker.
This is one badass
rice-and-beans-eatin'
motherfucker.
Born and bred in a hardcore community
with no opportunity,
so what can you do to me?

PoweRule

As one Chicano rapper put it, the Latin American experience is full of poets. Ad-libbed poetic commentary has flourished in Latino cultures throughout the Americas; from the pre-Columbian Aztecs, whose picture books depict the *flor y canto* (flower-and-song) style in the Nahuatl language, in which poetry was considered the key to knowledge and consciousness; from Spain's ten-line dueling verses called *décimas*; from Peru's *contrapuntos*, point-counterpoint challenges of poetry and dance; and from Cuba's one, two-three, four-five *clave* rhythms and *habanera* music derived from Africa-imported traditions. Rap is the newest form of improvised call-and-response set to tribal rhythms. Like other forms of Latin music—Puerto Rico's sung-newspaper *plenas* (derived from melodic folk *jíbaros* and percussive African *bombas*), Mexico's story-telling *corridos*, Cuba's topical *quarachas* (salsa, samba, mambo, tango, merengue, and so on)—raps by Latinos tell the stories of *la gente*, La Raza, Latino people.

The story of hip hop begins in the mid-1970s, in the ghettos and barrios of New York City. Street jams and block parties in schoolyards and parks were the cradle of a new style of art, music, dance, slang, and fashions that became world famous. Along with graffiti art and b-boying (breakdancing), rap was part of the new hip hop street culture that Latinos helped create.

Steve Clemente was only eleven when the scene started in his piece of the Bronx, circa 1976, when the jams were always mixed, Latino and black. "You know, you always get the misconception when you look at a rap video that it's all black people," he told me in an interview in the Bronx in 1991. "No, it wasn't all black people. There were many, many Hispanic people, and a lot of the early jams were held in Spanish Harlem and Spanish neighborhoods."

Clemente soon adopted the name Mr. Wiggles, performing vibrant electric-boogie dance routines with his partner, Fabel (Jorge Pabon), as part of the Magnificent Force and the legendary Rock Steady Crew of breakdancers and graffiti artists. The Crew danced on tour in the Middle East, Africa, Europe, and Latin America and were featured in such hip hop films as *Beat Street*, *Wild Style*, and *Style Wars*. Rock Steady's Crazy Legs (Richie Colon) broke the dancing into the big time in the movie *Flash Dance* (that was Crazy Legs spinning during the film's climax, not Jennifer Beals).

Crazy Legs recalled in an interview in New York City in 1991: "I got started in '77 at a Cold Crush jam . . . I had seen dance without music by my brother. I didn't know what he was doing, and I thought he looked like a fool. . . . When I got started, my cousin Lenny Nuñez started teaching me. My idol was a brother named Spy. A Puerto Rican. There was a certain mystique about him, the way everyone talked about him: a man with a thousand moves. I took his style for my footwork. It became my basic foundation."

Wiggles describes the scene in the early days, in the South Bronx, uptown, and on Harlem streets:

You had somebody come up, grab a mike and just start gettin' busy. First thing they always said is, "Yes yes, ya'll / To the beat, y'all / It's Hip-Hop, y'all / Ya don't stop / Keep, keep it on / Till the break of dawn / Keep-keepin' it on—ha! / Now, while I'm singin' my song."

And they'd go on with the crowd pleaser: "Everybody say yes, y'all / Say yes, y'all / Say hip hop (hip hop) / Say hip hop (hip hop) / Lemma hear you say hip hop / Shoowop da bop / Da bop da bop / Hidi bidi hop, hibbity hop, now." You know, that's where the hip hop term came from, 'cause everybody was runnin' that hip hop, hip hop stuff.

It was a time when artists like Lee Quiñones and Lady Pink (Sandra Fabara)—both of whom starred in *Wild Style*—T-Kid (Julius Cavero), Kel 139 (Randy Rodriguez) and his brother Mare 139 (Carlos Rodriguez), and Devious Doze (Jeffrey Greene) got busy with Krylon spray paint to create graffiti murals on subway trains and schoolyard walls, bombing with their name tags and cartoon figures on top-to-bottom masterpieces as though they were modern-day Orozcos, Siqueiras, or Diego Riveras. (While they probably got no direct inspiration from the Mexican muralists, the legacy of public art continued.) Crazy Legs and the rest of the Rock Steady Crew would throw down pieces of cardboard to spin on their heads, doing flips and glides and suicide dives like the acrobatic Brazilian *capoeira* dancers. Poppers like Wiggles and Fabel moved as though electric currents pulsated through every joint, while DJs like the Cold

Crush Brothers' Charlie Chase mixed and zigga-zigga scratched records back and forth. In front of turntables plugged into lampposts (until the cops rolled up), the rappers—the MCs—rocked the crowds, boasting and toasting, competing for juice.

"What made rap so inventive," says Cristina Verán, aka Dulce Love, breaking it down from a Bronx hip hop point of view, "is these guys would show up at a park, or wherever, they might look at the girls in the audience or rival MCs, and off the tops of their heads for twenty minutes at a time, come up with rhymes for them. That's where MC came from: They were the masters of ceremonies, keeping the crowds happy."[1]

> We got something new
> we want ya'll to hear
> So come a little closer
> and lend us your ear.

Mean Machine (1981)

After Kurtis Blow, the Fearless Four was the first rap group signed to a major record label (Elektra), creating hits that would become classics: "Rockin' It," "Problems of the World." The crew included a Puerto Rican named "Devastating Tito" Dones and DJ Oscar "O.C." Rodriguez, who had an early underground hit with Crazy Eddie called "Masters of Scratch." DJ Charlie Chase was also a Puerto Rican pioneer in hip hop, tearing it up on the turntable for the Cold Crush Brothers.

In 1981, an MC crew called the Mean Machine sparked the Spanish-speaking imaginations of hip hop kids when they recorded a rap for Sugar Hill titled "Disco Dream," the first bilingual rap set on vinyl.

> Wepa
> Wepa
> alli na' ma'
> Les abría las puertas a este ritmo
> si que tanto les fascinas
> Se lo trajen en español, mi gente,
> para America Latina.
> Si ustedes quieren gozar,
> y de la vida disfrutar,
> PUES—
> Olviden los problemas
> y empiezen a bailar
> haHaHA!
> Tiren sus manos al aire
> means
> Throw your hands in the air
> Y

Sigan con el baile
means
Dance your body like you just don't care.

Hey-O
Hey-O
Away from us, no more
We open the doors to this rhythm
if it fascinates you so
It comes to you in Spanish, my people,
for Latino America.
If you want to enjoy
and have fun in life,
WELL—
Forget about your problems
and just start to dance
haHaHA!

"Mean Machine was the first group to actually rap in Spanish, and to have a no-tified Spanish guy in a group," says Wiggles. "Because before then . . . we all know the many Spanish rappers there were: Charlie Chase, Ruby Dee of the Fantastic Five, you had Tito from Fearless Four, Master Don and the Death Committee had a brother in there who's Spanish."

Young Latinos had their heroes in the early, old-school rappers, not always recognizable as Latinos by the names they chose, like Prince Whipper Whip (James Whipper). Later on, the Real Roxanne (Joanne Martinez) and the Fat Boys' Prince Markie Dee (Mark Morales) increased the presence of Latino artists in the hip hop community.[2]

Multiculti musical merging

The Puerto Rican and Dominican b-boys joined forces with African American homeboys (the godfather of hip hop, Afrika Bambaataa, gives much respect to the Latino members of his worldwide Zulu Nation, then and now). "Basically, it was the blacks and the Latinos out there," DMC, of the crew Run DMC, recalled in a 1993 interview in New York City. "At the time, that was the complete fla-vor. It was who was in the ghetto, the inner city. As hip hop progressed, it got to be a black thing. Maybe there's more blacks doin' it, know what I'm sayin'? But it's all about who's got soul, who gots the flavor, who gots the raw freedom, the rebellious attitude in them."

Actress-dancer-choreographer Rosie Perez (*Do the Right Thing, White Men Can't Jump, Fearless,* etc.) remembers going to the clubs in the early eighties, where blacks and Puerto Ricans were "vibing with each other."[3] The blending of

cultures was nothing new in the ethnically diverse New York City neighborhoods. Juan Flores points to the 1940s, when Dizzy Gillespie and Count Basie
jammed with Machito, Mario Bauza, and Chano Pozo and Latin jazz was born.
He told me in an interview in Brooklyn in the summer of 1991, "You see there
that it's not just Latinos doing a black thing, but it's really them jamming together
and coming up with something that's not the same as either of the two they
started with. Something new comes out of the picture. It's not one plus one equals
two, but one plus one equals X. It's a different genre that emerges."

But the musical merging may have been even more natural in rap than when
"pachuco boogie" evolved in the zoot-suited 1940s, or when conga-spiced rock
and Latin soul grooved in the 1960s and 1970s, because the kids who created rap
were multicultural *to begin with*—sometimes black *and* Latino. Growing up listening to Celia Cruz salsas and Tito Puente mambos, Spanish ballads, and American rock and funk and soul and punk, the Latino hip hop pioneers lived in bicultural worlds, jumping back and forth between languages and traditions,
whether first generation or fifth in this country. Rap brought the African and indigenous American (North, Central, South) components of Latino culture into
a new fusion. To Wiggles and Fabel (now rappers in the crew Taino Tactics,
named for the Taino Indians in Puerto Rico), knowing the Latino roots of rap
dispels the common notion that rap is "a black thing. You wouldn't understand."

"It promotes some kind of racist attitude, saying 'This is a black thing' don't
even come close," Mare 139 says, surveying the ever-evolving masterpieces at the
Graffiti Hall of Fame in East Harlem's El Barrio. "What happens is a lot of young
blacks don't understand how the Puerto Rican experience relates to the black experience. When Latino rappers come out, they get sort of dissed, in the sense of
saying, 'Why you trying to do a black thing? Why you trying to act black?' I used
to have the mock necks and the shell toes, and the Pro-Keds, and my mom used
to be, like, 'What up? Why you want to be a Moreno?' But it's that integrating
that happens in the ghetto."

Wiggles elaborates: "It wasn't a black thing, it was a b-boy thing, 'cause when
you threw on your gear, you threw on *your* gear. My mom used to call me a light-
skinned black, blah-blah-blah. That was just another generation. They didn't understand. But to the brothers of Africa and Puerto Rico and all that, we all hung
together."

Kurious Jorge, a hard core MC of Puerto Rican and Cuban descent, claims hip
hop as a race in itself: The music is an urban thing, no color involved. "Hispanics
in general just get caught in the middle. We're not represented. That bothers me.
The industry could be racist, but talking about the fans, rap is totally color-blind."

Cristina "Dulce Love" Verán, a Peruvian-born writer and hip hop chronicler
down with the Rock Steady Crew, told me in an interview in New York City in
the summer of 1991 that Latinos, having had so much of their history denied,
erased, altered, or ignored by society, should not forget about their contributions
to the culture of hip hop. "We've lost so much of our cultural history, of Latin
American history too, that we can never get back. Hip hop is recent history, and
we can't afford to let it go unnoticed."

Verán and Crazy Legs are dedicated to preserving hip hop culture, throwing old-school jams every summer in Rock Steady Park in uptown Manhattan, and acting as hip hop activists. Carrying on the legacy is a responsibility Crazy Legs embraces. "Latin brothers come up and say, 'Yo. You brothers made it possible, being Puerto Rican.' "

In the early eighties, when Crazy Legs, Ken "Swift" Gabbert, Buck 4 (Gabriel Marcano), Doze, Daisy "Baby Love" Castro, Kuriaki (Lorenzo Soto), and other Rock Steady Crew b-boys toured the globe as hip hop ambassadors, they discovered that freestyling to rhythms was universal. "Our people come from all over the entire globe," says Wiggles. "I'll give you an example of what I mean. When I was sent to Morocco a couple of years ago, I met some Moroccan brothers. They did the same thing we did: banged on a drum with a beat. They did some acrobatic dancing, kicking verbalistic, and story telling. Not only that, they were writing on walls. Hieroglyphics. I hung out with some Aztecs in Mexico: same thing. You go anywhere in the world, go to anyplace with a lot of native people, the island or Caribbean people, they're all doing the same things. Only thing is, ours is a more media-controlled, commercial society."

As hip hop culture spread, it was rap, the culture's musical element, that by the late eighties became more commercialized. Graffiti artists also found their work appropriated and often exploited in the trendy art world, though some like Doze went on to have successful art careers. After those early days, subway graffiti art and breakdancing (which had been dominated by Latinos like those in the Rock Steady Crew, Dynamic Rockers, and New York City Breakers) got played out in the media after films like *Flash Dance*, *Beat Street*, *Wild Style*, and *Style Wars*. Dancers were relegated to background "color" in concerts and in videos. Crazy Legs remembers how the Rock Steady Crew danced for everyone from young Japanese teenagers to the queen of England. He noticed, too, that people from other countries often had a deeper appreciation for hip hop culture than did people in the United States, and he recalls achieving "ghetto celebrity status," props on the guest lists of clubs and the like, but not making any real money at first. Instead, he found people using b-boys to make a quick buck. "They bastardized the culture, they exploited us," he says, looking back. "I felt like I was an animal in a zoo. We were spectacles."

As rap began in the 1980s to develop a more political focus on black nationalism with the advent of Public Enemy, Boogie Down Productions, Brand Nubian, XCLAN, and other groups, the visibility of Latinos in hip hop faded. To reclaim turf, cousins Ricardo "Puerto Rock" Rodriguez and Anthony "KT" (Krazy Taino) Boston, two Boriqua b-boys who called themselves the Latin Empire, struck back in Spanglish:

The Puerto Ricans have landed
And
We're here to shift the crowd
From left to right,
so try not to get fouled.
And if you do,

Remember:
There's no fighting allowed
as we announce the title of this
j-a-m:
We're Puerto Rican and Proud,
Boyee,
We're Puerto Rican and Proud.

Inspired by their idols, the Mean Machine, the cousins broke into bilingual raps at South Bronx house parties and impressed blacks on the street with their Latino raps. Recalls Puerto Rock, "They actually complimented us."

KT says people need to broaden their horizons with more than one language. "At the time when we started performing, the reaction was: *Finally*. A Latin rap group that's showing pride. We've had audiences where they've actually cried and went crazy over us because we say we're Puerto Rican and proud. People are losing their pride. . . . Some of the kids now are not learning Spanish, they're learning English. And they don't wanna learn the Spanish. They think it's funny for them to speak in Spanish, so they turn away from it."

The fusion of Spanish and English in rhymes like the Latin Empire's have a rich spoken-word tradition. As Juan Flores noted in our 1991 interview of these linguistic possibilities, "As far as the actual genre of poetic delivery, you go back to the late sixties, early seventies, and you have people writing bilingually, doing a lot of the experiments that the rappers are now doing, with the language shifts . . . having a line in Spanish and a line in English, having a line start in English, and move over and have a Spanish word sprinkled in. Changing rhythmic patterns because of the different language structures and all that is really very rich poetic tradition. I believe it's the strongest, most interesting tradition in contemporary American poetry: the African American, and the bilingual."

Whether or not they realized it at first, the New York Latino rappers were following a tradition that in the sixties and seventies included Nuyorican poets like Miguel Piñero and Pedro Pietri, whose sensibilities echoed the Lower East Side (Loisaida) street life, and whose Spanglish slang injected a bicultural reality into their images of urban life.

Beware of signs that say
"Aquí Se Habla Español."
Do not go near those places
of smiling faces that do not smile
and bill collectors who are well trained
to forget how to hablar español
when you fall back on those weekly payments.

Pedro Pietri, "The Broken English Dream"

Two decades later, the Latin Empire would perform this rap at the same Nuyorican Poets Cafe that Piñero and Pietri helped found:

Tu sabe
que a lotta people wanna know
if you speak Spanish
—Un poquito
—Bust it!
I've been rapping for años
while you were still wettin' your paños.

By 1989, the Latin Empire's raps were spreading faster than a virus through-out New York, Puerto Rico, and the Dominican Republic. The group's music videos featured the Puerto Rican flag, cuchifrito stands, piragua vendors, bode-gas, and two-foot dolls dressed in street fashions: Kangol hats, high-top sneak-ers, medallions, baggy clothes, and all. Puerto Rock became a hip hop entre-preneur with the hip hop dolls he first created for his son Ricky, marketing them at Toys-Я-Us.

In Puerto Rico, the Latin Empire helped inspire *raperos* like Vico C, Rubén DJ, D-Squad, Lisa M, Brewsky MC, and Queen Latina, who began to rhyme en español moralistic tales about drugs, abortion, and SIDA (AIDS), among them "Ponte El Sombrero," slang for "wear a condom." In the Dominican Republic, in Colombia, Mexico, Cuba, young people who weren't into heavy metal, rock, or house were fans of rap music just as enthusiastically as their parents had been of merengue, cumbia, mambo, and salsa. But not before the Chicanos on the West Coast took up the Raza cause.

Chicano power

Hey Homey . . .
I'm gettin' tired of dudes just gettin' over on La Raza . . .
yeah . . .
This is for the Raza.
Kid Frost

Rapper Kid Frost began as Arturo Molina Jr., running his East L.A. streets with his barrio homeys. Molina remembers cruising in a lowriding 1972 Caprice with them the night one was "smoked" by a rival gang in the kind of drive-by shoot-ing that's become all too familiar in East Los Angeles. He himself has bullet scars from a 22-millimeter gun and an arm full of tattoos to show for his gang days. As Kid Frost, a protégé of Ice-T, Molina took revenge by spraying rhymes, not bul-lets. in 1990, he scored what became a new Chicano anthem "La Raza":

My gun is loaded;
It's full of balas
I put it in your face

and you won't say nada.
Vatos, cholos,
you call us what you will.
You say we are assassins,
you say we dress to kill.
It's in my blood to be
an Aztec Warrior.
Go to any extremes,
and hold no barriers.
Chicano.
And I'm Brown and proud.
Want this chingazo?
Simón.
Come on, let's get down.
Right now.
In the dirt.
What's the matter?
You 'fraid you gonna get hurt?

"La Raza," which Kid Frost describes as a "trip into the mind of a cholo," was the first rap hit to use the Chicano slang known as Calo (órale, simón, ese), slang used by the *veteranos* in the prisons, a language that often excludes and confuses the English-only.

"I consider myself a voice for Hispanics," said Frost in a 1991 interview in Los Angeles," a voice for La Raza, a voice for the young Chicano minority that's out there living in the streets."

Rapping over Tex-Mex saxophone riffs, wearing a "manhole-cover-sized" Aztec calendar around his neck and khakis, Frost onstage often referred to Aztlán, the mythical lands of the southwest United States said to have been stolen from the *indios*, lands that have come to embody the Chicano spirit.

In the same way the old-school Latinos identified with Boriqua nationalism, Frost followed a tradition of Chicano identification with the myths and symbols of ancient Meso-American cultures for national self-determination. In the sixties and seventies, during the height of the Chicano *movimiento*, when César Chavez was organizing farm workers for better wages and living conditions, when the Brown Berets were fighting oppression, racism, and war, poets like José Montoya, Alberto Alurista, J. L. Navarro, and Raul Salinas gave voice to Chicano revolution, pride, and identity. For example, Montoya's "El Louie" was an elegy to a dead pachuco, the Chicano antihero:

Kind of slim and drawn
there toward the end,
aging too fast from too much
booze y la vida dura. But
class to the end.

Frost's "trip into the mind of a cholo" is a descendant of Salinas's barrio poem "A Trip through the Mind Jail (for Eldridge)":

> Neighborhood of groups and clusters
> sniffing gas, drinking muscatel
> solidarity cement hardening
> the clan the family the neighborhood the gang
> NO MAS! . . .
> Neighborhood of could-be artists
> who plied their talents on the pool's
> bath-house walls / intricately adorned
> with esoteric symbols of their cult,
> the art form of our slums
> more meaningful & significant
> than Egypt's finest hieroglyphics.

Frost's raps gave voice to the modern-day pachuco, driving souped-up, lowriding cars, cruising with their homeboys. "First of all," he says, "you gotta realize that I come from the streets of East Los Angeles, California, where the gangs and stuff don't just band together for the name of a street or a barrio, but it's more of a *familia*. It's a family thing. And if you're down with the family, then you're protected. That's your family. It's not your mom and your dad, it's your homeboys.

"Now, a lot of people that stereotype us are the same people that we go after. Because we know it annoys them, so much of what we say. It just bothers them. So it's like ha! We're in your face anyway, because you don't really understand the reality of what we're kickin'. I'm just calling 'em how I see 'em."

Kid Frost's first LP, *Hispanic Causing Panic*, came under fire by critics of gangster rap's violent imagery. Jose Cuellar, chair of La Raza studies at San Francisco State University, admits messages of gangbanging aren't positive role-model devices, but at the same time, he sees rap as an empowering tool of self-expression from the barrios.

"I also agree," said Cuellar in a 1991 interview in San Francisco, "that when you give kids in the ghettos and barrios who live in this kind of context a microphone and a beat, they're writing lyrics about their lives. One of the things that will emerge will be that focus on those kinds of things. One of the things we hope to see, though, is that as these rappers evolve mentally and musically, they will begin to turn around and direct their critique and their glorification to other things that happen in the community . . . particularly nonviolence."

Frost defends himself: "I'm not glorifying or glamorizing the gang life and going out and telling these gangsters to go out there and gang bang and kill each other. In fact, what we're doing is the totally opposite, man. We're working with the Coalition to End Barrio Warfare, we work with the movement for La Raza, which is about uplifting the minds of young Hispanics, to take them to another level."

To try unifying Latino rappers in the early 1990s, Frost put together a Latin Alliance of rappers of Nicaraguan, Mexican, and Cuban origin, including Mellow Man Ace (who was the first to revive Spanglish rap on a commercial tip), ALT, Zulu Gremlin, Rayski, and United We Stand. "We Built something," says Frost, "and now we're just building it higher. We got the pyramid going, put it that way. And we're building a pyramid that's gonna be unstoppable."

"Oye mi rap"

The spring before Kid Frost started kicking his rhymes on wax, Cuban-born Ulpiano Sergio Reyes added a tropical touch to L.A. rap. In 1989, as Mellow Man Ace, he hit the black, rap, and pop charts with "Mentirosa," a bilingual scolding of a lying, cheating woman. He layered his rhyme over Santana's "Evil Ways," with a chorus sampled from "No One to Depend On":

Check this out, baby
Tenemos tremendo lío
Last night, you didn't go
a la casa du tu tío.
Resultase
Hey
You were at a party
Higher than the sky
Y borachada de Bacardi
—No I wasn't.
—I bet you didn't know que conocía al cantinero
—What?
—He told me you were drinkin'
and wastin' my dinero
talking 'bout
"Come and enjoy what a woman gives her hombre"
—Well, first of all,
I have to know your nombre.[4]

From his South Gate neighborhood, Reyes started out breakdancing and pitching baseball before he and brother Senen hit on the idea of throwing Spanish in raps. He recorded his first rap, "Más Pingon" (literally, more balls), for an independent label and found himself selling his tapes at swap meets. Reyes was still flipping hot dogs at Dodger Stadium when he was asked to record an album. Soon, he found himself singing smoothly, wearing a guayabera shirt, holding an unlit cigar, Panama hat covering his high-top fade, touring South and Central America as a "rhyme fighter."

"Whenever I go to a country, it's like, 'Listen to my rap. Oye mi rap. Oyelo. Oyelo. Que yo tambien rapeao en español,' " he said backstage at an antidrug rally in L.A. in 1991. "My goodness, I never would have thought it was gonna blow up to be where kids are coming up to me saying Spanish and bilingual raps, asking me what I really think about them. But it's great to know we've done something positive."

With a conga beat, Mellow Man reached back to an old Afro-Cuban style called *guaguancó* to come up with "Rap Guanco"; a visit from his uncle prompted him to pen "Brother with Two Tongues / El Brother de Dos Lenguas" (also the name of his second LP). As a "Calikid," he rapped about cruising and meeting "funky *muñecas*" (dolls or females) in the guise of a Spanish fly that lands in their drinks. While MCs often say their inspiration to rap comes from life on the mean streets, at least one rap came to Mellow Man Ace from watching TV reruns. "I like to watch [*I Love*] *Lucy*," he says. "One day I was watching, and Ricky was performing 'Babalu,' and he brought out little Ricky onstage. And little Ricky was like, 'Babalu Babalu-a-ay.' "

The Babalu Bad Boy, Mellow Man Ace, says he didn't allow anyone to tell him there was no market for Spanish and bilingual raps. He helped create the market, hoping to affirm his identity as a Latino. In "The Babalu Bad Boys," he even explains how he came to this country on a "liberty flight" to Miami:

I came all the way from Cuba
Just to Babalu ya
From a raft in the river,
From the river on to ya
Steppin' like a prisoner
who came por el Mariel
with a mission incomplete
'cause I didn't kill Fidel.
I brought a conga drum
and some Celia Cruz records
My mother had me dressed
in high-water pants with checkers
Talkin' 'bout, "oye, niño
No te hagate porfiado
Grow up and make some records
So you don't have to live quemado."

Some Latino hip hoppers are upset by what they fear has become the Ricky Ricardoization of other rappers who simply "e-speek e-Spaneesh" as a gimmick, prompted by record-company execs who have dollar signs in their eyes when looking toward the potential Latino market.[5] Many people were disturbed by the supermacho, sex-crazed "Latin-lover" images set forth by pop pseudorappers like Gerardo, whose machista mantra was "Rico Suave"—that is, tasty and smooth.

"That's how he sells records, on the strength of his image, not on his lyrical skills," says Bobby "Bobbito" Garcia, a hip hop exec with his own record label, Hoppoh. "His market is bonkers."

Cristina Verán adds, "He's portraying an exaggerated stereotype to an American public that already has no shortage of stereotypes of Latinos. We shouldn't do that to ourselves."

There's the danger that the culture vultures who don't understand the diversity of the Latino communities and of hip hop will continue to stereotype. Latino rap artists have been asked to do some Rico Suave licks. That, says Bobbito Garcia, is "a misrepresentation of what, let's say, someone who loves hip hop would want pop culture to see. People look at him and say, 'Oh, well, that's rap music.' A rapper like Gerardo. That's completely bonkers. The potential result of that is, okay, Gerardo sells eight billion records, so record companies want to have a sound like Gerardo. He's more radio playable."

Hip hop purists can't stand rap perpetrators who get paid "crazy" amounts while more talented MCs struggle for recognition. Most true Latino hip hoppers considered the Rico Suave phase a big joke. But in an MTV interview Ecuador-born dancer-actor-rapper Gerardo Mejia III laughed off criticism of his beefcake image. "It's like a parody," claimed the shirtless girl toy. "It's like I'm making fun of myself. I love women. Why would I put them down?"

Other Latino rappers are trying to counter the Latino-lover stereotype with messages about identity and image, in hopes that they're not treated as another fad and go the way of the lambada.

"We try to teach the youth you can be positive," says the Latin Empire's KT. "You can dress the way you want to, you can wear your hats to the side, looking all hoodlumlike. . . . It's our touch of style in the street. But that doesn't mean you gotta stop studyin'. You can still go to school; you can still get your diploma."

Homeboy Bobby "Bobbito" Garcia advocates Latinos controlling and setting their own media images in pop culture: Behind the scenes or on the mike, Latinos can change things. He's found himself surprising people sometimes when he tells them he graduated from Wesleyan, as though hip hop and Ivy League are incongruous concepts. A former Def Jam Records promoter, Garcia runs Hoppoh Records with partner Pete Nice. He represents Kurious Jorge and helps groups like New York crew PoweRule, with its Puerto Rican-Cuban-Dominican-Ecuadoran-Venezuelan mix, not only because he likes their music, but because he says he feels a responsibility as a Latino in the music industry.[6] "Yo. If I get my foot in the door, I'm not gonna turn around and forget where I came from. I'm gonna bring some people with me, you know? If I ever get to the top, I want my boys with me, you know? We'll be up there eatin' rice and beans."

Bronx Nuyorican David Perez, who has helped create images of Latino and non-Latino rap artists by directing music videos for Tribe Called Quest, Cypress Hill, House of Pain, Brand Nubian, Diamond D, Beastie Boys, KRS One, and others, says the issue is less one of stereotyping than of being real. "I look sort of white, so I have to establish myself. Gotta let them know where you're coming from, what you saw when you were growing up. Then all of a sudden, they look at you, and you're light skinned. You could be Italian, Jewish, Greek. Then after you establish yourself, you become authentic."

Kid Frost describes assimilated Latinos as "coconuts," brown on the outside, white on the inside. Mellow Man Ace calls for more unity: "I think if us as his-panics were more like the blacks, who get up and shout and scream and get what's ours, we'd be more successful . . . not only that, but came together, and worked with each other, instead of when somebody makes a little money, go and buy a car and gold and just leave, we could all grow as a people."

The nueva onda

From all the bragging about fast cars, money, gold, and women, rap in the nineties became politicized in the wake of more militant African American crews like Pub-lic Enemy. In Los Angeles, Latinos have spread their political messages through rhymes. MCs in A Lighter Shade of Brown, Robert Gutierrez (ODM: One Dope Mexican) and Bobby Ramirez (DTTX: Don't Try to XEROX), rap about cruising to Tijuana and being stopped by the border patrol. They've also been inspired to lay down some history on Mexican legends Pancho Villa and Emilio Zapata, though they revised those histories as they expanded their political consciousness.

"We started out brag-rapping, like most MCs, not having a message," says DTTX. "But then I heard Public Enemy, KRS One, who were teaching educa-tion to their people. I started looking into it. Now I'm trying to say how it is on *our* side of the street. We don't call girls bitches or hos, and we don't have to cuss to get our points across."

Latin Alliance's rappers explored sensitive topics like U.S. hypocrisy and "il-legal" immigration. To the question, What is an American? United We Stand's Zulu Gremlin (Steve Roybal) answers with "Latinos Unidos," a rap that calls on *la gente* to *vaya en paz* (go in peace),

> Free from any type of
> racial negativity,
> Nevertheless, we were blessed
> with a lighter shade of brown skin,
> a free country to live in.
> Cities with names that are Spanish.
> Tell me: who is the majority
> of Los Angeles?
> And then think
> but don't blink
> And don't let the Latin man become extinct.

In the spirit of La Raza raps, Chicano MCs in the politically correct San Fran-cisco Bay Area are reaffirming and reclaiming turf for what in California will be the majority population by 2000:

Bésame, cholo . . .
Yo. Check this out, man:
"If the immediate goal
for the young Chicano is to
rediscover Aztlán,
then the anthropological
and linguistic foundation
has been set."

Aztlán Nation

In 1969, three thousand young Chicanos met at a Liberation Youth Conference
to reclaim the symbol of Aztlán, a Mestizo nation: "We are a Bronze People with
a Bronze Culture." In El Plan Espiritual de Aztlán (the Spiritual Plan of Aztlán),
the students urged Chicanos to use their nationalism as the key to mass mobi-
lization, liberation from oppression, exploitation, and racism. "We must ensure
that our writers, poets, musicians, and artists produce literature and art that are
appealing to our people and relates to our revolutionary culture."

Today, that manifesto includes rap music, and the plan is being carried out
by crews in the Bay Area like the Aztlán Nation, DJ Beto, Nine Double M, MC
Machine Gun X, the A.S.P. (Ambassadors of Sound) Organization, the Funky
Aztecs, Mario Del Barrio, And DFTC (Down for the Cause).

I was born the son
of the Aztlán Nation
refused to live
on a reservation.
They keep me down
'cause my color is brown,
But now the time has come
to turn it all around.

Aztlán Nation

On the Friday night lowrider show *La Onda Bahita* on radio station KPFA in
Berkeley, California, rappers from the Aztlán Nation and A.S.P. Organization
talked about their politically active raps. "Some people of Caucasian persuasion
get offended. . . . I've had some inquiries into some of the lyrics. But the thing is,
they don't listen to all the lyrics. Like when I say, 'If you call me a wetback / You
better get back / all the way to Europe / 'Cause I don't play that,' they hear 'Get
back to Europe,' and that's all they focus on. They say, 'Why you tellin' me to go
back to Europe?' "

"It's *if* you call me a wetback. *If*."

"Chale con eso. From our point of view, this is the browning of las Americas."

"Our main message is: Chicanos, we're the future. You are the future. The
youth. Especially to the juventud, man. Young vatos in the streets and barrios,
you're our warriors."

"Like Che Guevara said, 'You don't sit around and wait for the revolution, you have to make it.' "

¡Orale! The Aztlán Nation's Albert Lopez, Michael Mostafa, Esteban Zul, and the "minister of knowledge," Martin Zul, say their purpose is to "instill pride of our Chicano and Mexican heritage, and to 'word-'em-up' on Aztlán." They rap about the census undercount of "minorities," the violent anti-immigration campaign to "Light Up the Borders" and drive back those who cross into this country. They talk of uniting the pueblo to stop Latinos from killing Latinos, to take back Aztlán. Their premise is based on the history of Chicano resistance through revolution.

"I didn't cross the border, the border crossed me," they rap in true Brown Beret style, straight from the land of the serpent and the eagle. Simón. Just kickin' poetic justice "till the border crumbles."

Martin Zul explains they are following in the oral tradition that preserves folklore, religion, history, mythology, geneology—a tradition in which rap is used as an antiestablishment tool to disguise political messages. Chicano rappers say they've been influenced more and more by the Movimiento Estudiantil Chicano de Aztlán (MEChA), which has been organizing Raza students since the seventies. Several MCs from the A.S.P. Organization were presidents of their campus MEChA. In homage, they wrote a MEChA rap. On the education tip, they promote bilingual education and voting. The Funky Aztecs, of Oakland, promote politically correct topics like practicing safe sex.

Jose Cuellar, aka "Dr. Loco" (whose Rockin' Jalapeño Band promotes Chicano themes through rock), notes the *nueva onda*, the new wave of Chicano activism by rappers. "There's a whole new generation of young folks that are still experiencing the same kinds of things: a high dropout rate, which was one of the things plaguing us in the 1960s, police oppression in the communities, the immigration service is still exploiting people, still deporting people," he says. "So I think young people in their teens and early twenties are still confronting the same problems and themes that were characterizing us twenty years ago."

Cypress hill flava

> Wanna feel the effects of the high
> I wanna feel the effects of the high
> You wanna feel the effects of the high?
> B-Real, light another.
> Cypress Hill, "Light Another"

By far, today's biggest rap crew with the Latino flava is Cypress Hill: Cubanos B-Real (Louis Freeze) and Sen Dog (Senen Reyes, Mellow Man Ace's brother), and their Italian partner, Muggs (Larry Muggerud). Their hip hop hits have gone beyond radio play and record sales, having scored sound track raps for such films as

Juice, *South Central*, *Last Action Hero*, and *The Meteor Man* (B-Real had a cameo in *Who's the Man?*).

Having helped revive the cannabis craze, "America's most blunted" rhyme about legalizing marijuana (fans write to them c/o The Buddha Club). Coverboys from *High Times* magazine, Cypress Hill was the first rap crew to champion the cause of the special-interest group N.O.R.M.L. With spliff-induced mellowness, B-Real, Sen Dog, and Muggs can break down the history and positive aspects of pot: how the government subsidized, then later suppressed weed crops; how hemp was the cheapest, strongest clothing fiber during World War II; how paper companies could use the marijuana crop instead of trees, thereby stopping the greenhouse effect; not to mention the medicinal benefits.

Feeling the effects of the high, they light another to rap in homage to the blunt in "Stoned Is the Way of the Walk."

> Hits from the bong
> Make me feel like Cheech
> and I'm kickin' it with Chong
> frontin' with ice cream
> Cypress Hill is here to give you a nice stream.

On the group's first LP, Sen Dog, "another proud Hispano, one of the many of the Latinos de este año," rapped to his fans some straight-up funky bilingual lines in "Latin Lingo." And in his unique nasalized style, B-Real delivered in "Pigs" a sarcastic rap response to the LAPD well before Rodney King exposed the widespread police brutality toward African Americans and Latinos.

> This pig harrassed the whole neighborhood
> well, this pig worked at the station.
> This pig, he killed my homeboy
> So that fucking pig
> went on a vacation.
> This pig, he is the chief
> Got a brother pig, Captain O'Malley
> He's got a son that's a pig, too
> He's collecting payoffs from a dark alley.

" 'Pigs' is our answer to constant harassment," says Sen Dog. The police, he says, "love to jack us, give us citations just for hanging a cigarette out from the window. It's ridiculous."

In front of the stucco houses that line their pacific-seeming South Gate streets, the Cypress Hill posse can point out which neighbors' houses have been sprayed with bullets by rivaling gangstas. Los Angeles, they argue, is like a wolf in sheep's clothing, more violent than the empty lots of New York. Driving up and down their street, Manchester Hill, B-Real and Sen Dog say they get stopped at least once a week just for being young, Latino, and in a car. "If you happen to be a kid with a goatee and a hat on, driving a car like a Cadillac that's dropped low with nice rims, they automatically assume you're a gang banger or a drug dealer. You're gonna get sweated."

Whether pointing out stereotypes or advocating marijuana, Cypress Hill carry out their mission with a common-man approach—an Afro-haired, stoned, common-man approach, like B-Real. "We're not trying to preach or teach," he says. "We're just kids from the street tellin' it like it is from *our* side of the picture."

The Cypress Hill family spawned another mostly Latino rap crew in L.A., Funk Doobiest, whose image has been described as "XXX butt naked funk," starring Son Doobiest (a lover of porno flicks), Tomahawk Funk, and DJ Ralph M, once known as "the Mixican." Funk Doobiest joined forces with Cypress Hill and House of Pain to become the Soul Assassins. *Beat Down* magazine's Elliot Wilson quoted Son Doobiest's take on the resurgence of the Latino rap movement: "I'm up on that Latino supremacy shit. I mean, we was there from the giddyup and nobody gave us funkin' no props [credit]. We perfected every funkin' art of Hip-Hop there was at the time. Whether it was breakdancing, the B-Boy shit, cazals, Lee jeans—all that stems from Latinos. Rap being a black thing, all that this year, we gonna squash that bullshit to the max."

Back in New York, where the whole thing started, in a June 1993 interview the Beat Nuts gave props to Cypress Hill for opening the door further to hard-core Latinos. After producing for Kurious Jorge, Pete Nice, Monie Love, Chi-Ali, and others, hard-core hedonists Ju-Ju (Jerry Tineo), Psyco Les (Lester Fernandez), Fashion (Berntony Smalls), and VIC (Victor Padilla) came out on their own, shouting, "I wanna fuck, drink beer, and smoke some shit." Boasting "more beats than a Puerto Rican's got cousins," the crew from Queens shops for beats in record and furniture stores throughout the world, bringing along a portable Fisher-Price turntable to sample their finds. Rapper Ju-Ju says he learned to appreciate music by listening to his Dominican mother's old salsa and merengue albums.

Ju-Ju says it's natural for him to throw Spanish in his raps, no gimmick. "But I ain't tryin' to stress that shit. I want to be respected as a talented hip hop artist, not a talented *Latino* hip hop artist. Of course, when we're up there we're gonna represent. We're never gonna deny where we come from. A lotta people think I'm black, know what I'm sayin'? I make it clear to them I'm not.

"I be gettin' upset when people act so surprised that we're Spanish. When a lotta people heard the music, they were like, 'Can't possibly be no Puerto Rican niggas doing this shit.' When they seen us, a lotta people bugged out. 'Oh shit. Niggas are Spanish?' Like they couldn't believe Spanish niggas could get down like that."

While previously English-only African American rappers like Nice 'N' Smooth (who added a Spanish remix to their "Hip-Hop Junkie"), Monie Love, and Main Source ("Vamos a Rapiar") sprinkled Spanish phrases and samples in their raps, Latinos like the Beat Nuts, Kurious Jorge, PoweRule, Fat Joe Da Gangsta, Funk Doobiest, and others are bringing rap back to its hard-core, true-to-the-culture roots. And not necessarily in Spanish.

Fat Joe Da Gangsta, who grew up in the South Bronx as president of the T.S. (Terror Squad, or Totally Spanish), said in a 1993 interview in New York City that it was definitely harder to get credit as a Latino rapper because promoters don't know what to do with a Latino who expresses himself or herself in English, not Spanish. "I can't really kick it in Spanish, I couldn't really feel the vibe, so I'm not even gonna try and make myself look stupid. Being Hispanic made it doper, because all they had was people rhyming, soundin' stupid with the accents and stuff like that."

"There's so many Latino people in the United States that don't speak Spanish, so they don't wanna hear that bilingual rap," says Prince PoweRule, Oscar Alfonso. "They're just like us; they're Americans."

"They wanna hear that hard-core, true-down, home-cookin' rap," says PoweRule's DJ Ax (Victor Maria).

"A hard-core, avid person who loves hip hop and lives it and has it in his heart," explains Bobbito Garcia, "they just wanna hear the skills, the inflection of the rhymes, the intonation, the different cadences, the wittiness of a metaphor, or an incredible using two words that you would have never thought would have rhymed together."

Cypress Hill's B-Real breaks it down even further: "Not hip-*pop*, hip hop. There's no gimmick here. Everything we do is from the heart, and we're true about it."

While Latinos are rhyming in English, and non-Latinos in Spanish, the influences of rap styles and rhythms are spreading even further. Groups like La Miami Band have created merengue and boogaloo raps; Panama's El General has found a niche with his reggae rap; Kurious Jorge experiments with jazz and rap; salsa-great Tito Puente puts rap to a conga beat; and rapper El Cacique (Men Tchaas Ur Sa-Ankh) jams with Manny Oquendo and the Conjunto Libre. Dr. Loco, who's following the growth of Latino rap and who often lectures about the subject in his Chicano studies classes, sees the trend blossoming. "The traditional salseros are using a rap. There's a Chicago group called La Sombra, that in the middle of one of their cumbias, they go into a rap. . . . There's a blending of rap into traditional Latino tropical and conjunto music." And so on.

So What Happens Now? was the title of a hip hop ghetto musical choreographed, written, and performed by members of the Rock Steady Crew (Crazy Legs, Ken Swift, Wiggles, Fabel, and others), who continue to preserve the culture. It's their history of and homage to the world-famous style that the multiculti kids from the Bronx helped create, a reminder of the contributions Latinos have made to hip hop. As this movement hip hops toward a new century populated by a brown majority, los raperos are a fuerza que no se puede ignore.

So what happens now? In English, Spanish, or Spanglish, Latinos in hip hop are kickin' the culture pa'lante.

As rapper Rayski Rockwell explains, "We're not trying to put any ethnic group down; we're just trying to bring ours up. Latinos Unidos."

Notes

1. Unless otherwise noted, quotations are taken from interviews conducted by the author for the purposes of the National Public Radio documentary on which this chapter is based.
2. Morales now has his own record label, "Soul Convention," through Columbia Records, which signed the group Menageri, featuring the former Devastating Tito of Fearless Four.
3. On the set of Fox-TV's *In Living Color*, actress Rosie Perez is known as the "harbinger of hip hop," having brought club and street dancing to mainstream America through her choreography and dancing in films and TV. In 1993, she executive produced a special series for HBO, *Society's Ride*, which featured hard-core rap acts. She fought with studio execs to air the concerts uncensored. She says, "It's sad that America and the media have made that connotation that rap is black. Rap is music and rap is soul, it's real. Music should never have a color appointed to it."
4. On the feminist tip, macho MCs have been challenged by underground rappers like Laura Segura in Salinas, California, and A Lighter Shade of Brown's Alexandra Quiroz ("Teardrop, the Brown Queen"). Both, in fact, took Mellow Man Ace to task in reply raps to "Mentirosa":

> Eres un Latino
> Yeah, you're all the same
> Quit playin' that game of macho
> 'cause I'll send you home in shame
> So let me tell you,
> straight up
> Time to school you with a lesson
> A woman's not a game
> much less a toy that you be messin'.

> **Laura Segura**

> So the girls think you're cute
> Hmmm.
> No me importa
> But you had to go chase girls
> and
> play me for a tonta
> So who's this girl named Lola?
> Yeah, the one who said hola.
> Every time she looks at you
> Detienes por la cola
> I heard she asked you out
> and of course, you said sí.
> Fueron a cenar
> and you forgot about me.
> You're a mentiroso,
> A big time baboso

Don't dare play me out
Porque eres un chismoso.

Teardrop

5. The term "Latin hip hop" became a misnomer for freestyle dance music: bubble-gum ballads over drum-machine beats by stars like Judy Torres, TKA, Trilogy, Cynthia, Johnny O, and manufactured pretty-women trios like the Cover Girls and Sweet Sensation. While the music tracks that accompanied them were descendants of the electro-funk music made popular by Afrika Bambaataa and the Soul Sonic Force, their sounds were far from being rap. Still, young Latino audiences grew large enough to encompass the two styles.
6. PoweRule's name comes from the term for Puerto Ricans given by the Five Percent Nation of Islam. In the Five Percent's Divine Mathematical Alphabet, P-Power, R-Rule; P.R. also signifies Puerto Rico and Puerto Rican.

puerto rocks: new york ricans stake their claim

juan flores

4 Hip hop has finally broken the language barrier. Though young Puerto Ricans from the South Bronx and El Barrio have been involved in breakdancing, graffiti writing, and rap music since the beginnings of hip hop back in the seventies, it is only in the early nineties that the Spanish language and Latin musical styles have come into their own as integral features of the rap vocabulary. By now, Mellow Man Ace, Kid Frost, Gerardo, and El General are household words among pop-music fans nationwide and internationally, as young audiences of all nationalities are delighting in the catchy Spanglish inflections and the *guaguancó* and merengue rhythms lacing the familiar rap formats. Mellow Man Ace's "Mentirosa" in the summer of 1990 was the first Latino rap record to go gold; Kid Frost's debut album *Hispanic Causing Panic* instantly became the rap anthem of La Raza in the same year; Gerardo as "Rico Suave" has his place as the inevitable Latin-lover sex symbol; and El General has established the immense popularity of Spanish-language reggae rap in the Caribbean and Latin America.

Who are these first Latin-rap superstars and where are they from? Mellow Man Ace was born in Cuba and raised in Los Angeles; Kid Frost is a Chicano from East L.A.; Gerardo is from Ecuador, and El General is Panamanian. But what about the Puerto Ricans, who with their African American homeboys created hip hop styles in the first place? They are, as usual, conspicuous for their absence, and the story of their omission is no less infuriating for its familiarity. Latin Empire, for example, the only Nuyorican act to gain some exposure among wider audiences, is still struggling for its first major record deal. Individual MCs and DJs have been scattered in well-known groups like the Fearless Four and the Fat Boys, their Puerto Rican backgrounds all but invisible. Even rap performers from Puerto Rico like Vico C, Lisa M, and Rubén DJ, who grew up far from the streets where hip hop originated, enjoy greater commercial success and media recognition than any of the Puerto Rican b-boys from the New York scene.

This omission, of course, is anything but fortuitous and has as much to do with the selective vagaries of the pop-music industry as with the social placement of the Puerto Rican community in the prevailing racial-cultural hierarchy. As commercialization involves extracting popular cultural expression from its original social context and function, it seems that the "Latinization" of hip hop has meant its distancing from the national and ethnic traditions to which it had most directly pertained. Instead of bemoaning this evident injustice or groping for elaborate explanations, it is perhaps more worthwhile to trace the history of the experience from the perspectives of some of the rappers themselves. For if New York Puerto Ricans have had scant play within the Hispanic-rap market, they have one thing that other Latino rappers do not: a history in hip hop since its beginnings as an emergent cultural practice among urban youth.

Such an emphasis is not meant to imply any inherent aesthetic judgment, nor does it necessarily involve a privileging of origins or presumed authenticity. Yet it is easy to understand and sympathize with the annoyance of a veteran Puerto Rican DJ like Charlie Chase at the haughty attitudes he encountered among some of the rap superstars from the island. "The thing about working with these Puerto Rican rappers," he commented recently, reflecting on his work producing records for the likes of Lisa M and Vico C, "they are very arrogant! You know, because they are from Puerto Rico, and I'm not, right? I feel kind of offended, but my comeback is like, well, yeah, if you want to be arrogant about that, then what are you doing in rap? You're not a rapper. You learned rap from listening to me and other people from New York!"[1] Actually this islanders' apprenticeship was probably less direct than Charlie Chase claims, since they more likely got to know rap through the recordings, videos, and concert appearances of Run DMC, L.L. Cool J, and Big Daddy Kane than through any familiarity with the New York hip hop scene of the early years.

Where did those first platinum-selling rappers themselves go to learn the basics of rap performance? Again, Charlie Chase can fill us in, remembering the shows he DJed with the Cold Crush Brothers back in the late 1970s and early 1980s. "When we were doing shows, you know who was in the audience? The Fat Boys. Whodini. Run DMC, L.L. Cool J, Big Daddy Kane. Big Daddy Kane told me a story one time, he said, 'You don't know how much I loved you guys.' He said, 'I wanted to see you guys so bad, and my mother told me not to go to Harlem World to see you guys perform because if she found out I did she'd kick my ass!' And he said, 'I didn't care, I went. And I went every week. And I wouldn't miss any of your shows.' That's how popular we were with the people who are the rappers today."

To speak of Puerto Ricans in rap means to defy the sense of instant amnesia that engulfs popular cultural expression once it is caught up in the logic of commercial representation. It involves sketching in historical contexts and sequences, tracing traditions and antecedents, and recognizing hip hop as more than the simulated images, poses, and formulas to which media entertainment tends to reduce it. The decade and more of hindsight provided by the Puerto Rican involvement shows that, rather than a new musical genre and its accompanying stylistic trappings, rap constitutes a space for articulating social experience. From this perspective, what has emerged as "Latin rap" first took shape as an expression of the cultural turf shared, and contended for, by African Americans and Puerto Ricans over their decades as neighbors, co-workers, and homies in the inner-city communities, part of a more extensive and intricate field of social practice. Not only is the social context wider, but the historical reach is deeper and richer: the black and Puerto Rican conjunction in the formation of rap is prefigured in doo-wop, Latin jazz, Nuyorican poetry, and a range of other testimonies to intensely overlapping and intermingling expressive repertoires. Thus when Latin Empire comes out with "We're Puerto Rican and Proud, Boyee!" the group is marking off a decisive moment in a tradition of cultural and political identification that goes back several generations.

I have gained access to this largely uncharted terrain by way of conversations and interviews with some of the protagonists of Puerto Rican rap. Early hip hop movies like *Wild Style* and *Style Wars*, which documented and dramatized the prominent participation of Puerto Ricans, sparked my initial interest and led to a burst of research (which hardly anyone took seriously at the time) and a short article published in various English and Spanish versions in the mid-1980s. At that time the only adequate written consideration of Puerto Ricans had to do with their role in the New York graffiti movement, as in the excellent book *Getting Up* by Craig Castleman and an important article by Herbert Kohl. Steve Hager's *Hip-Hop* (1984) includes a valuable social history of youth culture in the South Bronx and Harlem at the dawn of hip hop, with some attention to the part played by Puerto Ricans in graffiti, breakdance, and rap music.[2] Otherwise, and since those earlier accounts, coverage of Puerto Rican rap has been limited to an occasional article in the *Village Voice* or *Spin* magazine, generally as a sideline concern in discussions of wider style rubrics like "Hispanic," "Spanish," or "bilingual" rap. Primary historical evidence is even harder to come by, since Puerto Rican rhymes were never recorded for public distribution, and most have been forgotten even by their authors.

Chasin' the flash

Charlie Chase calls himself "New York's number one Puerto Rican DJ," and
that's how he's been known since the seventies when he was blasting the hottest
dance music on the waves of WBLS, and the early eighties when he was DJ for
the legendary Cold Crush Brothers. When he says "number one" he means not
only the best, but also the first: "When I started doing rap, there were no Hispanics doing it. If there were, I didn't know about it. Anyway, I was the first Hispanic to become popular doing what I did. I was a DJ."

Charlie was born in El Barrio in the fifties, and though his family moved a
lot it was always from one Puerto Rican and black neighborhood to another. "I
grew up in Williamsburg from the age of two to nine. I moved to the Bronx, on
Brook Avenue and 141st, ¡que eso por allí es candela! I grew up there from ten
to about thirteen, then I moved back to Brooklyn, over in Williamsburg, Mon-
trose Avenue, por allá on Broadway. Then we moved back to the Bronx again,
161st and Yankee Stadium. From there we went to 180th and Arthur, and from
there it was Grand Concourse and 183rd, then Valentine and 183rd, then back
to 180th. I mean, we moved, man! I've been all over the place, and it's like I've
had the worst of both worlds, you know what I mean?"

Charlie's parents came from Mayagüez, Puerto Rico. Though family visits to
the island were rare, that Puerto Rican background remained an active influence
throughout his upbringing. At home he was raised on Puerto Rican music. "You
see, I always listened to my mother's records. She was the one who bought all the
Latin records. She bought them all. She bought Tito Puento, she was into trios,
el Trio Los Condes." Even his career in music seems to have been handed down
to him as part of that ancestry. "I come from a family of musicians. My grandfather was a writer and a musician; he played in bands. So did my father; he played
in trios. So I kind of followed in their footsteps. My father left me when I was ten,
and I never learned music from him; he didn't teach me how to play instruments.
For some reason or other, it must have been in the blood, I just picked up the guitar and wanted to learn."

Charlie makes clear that he didn't start off in rap or as a DJ. "I'm a bass player.
I played in a Spanish ballad band, merengue band, salsa band, rock band, funk
band, Latin rock band. I produced my first album at the age of sixteen, and it was
a Spanish ballad album. We played with the best—Johnny Ventura, Johnny
Pacheco, Los Hijos del Rey, Tito Puente. The name of the group was Los Giramundos." So Charlie Chase, famed DJ for the Cold Crush Brothers, started off gig-
ging in a Latin band when he was fifteen years old and could have had a whole career in salsa. "Yeah," he recalls, "but there was no money in it. There were a lot of
people being ripped off. . . . I said, man, I want to do something else." Fortunately,
he did have somewhere to turn, for alongside his inherited Latin tradition there
was his dance music and R & B. Talking about his transition to DJing he remembers, "I was a music lover. I grew up listening to WABC, Cousin Brucie, Chuck
Leonard, all of these guys, and I was always into music. In school I would always

have the radio on. It was always a big influence in my life, and then I turned into a musician. I started playing with the band, and then a few years later I got into DJing, and then the DJing was making more money for me than the band."

It all seems to make sense, I thought, but what about that name? What's a thoroughbred Puerto Rican doing with a name like Charlie Chase? "My name was Carlos," he said. "Charlie is a nickname for Carlos." Behind the name Chase, he said, lies a story he had never told because his friend Grandmaster Flash would be "so souped." (Little was I to know how much this little story has to say about the situation of young Puerto Ricans in the early days of rap.) "I first saw Flash doing this, cutting and all of this, and I saw that and I said, aw, man, I can do this. I was DJing at the time, but I wasn't doing the scratching and shit, and I said, I can do this, man. I'll rock this, you know. And I practiced, I broke turntables, needles, everything. Now 'Chase' came because I'm like, damn, you need a good name, man. And Flash was on top and I was down here. So I was chasing that niggah. I wanted to be up where he was. So I said, let's go with Charlie Chase."

There's no telling how "souped" Grandmaster Flash will get when he finds out, but his friend and main rival (along with Grandmaster Theo) back in those days grew up as Carlos Mandes. "Not Méndez," Charlie emphasized. See, my roots come from Europe. My great-great-great-grandfather was French, and his wife was Jewish. Somewhere along the line the name changed. Her name was Mandel, and he had some French name; they combined it and came up with Mandes. Somewhere along the line they met up with some Puerto Ricans." Charlie Chase doesn't even like it when "Mandes" appears on the records he wrote. "Nobody knows my name was Carlos Mandes. They'd laugh. They'd snap on me."

Charlie might think that Mandes sounds corny now, but at the time the problem was that it didn't fit. He never tires of telling about how difficult it was to be accepted as a Puerto Rican in rap, especially as a DJ, and because he was so good. "A lot of blacks would not accept that I was Spanish. You know, a lot of times because of the way I played they thought I was black, because I rocked it so well." As a DJ he was usually seated in back, behind the MCs and out of sight. In the beginning, in fact, his invisibility was a key to success. "I became popular because of the tapes, and also because nobody could see me. Since they thought I was black, you know, because I was in the background." Even when they saw him, he says "they still wouldn't believe it. . . . A few years went by and they accepted it, you know. I was faced with a lot of that. You know, being Hispanic you're not accepted in rap. Because to them it's a black thing and something that's from their roots."

"What the fuck are you doing here, Puerto Rican?" Charlie remembers being faced with that challenge time and again when he went behind the ropes among the rappers at the early jams. He had to prove himself constantly, and he recalls vividly the times when it took his homeboy Tony Tone from DJ Breakout and Baron to step in and save his skin. Charlie himself knew that he wasn't out of place. "I always grew up with black people. . . . My daughter's godfather is black. He's like my brother, that guy."

But the best proof was that Charlie was with the Cold Crush Brothers, who were all black. "We all grew up in the streets, man. It's like a street thing. Once you see that the guy is cool, then you're accepted, everything flows correctly." And it's not that Charlie copied the other brothers to fit in. Aside from his *mancha de plátano*, those indelible earmarks of the Puerto Rican, he had his own style that he wasn't about to give up just to be one of the boys. He remembers about Cold Crush that "it was a trip when it came to the dressing bit. . . . I don't dress like the average hip hopper and never did. They wanted to wear Kangols, Martin X, and these British walkers and all that stuff at the time, and . . . I had a DA." Not only did he refuse to fit the mold, but Charlie's insistence helped the group arrive at the look "that everybody copied afterwards, which we felt comfortable with. It was the leather-and-stud look, which we popularized in rap, and through that look we became hard."

Besides, as alone as he was sometimes made to feel, Charlie knew that he wasn't the only Puerto Rican who was into rap. "Hispanics always liked rap, young Puerto Ricans were into it since the beginning . . . but they didn't have the talent, they just enjoyed it. Me, I wanted to do it." In its street beginnings, Puerto Ricans were an integral part of the rap scene, and not only as appreciative fans. Though their participation in production and performance was submerged (far more so than in breaking and graffiti), they were an essential and preponderant presence in the security crews that, in the gang environment, made the whole show possible. "It was rough, man," Charlie recalls. "All of my crew, the whole crew, were Spanish, maybe two or three black guys. They were all Spanish, and when we jammed we had bats. If you crossed the line or got stupid, you were going to get batted down, all right? And that was that." That was my crew, they would help me with records, they were security. The guys in my group were black, but the rest of the guys, security, were Hispanic."

When Charlie calls to mind other Puerto Rican rappers from those days, the names that surface are Prince Whipper Whip and Ruby Dee (Rubén García) from the Fantastic Five; O.C. from the Fearless Four with Tito Cepeda; Johnny, who was with Master Don and the Def Committee. "Then there was this one group," Charlie recalls, that wanted to do Latin rap songs, way back. And they had good ideas and they had great songs, but they just didn't have enough drive, you know? Robski and June Bug, those were the guys." Years before anybody started talking about "Latin rap," Robski and June Bug were busy working out Spanglish routines, even rendering some of the best rhymes of the time into Spanish. "It was weird, because they actually took everything we said and turned it into Spanish and made it rhyme. And they did a good job of it."

But in those days using Spanish in rap was still a rarity, especially in rhymes that were distributed on tapes and records. Not only lack of ambition kept Robski and June Bug from making it, "cause at that time," Charlie says, "a lot of people were doing it underground, but they couldn't come off doing it, they couldn't make money doing it. The people that did it, did it in parties, home stuff, the block, they were the stars in their ghetto." But Charlie himself, "chasing the

Flash," was with the first rap group to be signed by CBS Records, the first rap group to tour Japan, the group that played in the first hip hop movie, *Wild Style*. At that level, rapping in Spanish was still out of the question. Charlie explains what that constraint meant for him and gives a clear sense of the delicate generational process involved in the entry of bilingualism into commercially circumscribed rap discourse. "I always stressed the point that I was Hispanic doing rap music, but I couldn't do it in Spanish, you understand? But that was my way of opening the doors for everybody else to do what they're doing now. . . . I feel sorry that I couldn't do it then, but I want to do it now, and I'm making up for it, because now I can."

At that early stage in negotiating Puerto Rican identity in rap, the key issue was not language but what Charlie calls "the Latin point of view"; pushing rhymes in Spanish was not yet part of the precarious juggling act. "For me it's the Latin point of view. You see, what I emphasize is that I'm Hispanic in a black world. Not just surviving but making a name for myself and leaving a big impression. Everything that happened to me was always within the black music business, and I always was juggling stuff all of the time, because I had to be hip, I had to be a homeboy. But I also had to know how far to go without seeming like I was trying to kiss up or something, or 'he's just trying to be black.' When you deal with the people I deal with, especially at a time when rap was just hard core and raw, you're talking about guys who were hoodlums, you know, tough guys. I had to juggle that. I had to play my cards correct."

If Spanish wasn't yet part of the "Latin point of view," the music was, especially the rhythmic texture of the songs, which is where as the DJ Charlie was in control. He remembers sneaking in the beat from the number "Tú Coqueta" right "in the middle of a jam. I'm jamming, I throw that sucker in, just the beat alone, and they'd go off. They never knew it was a Spanish record. And if I told them that they'd get off the floor." Even the other rappers couldn't tell because the salsa cuts seemed to fit in so perfectly. "It was great! I would sneak in Spanish records. Beats only, and if the bass line was funky enough, I would do that too. Bobby Valentín stuff. He played bass with the Fania All-Stars, and he would do some funky stuff." As a bassist in Latin bands, Charlie knew the repertoire to choose from.

But he also knew that he had to walk a fine line and that he was ahead of his time, not only for the R & B–savvy rappers but for Latin musical tastes as well. In fact, not only the better pay but the resistance he faced from the Latin musicians had made Charlie decide to leave Los Giramundos and go into rap full time. "Sometimes I'd go to gigs and in between songs I'd start playing stuff from rap music and the drummer would like it too, and he'd start doing some stuff. And sometimes people would get up to dance to it, and the rest of the guys in the band would get furious at us. . . . They didn't want that stuff." Not that Charlie didn't try to interest Latin musicians in mixing some elements of rap into their sound. He especially remembers working on a record with Willie Colón. "He could have had the first Latin hip hop record out, and it would have been a hit. . . . He was singing, right, there was a little bit of rap, and I was scratching. I did the arrangements. What happened was, the project was being held and held and held. What happened? He put out the record, an instrumental! He took out all the raps, then he overdubbed. Killed the whole project."

But as Charlie learned early on, when it comes to the emergence of new styles in popular music it's all a matter of timing. He himself had trouble relating to the use of Spanish in rap when he first heard it on record. Back in 1981 the group Mean Machine came out with the first recorded Spanish rhymes in their "Disco Dream," a side that deeply impressed some present-day Latino rappers like Mellow Man Ace and Latin Empire when they first heard it some years after it was released. But Charlie knew Mean Machine when the group started and recalls his reaction when "Disco Dream" first came out. "It was strange, and it was new. At first I didn't jive with it because I was so used to and I myself got so caught up in that whole R & B thing." But with time tastes changed, as did Charlie's understanding of himself and his own role. "And then," he goes on, "something made me realize one day that, wait a minute, man, look at you, what are you? You don't rap like they do, but you're Hispanic just like them, trying to get a break in the business. And I said, if anything, this is something cool and new."

Seen in retrospect, Mean Machine was only a faint hint of what was to become Latino rap in the years ahead. The Spanish the group introduced amounted to a few party exhortations rather than an extended Spanish or bilingual text. Charlie draws this distinction and again points up the changing generations of Latino presence in rap. "The way that they did it was not like today. Today it's kind of political, opinionated, and commercial, and story telling. What they did was that they took a lot of Spanish phrases, like 'uepa' and 'dale fuego a la lata, fuego a la lata,' stuff like that, and turned them into a record." However perfunctory their bilingualism and fleeting their acclaim, Mean Machine's early dabbling with Spanglish rhymes did plant a seed. Puerto Rock of Latin Empire attests to the impact "Disco Dream" had on its members: "We were more or less doing it but in English and got crazy inspired when we heard that record. We was like, 'Oh, snap! He wrote the first Spanish rhyme!' We was skeptical if it was going to work, and when we heard the record we were like, 'It's going to work,' "[3]

The disbelief and strategic invisibility that surrounded Latino participation in rap performance in the early years gave way by the early 1990s to a fascination with something new and different. Charlie sees this process reflected in the changing fate of his own popularity among hip hop audiences. "It was kind of complicated," he recalls. If at first he became popular because "nobody could see me," he later became even more popular "when everyone found out I was Hispanic. And it was like, 'Yo, this kid is Spanish!' and 'What? Yo, we've got to see this!' " This sense of curiosity and openness marked a new stage in rap history, and Charlie was quick to recognize its potential, commercially and politically. He tells of how his enthusiasm infected some of the Latin musicians, especially his friend Tito Puente, who seem to be fondly reminded of their own breakthrough a generation ago. "These guys, they love it. Because for them it's getting back out into the limelight again, you know, in a different market. . . . The musicians are very impressed to see that somebody like me wants to work with them in my style of music. And when I tell them about my history they are very impressed because in their day, when they came out, they were the same way. When Tito Puente came out, he was doing the mambo and it was all something new. It was all new to him, too. So he can relate to what I'm doing. And for him it's almost like a second coming."

After the decade it has taken for Puerto Rican rap to come into its own, Charlie feels that the time is right for the two sides of his musical life to come together, and for full-fledged "salsa rap" to make its appearance. "For this next record I want to get all the East Coast rappers together, I want to get POW, I want to get Latin Empire, I want to get a few other guys that are unknown but that are good. . . . I want to bring in Luis 'Perico' Ortíz, I want to bring Tito, I want to bring Ray Barreto, you know. . . . My touch would be to bring in the rap loops, the beats, the bass lines, the programming. I'll program and also arrange it. And they will come in, Luis 'Perico' would do the whole horn section, Tito would come in and handle all the percussion section, and Ray Barreto would handle the congas. And I would get my friend Sergio who is a tremendous piano player, a young kid, he's about twenty-four, twenty-five now, he works for David Maldonado. I just want to kick this door wide open, once and for all, and that's the way I'm going to do it."

As ambitious as such a project may sound, bringing together Puerto Rican musicians across musical traditions is only half of Charlie's strategy for promoting Latino unity. For "if any Hispanics want to make it in this business," he claims, "they've got to learn to pull together, no matter where you're coming from, or it's not going to work. It's not going to work, man. Kid Frost on the West Coast right now, he's got a little thing going. He and I are working around a few things. He's got his Latin Alliance on the West Coast. I've got a lot of Latin people who work with me on this. I'm trying to form something here where we can merge, cover the whole United States. That's the best way we can do it, if we unify."

Yet with his repeated emphasis on Latino unity, Charlie has more than commercial success in mind. His own experience, he now feels, leads him to set his sights on the political and educational potential of his musical efforts. "Because what I did, I had to unite with black people to get my success and become Charlie Chase, New York's number one Puerto Rican DJ. Ironically, I did it with black people. Which proves, man, that anybody can get together and do it. If I did it with black people, then Hispanics can do it with Hispanics and do a much better job. That's my whole purpose right now. I mean, I have made my accomplishments, I have become famous doing my thing in rap, I have respect. Everybody knows me in the business. I have all of that already, man. I've tasted the good life. I've toured the world. I've done all of that. Now I want to do something meaningful and helpful. Hopefully, because a lot of kids are being steered the wrong way."

Puerto rocks

Moving into the 1990s, then, the prospects and context have changed for Latino rap. Critics have hailed hugely popular albums like *Latin Alliance*, *Dancehall Reggaespañol*, and *Cypress Hill* as a "polyphonic outburst" marking the emergence of "the 'real' Latin hip hop." Kid Frost's assembly of Latin Alliance is referred to as "a defining moment in the creation of a nationwide Latino/Americano hip hop aesthetic." Unity of Chicanos and Puerto Ricans, which has long eluded politicos and writers, is becoming a reality in rap, and its potential impact on the culture wars seems boundless: "Where once the folks on opposite coasts were strangers, they've become one nation kicking Latin lingo on top of a scratch', samplin' substrate. . . . There is no question that we are entering an era when the multicultural essence of Latino culture will allow for a kind of shaking-out process that will help define the Next Big Thing."[4] Not only are Spanish and bilingual rhyming accepted, but they have even become a theme in some of the best-known rap lyrics, like Kid Frost's "Ya Estuvo," Cypress Hill's "Funky Bilingo," and Latin Empire's "Palabras." Latino rappers are cropping up everywhere, from the tongue-twisting, "trabalengua" Spanglish of one Chicago group to the lively current of Tex-Mex rap in New Mexico and Arizona. Not only have the rappers themselves been building these bicultural bridges; Latin musical groups as varied as El Gran Combo, Wilfredo Vargas, Manny Oquendo's Libre, and Los Pleneros de la 21 have all incorporated rap segments and numbers into their repertoires.

But while he shares these high hopes, a seasoned veteran of "the business" like Charlie Chase remains acutely aware of the pitfalls and distortions involved. After all, he had witnessed firsthand what was probably the first and biggest scam in rap history, when Big Bad Hank and Sylvia Robinson of Sugar Hill Records used a rhyme by his close friend and fellow Cold Crush brother Grandmaster Cas on "Rapper's Delight" and never gave him credit. The story has been told elsewhere (see Steven Hager's book), but Charlie's is a lively version. "This is how it happened. Hank was working in a pizzeria in New Jersey, flipping pizza. And he's playing Cas's tape, right? Sylvia Robinson walks in, the president of Sugar Hill. She's listening to this, it's all new to her. Mind you, there were never any rap records. She says, 'Hey, man, who's this?' He says, 'I manage this guy. He's a rapper.' She says, 'Can you do this? Would you do this on a record for me?' And he said, 'Yeah, sure. No problem.' And she says, 'Okay, fine.' So he calls Cas up and says, 'Cas, can I use your rhymes on a record? Some lady wants to make a record.' You see what happened? Cas didn't have foresight. He couldn't see down the road. He never imagined in a million years what was going to come out of that. He didn't know, so he said, 'Sure, fine, go ahead.' With no papers, no nothing. And it went double platinum! Double platinum! 'Rapper's Delight.' A single. A double-platinum single, which is a hard thing to do."

Charlie doesn't even have to go that far back to reflect on how commercial interests tend to glamorize and, in his word, "civilize" rap sources. He tells of his

                                ■ 95
                                ■

own efforts to land a job as an A & R person with a record label. "All of this knowledge, all of this experience. I have the ear, I'm producing for all of these people. I mean, I know. You cannot get a more genuine person than me. I can't get a job." The gatekeepers of the industry could hardly be farther removed from the vitality of hip hop. "I go to record labels to play demos for A & R guys that don't know a thing about rap. They talk to me and they don't even know who I am. White guys that live in L.A. Forty years old, thirty-five years old, making seventy, a hundred thousand a year, and they don't know a thing! And they're picking records to sell, and half of what they're picking is bullshit. And I'm trying to get somewhere, and I can't do it."

As for promoting bilingual rap, the obstacles are of course compounded, all the talk of "pan-Latin unity" notwithstanding. "Not that long ago," Charlie says, "Latin Empire was having trouble with a Hispanic promoter at Atlantic Records who wouldn't promote their records. You know what he told them? (And he's a Latino.) He told them, 'Stick to one language.' And that's negative, man. You're up there, man, pull the brother up." And of course it's not only the limits on possible expressive idioms that signal a distortion but the media's ignorance of rap's origins. *Elle* magazine, for example, announced that Mellow Man Ace "has been crowned the initiator of Latin rap," their only evident source being Mellow Man himself: "I never thought it could be done. Then in 1985 I heard Mean Machine do a 20-second Spanish bit on their 'Disco Dream.' I bugged out." And the Spanish-language *Más* magazine reinforced the myth by proclaiming that it was Mellow Man Ace "quien concibió la idea de hacer rap en español" (who conceived the idea of doing rap in Spanish).[5]

The problem is that in moving "from the barrio to *Billboard*," as Kid Frost puts it, Latino rappers have faced an abrupt redefinition of function and practice. The ten-year delay in the acceptance of Spanish rhymes was due in no small part to the marketing of rap, through the mid-1980s, as a strictly African American musical style with a characteristically Afrocentric message. When Charlie Chase confronted this phenomenon even among some of his fellow rappers at the New Music Seminar in 1990, he drew upon his own historical authority to help set the record straight. "I broke on a big panel. Red Alert, Serch from 3rd Base, Chuck D, the guys from the West Coast, these are all my boys, mind you, these are all my friends. So I went off on these guys because they were like 'black this, and black music,' and I said 'Hold it!' I jumped up and I said, 'Hold up, man. What are you talking about, a black thing, man? I was part of the Cold Crush Brothers, man. We opened doors for all you guys.' And the crowd went berserk, man. And I grabbed the mike and I just started going off. I'm like, 'Not for nothing, man, but don't knock it. It's a street thing. I liked it because it came from the street and I'm from the street. I'm a product of the environment.' I said that to Serch, I pointed to Serch, cause that's his record from his album. And I said, 'Yo, man, rap is us. You're from the street, that's you man, that's rap. It ain't no black, white, or nothing thing, man. To me, rap is color-blind, that's that!' The niggahs were applauding me and stuff. I got a lot of respect for that."

Latin Empire has had to put forth the same argument in explaining their own project. As crew member Puerto Rock puts it, "When it comes to hip hop I never pictured it with a color." They too are a "product of the environment" and see no need to relinquish any of their Puerto Rican background. "Our influence," Puerto Rock says, "is the stuff you see around you. Things you always keep seeing in the ghetto. But they don't put it in art. It's streetwise. The styles, the fashions, the music is not just for one group. Everybody can do it. But too many Puerto Ricans don't understand. There's a big group of Latinos that's into hip hop, but most of them imitate black style or fall into a trance. They stop hanging out with Latin people and talking Spanish. I'm proving you can rap in Spanish and still be dope." Puerto Rock's cousin and partner in Latin Empire, MC KT (Anthony Boston), has had to deal even more directly with this stereotype of rap, as he is often mistaken for a young African American and was raised speaking more English than Spanish. KT's rhymes in "We're Puerto Rican and Proud, Boyee!" serve to clarify the issue:

> I rarely talk Spanish and a little trigueño
> People be swearin' I'm a moreno
> Pero guess what? I'm Puertorriqueño.
> Word 'em up.
> All jokes aside, I ain't tryin' to dis any race
> and
>
> Puerto Rock
>
> He'll announce everyplace . . .
>
> MC KT
>
> That I'll perform at, so chill, don't panic
> It is just me, Antonio, another desos Hispanics.

To drive the point home, the initials KT stand for "Krazy Taino." "It's fly," Puerto Rock comments. "With a *K*, and the *R* backwards like in Toys-Я-Us. In our next video he's going to wear all the chief feathers and that. Nice image. With all the medallions and all that we've got. Like in Kid Frost in his video, he wears the Mexican things. That's dope, I like that. Tainos have a lot to do with Puerto Ricans and all that, so we're going to boost it up too. Throw it in the lyrics."

But KT didn't always signal the Puerto Rican cultural heritage, and in fact the derivation of Latin Empire's names shows that the members' struggle for identity has been a response against stereotyped symbolism of rap culture. "MC KT is his name because before Latin Empire we were called the Solid Gold MCs. KT stood for karat, like in gold." The group gave up the faddish cliché Solid Gold because they had no jewelry and didn't like what it stood for anyway. When they started, in the early eighties, "We worked with a few different trend names. We started off with our name, our real names, our nicknames. Like Tony Tone, Ricky D, Ricky Rock, all of that. Everything that came out, Rick-ski, every fashion.

Double T, Silver T, all of these wild *T*s." After trying on all the conformist labels, Rick finally assumed the identity that was given him, as a Puerto Rican, in
the African American hip hop nomenclature itself; he came to affirm what
marked him off. "And then I wound up coming up with Puerto Rock, and I liked
that one. That's the one that clicked the most. The Puerto Ricans that are into
the trend of hip hop and all that, they call them Puerto rocks. They used to see
the Hispanics dressing up with the hat to the side and all hip hop down, and some
assumed that we're supposed to just stick to our own style of music and friends.
They thought rap music was only a black thing, and it wasn't. Puerto Ricans used
to be all crazy with their hats to the side and everything. So that's why they used
to call the Puerto Ricans when they would see them with the hats to the side,
'Yo, look at that Puerto rock, like he's trying to be down.' They used to call us
Puerto rocks, so that was a nickname, and I said, 'I'm going to stick with that.
Shut everybody up.'"

The name the group chose to replace Solid Gold, although arrived at somewhat more fortuitously, equally reflects the members' effort to situate themselves
in an increasingly multicultural hip hop landscape. "Riding around in the car
with our manager, DJ Corchado, we were trying to think of a Latin name. We
was like, the Three Amigos, the Latin Employees, for real, we came up with some
crazy names. We kept on, cause we didn't want to limit ourselves, with Puerto Rican something, yeah, the Puerto Rican MCs. We wanted Latin something, to represent all Latinos. So we was the Two Amigos, the Three Amigos, then we came
up with many other names, Latin Imperials, Latin Alliance. And then when we
were driving along the Grand Concourse my manager's car happened to hit a
bump when I came out with the Latin Employees. Joking around, we were just
making fun and when the car hit the bump my manager thought I said Empire. I
was like, what? Latin Empire! I was like, yo, that's it! As soon as they said it, it
clicked. It's like a strong title, like the Zulu Nation."

Groping for names that click, of course, is part of the larger process of positioning themselves in the changing cultural setting of the later eighties. The decision to start rhyming in Spanish was crucial and came more as an accommoda-
tion to their families and neighbors than from hearing Mean Machine or any
other trends emerging in hip hop. "In the beginning it was all in English and our
families, all they do is play salsa and merengue, they thought you were American.
They considered it noise. 'Ay, deja ese alboroto' [cut out that noise], you know.
We said, 'Let's try to do it in Spanish, so that they can understand it, instead of
complaining to us so much.' They liked it." When they tried out their Spanish
with the mostly black hip hop audiences, they were encouraged further. "We used
to walk around with the tapes and the big radios and the black people behind us,
'Yo, man, that sounds dope, that's fly!'. . . Then I used to try to do it in the street
jams, and the crowd went crazy."

Acceptance and encouragement from the record industry was a different
story, especially before Mellow Man Ace broke the commercial ice. Atlantic did
wind up issuing "We're Puerto Rican and Proud," but not until after "Mentirosa"

went gold, and then the company dragged its feet in promoting it. Since then, aside from their tours and the video "Así Es la Vida," which made the charts on MTV Internacional, Latin Empire has been back in the parks and community events. Its members believe wholeheartedly in the strong positive messages of some rap and have participated actively in both the Stop the Violence and Back to School movements. They pride themselves on practicing what they preach in their antidrug and antialcohol rhymes. They continue to be greeted with enthusiastic approval by audiences of all nationalities throughout the city, and on their tours to Puerto Rico, the Dominican Republic, and, most recently, Cuba.

Their main shortcoming, in the parlance of the business, is that they don't have an "act," a packaged product. As the author of "The Packaging of a Recording Artist" in the July 1992 issue of *Hispanic Business* suggests, "To 'make it' as a professional recording act, you must have all the right things in place. Every element of what a recording act is must be considered and exploited to that act's benefit. The sound, the image, the look—all these factors must be integrated into a single package and then properly marketed to the public." In the packaging and marketing process, the artists and the quality of their work become secondary; it's the managers, and the other gatekeepers, who make the act. "While quality singing and a good song are the product in this business, they don't count for much without strong management."[6]

The pages of *Hispanic Business* make no mention of Latin Empire, concentrating on the major Hispanic "products" like Gerardo, Exposé, and Angelica. What the article says about Kid Frost is most interesting, because here is a Latino rapper "on his way to stardom in the West Coast Hispanic community" who cannot be expected to "lighten up on who he is just to get that cross-over audience." Clearly the main danger to the artist crossing over is not, from this perspective, that he might thereby sacrifice his focus and cultural context, but that he could lose his segment of the market. "It's so tempting for an artist to do that once they've gained acceptance," Kid Frost says. "But you risk losing your base when you do that and you never want to be without your core audience. That's why we work as a team and always include our artists and their managers in the packaging and marketing process."[7]

Latin Empire can't seem to get their "act" together because they remain too tied to their base to endure "strong management." Their mission, especially since rap "went Latin," is to reinstate the history and geography of the New York Puerto Rican contribution to hip hop and counteract the sensationalist version perpetrated by the media. In more recent numbers like "El Barrio," "Mi Viejo South Bronx," and "The Big Manzana" the group takes us deep into the Puerto Rican neighborhoods and back, "way back, to the days of West Side Story," when the New York style originated. Tracing the transition from the gang era to the emergence of the "style wars" of hip hop, Latin Empire's members tell their own stories and dramatize their constant juggling act between black and Latino and between island and New York cultures. In a new rhyme, "Not Listed," they "take hip hop to another tamaño [level]" by emphasizing the particular Puerto Rican role in rap history and countering the false currency given new arrivals. They end by affirming these ignored roots and rescuing the many early Puerto Rican rappers from oblivion:

Y'all need to see a médico
but we don't accept Medicaid
we don't give no crédito
we only give credit where credit is due
we got to give it to the Mean Machine
and the other brothers who were out there
lookin' out for Latinos
some kept it up, some chose other caminos
but we can't pretend that they never existed
cause yo, they were out there, just not listed.[8]

In another of their latest rhymes the group addresses the music business itself, lashing out at the counterfeits and subterfuges facing Latin Empire in their "hungry" battle for a fair record deal. Some of "Kinda Hungry" sounds like this:

Yeah that's right I'm hungry,
in other words, yo tengo hambre.
Those who overslept caught a calambre.
Fake mc's have enough posiciones,
but all we keep hearing is bullshit canciones
. . . mis sueños.
You might be head of A & R but I want to meet the dueños.
So I can let 'em know como yo me siento
and update 'em on the Latino movimiento
cause I'm getting tired of imitadores
that shit is muerto, that's why I'm sending you flores
en diferentes colores.
I'm like an undertaker . . .
I still don't understand how they allowed you to make a
rap record que no sirve para nada
I'll eat 'em up like an ensalada.
Speakin' about food you want comida?
Na, that's not what I meant,
what I want is a record deal en seguida
so we can get this on a 24 track
so they're out on the market and bug out on the feedback.
Huh, tu no te dabas cuenta,
a nigga like me is in effect en los noventa.
Straight outta Vega Baja
I knock 'em out the caja,
knock 'em out the box because I'm not relajando

I truly feel it's time I started eliminando.
MC's given' us a bad nombre
I can't see TNT, you know my right hand hombre,
the Krazy Taino sellin' out,
there's no way, there's no how,
that's not what we're about.
All we're about is a couple of gente,
here's some food for thought, comida para la mente.

With all their "hunger" for recognition, Latin Empire also feel the burden of responsibility for being the only Nuyorican rap group given any commercial play at all. Its members realize that, being synonymous with Puerto Rican rap, they are forced to stand in for a whole historical experience and for the rich variety of street rappers condemned to omission by the very filtering process that they are confronting. A prime example for them of the "not listed" is the "right hand hombre" mentioned here, MC TNT. Virtually unknown outside the immediate hip hop community in the South Bronx, TNT is living proof that hard-core, streetwise rhyming continues and develops in spite of the diluting effects and choices of the managers and A & R departments. Over the past year or two Puerto Rock and KT have incorporated TNT into many of their routines, and his rhymes and delivery have added a strong sense of history and poetic language to their presentations.

Like Puerto Rock, TNT (Tomás Robles) was born in Puerto Rico and came to New York at an early age. But childhood in the rough neighborhoods on the island figures prominently in his raps, as in this autobiographical section interlaced with samples from Rubén Blades's "La Vida Te Da Sorpresas":

Este ritmo es un invento
Cuando empiezo a rimar le doy el 100 por ciento
No me llamo Chico, o Federico
Donde naciste? Santurce, Puerto Rico
Cuando era niño no salía 'fuera
porque mataban diario en la cantera
Esto es verdad realidad no un engaño
mi pae murió cuando yo tenía seis años
La muerte me afectó con mucho dolor
pues mi mae empaquetó y nos mudamos pa' Nueva York
cuando llegué era un ambiente diferente
pero no me repentí, seguí para frente
y por las noches recé a Dios y a la santa
porque en mi corazón el coquí siempre canta.[9]

This rhythm is an invention
When I start to rhyme I give it 100 percent
My name isn't Chico, or Federico
Where were you born? Santurce, Puerto Rico.

When I was a boy I didn't go outside
because they were killing in the quarry every day
This is true reality not a hoax
my father died when I was six years old
His death caused me a lot of pain
well my mother packed up and we moved to New York
when I arrived it was a very different atmosphere
but I didn't regret it, I moved ahead
and at night I prayed to God and the holy mother
because in my heart the *coqui* frog always sings

By the late seventies, as an adolescent, TNT was involved in the gang scene in the South Bronx and helped form Tough Bronx Action and the large Latino chapters of Zulu Nation. By that time he was already playing congas in the streets and schoolyards and improvising rhymes. When he first heard Mean Machine in 1981, he recalls, he already had notebooks of raps in Spanish, though mostly he preserved them in his memory.

More recently he has adopted the epithet "el rap siquiatra" (the psychiatric rapper): In his lively, story-telling rhymes he prides himself on his biting analysis of events and attitudes in the community. He responds to the charges of gangsterism by pointing to the ghetto conditions that force survival remedies on his people. "Livin' in a ghetto can turn you to a gangster" is one of his powerful social raps, and in "Get some money" he addresses the rich and powerful directly: "He threw us in the ghetto to see how long we lasted / then he calls us a little ghetto bastard." His "Ven acá tiguerito tiguerito," which compares with anything by Kid Frost and Latin Alliance for sheer verbal ingenuity, captures the intensity of a combative street scene in El Barrio and is laced with phrases from Dominican slang. His programmatic braggadocio is playful and ragamuffin in its effect, yet with a defiance that extends in the last line to the very accentuation of the language:

Soy un rap siquiatra un rap mecánico
óyeme la radio y causo un pánico
te rompo el sistema y te dejo inválido
con un shock nervioso te ves bien pálido
no puedes con mi rap
aléjate aléjate
tómata una Contac y acuéstate
o llame a los bomberos que te rescate

I'm a rap psychiatrist, a rap mechanic
hear me on the radio and I cause a panic
I break your system and I leave you an invalid
with a nervous shock you look pretty pale
you can't deal with my rap

go away go away
take a Contac and go to bed
or call the fire fighters to come rescue you

At twenty-seven, MC TNT is already a veteran of Spanish rap battles, still "unlisted" and awaiting his break yet still working on his rhymes and beats every moment he can shake off some of the pressure. He is the closest I have run across to a rapper in the tradition of Puerto Rican *plena* music, since like that of the master *pleneros* his work is taking shape as a newspaper of the barrios, a running ironic commentary on the everyday events of Puerto Rican life. When all the talk was of referendums and plebiscites to determine the political status of Puerto Rico, TNT had some advice for his people to contemplate:

Puerto Rico, una isla hermosa,
donde nacen bonitas rosas,
plátanos, guineos y yautía,
Sazón Goya le da sabor a la comida.
Y ¿quién cocina más que la tía mía?
Pero el gobierno es bien armado,
tratando de convertirla en un estado.
Es mejor la dejen libre (asociado?).
Cristobal¡Colón no fue nadie,
cruzó el mar con un bonche de salvajes.
Entraron a Puerto Rico rompiendo palmas,
asustando a los caciques con armas.
Chequéate los libros, esto es cierto,
pregúntale a un cacique pero ya está muerto.
¿Cómo él descubrió algo que ya está descubierto?
Boriqua, no te vendas!

Puerto Rico, a beautiful island
where there are pretty roses,
plantains, bananas and root vegetables,
Goya seasoning gives the food flavor.
And who cooks more than my own aunt?
But the government is well armed,
trying to convert it into a state
It's better to leave it free (associated?)
Christopher Columbus was nobody,
he crossed the sea with a bunch of savages.
They entered Puerto Rico destroying the palm trees,
terrifying the Indian chiefs with their weapons.
Check out the books, this is true,
ask one of the Indian chiefs but they're already dead.
How could he discover something already discovered?
Puerto Rico, don't sell yourself!

Like other Latino groups, Puerto Ricans are using rap as a vehicle for affirming their history, language, and culture under conditions of rampant discrimination and exclusion. The explosion of Spanish-language and bilingual rap onto the pop-music scene in recent years bears special significance in the face of the stubbornly monolingual tenor of today's public discourse, most evident in the crippling of bilingual programs and services and in the ominous gains of the English-only movement. And of course along with its Spanish and Spanglish rhymes, Latino rap carries an ensemble of alternative perspectives and an often divergent cultural ethos into the mainstream of U.S. social life. The mass diffusion, even if only for commercial purposes, of cultural expression in the "other" language, and above all its broad and warm reception by fans of all nationalities, may help to muffle the shrieks of alarm emanating from the official culture whenever mention is made of "America's fastest-growing minority." Latin rap lends volatile fuel to the cause of "multiculturalism" in our society, at least in the challenging, inclusionary sense of that embattled term.

For Puerto Ricans, though, rap is more than a newly opened window on their history; rap is their history, and Puerto Ricans are integral to the history of hip hop. As the "Puerto rocks" themselves testify in conversation and rhyme, rapping is one among many social and creative practices that express their collective historical position in the prevailing relations of power and privilege. Puerto Rican participation in the emergence of hip hop music needs to be understood in direct, interactive relation to Puerto Rican experience in gangs and other forms of association among inner-city youth through the devastating blight of the seventies. Puerto rocks are the children of impoverished colonial immigrants facing even tougher times than in earlier decades. They helped make rap what it was to become, as they played a constitutive role in the stylistic definition of graffiti writing and breakdancing.

In addition to these more obvious associations, the formative years of rap coincide with the development of both salsa and Nuyorican poetry, expressive modes that (especially for the young Puerto Ricans themselves) occupy the same creative constellation as the musical and lyrical project of bilingual and bicultural rap. Musically, rap practice among Puerto Ricans is also informed by the strong tradition of street drumming and, at only a slight remove, their parallel earlier role in styles like doo-wop, boogaloo, and Latin jazz. In terms of poetic language, Spanglish rap is embedded in the everyday speech practices of the larger community over the course of several generations, even echoing in more than faint ways the tones and cadences of lyric typical of *plena, bomba,* and other forms of popular Puerto Rican song.

Like these other contemporaneous and prefiguring cultural practices, the active presence of Puerto Ricans in the creation of rap bears further emphatic testimony to their long history of cultural interaction with African Americans. Hip hop emerged as a cultural space shared by Puerto Ricans and blacks, a sharing that once again articulates their congruent and intermingling placement in the impinging political and economic geography. It is also a sharing in which, as the story of rap reveals, the dissonances are as telling as the harmonies, and the distances as heartfelt as the intimacies. The Puerto Ricans' nagging intimation that they are treading on black turf and working in a tradition of performative expression most directly traceable to James Brown and Jimmy Castor, the dozens and the blues, makes rap a terrain that is as much contested as it is cohabitated on equal terms. Jamaican dubbing, with its strong Caribbean resonance, serves as a bridge in this respect, just as reggae in more recent years is helping to link rap to otherwise disparate musical trends, especially in its reggaespañol dance-hall versions. In the historical perspective of black and Puerto Rican interaction, rap is thus a lesson in cultural negotiation and transaction as much as in fusions and crossovers, especially as those terms are bandied about in mainstream parlance. If multiculturalism is to amount to anything more than the wishful fancy of a pluralist mosaic, the stories of the Puerto rocks show that adequate account must be taken of the intricate jostling and juggling involved along the seams of contemporary cultural life.

What is to become of Latino rap, and how we appreciate and understand its particular messages, will depend significantly on the continuities it forges to its roots among the Puerto rocks. Recuperating this history, explicitly or by example, and "inventing" a tradition divergent from the workings of the commercial culture, represents the only hope of reversing the instant amnesia that engulfs rap and all forms of emergent cultural discourse as they migrate into the world of pop hegemony. Charlie Chase, TNT, and the other Puerto rocks were not only pioneers in some nostalgic sense but helped set the social meaning of rap practice prior to and relatively independent of its mediated commercial meaning. That formative participation of Latinos in rap in its infancy is a healthy reminder that the rap attack, as David Toop argued some years ago, is but the latest outburst of "African jive," and that the age-old journey of jive has always been a motley and inclusive procession.[10] And as in Cuban-based salsa, the Puerto Rican conspiracy in the present volley shows how creatively a people can adopt and adapt what would seem a "foreign" tradition and make it, at least in part, its own. To return to the first Puerto rock I talked with more than ten years ago, I close with a little rhyme by MC Ruby Dee, Rubén García, from the South Bronx:

Now all you Puerto Ricans you're in for a treat,
cause this Puerto Rican can rock a funky beat.
If you fall on your butt and you start to bleed,
Ruby Dee is what all the Puerto Ricans need.
I'm a homeboy to them cause I know what to do,
cause Ruby Dee is down with the black people too.[11]

Notes

1. All quotes of Charlie Chase are from my interview with him, "It's a Street Thing!" published in *Calalloo* 15, 4 (Fall 1992): 999–1021.

2. Juan Flores, "Rappin', Writin' and Breakin': Black and Puerto Rican Street Culture in New York City," *Dissent* (Fall 1987): 580–584. (Also published in *Centro 2, 3* [Spring 1988]: 34–41.) A shortened version of the present essay appeared as " 'Puerto Rican and Proud, Boy-ee!': Rap, Roots, and Amnesia" in *Microphone Fiends: Youth Music and Youth Culture,* ed. Tricia Rose and Andrew Ross (New York: Routledge, 1994), 89–98. Craig Castleman, *Getting Up: Subway Graffiti in New York* (Cambridge: MIT Press, 1982). Herbert Kohl *Golden Boy as Anthony Cool: A Photo Essay on Naming and Graffiti* (New York: Dial, 1972). Steve Hager, *Hip-Hop: The Illustrated History of Break Dancing, Rap Music, and Graffiti* (New York: St. Martin's, 1984). See also David Toop, *The Rap Attack: African Jive to New York Hip-Hop* (Boston: South End, 1984).
3. All quotes of Latin Empire are from my interview with them, "Puerto Raps," published in *Centro* 3, 2 (Spring 1991): 77–85.
4. Ed Morales, "How Ya Like Nosotros Now?" *Village Voice,* November 26, 1991, 91.
5. Elizabeth Hanley, "Latin Raps: Nuevo Ritmo, A New Nation of Rap Emerges," *Elle,* March 1991, 196–198. C. A., "El rap latino tiene tumbao," *Más* 2, 2 (Winter 1990): 81.
6. Joseph Roland Reynolds, "The Packaging of a Recording Artist," *Hispanic Business* 14, 7 (July 1992): 28–30.
7. Ibid.
8. Latin Empire provided me with unpublished rhymes in personal communication.
9. I taped these and other lyrics of TNT's raps during my interview with him on July 21, 1992.
10. See Toop, *Rap Attack*. See also Peter Manuel, *Caribbean Currents: Caribbean Music from Rumba to Reggae* (Philadelphia: Temple University Press, 1995), 92–94.
11. Cited in "Rappin', Writin' and Breakin'," note 2 above.

Afrika Bambaataa, the godfather of hip hop and founder of the Zulu Nation. *Photo © Ernie Paniccioli.*

Grandmaster Flash, pioneering DJ, with **Kurtis Blow,** rap's first innovative MC. *Photo © Ernie Paniccioli.*

The two Roxannes, who initiated the first smash "hit and dis" recordings as a response to UTFO's "Roxanne, Roxanne." *Photo © Ernie Paniccioli.*

West Coast gangsta rapper Ice-T. *Photo © Ernie Paniccioli.*

Eclectic Brooklyn Afrocentric rappers **XCLAN**. *Photo © Ernie Paniccioli.*

Ice Cube's protégé and "phat" feminist rapper **Yo-Yo**, sporting the Intelligent Black Woman's Coalition logo. *Photo © Ernie Paniccioli.*

Rapper, businesswoman, and television and movie star **Queen Latifah**, soon after recording her debut album, *Ladies First. Photo © Ernie Paniccioli.*

MC **Serch**, *center*, and **Prime Minister Pete Nice**, *right*, of **3rd Bass**—hip hop's first "real" white act—with their DJ, *left*. *Photo © Ernie Paniccioli.*

Fat Joe, keeping it real. *Photo by Kristine Larsen*.

◀ **Krazy Taino** and **Puerto Rock**, hip hop's Latino founders.

The Beatnuts, fusing Latino flava
with the Age of Aquarius.
Photo by Michael Benabib.

■ genres

■

■

■

■

■

■

part II

▪ kickin' reality, kickin' ballistics:
▪ gangsta rap and postindustrial los angeles

▪ robin d. g. kelley

ForeWORD: south central los angeles, april 29, 1992

I began working on this essay well over a year before the Los Angeles rebellion of 1992, and at least two or three months before Rodney King was turned into a martyr by several police officers and a video camera owned by George Holliday. In fact, I had finished the essay and was about to send it out for comments when several thousand people seized the streets on May Day eve, in part to protest the acquittal of the four officers who brutally beat King thirteen months earlier.[1] Of course, the rebellion enriched and complicated my efforts to make sense of gangsta rap in late-twentieth-century Los Angeles, but I did not have to substantially change my original arguments. This particular genre of hip hop was, in some ways, an omen of the insurrection. The two years of "research" I had spent rocking, bopping, and wincing to gangsta narratives of everyday life were (if I may sample Mike Davis) very much like "excavating the future in Los Angeles."

Ice-T, truly the OG (original gangster) of L.A. gangsta rap, summed it up best in a 1992 *Rolling Stone* interview: "When rap came out of L.A., what you heard initially was my voice yelling about South Central. People thought, 'That shit's crazy,' and ignored it. Then NWA came and yelled, Ice Cube yelled about it. People said, 'Oh, that's just kids making a buck.' They didn't realize how many niggas with attitude there are out on the street. Now you see them."[2]

Although the mainstream media believes it all began with the beating of Rodney King neither the hip hop community nor residents of South Central Los Angeles were surprised by that event. Countless black Angelenos had experienced or witnessed this sort of terror before. When L.A. rapper Ice Cube was asked about the King incident on MTV, he responded simply, "It's been happening to us for years. It's just we didn't have a camcorder every time it happened." (Subsequently, Cube recorded "Who Got the Camera" on the 1992 album *The Predator*, a hilarious track in which he asks the police brutalizing him to hit him once more in order to get the event on film.)[3] Few black Angelenos could forget the killing of Eula Love in 1979, the sixteen deaths caused by LAPD choke holds, or numerous lesser-known incidents for which no officers were punished. Virtually every South Central resident experienced routine stops, if not outright harassment, and thousands of African American and Latino youths have had their names and addresses logged in the LAPD antigang task force data base—on a form, ironically, called a "rap sheet"—whether they were gang members or not.[4]

The L.A. rebellion merely underscores the fact that a good deal of gangsta rap is (aside from often very funky jeep music) a window into, and critique of, the criminalization of black youth. Of course, this is not unique to gangsta rap: all kinds of b-boys and b-girls—rappers, graffiti artists, breakdancers—have been dealing with and challenging police repression, the media's criminalization of inner-city youths, and the "just us" system from the get-go. Like the economy and the city itself, the criminal-justice system changed just when hip hop was born. Prisons are not designed to discipline but to corral bodies labeled menaces to society; policing is not designed to stop or reduce crime in inner-city communities but to manage it.[5] Moreover, economic restructuring resulting in massive unemployment *has* created criminals out of black youth, which is what gangsta rappers acknowledge. But rather than apologize or preach, they attempt to rationalize and explain. Most gangsta rappers write lyrics attacking law-enforcement agencies, the denial of their unfettered access to public space, and the media's complicity in making black youth out to be criminals. Yet these very stereotypes of the ghetto as "war zone" and the black youth as "criminal," as well as their (often adolescent) struggles with notions of masculinity and sexuality, also structure and constrain their efforts to create a counternarrative of life in the inner city.

Lest we get too sociological here, we must bear in mind that hip hop, irrespective of its particular flavor, is music. Few doubt it has a message, whether they interpret it as straight-up nihilism or the words of primitive rebels. Not many pay attention to rap as art—whether the rappers are mixing break beats from Funkadelic, gangsta limpin' in black hoodies, appropriating old-school "hustler's toasts," or simply trying to be funny. Although this essay admittedly emphasizes lyrics, it also tries to deal with form, style, and aesthetics. This is a lesson cultural critic Tricia Rose has been drumming into students of African American popular culture for some time. As she puts it, "Without historical contextualization, aesthetics are naturalized, and certain cultural practices are made to appear essential to a given group of people. On the other hand, without aesthetic considerations, black cultural practices are reduced to extensions of sociohistorical circumstances."[6]

Heeding Rose's call for a complex, more historical interpretation of cultural forms that takes account of context *and* aesthetics, politics *and* pleasure, I explore the cultural politics of gangsta rap—its lyrics, music, styles, roots, contradictions, and consistencies—and the place where it seems to have maintained its deepest roots: Los Angeles and its black environs. To do this right we need a historical perspective. We need to go back . . . way back, to the days of the OGs.

OGs in postindustrial los angeles: evolution of a style

L.A. might be the self-proclaimed home of gangsta rap, but black Angelenos didn't put the gangsta into hip hop. Gangsta lyrics and style were part of the whole hip hop scene from the very beginning. If you never hung out at the Hevalo Club on 173rd or at Cedar Park in the Bronx during the mid-1970s, just check out Charlie Ahearn's classic 1982 film *Wild Style* documenting the early graffiti and rap scene in New York. When Double Trouble steps on stage with the fly routine, they're decked out in white "pimp-style" suits, matching hats, and guns galore. Others are strapped as well, waving real guns as part of the act. The scene seems so contemporary, and yet it was shot over a decade before Onyx recorded "Throw Ya Guns in the Air." But we need to go back even further. Back before Lightnin' Rod (Jalal Uridin of the Last Poets) recorded *Hustler's Convention* in 1973; before Lloyd Price recorded "Stagger Lee" in 1958; even before Screamin' Jay Hawkins recorded his explicitly sexual comedy rap "Alligator Wine." We need to go back to the blues, to the baaadman tales of the late nineteenth century, and to the age-old tradition of "signifying" if we want to discover the roots of the gangsta aesthetic in hip hop.[7]

Nevertheless, while gangsta rap's roots are very old, it does have an identifiable style of its own, and in some respects it is a particular product of the mid-1980s. The inspiration for the specific style we now call gangsta rap seems to have come from the Bronx-based rapper KRS One and Boogie Down Productions, who released *Criminal Minded*, and Philadelphia's Schooly D, who made *Smoke Some Kill*. Both albums appeared in 1987, just a few months before Ice-T came out with his debut album, *Rhyme Pays*.[8] Ice-T was not only the first West Coast gangsta-style rapper on wax, but he was himself an experienced OG whose narratives were occasionally semiautobiographical or drawn from scenes he had witnessed or heard about on the street. A native of New Jersey who moved to Los Angeles as a child, T joined a gang while at Crenshaw High School and began a very short career as a criminal. He eventually graduated from Crenshaw, attended a junior college, and, in the midst of deindustrialization and rising unemployment, turned to the armed services. After four years in the service, he pursued his high-school dream to become a rapper and got his first break in the movie *Breakin'*.[9] Although Ice-T's early lyrics ranged from humorous boasts and tales of crime and violence to outright misogyny, they were decidedly shaped by his experiences. In "Squeeze the Trigger" on *Rhyme Pays* (1987), he leads off with a brief autobiographical composite sketch of his gangsta background, insisting all along that he is merely a product of a callous, brutal society.

As *Rhyme Pays* hit the record stores (though banned on the radio because of its explicit lyrics), according to NWA (Niggas with Attitude) member MC Ren, an underground gangsta hip hop community was forming in Compton and allegedly making and distributing underground tapes about street life. Among the participants was former drug dealer Eric Wright—better known as Ezy-E, who subsequently launched an independent label known as Ruthless Records and, along with his newly formed crew who made up Niggas with Attitude (MC Ren, Ice Cube, Yella, and Dr. Dre), moved gangsta rap into another phase. In 1987 and 1988, Ruthless produced a string of records, beginning with the twelve-inch *NWA and the Posse*, Ezy-E's solo album, *Eazy Duz It*, and the album that put NWA on the map, *Straight outta Compton* (1988).[10] NWA placed even more emphasis than did Ice-T on exaggerated descriptions of street life, militant resistance to authority, and outright sexist violence. Although songs like "Straight outta Compton" seemed more like modern-day versions of baaadman folklore, NWA's lyrics were far more brutal than any that had come before.

A distinctive West Coast style of gangsta rap, known for its rich descriptive story telling laid over heavy funk samples from the likes of George Clinton and the whole Parliament Funkadelic family, Sly Stone, Rick James, Ohio Players, Average White Band, Cameo, Zapp, and, of course, the Godfather himself—James Brown—evolved and proliferated rapidly soon after the appearance of Ice-T and NWA. The frequent use of Parliament Funkadelic samples led one critic to dub the music "G-Funk (gangsta attitude over P-funk beats)."[11] Within three years, dozens of Los Angeles–based groups came onto the scene, many having been produced by either Ezy-E's Ruthless Records; Ice-T and Afrika Islam's Rhyme Syndicate Productions; Ice Cube's post-NWA project, Street Knowledge Productions; and Dr. Dre's Death Row Records. The list of West Coast gangsta rappers includes Above the Law, Mob Style, Compton's Most Wanted, King Tee, the Rhyme Syndicate, Snoop Doggy Dogg, (Lady of) Rage, Poison Clan, Capital Punishment Organization (CPO), the predominantly Samoan Boo-Yaa Tribe, the DOC, DJ Quick, AMG, Hi-C, Low Profile, Nu Niggaz on the Block, South Central Cartel, Compton Cartel, 2nd II None, W. C. and the MAAD Circle, Cypress Hill, and Chicano rappers like Kid Frost and Proper Dos.

Although they have much in common with the larger hip hop community, gangsta rappers drew ire as well as praise from their colleagues. Indeed, gangsta rap has generated more debate within and without the hip hop world than any other genre.[12] Unfortunately, much of this debate, especially in the media, has only disseminated misinformation. Thus, it's important to clarify what gangsta rap is *not*. First, gangsta rappers have never merely celebrated gang violence, nor have they favored one gang over another. Gang bangin' itself has never even been a central theme in the music. Many of the violent lyrics are not intended literally. Rather, they are boasting raps in which the imagery of gang bangin' is used metaphorically to challenge competitors on the mic—an element common to all hard-core hip hop. The mic becomes a Tech-9 or AK-47, imaginary drive-bys occur from the stage, flowing lyrics become hollow-point shells. Classic examples are Ice Cube's "Jackin' for Beats," a humorous song that describes sampling other artists and producers as outright armed robbery; Ice-T's "Pulse of the Rhyme" or "Grand Larceny" (which brags about stealing a show); CPO's (Capital Punishment Organization) aptly titled warning to other perpetrating rappers, "Homicide"; NWA's "Real Niggaz"; Dr. Dre's "Lyrical Gangbang"; Ice Cube's "Now I Gotta Wet'cha"; and Compton's Most Wanted's "Wanted" and "Straight Check N' Em." Sometimes, as in the case of Ice-T's "I'm Your Pusher," an antidrug song that boasts of pushing "dope beats and lyrics / no beepers needed" gangsta-rap lyrics have been misinterpreted as advocating criminality and violence.[13]

When the imagery of crime and violence is not used metaphorically, exaggerated and invented boasts of criminal acts should be regarded as part of a larger set of signifying practices. Performances like the Rhyme Syndicate's "My Word Is Bond" or J.D.'s storytelling between songs on Ice Cube's *AmeriKKKa's Most Wanted* are supposed to be humorous and, to a certain extent, unbelievable. Growing out of a much older set of cultural practices, these masculinist narratives are essentially verbal duels over who is the "baddest motherfucker around." They are not meant as literal descriptions of violence and aggression, but connote the playful use of language itself. So when J.D. boasts about how he used to "jack them motherfuckers for them Nissan trucks," the point is less the stealing per se than the way in which he describes his bodaciousness. He would approach the driver in the drive-through line at McDonald's and announce, "Nigger, get your motherfuckin' food, leave it in the car, nigger get out!" (Ironically, in their brilliant film debut *Menace II Society*, the Hughes Brothers sampled this jack story as a representation of real live crime in South Central Los Angeles.)[14]

When gangsta rappers do write lyrics intended to convey social realism, their work loosely resembles a street ethnography of racist institutions and social practices, told more often than not in the first person. Whether gangsta rappers step into the character of a gang banger, hustler, or ordinary working person—that is, products and residents of the 'hood—they constitute an alternative voice to mainstream journalists and social scientists. In some ways, these descriptive narratives, under the guise of objective "street journalism," are no less polemical (hence political) than nineteenth-century slave narratives in defense of abolition. When Ice Cube was still with NWA, he explained, "We call ourselves underground street reporters. We just tell it how we see it, nothing more, nothing less."[15]

Of course, their reality is hardly objective in the sense of being detached; their standpoint is that of the ghetto dweller, the criminal, the victim of police repression, the teenage father, the crack slanger, the gang banger, and the female dominator. Much like the old baaadman narratives that have played an important role in black vernacular folklore, the characters they create appear at first glance to be apolitical individuals out only for themselves; and like the protagonist in Melvin Van Peebles's cinematic classic *Sweet Sweetback's Baaadass Song*, they are reluctant to trust anyone. It is hard to miss the influences of urban toasts and pimp narratives, which became popular during the late 1960s and early 1970s. In many instances the characters are almost identical, and on occasion rap artists pay tribute to toasting by lyrically sampling these early pimp narratives.[16]

Whereas verbal skills and creativity are the main attraction for the communities that created toasting, for some outsiders—middle-class white males, for instance—gangsta rap unintentionally plays the same role as the blaxploitation films of the 1970s or, for that matter, the gangster films of any generation. It attracts listeners for whom the ghetto is a place of adventure, unbridled violence, and erotic fantasy, or an imaginary alternative to suburban boredom. White music critic John Leland, who claimed that Ice Cube's political turn "killed rap music," praised NWA because it "dealt in evil as fantasy: killing cops, smoking hos, filling quiet nights with a flurry of senseless buckshot." This kind of voyeurism partly explains NWA's huge white following and why their album, *Efil4zaggin*, shot to the top of the charts as soon as it was released. As one critic put it, "NWA have more in common with a Charles Bronson movie than a PBS documentary on the plight of the inner-cities." NWA members have even admitted that some of their recent songs were not representations of reality in the 'hood but inspired by popular films like *Innocent Man* and *Tango and Cash*.[17]

While I'm aware that some rappers are merely "studio gangstas," and that the *primary* purpose of this music is to produce "funky dope rhymes" for our listening pleasure, we cannot ignore the ties of West Coast gangsta rap to the streets of L.A.'s black working-class communities where it originated. The generation who came of age in the 1980s during the Reagan-Bush era were products of devastating structural changes in the urban economy that date back at least to the late 1960s. While the city as a whole experienced unprecedented growth, the communities of Watts and Compton faced increased economic displacement, factory closures, and an unprecedented deepening of poverty. The uneven development of L.A.'s postindustrial economy meant an expansion of high-tech industries like Aerospace and Lockheed, and the disappearance of rubber- and steel-manufacturing firms, many of which were located in or near Compton and Watts. Deindustrialization, in other words, led to a spatial restructuring of the Los Angeles economy as high-tech firms were established in less populated regions like the Silicon Valley and Orange County. Developers and city and county government helped the process along by infusing massive capital into suburbanization while simultaneously cutting back expenditures for parks, recreation, and affordable housing in inner-city communities. Thus since 1980 economic conditions in

Watts have deteriorated on a greater scale than in any other L.A. community, and by some estimates Watts is in worse shape now than in 1965. A 1982 report from the California legislature revealed that South Central neighborhoods experienced a 50 percent rise in unemployment while purchasing power dropped by one-third. The median income for South Central L.A.'s residents was a paltry $5,900—that is, $2,500 below the median income for the black population in the late 1970s. Youth were the hardest hit. For all of Los Angeles County, the unemployment rate of black youth remained at about 45 percent, and in areas with concentrated poverty the rate was even higher. As the composition of L.A.'s urban poor becomes increasingly younger, programs for inner-city youth are being wiped out at an alarming rate. Both the Neighborhood Youth Corps and the Comprehensive Employment and Training Act (CETA) have been dismantled, and the Jobs Corps and Los Angeles Summer Job Program have been cut back substantially.[18]

Thus, on the eve of crack cocaine's arrival on the urban landscape, the decline in opportunities and growing poverty of black youth in L.A. led to a substantial rise in property crimes committed by juveniles and young adults. Even NWA recall the precrack illicit economy in a song titled "The Dayz of Wayback" on *Efil4zaggin* (1991) in which Dr. Dre and MC Ren wax nostalgic about the early to mid-1980s, when criminal activity consisted primarily of small-time muggings and robberies. Because of its unusually high crime rate, L.A. had by that time gained the dubious distinction of having the largest urban prison population in the country. When the crack economy made its presence felt in inner-city black communities, violence intensified as various gangs and groups of peddlers battled for control over markets. Yet in spite of the violence and financial vulnerability that went along with peddling crack, for many black youngsters it was the most viable sector of the economy.[19]

While the rise in crime and the ascendance of the crack economy might have put money into *some* people's pockets, for the majority it meant greater police repression. Watts, Compton, Northwest Pasadena, Carson, North Long Beach, and several other black working-class communities were turned into war zones during the mid to late 1980s. Police helicopters, complex electronic surveillance, even small tanks armed with battering rams became part of this increasingly militarized urban landscape. Housing projects, such as Imperial Courts, were renovated along the lines of minimum-security prisons and equipped with fortified fencing and an LAPD substation. Imperial Court residents were now required to carry identity cards, and visitors were routinely searched. Framed by the police murder of Eula Love, the rash of choke-hold killings of African Americans taken into LAPD's custody in the early 1980s, and the videotaped beating of Rodney King, the past decade has been one of rising police brutality. As popular media coverage of the inner city associated drugs and violence with black youth, young African Americans by virtue of being residents of South Central L.A. and Compton were subject to police harassment and in some cases became the source of neighborhood distrust.[20]

Along with the social and economic disintegration of black urban life, the combination of joblessness and poverty under Reagan-Bush, the growing viability of the crack economy and other illicit forms of economic activity, and the intensification of racist police repression, the general erosion of notions of justice, law, and order have generated penetrating critiques by gangsta rappers. MC Ren, for example, blames "the people who are holding the dollars in the city" for the expansion of gang violence and crime, arguing that if black youth had decent jobs, they would not need to participate in the illicit economy. "It's their fault simply because they refused to employ black people. How would you feel if you went for job after job and each time, for no good reason, you're turned down?"[21] Ice-T blames capitalism entirely, which he defines as much more than alienating wage labor; the marketplace itself as well as a variety of social institutions are intended to exercise social control over African Americans. "Capitalism says you must have an upper class, a middle class, and a lower class. . . . Now the only way to guarantee a lower class, is to keep y'all uneducated and as high as possible."[22] According to Ice-T, the ghetto is, at worst, the product of deliberately oppressive policies, at best, the result of racist neglect. Nowhere is this clearer than in his song "Escape from the Killing Fields" on OG: Original Gangsta (1991), which uses the title of a recent film about the conflict in Cambodia as a metaphor for the warlike conditions in today's ghettos.

Rather than attempt to explain in global terms the relationship between joblessness, racism, and the rise of crime in inner-city communities, gangsta rappers construct a variety of first-person narratives to illustrate how social and economic realities in late-capitalist L.A. affect young black men. Although the use of first-person narratives is rooted in a long tradition of black aesthetic practices, the use of "I" to signify both personal and collective experiences also enables gangsta rappers to navigate a complicated course between what social scientists call "structure" and "agency."[23] In gangsta rap there is almost always a relationship between the conditions in which characters live and the decisions they make. Some gangsta rappers—Ice Cube in particular—are especially brilliant at showing how, if I may paraphrase Marx, young urban black men make their own history, but not under circumstances of their own choosing.

"Broke niggas make the best crooks"

"The press is used to make the victim look like the criminal and make the criminal look like the victim," said Malcom X.[24] In an era when the popular media, conservative policy specialists, and some social scientists are claiming that the increase in street crime can be explained by some pathological culture of violence bereft of the moderating influences of a black middle class who only recently fled to the suburbs, L.A.'s gangsta rappers keep returning to the idea that joblessness and crime are directly related.[25] Indeed, this is partly why their first-person narratives are not dominated by more socially responsible criminals, those "social bandits" who rob from the rich and give to the poor.

Consider W.C. and the MAAD (Minority Alliance of Anti-Discrimination) Circle's manifesto on the roots of inner-city crime, "If You Don't Work, U Don't Eat," on their 1991 album *Ain't a Damn Thing Changed;* the song appropriates the title of Bobby Byrd's late 1960s hit (which is also sampled) but replicates a very popular Old Left adage. Describing the song in a recent interview, W.C. explained the context in which it was conceived: "I've got to feed a family. Because I don't have [job] skills I have no alternative but to turn this way. My little girl don't take no for an answer, my little boy don't take no for an answer, my woman's not going to take no for an answer, so I gotta go out and make my money."[26] In the song, members from his own crew as well as guest artists (MC Eiht from Compton's Most Wanted (CMW) and J.D. from Ice Cube's posse, Da Lench Mob) each give their personal perspective on how they (or their character) became criminals. For MAAD Circle rapper Coolio, crime is clearly a means of survival, though he is fully cognizant that each job he pulls might lead to death or incarceration. Especially noteworthy are his swipes at racism and liberal democracy, which imply that legitimate opportunities to make decent money are denied him by race and class, and that the kind of freedom he is able to pursue won't pay his bills: "Money ain't everything, but neither is brokeness / Give me a knife, cause I can't live off happiness." MC Eiht openly declares that crime is his way of resisting wage labor ("I ain't punchin' a clock") but admits with some remorse that his victims are usually regular black folk in the 'hood. Unless conditions change, he insists, neighborhood crime will continue to be a way of life.

Ice Cube's "A Bird in the Hand" from his controversial album *Death Certificate* is a brilliant examination of the making of a young drug peddler. Cube plays a working-class black man just out of high school who can't afford college and is regularly turned down for medium-wage service-sector jobs. Because he is also a father trying to provide at least financial support for his girlfriend and their baby, he decides to take the only "slave" available—McDonald's is his spot. As the bass line is thumpin' over well-placed samples of screaming babies in the background, Ice Cube looks for another way out. It does not take much reflection for him to realize that the drug dealers are the only people in his neighborhood making decent money. Although his immediate material conditions improve, he now must face constant hounding from police and the mass media: "Now you put the feds against me / Cause I couldn't follow the plan of the presidency / I'm never gettin' love again / But blacks are too fuckin' broke to be Republican." In the end, the blame for the rapid expansion of crack is placed squarely with the Reagan and Bush administrations. "Sorry, but this is our only room to walk / Cause we don't want to drug push / But a bird in the hand, is worth more than a Bush."

While critics who want more socially conscious criminals often misinterpret painful descriptions of "black-on-black" crime as celebratory, most gangsta stories emphasize that poverty and oppression do not automatically breed either revolution or selfish individualism. If we are to understand the work of gangsta rappers, we might do well to heed historian Peter Linebaugh's advice about studying working-class criminals in London during the eighteenth century: "If we catego-

rize them too quickly as social criminals taking from the rich, or criminals stealing from the poor, in the process of making these judgments we cloud our atten-
tiveness to theirs."[27] Like the working-class thieves three centuries and an ocean
away whom Linebaugh lifts from the forgotten stories of London's hanged, the
characters in gangsta narratives defy our attempts to define them as social bandits or "criminal-criminals." The very same voices we hear beating or arresting
other brothers and sisters occasionally call on male gangsters to turn their talents
toward the state. In "Get Up Off That Funk" on *Ain't a Damn Thing Changed*,
W.C. and the MAAD Circle take a Robin Hood stand, declaring that their own
agenda includes jackin' the powerful and distributing the wealth. Rapping over a
heavy bass and trap drum reminiscent of the hard-core go-go music one hears on
the darker side of the nation's capital, W.C. describes the Minority Alliance of
Anti-Discrimination as an organization intent on stealing from the rich to give
"to the poor folks in the slums."

Ice Cube takes the Robin Hood metaphor a step further, calling for the "ultimate drive-by" to be aimed at the U.S. government. In a recent interview, he
even suggested that gang bangers "are our warriors. . . . It's just they're fighting
the wrong gang." The gang they ought to be fighting, he tells us, is "the government of the United States."[28] "I Wanna Kill Sam" on his album *Death Certificate*
is his declaration of gang warfare on America. It begins with Cube loading up his
gat in anticipation of taking out the elusive Uncle Sam. Following a fictional pub-
lic-service announcement on behalf of the armed services, Cube gives us his own
version of U.S. history, collapsing the slave trade, forced labor in the era of freedom, and army recruitment into a dramatic transhistorical narrative of racist repression and exploitation. He then connects the "pasts" to the present, suggesting that while the same old racism still lingers, the victims are unwilling to accept
the terms of the existing order. No more retreats. No more nonviolent protests.
Just straight jackin', gangsta style. On *Guerrillas in the Mist* (Priority, 1992), Da
Lench Mob's title cut puns on the infamous LAPD dispatch describing African
Americans in the vicinity, which itself puns on the popular film set in Africa titled "Gorillas in the Mist." But for Da Lench Mob, the "gorillas" are America's
nightmare, organized and armed gangstas ready for the Big Payback.

Of course, the idea of the Crips and Bloods becoming a revolutionary guer-
rilla army seems ludicrous, especially given the role street gangs have assumed as
protectors of the illicit economy. Consider the words of a Chicano gang member
from Los Angeles: "I act like they do in the big time, no different. There ain't no
corporation that acts with morals and that ethics shit and I ain't about to either.
As they say, if it's good for General Motors, it's good enough for me."[29] Hardly
the stuff one would expect from an inner-city rebel. Nevertheless, we need to
keep in mind that the hip hop generation consumed films like "The Spook Who
Sat by the Door," and some even read the book. *The Autobiography of Malcolm X*
convinced unknown numbers of kids that even second-rate gangsters can become
political radicals. It's possible that a few black Angelenos absorbed some OG oral
history about the gang roots of the Black Panther Party. L.A. Panther leaders

Bunchy Carter and John Huggins were former Slausons, and their fellow banger, Brother Crook (Ron Wilkins), founded the Community Alert Patrol to challenge police brutality in the late 1960s. And the postrebellion role of gang leaders in drafting and proposing the first viable plan of action to rebuild South Central Los Angeles cannot be overlooked. Indeed, much like today, both the presence of the Nation of Islam and the rise in police brutality played pivotal roles in politicizing individual gang members.[30]

By treating crime as a mode of survival and as a form of rebellion, gangsta rappers obviously run the risk of idealizing criminal activity. However, they use the same narrative strategies—first-person autobiographical accounts or the ostensibly more objective "street journalism"—to criticize inner-city crime and violence. Songs like Ice-T's "Pain," "6 in the Mornin'," "Colors," "New Jack Hustler," and "High Rollers"; Ice Cube's "Dead Homiez" and "Color Blind"; NWA's "Alwayz into Somethin' "; Cypress Hill's "Hand on the Pump" and "Hole in the Head"; and "We're All in the Same Gang" by a collection of gangsta groups express clear messages that gangbanging and jackin' for a living usually end in death or incarceration—that is, if you're caught.[31] CPO's "The Wall" (as well as "The Movement," and sections from "Gangsta Melody," all on 1990's *To Hell and Black*), performed by their quick-tongued lead lyricist, Lil Nation, rails against drive-by shootings, the rising rate of black-on-black homicide, and brothers who try to escape reality by "cold drinkin' 8-ball." Lil Nation even breaks with the majority of his fellow gangsta rappers by announcing that black youth today need more religion, a better set of values, and a radical social movement to bring about change—which is precisely what "the wall" represents. Even a group as hard as Da Lench Mob suggests that black urban youth should become more religious.

Most gangsta rappers are not so quick to denounce violence, arguing that it is the way of the street. This reticence is certainly evident in Ice Cube's advice that "if you is or ain't a gang banger / keep one in the chamber" as well as his tongue-in-cheek call to replace guard dogs with guns ("A Man's Best Friend"). Even his antigang song, "Color Blind," implies that inner-city residents should be armed and ready in the event of a shoot-out or attempted robbery. MAAD Circle rappers Coolio and W.C. likewise emphasize the need for protection. Although they both agree that gang banging will ultimately lead to death or prison, they also realize that rolling with a crew serves the same purpose as carrying a gun. As Coolio points out, "They say on the radio and TV that you have a choice, but it's bullshit. If you're getting your ass whipped everyday, you've got to have some protection."[32]

The gendering of crime also helps explain why gangsta rappers are reluctant to denounce violence, as well as why the criminals in their narratives are almost always men, and why, in part, violence against women appears consistently in the music of many gangsta groups. First, as criminologist James Messerschmidt reminds us, "throughout our society . . . violence is associated with power and males, and for some youth this association is reinforced as part of family life. As a result, most young males come to identify the connection between masculinity-power-aggression-violence as part of their own developing male identities." Being a man, therefore, means not "taking any shit" from anyone, which is why the characters in gangsta rap prefer to use a gat rather than flee the scene, and why drive-by shootings often occur over public humiliations. Second, although it might be argued that men dominate these narratives because they are the ones who construct them, it is also true that the preponderance of street crime is committed by marginalized males. The matter is far too complicated to discuss in detail here, but several scholars attribute these patterns to males' higher rates of unemployment and greater freedom from the restraints of the household compared to females (and thus more opportunity to engage in criminal activity), and to a patriarchal culture that makes earning power a measure of manhood.[33]

Whereas most gangsta rappers take violence against women for granted, they do attempt to show the dark, nasty side of *male-on-male* street violence. Sir Jinx's use of documentary-style recordings of simulated drive-bys and fights that escalate into gun battles is intended to deromanticize gang violence.[34] A much more clear-cut example is CMW's "Drive-by Miss Daisy," a powerful, complex depiction of the ways in which ordinary bystanders can become victims of intergang warfare. The first story begins with a young man assigned to assassinate a rival gang banger who had just killed his homie. Afraid and intimidated, he decides to get drunk before calling his posse together for the drive-by. When they finally pull up in front of the house, he is apparently unaware that the boy's mother is in the kitchen cooking dinner. Just before he pulls the trigger, his conscience intervenes for a second: "He hears a fucking little voice in his brain / It says, 'Don't kill, we're all in the same gang' / He tells it back, 'That ain't the gang I'm in' / Cause the gang I'm in is like in it to win." In the second story, another "Miss Daisy" happens to be pumping gas at a Mobil station when a shoot-out ensues between two young men. What makes the song so compelling is less the lyrics than the music. Although CMW had already established a reputation among gangsta rappers for employing more laid-back jazz and quiet storm tracks than hard-core funk, their choice of music in "Drive-by" was clearly intended to heighten the intensity rather than provide an understated backdrop for their lead rapper. Thus we hear straight-ahead modal jazz circa the 1960s—heavy ride and crash cymbals and acoustic bass beneath the laid-back and strangely cartoonish, high-pitched voice of MC Eiht. The two instrumental interludes are even more powerful. The bass and cymbal combination is violently invaded by an acoustic piano playing strong, dissonant block chords in the vein of Don Pullen or Stanley Cowell. Mixed in are the sounds of automatic weapons, a looped sample of blood-curdling screams that has the effect of creating an echo without reverberation, and samples of would-be assassins hollering, "You die, motherfucker." This disturbing cacophony of sound captures the fragility of human life, the chaos of violent death, and the intense emotions young murderers and their victims must feel.[35]

Ice Cube's "Dead Homiez" on *Kill at Will* reflects on the tragedy of inner-city homicide in a graveyard, its final social site. An able storyteller, Cube paints a detailed picture of his homie's funeral, interrupting periodically with loving as well as frustrating memories of his dead friend. No matter how many forty-ounce bottles of malt liquor he downs, his friend's death continues to haunt him: "Still hear the screams from his mother / as my nigger lay dead in the gutter." His most powerful message is what a youth's death means to the living. The anger, pain, confusion, and fear of those left behind are all inscribed in the ritual of mourning.

Drug dealers have been a common target of gangsta rap from the beginning. One of NWA's first releases, "Dope Man," on *NWA and the Posse* (1988), offers some brutal insights into the effects of the rising crack-cocaine economy. Screamed over electronic drum tracks and a Middle Eastern–sounding reed instrument, Dr. Dre declares, "If you smoke 'caine you a stupid motherfucker" and goes on to describe some nameless "crackhead" whose habit forced him into a life of crime. CPO's "The Movement" and "The Wall" on *To Hell and Black* wage frontal attacks on all pushers, whom Lil Nation accuses of committing genocide against black people; he advocates a social movement to wipe pushers out, since law enforcement is half-hearted and the justice system is both inept and corrupt.

Because most gangsta rappers try to explain why people turn to drug dealing and other assorted crimes and simultaneously attack drug dealers for the damage they do to poor black communities, they have often been accused of being inconsistent, contradictory, or even schizophrenic. For example, on *Death Certificate*, the album that includes "A Bird in the Hand," Ice Cube calls drug dealers "killers" and insists that they exploit black people "like the caucasians did." That Cube finds nothing redeeming in the activities of crack peddlers, however, does not contradict the clear message in "A Bird in the Hand." His effort to explain why the drug trade is so appealing to some inner-city residents is not an uncritical acceptance of it. Indeed, a third *Death Certificate* song about the crack economy not only reveals the violence that goes along with carving out new markets but borrows from dominant images of legitimate entrepreneurship to further underscore the similarities between the illicit and legal economies. "My Summer Vacation" is about a hostile takeover of the St. Louis, Missouri, drug economy by "four gangbangers, professional crack slangers" from Los Angeles. Their decision to break into the St. Louis drug trade was precipitated by a police crackdown and intense competition in the City of Angels. After moving into the seediest section of the black community, they forcibly seize critical street corners. The campaign was so calculated that it could have been drawn from a page in Karl Marx's chapter on "primitive accumulation" in *Capital*, and so successful that, in another context, it might be regarded as an exemplar of American enterprise. Once in charge, the four begin to turn an enormous profit; everything is working as planned until "St. Louis niggas want they corner back." As the struggle leads to escalating violence they decide to set up shop in Seattle, but they're caught and imprisoned before leaving town.

Arguably the scenario in "My Summer Vacation" is no different from any typical gangster movie such as *The Godfather* or *New Jack City*; the protagonist even describes himself as a "1991 Tony Montana," referring to the film *Scarface*. What is most interesting about the song, however, is the parallel Cube draws be-

tween legitimate corporate struggles for power and the crack economy. By "reversing" dominant discourses legitimating entrepreneurship, hostile takeovers,
and a global corporate culture more concerned with profits than committed to a
national community, Cube and other gangsta rappers hold up the illicit economy
as a mirror image of American capitalism. Ice-T, in the role of "New Jack Hustler" on OG: *The Original Gangster,* not only suffers from a "capitalist migraine"
but asks if the luxury he enjoys as a big-time drug dealer is "a nightmare, or the
American dream." His implication is clear, for this particular enterprise leads to
death, destruction, and violence rather than to accumulation and development.

These economic critiques resist labels; the recasting of capitalism as gangsterism is not intended simply to legitimate the illicit economy or delegitimate
capitalist exploitation. Gangsta rappers discuss capitalism in varying contexts,
and to portray them as uniformly or consistently anticapitalist would certainly
misrepresent them. All groups emphasize getting paid, and the more successful
artists tend to invest in their own production companies. They understand better than their audiences that music is a business and rapping is a job. At the same
time, their acceptance of compensation does not mean that they like the current
economic arrangements or that their music lacks integrity. On the contrary, for
many black and Latino working-class youth who turned to hip hop music, rapping, DJing, and producing are ways to avoid low-wage labor or, possibly, incarceration. As Cube said of his own crew in "Rollin' wit the Lench Mob" on
AmeriKKKa's Most Wanted, "You can either sell dope or get your ass a job / I'd
rather roll with the Lench Mob."

Their ambivalence toward capitalism notwithstanding, gangsta rappers consistently trace criminal behavior and vicious individualism to mainstream American culture. Contrary to the new "culture of poverty" theorists who claim that the
life-styles of the so-called black underclass constitute a significant deviation from
mainstream values, most gangsta rappers insist that the characters they rap about
epitomize what America has been and continues to be. In challenging the tendency
to equate criminality with some black "underclass" culture, Ice-T retorts in
"Straight Up Nigga" on OG: *Original Gangster,* "America stole from the Indians,
sure and prove / What's that? A straight up nigga move!" Similarly, in
"AmeriKKKa's Most Wanted" on the album of the same name, Ice Cube considers crime as American as apple pie: "It's the American way / I'm a G-A-N-G-S-T-A."
He even takes a swipe at the purest of American popular heroes, Superman. The
man who stands for Truth, Justice, and the American Way is appropriated and
then inverted as Public Enemy Number One. From Ice Cube's perspective, Superman is a hero because the Americanism he represents is nothing but gangsterism. Donning the cape himself, Cube declares, "I'm not a rebel or a renegade
on a quest, I'm a Nigga with an 'S' / So in case you get the kryptonite / I'm gonna
rip tonight cause I'm scaring ya / Wanted by America."

These artists are even less ambiguous when applying the gangster metaphor
to the people and institutions that control their lives—expressly politicians, the
state, and police departments. Ice-T's "Street Killer," for example, is a brief

monologue that sounds like the boasts of a heartless gang banger but turns out to be cop. In a recent interview, Coolio and W.C. of the MAAD Circle reverse the dominant discourse about criminals, insisting that the powerful, not powerless ghetto dwellers, are the real gangsters:

> *Coolio:* Who's the real gangsta, the brotha with the khakis on, the brotha with the Levis on or the muthafucka in the suit? Who's the real gangsta? *W.C.:* Well, the suit is running the world, that's the real gangsta right there.[36]

In other words, the *real* gangstas are in the White House. Dozens of rap artists, both inside and outside of L.A., indict "America" for stealing land, facilitating the drug trade either through inaction or active participation of the CIA and friendly dictators, and waging large-scale "drive-by shootings" against little countries such as Panama and Iraq. In the aftermath of the L.A. uprising, while politicians and media spokespersons called black participants "criminals" and "animals," Ice Cube reminded whoever would listen that "the looting . . . in South-Central was nothing like the looting done by the savings and loans." Cube's MTV video for "Who's the Mack," which reveals a photo of George Bush playing golf over the caption "President Mack" and a graffiti American flag with skull and crossbones replacing the stars, further underscored the argument that violence and gangsterism are best exemplified by the state, not by young inner-city residents.[37]

Police repression remains gangsta rap's primary target. We must bear in mind that this subgenre was born amidst the militarization of Compton, Watts, and other black communities since at least the early 1980s, when Los Angeles became a primary site of the so-called war on drugs. The recasting of South Central as a U.S. war zone was brought to us on *NBC Nightly News* on Dan Rather's special report, "48 Hours: On Gang Street"; in Hollywood films like *Colors* and *Boyz in the Hood;* and in a massive media blitz that has been indispensable in creating and criminalizing the so-called underclass. *Straight outta Compton*, for example, was released about the time Chief Darryl Gates implemented "Operation HAMMER," when almost 1,500 black youth in South Central were picked up for "looking suspicious." While most were charged with minor offenses like curfew and traffic violations, some were not charged at all but simply had their names and addresses logged in the LAPD antigang task force data base.[38] In this context NWA released their now classic anthem, "———— the Police," on *Straight outta Compton*. Opening with a mock trial in which NWA is the judge and jury and the police are the defendants, each member of the group offers his own testimony. After promising to tell "the whole truth and nothing but the truth," Ice Cube takes the stand and explodes with an indictment against racism, repression, and the practice of criminalizing all black youth. NWA emphasizes that police repression is no longer a simple matter of white racists with a badge, for black cops are as bad, if not worse, than white cops.[39]

L.A. rappers since Toddy Tee and NWA have expanded their critique of the relationship between police repression and their own political and economic powerlessness. Besides Ice Cube's solo effort and NWA's most recent album, groups like Compton's Most Wanted on *Straight Check N' Em* ("They Still Gafflin"), Cyrpress Hill on *Cypress Hill* ("Pigs" and "How I Could Just Kill a Man"), and Kid Frost on 1992's *East Side Story* ("I Got Pulled Over" and "Penitentiary"), to name but a few, try to place their descriptions of police repression within a broader context of social control. One Times or Five-Ohs, as the police are called in L.A., are portrayed as part of a larger system of racist and class domination that includes black officers. For W.C. and the MAAD Circle, policing as a form of racial and class oppression belongs to a historical tradition etched in the collective memory of African Americans. "Behind Closed Doors" on *Ain't a Damn Thing Changed* begins with lead rapper W.C. writing a letter of complaint to the chief of police describing an incident in which he was beaten and subsequently shot by officers with no provocation; one cannot help but notice what George Lipsitz calls "sedimented historical currents" running throughout his narrative. In just a few lines W.C. links antebellum slavery and depression-era fascism to the police beating of Rodney King.[40]

Mirroring much current political discourse in urban black America, some gangsta rappers implicitly or explicitly suggest that police repression against black men is part of genocidal war.[41] "Real Niggaz Don't Die," which samples the Last Poets' live performance of "Die Nigger," and Ice Cube's "Endangered Species (Tales from the Darkside)" on *AmeriKKKa's Most Wanted* (and remixed on *Kill at Will*) construct black males as prey of vicious, racist police officers. Cube's lyrics underscore the point that the role of law enforcement is to protect the status quo and keep black folks in check:

> Every cop killer goes ignored,
> They just send another nigger to the morgue.
> A point scored. They could give a fuck about us.
> They'd rather catch us with guns and white powder. . . .
> They'll kill ten of me to get the job correct
> To serve, protect, and break a nigga's neck.

In the title track to *AmeriKKKa's Most Wanted*, in which he assumes the role of an inner-city criminal who ventured into the suburbs, Cube closes the song having learned a valuable lesson about community differences in policing: "I think back when I was robbing my own kind / The police didn't pay it no mind / But when I started robbing the white folks / Now I'm in the pen with the soap on the rope."

"Behind Closed Doors" by W.C. and the MAAD Circle speaks to the less dramatic incidents of police repression, which frequently have greater resonance among black youth. In one of the stories, Circle rapper Coolio is a recently discharged ex-convict working hard to survive legitimately, until he is stopped and harassed for no apparent reason by "the same crooked cop from a long time ago / Who planted an ounce in my homie's El Camino." He and the cop exchange blows, but instead of taking him into custody the officer and his partner decide to drop him off in hostile gang territory in order to incite violence. Coolio's narrative is more than plausible: Among the tactics adopted by Chief Darryl Gates in his antigang sweeps was to draw out gang bangers by "leaving suspects on enemy turfs, writing over Crip graffiti with Blood colors (or vice versa) and spreading incendiary rumors."[42]

Even more common to the collective experience of young black residents of L.A.'s inner city was the police policy of identifying presumably suspicious characters on the basis of clothes styles. Indeed, officers who were part of the Gang Related Active Trafficker Suppression program were told to "interrogate anyone who they suspect is a gang member, basing their assumptions on their dress or their use of gang hand signals."[43] Opposition to this kind of marking, which in effect is a battle for the right to free expression and unfettered mobility in public spaces, has been a central subtheme in gangsta rap's discursive war of position against police repression. In CMW's cut "Still Gafflin'," lead rapper MC Eiht complains that the police are "on my dick trying to jack me / I guess because I sport a hat and the khakis." Perhaps the sharpest critique is W.C. and the MAAD Circle's "Dress Code" on *Ain't a Damn Thing Changed*. Directed at ordinary white citizens and club owners as well as police officers, the Circle members tell stories of being stereotyped as common criminals or gang bangers by complete strangers, all of whom presume that "if you dress like me, you gotta run with a crew." Clothing also signifies status, as is evident in the way W.C. is treated when he tries to get into a club: "Gotta wear a silk shirt / just to dance to a funky song." Nevertheless, not only do he and his crew refuse to apologize for their appearance, insisting that young working-class black men have the right to dress as they please without being treated with fear or contempt, but W.C. also attributes his styles to his class position. Because he "can't afford to shop at Macy's or Penney's . . . it's off to the swap meet for a fresh pair of dickys [khaki pants]."

Of course, style politics are much more complicated. Even the most impoverished black youth do not choose styles solely on the basis of what is affordable. Young men wear starter jackets, hoodies, L.A. Raiders caps, baggy khaki pants, and occasionally gold chains not only because they are in style, but because it enables them to create a collective identity that is distinct from, and even oppositional to, the dominant culture. While these accoutrements are products of the dominant culture, black youth has appropriated, transformed, and reinscribed onto these styles what Dick Hebdige identifies as "secret" meanings that "express, in code, a form of resistance to the order which guarantees their continued subordination."[44] It is naive to believe, for example, that young blacks merely sport Raiders paraphernalia because they are all hard-core fans. Besides, as soon as NWA and more recent L.A. groups came on the scene sporting Raiders caps, the style became even more directly associated with the gangsta rappers than with the team itself, and the police regarded the caps, beanies, hoods, and starter jackets as gang attire.

What we always need to keep in mind is the degree of self-consciousness with which black urban youths—most of whom neither belong to gangs nor engage in violent crime—insist on wearing the styles that tend to draw police attention. By associating certain black youth styles with criminality, violence, and (indirectly) police repression, the dominant media unintentionally popularizes these styles among young men who reinterpret these images as acts of rebellion or outright racist terror.[45] The styles also suggest implicit acceptance of an "outlaw" status that capitalist transformation and the militarization of black Los Angeles has brought about. Hence, the adoption and recasting of "G" as a friendly form of address among young African American men and, to a lesser degree, women. While the origins of "G" apparently go back to the Five Percent Nation on the East Coast where it was an abbreviation for "God," among youth in California and elsewhere it currently stands for "gangsta."[46] Finally, my own discussions with black youths in L.A. reveal that the black-and-silver Los Angeles Kings caps associated with artists like King Tee, NWA, and other gangsta groups have become even more popular following the Rodney King beating and the subsequent uprising—and hockey clearly has nothing to do with it. These caps signify very powerfully that all young African Americans are potential "L.A. [Rodney] Kings." (We must be careful not to presume that these styles are merely the authentic expressions of poor black urban youth. Many middle-class suburban black kids and many more white kids—males and females—can be found sporting the "G" style at college and high school campuses, malls, and playgrounds throughout the country. What this means deserves an essay in itself.)

In the streets of Los Angeles, as well as in other cities across the country, hip hop's challenge to police brutality sometimes moves beyond the discursive arena. Because the Vietnam-like conditions in their communities and the pervasive racism throughout the whole city (and country) circumscribe the movement of young blacks, their music and expressive styles have literally become weapons in a battle over the right to occupy public space. Frequently employing high-decibel car stereos and boom boxes, they "pump up the volume" not only for their own listening pleasure but also as part of an indirect, ad hoc war of position to take back public space. The "noise" constitutes a form of cultural resistance that should not be ignored, especially when we add those resistive lyrics about destroying the state or retaliating against the police. Imagine a convertible Impala or a Suzuki pulling up alongside a "black-and-white," pumping the revenge fantasy segment of Ice Cube's "The Wrong Nigga to Fuck wit" from *Death Certificate*, which promises to break Chief Darryl Gates's "spine like a jellyfish," or Cypress Hill's "Pigs" from *Cypress Hill*, vowing to turn "pigs" into "sausage." Furthermore, hip hop producers have increased the stakes by pioneering technologies that extend and "fatten" the bass in order to improve clarity at louder decibels (appropriately called "jeep beats"). Although the political dimension of these "sonic forces," to quote Tricia Rose, is ambiguous, the ways in which hip hop cultural politics manifests itself as everyday social practices needs to be explored. We cannot easily dismiss Ice Cube when he declares, "I'm the one with a trunk of funk / and 'Fuck the Police' in the tape deck."[47]

The criminalization of black male bodies produces and is produced by the shockingly high incarceration rates of African American men, a phenomenon that has not escaped the attention of the entire hip hop community. In 1989, 23 percent of black males ages twenty to twenty-nine were either behind bars or on legal probation or parole. There is substantial evidence that the racially biased structure of the criminal-justice system is partly responsible for the higher arrest and incarceration rates for black and Latino men compared to white men: Studies have shown, for example, that black men convicted of the same crime as whites receive longer sentences on average.[48] Statistics aside, many rappers take up the subject of incarceration because they know people who are "locked down," and a few rap artists have actually served time in the penitentiary, for example, MAAD Circle rapper Coolio and East Coast rappers Intelligent Hoodlum (Percy Chapman), K-Solo, and the currently incarcerated Lifer's Group.

Through thick descriptions of prison life and samples of the actual voices of convicts (e.g., Ice-T, "The Tower"; W.C. and the MAAD Circle, "Out on a Furlough"; and Kid Frost, "The Penitentiary"), gangsta rappers come close to providing what Michel Foucault calls a "counter-discourse of prisoners." As Foucault explains, "When prisoners began to speak, they possessed an individual theory of prisons, the penal system, and justice. It is this form of discourse which ultimately matters, a discourse against power, the counter-discourse of prisoners and those we call delinquents—and not a theory *about* delinquency."[49] Most rappers—especially gangsta rappers—treat prisons as virtual fascist institutions. In "You Shoulda Killed Me Last Year" at the end of his OG album, Ice-T suggests that prisons constitute a form of modern-day bondage: "They say slavery has been abolished except for the convicted felon. Y'all need to think about that, unless you know what the fuckin' Constitution really is about." Moreover, mirroring the sentiments of a significant segment of the black community, several rappers suggest that the high incarceration rate of black males is part of a conspiracy. In "The Nigga Ya Love to Hate" on *AmeriKKKa's Most Wanted*, Ice Cube asks, "Why [are] there more niggas in the pen than in college?"[50] He even suggests in "The Product" on *Kill at Will* that prison is the inevitable outcome for young black men who fail or refuse to conform to the dominant culture. Inmates, he argues, are "products" of joblessness, police repression, and an inferior and racist educational system.[51]

Gangsta rappers tend toward a "scared straight" approach to describing actual prison life. But unlike, say, the Lifer's Group, their descriptions of prison are not intended merely to deter black youth from crime, for that would imply an acceptance of prisons as primarily institutions to punish and reform "criminals." Instead, their descriptions of prison life essentially reverse the popular image of black prisoners as Willie Hortons and paint a richer portrait of inmates as real human beings trying to survive under inhuman conditions. While they do not ignore the physical and sexual violence between prisoners, they do suggest that prison conditions are at the root of such behavior.[52] Again, from Ice Cube's "The Product" on *Kill at Will*:

Livin' in a concrete ho house,
Where all the products go, no doubt.

Yo, momma, I got to do eleven,
Livin' in a five by seven.
Dear babe, your man's gettin worn out
Seeing young boys gettin' their assholes torn out . . .

It's driving me batty,
Cause my little boy is missing daddy.
I'm ashamed but the fact is,
I wish pops let me off on the mattress [i.e., wishes he was never conceived],
Or should I just hang from the top bunk?
But that's going out like a punk.
My life is fucked. But it ain't my fault
Cause I'm a motherfuckin' product.

Ice-T's "The Tower" on OG: Original Gangster suggests that violence between inmates, especially racial conflict, is permitted if not instigated by guards and ad-
ministrators as a means of controlling "the yard." The song consists of several
first-person anecdotes rapped over a haunting snythesized cello track and punctuated by "audio verité" samples of presumably authentic prisoners telling their
own stories of violence in the pen. By focusing on prison architecture rather than
on the inmates themselves, the video for "The Tower" emphasizes how the structural and spatial arrangements themselves reproduce the prisoners' powerlessness.
After each verse, Ice-T asks, "Who had the power? / The whites, the blacks, or
just the gun tower?"

The criminalization, surveillance, incarceration, and poverty of black youth
in the postindustrial city have been the central themes in gangsta rap and thus
constitute the primary experiences from which cultural identities are constructed. Whereas Afrocentric rappers build an imagined community by invoking images of ancient African civilizations, gangsta rappers are more prone to Eric
B. and Rakum's dictum, "It ain't where you're from, it's where you're at." When
they are not describing prison or death, they foreground daily life in the ghetto—
an overcrowded world of deteriorating tenement apartments or tiny cement-
block, prisonlike projects, streets filthy from the lack of city services, liquor stores
and billboards selling malt liquor and cigarettes. The construction of the ghetto
as a living nightmare and gangstas as products of that nightmare has given rise to
what I call a new "ghettocentric" identity in which the specific class, race, and
gendered experiences in late-capitalist urban centers coalesce to create a new
identity—"Nigga."

Niggas in post—civil rights america

Although Claude Brown wrote that "perhaps the most soulful word in the world
is 'nigger,' " gangsta rappers have drawn a lot of fire for their persistent use of
"Nigga," as in Ice-T's "Straight Up Nigga" on OG: Original Gangster: "I'm a nig-

ger, not a colored man or a black / or a Negro or an Afro-American—I'm all that / Yes, I was born in America too. / But does South Central look like America to you?"[53] Even the *New York Times* and popular magazines like *Emerge* have entered the debate, carrying articles about the growing popularity of the "N-word" among young people. Rap artists are accused of inculcating self-hatred and playing into white racism. Those who insist that the use of "Nigga" in rap demonstrates self-hatred and ignorance of African American history generally do not impose the same race-conscious litmus test to otherwise celebrated cultural traditions where "nigger" is used as a neutral or even friendly appellation. Besides, one need only look to the whole body of black humor and folklore for numerous examples, or simply to ordinary vernacular speech among African Americans. In these latter circumstances, "nigger" was and is uttered and interpreted among black folk within a specific, clearly defined context, tone, and set of codes rooted in black vernacular language. As anthropologist Claudia Mitchell-Kernan explained, "The use of 'nigger' with other black English markers has the effect of 'smiling when you say that.' The use of standard English with 'nigger,' in the words of an informant, is 'the wrong tone of voice' and may be taken as abusive."[54]

To comprehend the politics of ghettocentricity, we must understand the myriad ways in which the most ghettocentric segments of the West Coast hip hop community have employed the term "Nigga." Gangsta rappers, in particular, are struggling to ascribe new, potentially empowering meanings to the word. Indeed, the increasingly common practice of spelling it N-i-g-g-a suggests a revisioning. For example, Bay Area rapper and former Digital Underground member 2Pac (Tupac Shakur) insists on his 1991 album *2Pacalypse Now* that "Nigga" stands for "Never Ignorant, Getting Goals Accomplished." More common, however, is the use of "Nigga" to describe a condition rather than skin color or culture. Above all, "Nigga" speaks to a collective identity shaped by class consciousness, the character of inner-city space, police repression, poverty, and the constant threat of intraracial violence fed by a dying economy. Part of NWA's "Niggaz4Life" on *Efil4zaggin*, for instance, uses "Nigga" almost as a synonym for "oppressed."

In other words, "Nigga" is not merely *another* word for black. Products of the postindustrial ghetto, the characters in gangsta rap constantly remind listeners that they are still second-class citizens—"Niggaz"—whose collective lived experiences suggest that nothing has changed *for them* as opposed to the black middle class. In fact, "Nigga" is frequently employed to distinguish urban black working-class males from the black bourgeoisie and African Americans in positions of institutional authority. The point is simple: The experiences of young black men in the inner city are not those of all black people, and, in fact, gangsta rappers, like other young blacks, recognize that some African Americans play a role in perpetuating their oppression. To be a "real Nigga" is to have been a product of the ghetto. Thus by linking their identity to the 'hood instead of simply to skin color, gangsta rappers acknowledge the limitations of racial politics—black middle-class reformism as well as black nationalism. Again, this is not new. "Nigger" as a signifier of class and race oppression has been a common part of black rural and working-class language throughout the twentieth century, if not longer. In fact, because of its power to distinguish the black urban poor from upwardly mobile middle-class blacks, "nigger" made a huge comeback at the height of the Black Power movement. Robert DeCoy's infamous book, *The Nigger Bible*, published in 1967, distinguishes "Nigger" from "Negroes"—the latter a derogatory term for sell-outs. DeCoy defined "Negro" as a "vulgar but accepted description of the Nigrite or Nigger. Referring to an American Nigger of decency and status. A White-Nigger. Or a brainwashed Black who would be Caucasian if possible." And in 1968 one Los Angeles–based black nationalist artist collective, the Ashanti Art Service, launched a journal called *Nigger Uprising*.[55]

Perhaps not since the days of the blues singer Leadbelly has the word "bourgeois" been so commonly used by black musicians. It has become common lingo among hip hop artists to refer to black-owned radio stations and, more generally, middle-class African Americans who exhibit disgust or indifference toward young working-class blacks. For Ice-T, living in the lap of luxury is not what renders the black bourgeoisie bankrupt, but rather their inability to understand the world of the ghetto, black youth culture, and rap music. In an interview a few years back he explained, "I don't think the negative propaganda about rap comes from the true black community—it comes from the bourgeois black community, which I hate. Those are the blacks who have an attitude that because I wear a hat and a gold chain, I'm a nigger and they're better than me." More recently, on his album *The Iceberg/Freedom of Speech . . . Just Watch What You Say*, he expressed similar sentiments: "I'm trying to save my community, but these bourgeois blacks keep on doggin' me. . . . You just a bunch of punk, bourgeois black suckers."[56] W.C. and the MAAD Circle level an even more sustained attack on those they call "bourgeois Negroes." Proclaiming on *Ain't a Damn Thing Changed* that the Circle's sympathies lie with "poor folks in the slums," W.C. writes off suburban middle-class African Americans as turncoats and cowards.

Although some might argue that these snipes at the black middle class are misdirected, we need to remember their political and demographic context. Not only is there greater intraracial class segregation with the increasing suburbanization of middle-class blacks, but petit-bourgeois blacks are sometimes guilty of the kind of social labeling associated with white suburbanites and police. One need only visit predominantly black public spaces with considerable cross-class mixing (e.g., L.A.'s venerable Fox Hills Mall) to notice the considerable disdain many middle-class African Americans exhibit toward youth who are dressed a certain way or elect to walk in groups. Moreover, having come of age under a black mayor, black police officers, and a city council and legislature with a small but significant black presence, L.A. gangsta rappers have difficulty overlooking the complicity of black politicians and other authority figures—many of whom do not live in South Central or Compton—in maintaining the near-fascist conditions that prevail in poor communities. With the rise of the crack economy, for example, a number of leading black "liberal" politicians and spokespersons actually supported the police crackdown on black youth.[57]

L.A. gangsta rappers are frequent critics of black nationalists as well. They contend that the nationalists' focus on Africa—both past and present—obscures the daily battles poor black folk have to wage in contemporary America. In what proved to be a highly controversial statement, Ezy-E declared: "Fuck that black power shit: we don't give a fuck. Free South Africa: we don't give a fuck. I bet there ain't nobody in South Africa wearing a button saying 'Free Compton' or 'Free California.' "[58] Ice Cube poses the same issue in "Tales from the Darkside" on *AmeriKKKa's Most Wanted*, but in a less dismissive and more meaningful manner:

> You want to free Africa,
> I'll stare at ya'
> Cause we ain't got it too good in America.
> I can't fuck with 'em overseas
> My homeboy died over kee's [kilos of cocaine].

To say that gangsta rappers are *anti*nationalist overstates the case. Indeed, rappers like CPO and, more recently, Ice Cube, express some explicit nationalist positions, though L.A. groups have shown less inclination than their East Coast counterparts to openly support the Nation of Islam or the Five Percent Nation. West Coast gangsta groups tend to be more weary of nationalism, given the real divisions that exist among African Americans, the Afrocentric celebration of a past that, to them, has no direct bearing on the present, and the hypocrisy and inconsistency exhibited by individual black nationalists. The last point is the subject of W.C. and the MAAD Circle's "Caught 'N a Fad" on *Ain't a Damn Thing Changed*, wherein they tell the story of a hustler who joined the Nation and wore African garb because it was in style but never changed his ways. He was "popping that 'too black, too strong' / But he was the first to get the dice game going on." Likewise, in "The Nigga Ya Love to Hate" on *AmeriKKKa's Most Wanted*, Ice Cube takes a swipe at the Afrocentrists who speak of returning to Africa: "All those motherfuckers who say they're too black / Put 'em overseas, they be beggin' to come back."

For all its oppositional potential, ghettocentricity, like Afrocentricity, draws its arsenal from the dominant ideology. As products of sustained violence, the characters in gangsta rap are constantly prepared to retaliate with violence, whether against a cop or another brother; those unwilling are considered "cowards," "punks," or, as Ice-T would say, "bitches." In other words, "real Niggaz" are not only victims of race and class domination but agents—dangerous agents, nightmarish caricatures of the worst of the dispossessed. What is most striking about gangsta rappers' construction of "Nigga" as the embodiment of violence is the extent to which this highly masculinist imagery draws from existing stereotypes. Once again, we find members of the black youth subculture reconstructing dominant representations of who they are in order to "remake" their image in popular discourse.[59] Negative stereotypes of black men as violent, pathological, and lazy are recontextualized: Criminal acts are turned into brilliant capers and a way to *avoid* work; white fear of black male violence becomes evidence of black power; fearlessness is treated as a measure of masculinity. A large part of Ezy-E's repetoire has him proving his manhood and authenticity as a "real Nigga" by bustin' caps on anyone who stands in his way.[60] Following a long tradition of black humor, both Ice-T and Ezy-E appropriate and recast stereotypes of black men as hypersexual beings with large penises.[61] Ezy-E explains "Niggaz4Life" on *Efil4zaggin* that one of the reasons he calls *himself* a "Nigga" is that he "can reach in my draws and pull out a bigger dick." Ice-T, who refers to himself in "Straight Up Nigga" on *OG: Original Gangster* as a "white woman's dream / Big dick straight up Nigga," combines several stereotypes in the following passage:

> I'm loud and proud,
> Well endowed with the big beef.
> Out on the corner,
> I hang out like a house thief.
> So you can call me dumb or crazy,
> Ignorant, stupid, inferior, or lazy,
> Silly or foolish,
> But I'm badder and bigger,
> And most of all
> I'm a straight up Nigga.

While the meanings of these appropriations and reversals of racial stereotypes constantly shift with different contexts, in many cases they ultimately reinforce dominant images of African Americans. Moreover, the kinds of stereotypes they choose to appropriate—hypermasculinity, sexual power, and violence as a "natural" response—not only reproduce male domination over women but often do so in an especially brutal manner.

"Pimpin' ain't easy": women in the gangsta imagination

While young African American males are both products of and sometimes active participants in the creation of a new masculinist, antifeminist identity politics, we cannot be too quick to interpret sexist and misogynist lyrics as simply products of the current crisis in patriarchy. African American vernacular culture has a very long and ignoble tradition of sexism evidenced in daily language and other more formal variants such as "the dozens," "toasts," and the age-old baaadman narratives. A word like "bitch," for example, was not suddenly imported into African American male vocabularly by rap music, as in Ezy-E's "One Less Bitch" on *Efil4zaggin*: "To me, all bitches are the same: money-hungry, scandalous, groupie hos that's always riding on a nigger's dick, always in a nigger's pocket." In the late 1950s, it was such a common reference to women that folklorist Roger

Abrahams, in his study of black oral culture in Philadelphia, defined it in his glossary of terms as "any woman. As used here, usually without usual pejorative connotations."[62] Some of the toasts that are at least a few decades old are more venomous than much of what we find today in hip hop. In 1966, Bruce Jackson recorded a toast titled "The Lame and the Whore" in which a veteran pimp teaches a "weak" mack daddy how to treat his women: "Say, you got to rule that bitch, you got to school that bitch, you got to teach her the Golden Rule, you got to stomp that bitch, you got to tromp that bitch, and use her like you would a tool."[63] Aside from narratives that have been recovered by historians and folklorists, I personally remember having learned by heart "Imp the Skimp, the Tennis Shoe Pimp," a long first-person narrative in which we bragged incessantly of being "the baby maker / the booty taker." "Imp" became part of my verbal repertoire around 1971; I was nine years old. Unlike rap music, however, our sexist and misogynist street rhymes were never discussed on Ted Koppel's *Nightline* because they never made it to wax; they remained where our mamas said they should—in the streets.[64]

But the story is a bit more complicated than black youth recording and distributing an oral tradition of "hustler poetry." During the late 1960s and early 1970s, as the United States became an increasingly "sexualized society," we witnessed an explosion of recorded sexually explicit comedy routines by black comics like Rudy Ray Moore, Redd Foxx, and Richard Pryor, as well as the publication and popularization of so-called genuine pimp narratives. The *pimp*, not just any baaadman, became an emblematic figure of the period, elevated to the status of hero and invoked by Hollywood as well as in the writings of black-nationalist militants like H. Rap Brown, Eldridge Cleaver, Bobby Seale, and Huey P. Newton. Aside from film and popular literature, the pimp appeared in a proliferation of sensationalist autobiographies, scholarly ethnographies, and "urban folklore" collections of incarcerated hustlers.[65]

Old-school rappers like Ice-T and Philly's Schooly D were strongly influenced by some of these published reminiscences of hustlers. Ice-T recalls, "I used to read books by Iceberg Slim. . . . He would talk in rhyme—hustler-like stuff—and I would memorize lines." The classic recording of *Hustler's Convention* in 1973 by an ex-prisoner who would eventually help found the Last Poets and the celebrated status of the pimp in blaxploitation films also had a profound impact on gangsta rap. In fact, the word "gangsta" is frequently used interchangeably with terms like "pimp," "Mack Daddy," "Daddy Mack," and "hustler." One can hear the influence of the pimp narratives and black comedians on several Ice-T cuts, especially "Somebody's Gotta Do It [Pimpin' Ain't Easy]," "I Love Ladies," and "Sex," which were recorded on his first album, *Rhyme Pays*. Boasts about his ability to sexually please women, the number of women he sleeps with, and the money he is making in the process, these kinds of rhymes are not descriptions of social reality but recorded versions of what anthropologist Ulf Hannerz calls "streetcorner mythmaking" or what hip hop critic Dan Charnas calls simply "bullshit, schoolboy humor."[66]

The critical question, it seems to me, is Why has the pimp returned to an exalted status in black male popular culture in the 1990s? Why has the pimp figured so prominently in the late 1960s/early 1970s and the late 1980s/early 1990s, periods of rising black nationalism and patriarchal backlash? Was the celebration of the pimp in popular culture during the Black Power era a response to the image of black female dominance created by the Moynihan report? Did young black men identify with the pimp because he represented the ultimate dominator, turning matriarchy on its head? Was the valorization of the pimp just another example of black militants celebrating a "lumpen" life-style?

These questions eventually need answers. But for now, they underscore the need to historicize and contextualize the emergence of the pimp figure in black popular culture. The question for us, then, becomes Why has the pimp made such a strong return via gangsta rap in an age where the dominant discourse—from Reagan conservatives to African American nationalists—demands the restoration of the patriarchal family? Another question might be Why do gangsta rappers (not unlike other male hip hop performers) exhibit a profound fear of black female sexuality, which manifests itself as open distrust or, in some cases, as aggressive hatred of women?[67]

I am not in a position to offer answers to these questions, nor am I in a position to confidently provide a sociological explanation—if one is even appropriate. Given the central place that misogyny occupies in the gangsta/baaadman aesthetic, it is hard to trust straight sociological interpretations. Furthermore, I do not believe rap music can or ever intended to represent the true and complex character of male/female relations among black urban youth. Too many critics have taken the easy way out by reading rap lyrics literally rather than researching actual social relations among young people, in all of their diversity and complexity. And there is no reason in the world to believe that any music constitutes a mirror of social relations that can be generalized for entire groups of people.

Nevertheless, I do think that there is a specific social context that provides some insights into the *popularity* of gangsta rap and the particular forms its misogyny takes. For example, although the "traditional" family itself might be fading, neither the ideology of male dominance nor the kinds of economic negotiations that have always been a part of intrafamily conflict have disappeared. As is evident in both contemporary popular culture and current policy debates, the last decade or so has witnessed a reassertion of masculinity and the increasing commodification of sexual relations. Moreover, gangsta rappers, the mass media, and mainstream black leadership commonly cast the problems of the inner city as a problem of black males, even if their interpretations differ. Some intellectuals and politicians propose saving the "underclass" by eliminating welfare, retraining young black men in all-male schools, and reinstituting the nuclear family—implying, of course, that the cause of the current crisis lies not with capitalism but with the collapse of the patriarchal family.[68]

Given the political context, young working-class African American women are often blamed for the current state of affairs, portrayed as welfare queens making babies merely to stay on public assistance or as "gold diggers" who use their sexuality to take black men's meager earnings. This image, hardly new, has become an increasingly prominent theme in hip hop over the last ten years or so. In a partly tongue-in-cheek verbal duel with female rapper Yo-Yo, Ice Cube kicks some lyrics in "It's a Man's World" on *AmeriKKKa's Most Wanted* that nonetheless reflect the thinking of many of his black male compatriots: "I hear females always talking 'bout women's lib / Then get your own crib, and stay there / Instead of having more babies for the welfare / Cause if you don't I'll label you a gold digger."

Part of the attack has to do with what these rappers feel are young black women's unrealistically high expectations of black men. Thinking back to their precelebrity days when they were reportedly jobless or worked for minimum wages, a number of male rappers have criticized women who wanted to go out only with men who were stable or fairly well-off financially. Given the lack of employment opportunities available for young black women due to race and gender segmentation in the labor market, and the still hegemonic notion that males ought to be the primary wage earners, these expectations could hardly be considered unreasonable. Yet, in interviews and in their music, most gangsta rappers label such women "bitches," "hos," or "skeezers." W.C. of the MAAD Circle, who is unique for avoiding these epithets on his debut album, tries to be slightly more conscientious by blaming "society" for imbuing women with materialistic values. Nevertheless, he throws up a weak argument for the use of the term "bitch": "Well, society has us all believing that if you don't fit up to their standard, then you're not shit. . . . If you have that attitude, then W.C. is calling you a bitch. But I'll never call a *woman* a bitch, because a real women doesn't think with that mentality. This society has us believing that if you don't drive a brand new car, if you drive a bucket, you're not shit."[69]

Although some might argue from this evidence that gangsta rap's distrust and even hatred of black women mask the "hidden injuries of class," such a simplistic materialist approach misses the point that labeling women "bitches" or "hos," irrespective of their reasoning, is a direct form of male domination. Disstinguishing "bad" women from "good" women (or, in W.C.'s case, from "real" women) ultimately serves to justify violence against women by devaluing them.[70] The most obvious examples can be found on NWA's album *Efil4zaggin*. Songs like "One Less Bitch" and the audio-verité recording "To Kill a Hooker" justify outright brutality and murder by using labels intended to strip women of any humanity. Hardly the stuff of everyday life in the ghetto, these draconian fantasy performances are more akin to snuff films than the kind of ethnographic observations NWA claim as their raw material. And like violent pornography, NWA's misogynist narratives are essentially about the degradation and complete domination of women. On the one hand, like the vast array of cultural images, they reinforce existing forms of patriarchal power; on the other hand, they create misogynist dystopian space by constructing scenes of uncontested domination and acts of violence against women for which the perpetrators are never held accountable. In "One Less Bitch," Dr. Dre assumes the role of a pimp who discovers that his prostitute is trying to "steal" from him by retaining some of the money she earned. Reminiscent of "The Lame and the Whore" (or a snuff film—take your pick), Dre orchestrates what is best described as a lynching. Each story of mayhem and murder is followed by a chorus of the entire NWA crew chanting: "One Less, one less, one less bitch you gotta worry about."

Economic conflict and a reassertion of male dominance in response to shifting gender and family relations still does not fully explain such misogyny. Another part of the answer can be found in Tricia Rose's provocative and compelling argument that misogynist lyrics in rap reflect black male fears of black women's sexuality. Unlike male utopian spaces like "playboy clubs" where women are paid to be packaged fantasies, in inner cities young black men have to deal with black women with real voices, demands, expectations, and complaints—women with agency. In the everyday lives of young black men, sexuality is always a process of negotiation. Rose suggests that "many men are hostile toward women because the fulfillment of male heterosexual desire is significantly checked by women's capacity for sexual rejection and/or manipulation of men." Manipulation, in this context, refers to the perceived power of black women to obtain money and goods in exchange for sex.[71]

Pregnancy is one way women allegedly exact attention and financial support, as is depicted in Ice Cube's "You Can't Fade Me" from *AmeriKKKa's Most Wanted*. The narrative opens with Cube's character, who is on the corner drinking with his homies, discovering that he might have fathered a child by a young woman with whom he had a one-night stand. His initial impulse, not surprisingly, is to blame her rather than take responsibility. As the story progresses, he recounts that one fateful night in stark, unflattering terms stripped completely of sensuality or pleasure. Because he saw her as physically unattractive, he felt compelled to sneak around in order to have sex with her while preserving his reputation. When they finally found a safe place to have intercourse—in the backseat of his "homie's Impala"—both the sex and the end of their "date" were anticlimactic: "I dropped her off man, and I'm knowing, / That I'm a hate myself in the morning. / I got drunk to help me forget, / Another day, another hit, shit, I'm getting faded." But once he returns to the present and she's about to have the child, the character Cube plays turns all of his anger and frustration upon her, threatening to beat her down and perform an abortion himself. In the end, the baby turns out not to be his, but the whole ordeal illustrates the possible consequences of his actions, even if the character Cube plays failed to learn anything from it. Sex as an act of conquest can also degrade men. Moreover, the end result of sexual conquest might be pregnancy, leading to the very thing the playboy ethic tries to avoid: commitment. In short, like all forms of power, male domination not only produces its own limits but is constantly contested.

While songs like "You Can't Fade Me" are decidedly sexist, Ice Cube is unique among L.A. gangsta rappers for incorporating women's voices that contest his own lyrics. On *AmeriKKKa's Most Wanted*, for example, we hear not only a young woman's voice disrupt "The Nigga You Love to Hate" with vehement protests over the use of the word "bitch," but also Yo-Yo, an extraordinary young female rapper concerned with building a progressive movement of black women, engaging Cube in a verbal battle of the sexes in "It's a Man's World." In this classic "dis" tune, their duet is rooted in the "dozens" tradition and thus intended to be humorous. But it also reminds us that the discursive space in which young black men assert their masculinity and dominance over women is always highly contested terrain. The song opens with literally dozens of sampled voices saying "bitch"—ranging from Richard Pryor to Ezy-E and the controversial comedian Andrew "Dice" Clay—a machine-gun-like assault of sexist epithets that closes with a lone male voice: "Don't talk about my mamma!" Ice Cube launches into what is supposed to be a monologue about what women are "good for," when Yo-Yo seems to come out of nowhere and interrupts with, "What the hell you think you're talkin' about?" Because her intervention takes place away from the microphone in a sort of echo mode, her interruption is presented as an unexpected penetration into all-male discursive space, reminding the "brothas" just how vulnerable "the circle" is to female invasion and disruption. From that point on, Yo-Yo criticizes Cube's ability to rap, questions his manhood, and even makes fun of the size of his penis.[72]

Finally, I must caution against interpreting the misogyny in gangsta rap as merely a reflection of daily gender conflicts and negotiations among inner-city black youth. In many instances, the narratives are based on rappers' lived experiences as *performers* whose status as cultural icons gives them an enormous amount of sexual power and freedom. The long version of Ice Cube's "Get Off My Dick Nigger—and Tell Yo' B—— to Come Here," which is primarily an attack on male "groupies," simultaneously celebrates his new status and ridicules star-struck teenage women who ultimately become the prey of male performers. In a line that falls somewhere between masculinist boast and paternal warning, Cube tells these women, "See for a fact, I do damage / They think I'm a star, so I take advantage."[73] Several songs on NWA's *Efil4zaggin* assert both the newfound power the group holds over impressionable and sexually curious young female fans and the brutality that can result from such power. One of the more vicious segments in "She Swallowed It" is the story of a woman who "did the whole crew." As NWA tried to make the difficult shift from "street Niggas" to fame and fortune, it became increasingly clear that they not only saw their newfound power as boundless but had no qualms about practicing what they "preach." Dr. Dre's assault on Dee Barnes, the host of the video show *Pump It Up* and member of the rap duo "Body and Soul," is a case in point. Angered by an interview Barnes did with Ice Cube that allegedly made NWA look bad, Dre viciously assaulted her in a crowded club. When asked about the incident, both Ezy-E and Ren agreed that the "bitch deserved it." Dre seemed unfazed that Barnes has filed a multimillion dollar lawsuit: "People talk all this shit, but you know, somebody fucks with me, I'm gonna fuck them. I just did it, you know. Ain't nothing you can do now by talking about it. Besides, it ain't no big thing—I just threw her through a door."

The course of these events should be instructive to those who read all of NWA's lyrics describing violence against women as fantasy or metaphor; in light of the Dee Barnes incident, Dr. Dre's line in "Findum, Fuckum, and Flee" sounds like an eerie premonition of things to come: "If a bitch tried to dis me while I'm full of liquor / I'll smack the bitch up and shoot the nigger that's with her."[74]

Are there any potential cracks or ruptures in the gangsta rappers' constructions of women or in their efforts to reassert male power through violence and sexual domination? Given gangsta rap's emphasis on "reality," such ruptures do occur when young black men or their peers are themselves victims of patriarchy. Indeed, Ice-T's "The House" demands an end to violence against children within the family context, and W.C. and the MAAD Circle critique domestic violence against women. The medium-tempo, hauntingly funky "Fuck My Daddy" on *Ain't a Damn Thing Changed* shows the flip side of the world NWA raps about:

> I'm giving peace to moms
> Cause moms was the strongest. . . .
> Dad was a wino, as sick as a psycho.
> I used to hide under the covers with my eyes closed.
> Crying and hoping tonight that daddy didn't trip,
> Cause mama already needs stitches in her top lip. . . .
> I used to pray and hope that daddy would die,
> Cause over nothing mama suffered from a swole up black eye.
> And at the end of my prayers cry myself to sleep
> All I could think about was "Fuck my daddy."

While W.C.'s lyrics mark a significant break from those of earlier gangsta groups, by focusing on his own mother as victim he does not directly challenge the dichotomy between "good" and "bad" women, which, as we have seen, is used to justify violence against women.[75] Moreover, neither of these examples challenges male domination, and reflections on lived experience are unlikely to convince even the most progressive of the gangsta rappers that the overthrow of patriarchy should be part of an emancipatory agenda. However, the introduction of new *discourses* can, and has, proven an important influence on the politics of rap music. Not only have black women rappers played a crucial role in reshaping the attitudes toward women among a substantial segment of the hip hop community, they are also largely responsible for raising the issue of sexism within rap. Insofar as recording technology has conveyed the voices of ghetto youth (or those who claim the "authenticity" of ghetto living) to a national audience, it has brought rappers face to face with other critical communities, including feminists, left-wing radicals, suburban white youth, and Christian Fundamentalists. The heated debates surrounding rap music have found their way into mainstream media where either rap is generally misunderstood or gangsta rap is regarded as a real description of daily life in the ghetto. More significantly, the racist undercurrents of the media critique of sexism in hip hop have obscured or ignored the degree to which these discursive assaults against women mirror mainstream mass culture, thus suppressing an opportunity to extend public discussions about sexism to modes of discourse that have achieved respectability. Yet, although the dialogue itself is limited, public discussions about rap's sexism have disrupted or challenged the narrow and localized assumptions of young black males. In other words, if rap had never become a commodity but remained forever in the streets and house parties of urban America, derogatory terms like "bitch" and misogyny within black communities would probably not have been so widely and forcefully debated. By turning what is frequently street talk into a national discussion that crosses gender, class, and racial boundaries, new discourses have the potential of at least challenging misogyny and possibly enabling black youth to penetrate the ideology of male dominance, even if much of acceptable mass culture escapes criticism.

AfterWORD: a genre spent?

"I don't like the trend toward so many gangster records in rap, but I am an art dealer and that's what is selling now," explains Russell Simmons, CEO of Rush Communications, while Cypress Hill's B-Real warns that "after the National Guard leaves, there's still gonna be angry, psycho motherfuckers out there." If you recognize the name Snoop Doggy Dogg, the latest superstar addition to Dr. Dre's stable on Deathrow Records, a gangsta rapper from Long Beach with the coolest, slickest "Calabama" voice I've ever heard, you probably know his name because his recent arrest for the fatal shooting of a young black man became national news.[76] While his picture never made the post office, Snoop's face graced the cover of *Newsweek* and almost every major music magazine and gained notoriety on a variety of television news programs. That Snoop's murder charges coincided with the release of his debut CD/album did not seem to hurt record sales one bit. On the contrary, the shooting simply confirmed his claims to be a "real" gangsta, to have committed more "dirt" than the next man. The hype around the man is clearly responsible for pushing *Doggy Style* to the top of the charts *before* it was released. Most of his lyrics represent nothing but senseless, banal nihilism. The misogyny is so dense that it sounds more like little kids discovering nasty words for the first time than full-blown male pathos. It is pure profanity bereft of the rich story telling and use of metaphor and simile that have been cornerstones of rap music since its origins.

While I still contend that most of the early gangsta rappers did not set out to glamorize crime, by the summer of 1993 gangsta rap had been reduced to "nihilism for nihilism's sake." For a moment, the hardest core, most fantastic misogynist and nihilistic music outsold almost everything on the rap scene, burying the most politically correct. In some respects, this development should not be surprising. Hard-core gangsta rap has become so formulaic that capturing even a modicum of reality no longer seems to be a priority. Ironically, the massive popularity of gangsta rap coincided with a fairly substantial increase in white surburban consumers of rap. This is in spite of the post–L.A. rebellion political climate when many commentators and cultural critics had hopes for a progressive turn in ghettocentric music, and a militant backlash against gangsta rap specifically and hip hop more generally (led mainly by middle-class male spokespersons like the Reverend Calvin Butts of Abyssinian Baptist Church in New York, African American feminist groups, and some black working-class communities concerned about violence in their midst). And, as I pointed out elsewhere in this essay, some of the most vociferous critics of gangsta rap come from within the hip hop community itself.[77]

In the early 1990s one cannot help but notice how rap music generally, and gangsta rap in particular, has become the scapegoat for some very serious problems facing urban America. Besieged communities who are truly drowning in poverty and violence, it seems, are grasping at straws. Spokespersons for these antirap movements invoke a mythic past in which middle-class values supposedly ruled. They point to a "golden age" of good behavior, when the young respected their elders, worked hard, did not live their lives for leisure, took education seriously, and respected their neighbor's property. But this has been the claim of every generation of black intellectuals and self-appointed leaders since the end of Reconstruction. The critique of the middle class that was so powerful in some glimmers of early gangsta rap is now silenced, as is the critique of what the economy has done to people. The door is open wider than ever to more all-male schools, heavier discipline, more policing, censorship, dress codes—what amounts to an all-out war on African American youth. On the other hand, the money is still flowing for gangsta rappers, many of whom now live in the hills overlooking the ghetto. The tragedy of all this is that the gangsta rappers have gotten harder and harder, kicking more ballistics than "reality"; critics and opponents have become harder and more sweeping in their criticism, dismissing not only the gangsta stuff but the entire body of rap; and the very conditions they are concerned about remain the same.

Gangsta rap might be on its last legs, a completely spent genre that now exists in a cul-de-sac of posturing, adolescent misogyny and blood-and-guts narratives. But it would be a mistake to dismiss gangsta rap and other genres of hip hop as useless creations of the marketplace. If we want to know the political climate among urban youth, we still should listen to the music and, most importantly, to the young people who fill the deadened, congested spaces of the city with these sonic forces. And as we all probably realize, the world from which this music emerged, and to which it partially speaks, inevitably faces the further deterioration of already unlivable neighborhoods, more street crime, and increased police repression. To take their voices seriously, however, is not to suggest that they are progressive or correct, or that every word, gesture, or beat is dripping with social significance. More often than not, "G-boys" are simply out to get paid, making funky jeep music, practicing the ancient art of playing the dozens, trying to be funny, and giving the people what they want. And when they address the problems of inner-city communities, we have to keep in mind that their sharpest cri-

tiques of capitalist America are derived from the same social and economic contexts that led a lot of homies to distrust black women and each other. Nevertheless, if we learned anything from that fateful April 29 in Los Angeles, it is that,
whether we like the message or not, we must read the graffiti on the walls and, as
Ice-T puts it, "check the pulse of the rhyme flow."

Kickin' reality, kickin' ballistics (remix version)

A nice, neat ending to be sure, but I can't go out like that. To write about the "politics" of gangsta rap is only part of the story. Let's face it: Listening to gangsta rap,
or any hard-core hip hop, is not exactly like reading an alternative version of the
Times (New York or L.A.). Hip hop is first and foremost music, "noize" produced
and purchased to drive to, rock to, chill to, drink to, and occasionally dance to.
To the hard core, how many people get fucked up in a song is less important than
an MC's verbal facility on the mic, the creative and often hilarious use of puns,
metaphors, and similes, not to mention the ability to kick some serious slang and
some serious ass on the microphone. A dope MC leaves a trail of victims to rot in
body bags, perpetrators who had the audacity to front like they could flow. This is
why I insisted from the get-go that gangsterism is integral to all hard-core hip hop,
from EPMD to MC Lyte, from Big Daddy Kane to Nice 'N' Smooth, just as
gangstas have been integral to all African American and, for that matter, black
Atlantic oral traditions. Moreover, as microphone fiend Rakim might put it, hip
hop ain't hip hop if you can't "move the crowd." In my book, the most politically
correct rappers will never get my hard-earned ducats if they ain't kickin' some
boomin' drum tracks, a fat bass line, a few well-placed JB-style guitar riffs, and some
stupid, nasty turntable action. If it claims to be hip hop, it has to have, as Pete
Rock says, "the breaks . . . the funky breaks . . . the funky breaks."

I wrote this little refrain not to contradict my analysis but to go out with a
dose of reality while giving a shout out to the hard core. For all the implicit and
explicit politics of rap lyrics, hip hop must be understood as a sonic force more
than anything else. You can't simply read about it; it has to be heard, volume
pumping, bass in full effect, index finger in reach of the rewind button when a
compelling sample, break beat, or lyric catches your attention. This is why, for all
my left-wing politics, when you see me driving by in my Subaru wagon, windows
wide open, digging in the seams with the gangsta lean, rear-view mirror trembling
from the sonic forces, I'll probably be rockin' to the likes of EPMD, Pete Rock
and C. L. Smooth, Das EFX, Pharcyde, Cypress Hill, Boss, Lords of the Underground, MC Lyte, Ice-T, Jeruda Damaja, Nas, Guru, and, yes, Ice Cube. Keep the
crossover and save most of the "PC" morality rap for those who act like they *don't*
know. I'm still rollin' with Da Lench Mob, chillin' with the Hit Squad, kickin' it
with the Rhyme Syndicate, hanging out in the Basement with Pete Rock and the
rest, and, like Das EFX, I'm coming straight from the Sewer.

I'm out . . . Peace.

Notes

1. There has been a flood of articles on the L.A. rebellion. Useful analyses can be found in Mike Davis, "In L.A., Burning All Illusions," *The Nation*, June 1, 1992, 743–746; *L.A. Weekly*, May 8–14, 1992; *Understanding the Riots: Los Angeles before and after the Rodney King Case* (Los Angeles: Los Angeles Times, 1992); Robert Gooding-Williams, ed., *Reading Rodney King, Reading Urban Uprising* (New York: Routledge, 1993); Brenda Wall, *The Rodney King Rebellion: A Psychopolitical Analysis of Racial Despair and Hope* (Chicago: African American Images, 1992); Haki R. Madhubuti, ed., *Why L.A. Happened: Implications of the '92 Los Angeles Rebellion* (Chicago: Third World Press, 1993).

2. Alan Light, "L.A. Rappers Speak Out," *Rolling Stone*, June 25, 1992, 21; see also Light's "Rappers Sounded Warning," *Rolling Stone* July 9–23, 1992, 15–17, which appeared a month after my own article, "Straight from Underground," *The Nation*, June 8, 1992, 793–796.

3. Ice Cube interview, MTV News, May 3, 1992.

4. The best sources on recent police-brutality cases in Los Angeles are the Independent Commission on the Los Angeles Police Department, *Report of the Independent Commission on the Los Angeles Police Deparment* (Los Angeles, 1991), hereafter cited as *The Christopher Report*; Mike Davis, *City of Quartz: Excavating the Future in Los Angeles* (London: Verso, 1990), 267–292; see also Douglas G. Glasgow, *The Black Underclass: Poverty, Unemployment, and Entrapment of Ghetto Youth* (New York: Jossey-Bass, 1980), 101; M. W. Meyer, "Police Shootings at Minorities: The Case of Los Angeles," *Annals* 452 (1980): 98–110; for other local and national examples, S. Harring, T. Platt, R. Speiglman, and P. Takagi, "The Management of Police Killings," *Crime and Social Justice* 8 (1977): 34–43; P. Takagi, "A Garrison State in 'Democratic Society,' " *Crime and Social Justice* (Spring–Summer 1978): 2–25; C. Milton, *The Police Use of Deadly Force* (Washington, D.C., 1977); Jerry G. Watts, "It Just Ain't Righteous: On Witnessing Black Crooks and White Cops," *Dissent* 90 (1983): 347–353; Bruce Pierce, "Blacks and Law Enforcement: Towards Police Brutality Reduction," *Black Scholar* 17 (1986): 49–54; A. L. Kobler, "Figures (and Perhaps Some Facts) on Police Killing of Civilians in the United States, 1965–1969," *Journal of Social Issues* 31 (1975): 163–191; J. J. Fyfe, "Blind Justice: Police Shootings in Memphis," *Journal of Criminal Law and Criminology* 73 (1982); 707–722; Bernard D. Headley, " 'Black on Black' Crime: The Myth and the Reality," *Crime and Social Justice* 20 (1983): 52–53.

5. For this anlaysis, which runs throughout much of the essay, I am indebted to my conversations with Charles Bright and to reading John Irwin, *The Jail: Managing the Underclass in American Society* (Berkeley and Los Angeles: University of California Press, 1985); Diana R. Gordon, *The Justice Juggernaut: Fighting Street Crime, Controlling Citizens* (New Brunswick, N.J.: Rutgers University Press, 1990); Michel Foucault, *Discipline and Punish: The Birth of the Prison*, trans. Alan Sheridan (New York: Pantheon, 1979), esp. 195–228.

6. Tricia Rose, "Black Texts/Black Contexts," in *Black Popular Culture*, ed. Gina Dent, (Seattle: Bay Press, 1992).

7. See David Toop, *Rap Attack 2* (London: Serpent's Tail, 1992), 40; on the baaadman narratives, see John W. Roberts, *From Trickster to Badman: The Black Folk Hero in Slavery and Freedom* (Philadelphia: University of Pennsylvania Press, 1989),

171–215; and on signifying, see Henry Louis Gates, Jr., *The Signifying Monkey: A Theory of African-American Literary Criticism* (New York: Oxford University Press, 1988), esp. 64–88; Claudia Mitchell-Kernan, "Signifying, Loud-talking, and Marking," in *Rappin and Stylin' Out: Communication in Urban Black America* (Urbana and Chicago: University of Illinois Press, 1972).

8. Darryl James, "Ice-T the Ex-Gangster," *Rappin'*, January 1991, 37; Havelock Nelson and Michael A. Gonzales, *Bring the Noise: A Guide to Rap Music and Hip Hop Culture* (New York: Harmony Books, 1991), 30–31. Ice-T had been on the scene for a while. However, his first single, "The Coldest Rap" (1981), does not fall within the gangsta style.

9. James, "Ice-T the Ex-Ganster," 37; "T for Two," *Details*, July 1991, 51–55; Alan Light, "Rapper Ice-T Busts A Movie," *Rolling Stone*, May 16, 1991, 85; David Mills, "The Gangsta Rapper: Violent Hero or Negative Role Model?" *The Source*, December 1990, 32.

10. Mills, "The Gangsta Rapper," 32; Frank Owen, "Hanging Tough," *Spin* 6 (April, 1990): 34; Nelson and Gonzales, *Bring the Noise*, 80–81, 165–167.

11. "1993 Summer Jeep Slammers," *Source*, July 1993, 76. The most obvious exception is Compton's Most Wanted, which is more inclined toward jazz and quiet storm tracks (see especially CMW, *Straight Check N' Em* (Orpheus Records, 1991). Nevertheless, funk dominates West Coast gangsta rap to the point where house music is practically absent and reggae and jazz have been slow in coming.

12. The larger hip hop community has maintained an ambivalent, and occasionally critical, stance toward most gangsta rappers. See, for instance, the criticisms of Kool Moe Dee, YZ, and others in "Droppin' Science," *Spin*, August 1989, 49–50; The J, "If You Don't Know Your Culture, You Don't Know Nothin'! YZ Claims He's Thinking of a Master Plan' for Black Awareness," *RapPages*, December 1991, 64; "Views on Gangsta-ism," *The Source*, December 1990, 36, 39, 40; as well as critical perspectives in the music itself, e.g., Del tha Funkee Homosapien, "Hoodz Come in Dozens," *I Wish My Brother George Was Here* (Priority Records, 1991); Public Enemy, "No Nigga," *Apocalypse '91* (Def Jam, 1991); Arrested Development, "People Everyday" and "Give a Man a Fish," *3 Years, 5 Months, and 2 Days in the Life Of. . .* (Chrysalis Records, 1992); the Disposable Heroes of Hipoprisy, especially "Famous and Dandy (Like Amos n' Andy)," *Hypocrisy Is the Greatest Luxury* (Island Records, 1992); the Coup, *Kill My Landlord* (Wild Pitch Records, 1993).

13. Ice-T, *OG: Original Gangster* (Sire Records, 1991); Ice Cube, *Kill at Will* (Priority Records, 1992); Ice-T, *Power* (Warner Bros., 1988); CPO, *To Hell and Black* (Capitol Records, 1990); NWA, *100 Miles and Runnin'* (Ruthless, 1990); CMW, *Straight Check N' Em* (Orpheus Records, 1991); Ice Cube, *The Predator* (Priority Records, 1992); Dr. Dre, *The Chronic* (Interscope Records, 1992). How Ice-T's lyrics from "I'm Your Pusher" were misinterpreted was discussed on McNeil-Lehrer on a special segment on rap music.

14. Ice-T [and the Rhyme Syndicate], "My Word Is Bond," *The Iceberg/Freedom of Speech . . . Just Watch What You Say* (Sire Records, 1989); Ice Cube, "J.D.'s Gafflin'," *AmeriKKKa's Most Wanted* (Priority Records, 1990). West Coast rappers also create humorous countercritiques of gangsterism; the most penetrating is perhaps Del tha Funkee Homosapien's hilarious, "Hoodz Come in Dozens," *I Wish My Brother George Was Here* (Priority Records, 1991).

15. Mills, "The Gangsta Rapper," 39; see also Dan Charnas, "A Gangsta's World View," *The Source*, Summer 1990, 21–22; "Niggers with Attitude," *Melody Maker*, Novem-

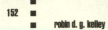
ber 4, 1989, 33; and the Geto Boys' Bushwick Bill's explanation in J. Sultan, "The Geto Boys," *The Source*, December 1990, 33.

16. Digital Underground's "Good Thing We're Rappin'," *Sons of the P* (Tommy Boy, 1991), is nothing if not a tribute to the pimp narratives. One hears elements of classic toasts, including "The Pimp," "Dogass Pimp," "Pimping Sam," "Wicked Nell," "The Lame and the Whore," and perhaps others. Even the meter is very much in the toasting tradition. (For transcriptions of these toasts, see Bruce Jackson, *"Get Your Ass in the Water and Swim Like Me": Narrative Poetry from Black Oral Tradition* [Cambridge: Harvard University Press, 1974], 106–130.) Similar examples that resemble the more comical pimp narratives include Ice Cube, "I'm Only Out for One Thing," *AmeriKKKa's Most Wanted* (Priority, 1990), and Son of Bazerk, "Sex, Sex, and More Sex," *Son of Bazerk* (MCA, 1991).

17. See John Leland, "Rap: Can It Survive Self-Importance?" *Details*, July 1991, 108; Frank Owen, "Hanging Tough," *Spin* 6, April 1990, 34; James Bernard, "NWA," *The Source*, December 1990, 34. In fact, Ice Cube left NWA in part because they were not "political" enough. Though most accounts indicate that financial disputes between Cube and manager Jerry Heller caused the split, in at least one interview he implied that politics had something to do with it as well. As early as *Straight outta Compton*, Cube wanted to include more raps like "——— the Police," and when the FBI sent a warning to NWA about inflammatory lyrics, Cube planned to put out a twelve-minute remix in response. Of course, neither happened. It finally became clear to Cube that he could not remain in NWA after Jerry Heller kept the group from appearing on Jesse Jackson's weekly TV show. Darryl James, "Ice Cube Leaves NWA to Become Amerikkka's Most Wanted," *Rappin'*, January 1991, 20.

18. Davis, *City of Quartz*, 304–307; Edward Soja, *Postmodern Geographies: The Reassertion of Space in Critical Social Theory* (London: Verso, 1989), 197, 201.

19. The idea that unemployed black youth turn to crime because it is more rewarding than minimum-wage service-oriented work has been explored by a number of social scientists. See, for example, Richard B. Freeman, "The Relation of Criminal Activity to Black Youth Employment," 99–107, and Llad Phillips and Harold Votey, Jr., "Rational Choice Models of Crimes by Youth," 129–187, both in *The Economics of Race and Crime*, ed. Margaret C. Simms and Samuel L. Myers (New Brunswick, N.J.: Transaction Books, 1988); Llad Phillips, H. L. Votey, Jr., and D. Maxwell, "Crime, Youth, and the Labor Market," *Journal of Political Economy* 80 (1972): 491–504; Philip Moss and Chris Tilly, *Why Black Men Are Doing Worse in the Labor Market: A Review of Supply-Side and Demand-Side Explanations* (New York: Social Science Research Council Committee for Research on the Underclass, Working Paper, 1991), 90–93. Steven Box, *Recession, Crime, and Punishment* (Totowa, N.J.: Barnes and Noble, 1987); Elliot Currie, *Confronting Crime: An American Challenge* (New York: Pantheon, 1985), 146; James W. Messerschmidt, *Capitalism, Patriarchy, and Crime* (Totowa, N.J.: Rowman and Littlefield, 1986), 54–58. For a discussion of the role of gangs in the illicit economy, see Martin Sanchez Jankowski, *Islands in the Street: Gangs and American Urban Society* (Berkeley and Los Angeles: University of California Press, 1991), 119–131. Despite the general perception that dealers made an enormous amount of money, at least one study suggests that the average crack peddler only makes about $700 per month. See Peter Reuter, Robert MacCoun, and Patrick Murphy, *Money for Crime: A Study of the Economics of Drug Dealing in Washington, D.C.* (Santa Monica, Calif.: Rand Drug Policy Research Center, 1990); Davis, *City of Quartz*, 322.

20. For discussions of the ways in which the mass media depicts black youth gangs, violence, and the crack economy in inner-city neighborhoods, see Jankowski, *Islands in the Street*, 284–302; Jimmie L. Reeves and Richard Campbell, *Cracked Coverage: Television News, the Anti-cocaine Crusade, and the Reagan Legacy* (Durham, N.C.: Duke University Press, 1994); Herman Gray, "Race Relations as News: Content Analysis," *American Behavioral Scientist* 30 (March–April 1987): 381–396; Craig Reinarman and Harry G. Levine, "The Crack Attack: Politics and Media in America's Latest Drug Scare," in *Images of Issues: Typifying Contemporary Social Problems*, ed. Joel Best (New York: Aldine de Gruyter, 1989), 115–135; Clarence Lusane, *Pipe Dream Blues: Racism and the War on Drugs* (Boston: South End, 1991).

21. "Niggers with Attitude," *Melody Maker*, November 4, 1989, 33.

22. James, "Ice-T the Ex-Gangster," 38. Of course, the last part of Ice-T's pronouncements echoes a range of conspiracy theories that continue to float among communities under siege and even found a voice in Furious Styles, a lead character in John Singleton's *Boyz in the Hood*. But T's assertion cannot be dismissed so easily, since there are more liquor stores per capita and per square mile in low-income inner-city neighborhoods than anywhere else in the United States. See George A. Hacker, *Marketing Booze to Blacks* (Washington, D.C.: Center for Science in the Public Interest, 1987); Manning Marable, *How Capitalism Underdeveloped Black America: Problems in Race, Political Economy, and Society* (Boston: South End, 1983).

23. On black aesthetic tradition, see the interview with Bernice Johnson Reagon by Bill Moyers, PBS; Roger Abrahams, *Deep down in the Jungle Negro Narrative Folklore from the Streets of Philadelphia* (Chicago: Aldine, 1970), 58–59; Mark Zanger, "The Intelligent Forty-Year-Old's Guide to Rap," *Boston Review*, December 1991, 34.

24. Malcolm X, *Malcolm X: The Last Speeches*, ed. Bruce Perry (New York: Pathfinder, 1989), 161.

25. This argument has been made by numerous scholars. A sampling: Ken Auletta, *The Underclass* (New York: Random House, 1982), 90–108 passim; Charles Murray, *Losing Ground: American Social Policy, 1950–1980* (New York: Basic Books, 1984); see also Roger Lane's more historical but equally flawed treatment in *Roots of Violence in Black Philadelphia, 1860–1900* (Cambridge: Harvard University Press, 1986).

26. D-Dub, "We're Not Glamorizin'—But We're Factualizin'," *RapPages*, December 1991, 55–56. For Bobby Byrd, however, a job is not something one pulls, but something one has. His lyrics are clearly about wage labor: "You got to have a job / Put meat on the table / You got to have a job / to keep the family stable." Quoted in Michael Haralambos, *Soul Music: The Birth of a Sound in America* (New York: De Capo, 1974), 115.

27. Peter Linebaugh, *The London Hanged: Crime and Civil Society in the Eighteenth Century* (London: Penguin, 1991), xxiii.

28. James Bernard, "Ice Cube: Building a Nation," *The Source*, December 1991, 34.

29. Quoted in Jankowski, *Islands in the Street*, 103.

30. Davis, *City of Quartz*, 297; *Los Angeles Times*, May 25, 1992; Alexander Cockburn, "Beat the Devil," *The Nation*, June 1, 1992, 738–739.

31. Ice-T, "Pain" and "6 in the Mornin" from *Rhyme Pays*, "High Rollers" from *Power*, and "New Jack Hustler" from *OG: Original Gangster*; Ice Cube, "Dead Homiez" from *Kill at Will*, "Color Blind" from *Death Certificate*; NWA, "Alwayz into Somethin" from *Efil4zaggin*; Cypress Hill, *Cypress Hill* (Columbia, 1991).

32. D-Dub, "We're Not Glamorizin'," 57.

33. Messerschmidt, *Capitalism, Patriarchy, and Crime*, 58–60, quote on 59; Tony Platt, " 'Street Crime': A View from the Left," *Crime and Social Justice* 9 (Spring–Summer 1978): 26–34; Walter J. Ong, *Fighting for Life: Contest, Sexuality, and Consciousness* (Ithaca, N.Y.: Cornell University Press, 1981), 68–69; R. W. Connell, *Gender and Power: Society, the Person, and Sexual Politics* (Stanford, Calif.: Stanford University Press, 1987), 57–58, 85–86; R. E. Dobash and R. P. Dobash, *Violence against Wives: A Case against Patriarchy* (New York: Free Press, 1979). One very obvious example of a gangsta rapper measuring masculinity by his ability and willingness to fight is Ice-T's "Bitches 2" from *OG: Original Gangster*. One woman's gangsta group whose music talks about women engaging in drive-by shootings and taking out police in a flurry of buckshot is the New York–based Bytches with Problems; see "We're Coming Back Strapped" and "Wanted," *The Bytches* (Def Jam, 1991).

34. See "The Drive By," *AmeriKKKa's Most Wanted* and *Kill at Will*.

35. Compton's Most Wanted, *Straight Check N' Em* (Sony, 1991). Hip hop critic Reginald C. Dennis, who shares these gangsta rappers' sensitivity to both the logic of crime and its detrimental effects, has made a plea for criminals to be socially responsible when engaging in violence: "If you have chosen the lifestyle of the 'gangsta' you can still contribute to the cause by making sure the blood of innocents is not randomly spilled because of your irresponsibility. Do what you gotta do, but keep it limited to your social circle. If you must be criminal minded be professional and responsible—don't drag children and other innocents down with you. . . . In this way we can attempt to find some common ground between the criminal and the activist, and in diverse ways, work towards the same goal." Dennis, "After all . . . We Are the Ones Who Are Dying: Inner City Crime," *The Source*, February 1991, 34.

36. D-Dub, "We're Not Glamorizin'," 56–57.

37. Cube quoted in Robert Hilburn, "The Rap Is: Justice," *Los Angeles Times*, May 31, 1992; see also Niggers with Attitude," *Melody Maker*, November 4, 1989, 34. Of course, the complicity of the U.S. government in the distribution of drugs into the black community is not a new theme or one unique to hip hop. See Sir Mix-a-Lot, "National Anthem," lyrics reprinted in Lawrence A. Stanley, ed., *Rap: The Lyrics* (New York and London: Viking Penguin, 1992), 294; 2 Black, 2 Strong MMG, "War on Drugs," *Doin' Hard Time on Planet Earth* (Relativity Records, 1991); Geto Boys, "City under Siege," *The Geto Boys* (Def American Records, 1989).

38. Davis, *City of Quartz*, 268; Jankowski, *Islands in the Street*, 252, 254; also see Glasgow, *The Black Underclass*, 100–101.

39. Owen, "Hanging Tough," 34.

40. George Lipsitz, *Time Passages: Collective Memory and American Popular Culture* (Minneapolis: University of Minnesota Press, 1990), 5.

41. Although young black women also were victims of police marking and experienced outright brutality, L.A. gangsta rappers have been silent on the policing of women. Combined with a dominant black political ideology that has framed the issues solely in terms of the problems of black males, the refusal to acknowledge black women's experiences with state-sanctioned violence has effectively rendered them invisible in the whole discourse about police brutality in the aftermath of Rodney King. Even black female rappers have ignored the issue of state-sanctioned violence against women—one exception being "Wanted" by the New York–based rap group Bytches with Problems. "Wanted" not only reminds listeners that women are victims of police harassment but briefly adds the dimension of sexual abuse in its descriptions of

day-to-day repression. BWP, *The Bytches* (Def Jam, 1991). While far more black males than females are victims of police repression, the most important police homicide and brutality cases over the past decade have had black female victims: Eula Love, Eleanor Bumpurs, Tawana Brawley, to name a few. Unfortunately, scholarship on policing is equally male focused and thus complicit in rendering black women's experiences invisible. One recent exception is Ruth Chigwada's study of black women in Britain, "The Policing of Black Women," in *Out of Order? Policing Black People*, ed. Ellis Cashmore and Eugene McLaughlin (London and New York: Routledge, 1991), 134–150.

42. Davis, *City of Quartz*, 274.

43. Ibid., 272. Of course, L.A. is not unique in this respect. See, for example, Box, *Recession, Crime, and Punishment*, 46–47; Lee P. Brown, "Bridges over Troubled Waters: A Perspective on Policing in the Black Community," in *Black Perspectives on Crime and the Criminal Justice System*, ed. Robert L. Woodson (Boston: Hall, 1977), 87–88; Elijah Anderson, *Streetwise: Race, Class, and Change in an Urban Community* (Chicago: University of Chicago Press, 1990), 194–196.

44. Dick Hebdige, *Subculture: The Meaning of Style* (London: Methuen, 1979), 18.

45. This interpretation is derived from a reading of Stuart Hall, "Culture, Media, and the 'Ideological Effect,' " in *Mass Communication and Society*, ed. James Curran, Michael Gurevitch, and Janet Woolacott (Beverly Hills: Sage, 1979).

46. Founded in the mid-1960s, the Five Percenters believe that every person is God. Less commonly, "G" is used as a shorthand term for "money," which is also used as a form of address. Although my point that this terminology cuts across gender lines is drawn from very unscientific participant observation, one might listen to the music of Yo-Yo, MC Lyte, or Queen Latifah for their employment of "G" as a form of address.

47. Tricia Rose, *Black Noise: Rap Music and Black Culture in Contemporary America* (Hanover, N.H.: University Press of New England, 1994), 63; Ice Cube, "The Wrong Nigga to Fuck Wit," *Death Certificate*, and "Tales from the Darkside (Endangered Species)," *AmeriKKKa's Most Wanted*.

48. Marc Mauer, *Young Black Men and the Criminal Justice System: A Growing National Problem* (Washington, D.C.: Sentencing Project, 1990), 1–11; Irwin, *The Jail*; Gordon, *The Justice Juggernaut*; Messerschmidt, *Capitalism, Patriarachy, and Crime*, 52–53; Jeffrey Reiman, *The Rich Get Richer and the Poor Get Prison* (New York: Wiley, 1984); R. Sheldon, *Criminal Justice in America: A Sociological Approach* (Boston: Little, Brown, 1982), 39–50; Brown, "Bridges over Troubled Waters," 87–88.

49. Michel Foucault, "Intellectuals and Power," in *Language, Counter-memory, Practice: Selected Essays and Interviews by Michel Foucault*, ed. Donald F. Bouchard, trans. Donald F. Bouchard and Sherry Simon (Ithaca, N.Y.: Cornell University Press, 1977), 209.

50. Other examples include 2Pac, "Trapped," *2Pacalypse Now*; Public Enemy, "Black Steel in the Hour of Chaos," *It Takes a Nation of Millions to Hold Us Back* (Def Jam, 1988); MMG, 2 Black, 2 Strong, "Up in the Mountains," *Doin' Hard Time on Planet Earth* (Relativity, 1991). Popular texts that suggest that incarceration reflects part of a conspiracy include Jawanza Kunjufu, *Countering the Conspiracy to Destroy Black Boys* (Chicago: African American Images, 1985–86), 3 vols.; Baba Zak A. Kondo, *For Homeboys Only: Arming and Strengthening Young Brothers for Black Manhood* (Washington, D.C.: Nubia, 1991). Although women's voices are absent in these narratives about incarceration, we should keep in mind that 96 percent of the nation's prison

population is male. Franklin E. Zimring and Gordon Hawkins, *The Scale of Imprisonment* (Chicago: University of Chicago Press, 1991), 73.

51. A similar point is made in W.C. and the MAAD Circle's "Out on a Furlough," *Ain't a Damn Thing Changed*.

52. Clearly, the roots of homophobia among African American males lie elsewhere, but it is interesting to note how frequently homosexuality is talked about in terms of prison rape. This pervasive image must shape the particular character of homophobia in African American urban communities.

53. Claude Brown, "The Language of Soul," *Esquire Magazine*, April 1968, 88.

54. Mitchell-Kernan, "Signifying, Loud-talking, and Marking," 328; for numerous examples from folklore, see Lawrence Levine, *Black Culture and Black Consciousness* (New York: Oxford University Press, 1977); Roberts, *From Trickster to Badman*. When used in this context, very few African Americans would point to such dialogues as examples of "self-hatred." And yet this is what Ice Cube (before splitting with NWA) was trying to get at in an interview: "Look, when we call each other nigger it means no harm, in fact, in Compton, it's a friendly word. But if a white person uses it, it's something different, it's a racist word" "Niggers with Attitude," *Melody Maker*, November 4, 1989, 33. Cube's defense of "nigger" tells us very little, however, primarily because his response is structured by critics whose discursive terrain is limited to the use of the word itself rather than the context in which gangsta rappers employ "nigger." As Ice Cube slowly moves away from gangsta rap, influenced largely by the Nation of Islam, his views on the use of the word seem to have undergone a substantial shift. In a recent interview he told hip hop journalist James Bernard, "The reason I say 'nigger' is because we are still 'niggers' cuz we got this white man in our heads. Until we get him out our heads, that's when we become Black men and that's when I'll stop using the word" (James Bernard, "Ice Cube: Building a Nation," *The Source*, December 1991, 32. Although most cultural nationalist groups critique or avoid the term "Nigga" altogether, XCLAN apparently embraces the phrase as an ironic, often humorous, comment on white fears of black militancy. See especially their album *Xodus: The New Testament* (Polygram Records, 1992).

55. Robert H. DeCoy, *The Nigger Bible* (Los Angeles: Holloway House, 1967), 33; William L. Van Deburg, *New Day in Babylon: The Black Power Movement and American Culture, 1965–1975* (Chicago: University of Chicago Press, 1992), 218. There are dozens of examples. We might point to the light-skinned character in the film version of "The Spook Who Sat by the Door," who claimed his authenticity by calling himself a "Nigger," or Cecil Brown's reference to James Brown's music as "Nigger feeling" in his brilliant essay "James Brown, Hoodoo, and Black Culture," *Black Review* (1971), 182. We might also consider the prize-winning and celebrated narrative compiled by Theodore Rosengarten, *All God's Dangers: The Life of Nate Shaw* (New York: Avon, 1974). When Shaw (whose real name was Ned Cobb) used the word "nigger" as a form of self-designation, it signified more than color. In making distinctions between "niggers" and "better-class Negroes," he represented the impoverished, the exploited, the working person.

56. Quoted in Michael Eric Dyson, "The Culture of Hip Hop," in *Reflecting Black: African-American Cultural Criticism* (Minneapolis: University of Minnesota Press, 1993); see also Ice-T, "Radio Suckers," *Power* (Sire Records, 1988), "This One's for Me," *The Iceberg/Freedom of Speech . . . Just Watch What You Say*; Ice Cube, "Turn off the Radio," *AmeriKKKa's Most Wanted*.

57. Davis, *City of Quartz*, 290–292.

58. Owen, "Hanging Tough," 34. A comparable line can be found in MC Ren's contribution to "Niggaz 4 Life," *Efil4zaggin*.

59. Hebdige, *Subculture*, 86.

60. Examples can be found in most gangsta rap, but see especially *Eazy-Duz-It* (Ruthless, 1988); *Straight outta Compton*, *100 Miles and Running*, and "Niggaz 4 Life," *Efil4zaggin*.

61. The black male celebration of stereotypes of black sexuality is common in much black humor. Lawrence Levine writes, "Black humor reflected an awareness that the pervasive stereotype of Negroes as oversexed, hyper-virile, and uninhibitedly promiscuous was not purely a negative image; that it contained envy as well as disdain, that it was a projection of desire as well as fear." *Black Culture*, 338.

62. Abrahams, *Deep down in the Jungle*, 258.

63. Jackson, "*Get Your Ass in the Water and Swim Like Me*," 129; see also several other toasts in Jackson's collection as well as Dennis Wepman, Ronald B. Newman, and Murray Binderman, *The Life: The Lore and Folk Poetry of the Black Hustler* (Philadelphia: University of Pennsylvania Press, 1976).

64. Henry Louis Gates, Jr., "Two Live Crew De-Coded," *New York Times*, June 19, 1990; on urban toasts and "baaadman" narratives, see especially Jackson, "*Gut Your Ass in the Water*"; Levine, *Black Culture*, 407–420; Roberts, *From Trickster to Badman*, 171–215; Abrahams, *Deep down in the Jungle*; Anthony Reynolds, "Urban Negro Toasts: A Hustler's View from Los Angeles," *Western Folklore* 33 (October 1974): 267–300; Wepman, Newman, and Binderman, *The Life*.

65. "Sexualized society" is borrowed from John D'Emilio and Estelle Freedman, *Intimate Matters: A History of Sexuality in America* (New York: Harper & Row, 1988), 326–330. The more popular pimp narratives include Iceberg Slim [Robert Beck], *Pimp: The Story of My Life* (Los Angeles: Holloway House, 1969); Christina Milner and Richard Milner, *Black Players: The Secret World of Black Pimps* (New York: Little, Brown, 1973). On the pimp in popular film, see Donald Bogle, *Toms, Coons, Mullatoes, Mammies, and Bucks: An Interpretive History of Blacks in American Films*, 2d ed. (New York: Continuum, 1989), 234–242; Daniel Leab, *From Sambo to Superspade: The Black Experience in Motion Pictures* (Boston: Houghton Mifflin, 1975); David E. James, "Chained to Devilpictures: Cinema and Black Liberation in the Sixties," in *The Year Left 2: Toward a Rainbow Socialism—Essays on Race, Ethnicity, Class, and Gender*, ed. Mike Davis et al. (London: Verso, 1987), 125–138. Black nationalist narratives that tend to celebrate or romanticize the pimp in African American communities include H. Rap Brown, *Die, Nigger, Die* (New York: Dial, 1969); Bobby Seale, *Seize the Time* (New York: Random House, 1970) and *Lonely Rage* (New York: Times Books, 1978), in which Seale himself takes on the characteristics of a pimp; Huey P. Newton, *Revolutionary Suicide* (New York: Harcourt Brace Jovanovich, 1973); Eldridge Cleaver, *Soul on Ice* (New York: McGraw Hill, 1968).

66. Ice-T quoted in Havelock and Gonzales, *Bring the Noise*, 110; Ulf Hannerz, *Soulside: Inquiries into Ghettoe Culture and Community* (New York: Columbia University Press, 1969), 105–107; Charnas, "A Gangsta's World View," 22.

67. In the discussion following I limit my critique of sexism to L.A. gangsta rap and thus do not deal with better-known controversies (e.g., the 2 Live Crew obscenity trial). See, for example, Tricia Rose, "Never Trust a Big Butt and a Smile," *Camera Obscura* 23 (1991): 109–131; Kimberle Crenshaw, "Beyond Racism and Misogyny: Black

Feminism and 2 Live Crew," *Boston Review*, December 1991; Michelle Wallace, "When Black Feminism Faces the Music and the Music Is Rap," *New York Times*, July 29, 1990; Michael Eric Dyson, "As Complex as They Wanna Be: 2 Live Crew," *Zeta Magazine*, January 1991, 76–78; Paulla Ebron, "Rapping between Men: Performing Gender," *Radical America* 23 (June 1991): 23–27.

68. For example, see *Los Angeles Times*, August 22, 1991; Jewell T. Gibbs, *Young, Black, and Male in America: An Endangered Species* (Dover, Mass.: Auburn House, 1988); Harry Edwards interview, *San Francisco Focus*, March 1984, 100; Murray, *Losing Ground*; Lawrence Mead, *Beyond Entitlement: The Social Obligation of Citizenship* (New York: Free Press, 1985); and for a liberal approach that also suggests that family structure is partly to blame for persistent poverty, see Eleanor Holmes Norton, "Restoring the Traditional Black Family," *New York Times Magazine*, June 2, 1985.

69. D. Dub, "We're Not Glamorizin'," 57; Ice Cube made a similar point in Bernard, "Ice Cube: Building a Nation," 32.

70. Messerschmidt, *Capitalism, Patriarchy, and Crime*, 134.

71. Rose, "Never Trust a Big Butt," 115. A clear example is Ice-T, "I Love Ladies," *Rhyme Pays*.

72. I am grateful to Tricia Rose for her insights into the ways in which Yo-Yo's intervention disrupts Cube's masculinist discourse (conversation with Tricia Rose, December 26, 1991). See also Yo-Yo's other lyrical challenges to sexism on *Make Way for the Motherlode* (Priority, 1991). Some of the most antisexist lyrics on Yo-Yo's album were written by Ice Cube.

73. *Kill at Will* (Priority, 1991); a shorter version appeared first on *AmeriKKKa's Most Wanted*.

74. Alan Light, "Beating Up the Charts," *Rolling Stone*, August 8, 1991, 66.

75. See "The House," *OG: Original Gangster*; "Fuck My Daddy," *Ain't a Damn Thing Changed*. Bay Area gangsta rapper 2Pac has recently dealt critically with issues such as incest ("Brenda Has a Baby") and the rape of young women by their stepfathers ("Part-Time Mutha") on *2Pacalypse Now*.

76. I credit the music critic Toure with the term "Calabama"; at least that's who I got it from. It's hard to describe other than a kind of West Coast "twang," a Texas-meets-California accent.

77. Brent Staples, "The Politics of Gangster Rap: A Music Celebrating Murder and Misogyny," *New York Times*, August 27, 1993; Michel Marriot, "Harsh Rap Lyrics Provoke Black Backlash," *New York Times*, August 15, 1993; Calvin Sims, "Gangster Rappers: The Lives, the Lyrics," *New York Times*, November 1993; Donna Britt, "A One-Word Assault on Women," *Washington Post*, November 30, 1993; Scott Armstrong, "Backlash Is Brewing over 'Gangsta Rap' Lyrics as Public Says 'Enough,' " *Christian Science Monitor*, December 13, 1993; Michael Farquhar, "Gangsta Rap Ripped by Protesters: Black Women's Group Arrested at D.C. Store," *Washington Post*, December 22, 1993.

making the strong survive: the contours and
contradictions of message rap

ernest allen, jr.

Yes, I'm that kind of nigga that they can't stand
The one that taught African how to say Black Man
The one you can plainly see
With nationalist colors of red, black and green
The one who cut Tarzan's vine
And ran his ass out of the jungle with his homeboy swine.

XCLAN, "Fire and Earth"

I can't wait, time's quickly running out
Call to arms, revolution's in the house
Unforgettable, the words of wisdom
Brought to life by the ten-point system
Freedom and power to determine our destiny
Full employment for the black community
Fight the capitalist with a raised fist
B-U-Y black and stack awareness . . .

Black juries when our brothers are tried in court
And in addition to all this we want
Land, bread, housing, and education
To go with justice and peace for the black nation.

Paris, "Escape from Babylon"

Members of old-school generations venturous enough to switch on their televisions these days are no doubt aware of the resurgence of a nationalism and political progressivism reminiscent of African American popular culture in the late 1960s and early 1970s. But in place of organizational structures such as the Student Non-Violent Coordinating Committee, the Black Panther Party, or the Spirit House Movers, for example, the principal generative form of a reawakened black consciousness of the eighties and nineties has arrived, rather incredibly, via a poetic/musical form known as "rap." Sharing the stage with more entertainment-oriented rappers such as Hammer, Heavy D and the Boys, as well as many others, are Queen Mother Rage, Eric B. & Rakim, Isis, Poor Righteous Teachers, Public Enemy, Lakim Shabazz, Ed O. G. & Da Bulldogs, KMD, Two Kings in a Cypher, and A Tribe Called Quest—only some of the rap groups or single artists contributing to the message of the present era.

Although political rap, or message rap, as it is more commonly called, constitutes only a small segment of the genre, it exerts a powerful political and artistic influence on its youthful listeners as well as on rap artists in general. Today rap music has become one of the principle vehicles by which young African

Americans express their views of the world, attempting to create a sense of order out of the mayhem and disorder of contemporary urban life. Such efforts, however have not been without severe contradictions. On the positive tip, one notes the forward-looking attempts of message rap to address existing catastrophic social problems facing African Americans. No theme—be it education, family structure, poverty, teenage pregnancy, incest, AIDS, crack cocaine, or alcoholism—is too sensitive for unreserved public discussion. In an epoch where adult leadership appears to have collapsed, and where a sense of hopelessness rivets African American life in a way perhaps unmatched since the post-Reconstruction era, we need to heartily encourage the efforts of message rappers to instill a sense of optimism and resistance in the minds and actions of black youth. "Nothin' wrong with a song to make the strong survive," in the words of Public Enemy.

Since the world inhabited by urban youth is predatory and oppressive, however, one can never assume that a given message will transcend the corrosiveness of life in the 'hood. Message rap tends to carry with it considerable antisocial baggage characteristic of, but hardly limited to, the rap phenomenon in general: misogyny, homophobia, vainglorious trippings, interethnic malevolence, and—if these were not sufficient—a moral relativism that repudiates any responsibility for one's own actions, including all of the above. Politically conscious or otherwise, at the core of this righteous rebellion of African American youth lies an obsessive, generational preoccupation with social acknowledgment and respect—a thin-skinned quest to preserve the self against any hint of disrespect, real or imagined, from whatever source. If the seventies produced the "me" generation, the nineties is where industrial-strength "attitude" occupies the throne.

Overall, the message tends to portray, in vivid and urgent terms, the contours of existing social breakdown, and in the best of cases may offer a vision of a new and more just way of life. But all too frequently these youthful assertions of social identity and envisioned social order degenerate into a malevolent disparaging of other groups, based upon differences rooted in gender, ethnicity, or sexual preference. In the process they often obscure and contaminate the legitimate demand for African American justice in a white-dominated capitalist world. In the face of prevailing social conditions one is led to ask, How can it be otherwise?[1]

Moreover, because the medium of rap—its production and distribution—is filtered through the corporate pipeline, it is to be expected and lamented that market forces will play a decisive role in shaping and propagating the message itself. In an era characterized by the collapse of significant political life and by the relative success of media forces in defining symbolic meaning for large numbers of African Americans, message rap remains decapitated from any mass political movement for social change, and overwhelmingly dependent on the market for dissemination—a significant political weakness. (On the other hand, it is likely that message rap has been allowed to expand as a profit engine to the entertainment business precisely *because* of the current political disarray of African Americans.) Efforts on the part of many rap artists to reach the crossover dollars of a larger market have generally led to artistic and political compromises or distortions, if not wider acceptance of the "product," leading to an intense and interesting struggle among rap artists themselves as to which expressions of rap are legitimate. Moreover, the medium's comprehension of and message to the world remain literally fragmented by electronic audio/video "sampling," its parameters determined primarily by artistic criteria. It is not uncommon to find, for example, repetitive soundbites from Malcolm X, Martin Luther King, or Louis Farrakhan strewn together behind God-knows-what "dope" rhyme, leaving even the most sophisticated listener to ponder the significance of it all—above and beyond a respect for its underlying, creative genius. However, celebrated as the innovative, African American contribution to postmodernism that rap is, such fragmentation also tends to retard the maturation of the mass political consciousness to which it initially gave birth. And, finally, the politics of message rap remain largely the captive of intersubjective approaches to social relations and social structure—a "politics of recognition" whose shortcomings I intend to make clear in this essay.

The emergence of message rap

Artistically speaking, the immediate roots of message rap are to be found, in part, in the black poetry movement of the sixties, its specific content traceable to the sociopolitical thought of African Americans from that period to the present.[2] As William Eric Perkins has noted, the ritualized verbal combat of inner-city "signifying" and the stylized "rap" of black radio DJs have also contributed heavily to the genre.[3] Although most African American youth are probably unaware, except perhaps in a peripheral way, of the existence of such poets as Sonia Sanchez, Askia Muhammad Touré, June Jordan, Larry Neal, or even Amiri Baraka, to name but a few of the more illustrious black bards who emerged a generation ago, some will more likely be familiar with performing artists such as The Last Poets and Gil Scott-Heron—if only because the latter's audio recordings have been sampled by rappers as well as recently been made available in their original form.[4]

Other essays in this volume cover the development of the rap form itself, and there is general agreement that the genre evolved in three waves.[5] Although earlier manifestations can readily be cited, political message rap fundamentally belongs to the third period of the hip hop wave, which began on the "hard" side with the release of Public Enemy's Yo! Bum Rush the Show in 1987. This was quickly followed by, for example, the softer sound of DJ Jazzy Jeff and the Fresh Prince, as well as the strongly dance-oriented tunes of M.C. Hammer, both in 1988. With a few exceptions the emergence of white rappers such as Vanilla Ice and others tended to push the soft-core rap even softer; the polishing up of gangsta rap by NWA (Niggas with Attitude) and its successors, on the other hand, put an edge on hard-core rap that will never be surpassed—or more accurately, one "crams to understand" how it might be transcended in terms of its nihilism. The third wave is also characterized by a black feminist response to negative characterizations of females by male rappers, and by attempts by female rappers to address the question of male/female as well as female/female relations in the African American community.

Political rap manifests in three relatively distinct though interrelated expressions: (1) the Islamic nationalist orientation of rappers such as Pete Rock and C. L. Smooth, Lakim Shabazz, Poor Righteous Teachers, Eric B. and Rakim, Brand Nubian, and many others; (2) the cultural-political nationalism of Public Enemy, Boogie Down Productions, Kool Moe Dee, XCLAN, Ed O. G. & Da Bulldogs, Paris, and the Jungle Brothers, for example; and (3) specific, message-oriented expressions embedded in the more earthy gangsta rap of NWA, Ice Cube, Ice-T, Criminal Nation, Schooly D, the Geto Boys, and the like.[6]

But where, specifically, do the messages of message rap come from? At its core, the social base of the rapper worldview is to be found among black urban youth—unemployed/underemployed, politically powerless. That is not to say, of course, that every successful rapper is a former gang member or potential gangster, or even that his or her social origins are necessarily to be found in the inner city—witness the suburban-raised, college-bred Public Enemy. My point is rather that, generally speaking, core values articulated in a given rap message, no matter the origin of individual rappers, tend to be socially rooted in the daily lives of marginalized African American youth—in contrast to, say, those of black industrial workers or of the educated black middle class.

Youth gangs and the gangsta mentality

For a look into the worldviews of marginalized youth, a brief history of Los Angeles youth gangs proves invaluable.[7] The first such groups were formed in the early 1940s in L.A.'s Chicano community. By the 1950s and 1960s, a small number of African American youth gangs appeared, claiming names such as the Businessmen, the Gladiators, the Black Cobras, the Swamp Boys, the Boozies, the Slausons, and the Watts. "There were few shootings," however, "and crimes were relatively petty by today's standards." The August 1965 Los Angeles rebellion transformed the playing field altogether. Following that event, many gang members became politicized, joining the Black Panther Party or US organization; reflecting this constituency, the daily practices of the Black Panthers, especially on the West Coast, belied a tendency toward gangsterism. But in the wake of FBI-sponsored assassinations of BPP leaders Bunchy Carter and John Huggins by US-organization members George Stiner, Larry Stiner, and Claude Hubert in January 1969, L.A. youth-gang activity was rekindled, but with an unprecedented resort to weaponry that probably owed as much to the Panther "picking-up-the-gun" culture as it did to the paramilitary structure of Los Angeles's so-called law enforcement organizations. In the process there emerged a new generation of African American youth—highly cynical and largely depoliticized, but not completely so on either count. And central to this story was the emergence of a gang known as the Crips:

> Accounts vary widely, but oral historians agree on one of the founders. He was Raymond Washington, a Fremont High School student who had been too young to be a Black Panther but had soaked up some of the Panther rhetoric about community control of neighborhoods.
>
> After Washington was kicked out of Fremont, he wound up at Washington High, and something began to jell in the neighborhood where he lived, around 107th and Hoover streets. Whether it was simply a gang of street kids or an attempt to organize the neighborhood is not clear.[8]

Washington died in a state prison in the mid-1980s, but Crips and Bloods "sets" or 'hoods, as gang-claimed neighborhoods were called, proliferated throughout Los Angeles, counting some twenty-four thousand members spread among 260 or so gangs.[9] Rising permanent unemployment and the introduction of cheap crack cocaine in that same period hardened the economic underpinnings of gang activity, leading to homicides on an unprecedented scale.[10] Out of the turmoil of poverty, drugs, and death emerged an African American youth worldview at considerable odds with those of the more stable black working and middle classes. In place of a tendency toward "mutual respect unless proved otherwise," the new youth culture demanded immediate "props," or proper respect, giving sanction to the elimination of those misfortunate enough to "diss," or disrespect, others, however unintentionally. Misogyny and homophobia, though always present to some degree in African American life, became principal vehicles in the formation of youthful black male identity. In lieu of the all-encompassing African American group identity forged during the 1950s and 1960s, the new youth culture offered the primacy of "turf," of neighborhood territoriality, as the basis of social identification. With diminished practical reinforcement of life-affirming values emerged a callous and resigned attitude toward violence and death. And, finally, on the moral plane, devotion to individuals rapidly overcame devotion to principle, with a concomitant repudiation of individual responsibility.

But the content of message rap draws upon not only the brutal realities of present-day urban life, but the more affirmative sacred and secular influences of the late sixties and early seventies as well. The cultural and political nationalist tendencies expressed by the message constitute a direct outgrowth of parallel trends manifested in the earlier era—absent the ideological tensions that may have formerly existed. (For example, take today's reductionist pairing of Malcolm and Martin, or the relatively peaceful coexistence of cultural nationalist and revolutionary viewpoints.) On the cultural side, following the identity-oriented expressions of the sixties' Black Arts movement, the Spirit House Movers, US organization, and the like, one finds a strong identification with Africa, an emphasis on a black social identity at the expense of an American one, and an extolling of black cultural heroes. On the political plane one sees an emphasis on the struggle for African American human rights, resistance to the role of local police as occupying armies within black communities, and support for self-determination in one form or another. Here one rediscovers the secular legacies of the preceding generation: of Malcolm X in his role as political spokesman for African Americans; of the Black Power phase of the Student Non-Violent Coordinating Committee; as well as those of the Panthers, the Black Liberation Army, and others. On the sacred side we find, principally, elements of the Islamic nationalism spawned by Elijah Muhammad's Nation of Islam or NOI (1930–1975) and its off-shoots: since 1964, the Five Percenters and from 1978 onward, the reconstituted NOI itself, led by Louis Farrakhan.[11]

Overall, the strength and appeal of visionary message rap for African American youth is that, in the absence of organized political life, it not only describes and explains the existing dismal state of affairs with varying degrees of success but also imposes a stable if not rigid sense of order upon a menacing universe, with prescribed solutions to all of its ills. But where the messages of gangsta rap are content to describe in a fatalistic way the world "as it is," disclaiming any responsibility for the negativism to which gangsters themselves contribute, the nationalism of politically, culturally, or religiously oriented rappers tends toward a grand, often millennial, vision of how things might or ought to be. It is from the ranks of Islamic rappers that the sense of an ordered world—for better or for worse—remains the most elaborate, a factor which, above and beyond undeniable questions of artistry, helps to explain the popularity of this genre. By far the most potent and least-understood force in all of message rap, the Islamic connection requires particular elucidation.

Islamic nationalism: mecca and the soul brother/sister

From the 1920s onward, Islam's primary appeal to African Americans has come via its relatively color-blind approach to religious affairs.[12] Based only indirectly on Qur'anic teachings, two proto-Islamic heritages feed contemporary rap: on the one hand, that of Elijah Muhammad's Nation of Islam and its direct descendant, the NOI of Louis Farrakhan; and on the other, an NOI spinoff, the Five Per-centers—the greatest single influence in this vein. NOI ideology, launched in 1930 by the enigmatic W. D. Fard and elaborated by his eventual successor, Elijah Muhammad, from 1932 to 1975, is characterized by an apocalyptic and prophetic vision of the world. The doctrine holds that the African American, the "original" or "Asiatic" black man, fell into a state of social domination that began with slavery—a direct result of the machinations of an evil black scientist, Yakub, who grafted white people, also known as "devils," from original black people some six thousand years ago. God granted whites six thousand years to rule the planet, after which time a fiery battle was to take place in the sky, where whites would suffer defeat, and the original sense of order would be restored to earth. The devils' rule was actually up in 1914, with an additional grace period granted by Allah in order to allow the Nation of Islam to save and convert as many African Americans as possible to their true religion. A number of NOI doctrinal elements, notably those asserting a mythical Asiatic identity for African Americans, the notion that all black men are gods, that human beings create their own heaven and hell, and that Islam was the original religion of black people, were most likely extracted from Moorish Science teachings.[13] But unlike the Moorish Science Temple, by the 1950s the doctrine of Lost/Found Islam actually drew upon the Holy Qur'an for inspiration—despite the Bible's role as an even more frequent source of quotes in the elucidations of NOI leaders.

In 1958 the Nation of Islam began a thoroughgoing internal process of modernizing and mainstreaming what had been, up to that time, little more than a small, inward-looking parochial order. The ensuing development of economic resources and projects was accompanied by an economic nationalism reminiscent of Marcus Garvey's Universal Negro Improvement Association in the 1920s.[14] This newly established economic orientation, linked to a subsequent organizational influx of substantial numbers of African American middle-class professionals as well as more formally educated Muslim ministers, permanently transformed the NOI's social character. It also produced considerable internal tensions in the process. NOI ideology itself became dichotomized along sacred/secular lines, with Elijah Muhammad remaining the NOI's overarching religious patriarch and Malcolm X becoming its secular spokesman. This dichotomy was furthered by Mr. Muhammad's hiring, from the outside, a group of black editors with affiliations to the Old Left, who transformed the organization's newspaper, *Muhammad Speaks*, into the most powerful anticolonial and anti-imperialist voice on the North American continent. Its center pages, however, were properly reserved for the religious exegeses of the Honorable Elijah Muhammad.[15] By the early sixties the Nation of Islam had become a highly structured, hierarchical, and more secular-oriented association—a situation with which some of its followers may not have been entirely comfortable, even as they reaped the overall benefits of membership. Such, apparently, was the situation of Clarence Jowars Smith, otherwise known as Clarence 13X, who was reputedly expelled from the NOI's Harlem Temple No. 7 either for his gambling activities or for teaching, in an unqualified way, that "all black men are gods."[16] Although Elijah Muhammad had taught a similar truth, he also emphasized that, above all, there existed a supreme God, of which Mr. Muhammad himself was the Messenger. To affirm the godliness of all black men without qualification was to relativize divine authority, denying to any one individual the prerogative of spiritual command on earth. Inimical to the centralized leadership of Mr. Muhammad and his ministers, such thoughts would have hardly curried favor in the NOI's upper circles.[17]

But despite the unclarity surrounding the precise cause and timing of his organizational break with the NOI, we do know that when Clarence 13X left the organization, he carried with him its internally transmitted catechisms. These would provide the basis for the emergence of a new Islamic nationalist movement destined to take hold among scores of African American youth a quarter-century later. By 1964 Clarence 13X had established an alternative, more loose-knit organization of Harlem street youth—some would say "gang"—known as the Five Percenters. Doctrinally rooted in the early, "secret" writings of NOI founder W. D. Fard but committed to a relativization of male divinity, the Five Percenters proffered additional metaphysical novelties in the form of a Supreme Alphabet and Supreme Mathematics.[18] In the blink of a third eye the Five Percent founder was transformed into "Allah," Harlem was renamed Mecca, and Brooklyn became Medina following "Allah's" later relocation there. Women metamorphosed into Moons who basked in the luminous wisdom of male Suns. The counterparts of masculine Gods, females were also Earths who dutifully prepared their bodies for the implantation of divine seed. And "G," the seventh letter of the Supreme Alphabet, which stood for God, became the appellation by which young black men would heartily greet one another on the street. Describing the group in these early years, an FBI informant noted: "The 'Five Percenters,' who are, on occasion, referred to as the 'Brotherhood of Blackmen' or the 'Brotherhood of Allah,' is a loosely knit group of Negro youth gangs in the Harlem section of New York City."[19] Another informant estimated the total number of members to be around 200: 125 in Harlem and an additional 75 spread throughout the Bronx, Brooklyn, and Queens boroughs, with the majority concentrated in the Fort Greene area of Brooklyn and the St. Mary's Park section of the Bronx.

Like much of Five Percent doctrine, the original meaning of "five percent" itself was culled from Nation of Islam teachings—in this case a forty-question NOI catechism, "Lost Found Moslem Lesson No. 2," written in 1934 by Nation of Islam founder W. D. Fard:

14. Question: Who is the 85%?
    Answer: The uncivilized people, poison animal eaters, slaves from mental death and power.

    People who do not know the living god or their origin in this world and they worship that they know not what, and who are easily led in the wrong direction but hard to lead into the right direction.

15. Question: Who is the 10%?
    Answer: The rich, the slave makers of the poor, who teach the poor lies to believe that the almighty true and living god is a spook and cannot be seen with the physical eye. Otherwise known as the bloodsucker of the poor.

16. Question: Who is the 5% on this poor part of the earth?
    Answer: They are the poor, righteous teachers who do not believe in the teaching of the 10% and are all wise and know who the living god is and teach that the living god is the Son of Man, the supreme being, the black man of Asia; and teach freedom, justice and equality to all the human families of the planet earth, otherwise known as civilized people, also is Moslem and Moslem sons.[20]

A loosely structured crew, Five Percenters interpreted their organizational name in creatively ambiguous ways. For example, in the mid-1960s they reportedly described themselves as "the five percent of Muslims who smoke and drink." Another version held that 85 percent of blacks were cattle, 10 percent were "Uncle Toms," and the remaining 5 percent were the "poor righteous teachers"—the real leaders of black Americans.[21] In yet another version—much closer to the original—Five Percenters held that 10 percent of the population were responsible for the suffering of all the rest. Five percent, however, were "poor, righteous teachers" fully cognizant of the situation, and willing to sacrifice their lives in order to bring about a new society. The remaining 85 percent were "deaf, dumb, and blind," and needed the 5 percent in order to show them the way out of their suffering.[22] In "The Lost Tribe of Shabazz," from the title track of his 1991 album, Islamic rapper Lakim Shabazz runs down the Five Percent ethos:

My people were took from the motherland by the other man
Brought to the wilderness like a ventriloquist
Played my people like puppets by playing fear in their heart
Nowadays most of us don't know where to start.

Ten percent of us can help, but don't feel the need
They love greed, and this really bothers me
Eighty-five percent of us are totally ignorant
Walkin' around with a nigga mentality
Five percent of us are ready to die
for the cause, so pause, the source is Elijah.

The death of Elijah Muhammad in February 1975 wrought far-reaching changes to the original Nation of Islam. Muhammad's son and spiritual/political heir, Wallace Muhammad, dropped the NOI name and quickly propelled the organization toward more traditional Islamic moorings. Members dissatisfied with these changes eventually rallied behind Minister Louis Farrakhan, who formed a reconstituted Nation of Islam in 1978, adopting all the ideological tenets of the original association.[23] Like that of its parent organization, the attraction of the new NOI lay in a mythical vision of the world that explained that world's origins, established the identity and "place" of the African American in it, and foretold the coming of imminent, divine retribution; a promise of African American economic self-sufficiency; and a sense of personal "safety" and structure for those willing to submit to NOI ritual and discipline. Five Percenters, on the other hand, drew and still draw freely upon the NOI's creation mythology, millennial vision, and fictive Asiatic identity, but without having to subject themselves to its strict internal rules. Absent any consequent organizational structure or recognized leader of stature, its members continue to pay nominal respect to Louis Farrakhan and Elijah Muhammad as well, all the while preserving the memory of their group's founder, "Father Allah."[24]

Spreading from its 1960s New York City origins, the amorphous association is now well established in a number of urban areas throughout New Jersey, and beyond. In fact, today it is probably incorrect to refer to the Five Percenters as a single organization. This extraordinary growth of the Five Percent following Clarence 13X's assassination in June 1969 remains, for the most part, an undocumented process. And it is, of course, the followers of Five Percent Islam who make up the great majority of Islamic rappers today: Grand Puba, Poor Righteous Teachers, Lakim Shabazz, King Sun, Eric B. & Rakim, Movement X, KMD, Two Kings in a Cypher, A Tribe Called Quest, and many other lesser known groups and individuals.[25] Even Big Daddy Kane ("Pimping Ain't Easy") claims Five Percent allegiance.

While the principle alignment of most Islamic-based rappers lies with the Five Percenters, a few have gravitated toward the orbit of Farrakhan's Nation. Some, like NOI supporters Public Enemy and Professor Griff, former minister of information for PE, have remained outside the organization proper.[26] Others, like Chicago-based Prince Akeem, who, prior to Ice Cube's recent conversion, had been the only bona fide member of Farrakhan's NOI to achieve prominence as a rapper, have shown themselves willing to submit to a collective will. Listen as Prince Akeem throws down regarding the government plot against African Americans:

The government
Is schemin' on the Black Man
Disguisin' drugs, so he can
Paint a picture of youth
Slangin', gang bangin'
Hangin', Cone is just black
The plans at hand
To destroy the Black Man
I push on Bush because I can
Lay out the plot, come on now
Take ya for a ride
The plan is this, they call it genocide.[27]

The message: intersecting themes of resignation and resistance, raunch and redemption

The various themes of message rap are themselves defined by opposing tendencies, with message-bearing gangsta rappers tending to coalesce at one pole of the spectrum, and those holding more visionary spiritual or political outlooks commingling at the other. Here one encounters at least three predilections: a morality rooted in interpersonal loyalties on one side contrasted to one that is grounded in more universally applied principles; a shameless exploitation of negative African American stereotypes in the pursuit of crossover record sales on one hand, as opposed to the explicit rejection of such stereotypes and cultivation of positive black images on the other; and a fatalistic and cynical view of the world ("that's just how things are") at one end countered by one that leans toward visionary possibilities at the other ("here is how things might be").[28] Where both visionary and gangsta rap may manifest an antisocial character with respect to the dominant society, gangsta rap is antisocial with respect to the black community itself. (One can flee from the police or the FBI for a wide variety of reasons, not all of them explicitly political.) And where gangsters seem to fall back on individualistic solutions to social problems, the vision oriented tend toward more collective ones.

Nonetheless, gangsta and visionary message rap are not as far apart as they may at first appear. For example, where gangsta males denigrate women in the worst way ("Bitch Better Have My Money"), and the more idealistic place them on pedestals ("Black Queen of the Universe"), both positions reinforce the subjugation of women. Indeed, masculine identity in either case is defined at the expense of women in general and gay men in particular (lesbians are virtually ignored). Today, in many ways, rap plays a role with respect to these two groups that D. W. Griffith's infamous film *Birth of a Nation* enjoyed with respect to African Americans overall circa World War I: artistic innovation and creativity, to be sure, but with an antihumanist content.

The centrality of the rebel figure to both genres has already been noted. Moreover, the interconnections between gangsta and visionary rap are rendered even more concrete through the discovery that popular artists like KRS One and Ice Cube, for example, freely glide back and forth between the two categories. In fact, with the 1992 issue of *Sex and Violence*, KRS One/BDP came full circle, since "9mm Goes Bang" from their album *Criminal Minded* belongs to the pioneering ranks of gangsta rap.[29] Since his enlistment into the ranks of the Nation of Islam, on the other hand, Ice Cube has not so much left behind gangsterism as he has fused it with NOI eschatology, giving birth to a novel form that might properly be called "gangsta armageddon," where apocalyptic vision is indistinguishable from negative, contemporary reality.[30]

On the salutary side, virtually all manifestations of message rap bear witness to resistance against overt external oppression—especially that coming from occupying forces in blue. The role of the police all too often is, as Ice-T observes, "To serve, protect, and break a niggaz neck." In "——— the Police," from *Straight outta Compton* (1988), NWA condemn the unrelenting police harassment of young African Americans:

> Fuck the police, comin' straight from the underground
> A young nigga got it bad, cause I'm brown
> And not the other color, so police think
> They have the authority to kill a minority.

Unleashing a torrent of words that falls somewhere between rapping and a jeremiad with a beat, Sister Souljah warns in the album *360 Degrees of Power* (1992) in "The Final Solution" that slavery's back in effect":

We are at war!
That's what I told ya!
I know you heard what the president said
And if the nigger don't move, then he's dead
It's time for us to take a stand
Woman to woman and man to man
Blood rushes through your veins, you feel the fear
Who would've thought that this would happen here
In the land of the free, home of the brave
The year is '95, you're a slave.

And citing Boston's Charles Stuart case as an example, Ed O.G. runs down the racial disparities in the criminal justice system:

Here's the reason that I've been upset for a while
Cause if you're black, you get life
But if you're white, you're on trial.
Ain't nothin' to it, just like that chump Charles Stuart
They always claim that the devil made me do it.
For insurance he killed his wife and his child
And blamed it on a brother and the racists went buck wild.[31]

One observes as well the celebration of the rebel, political or otherwise, who dares to flaunt societal norms that operate to the detriment (and also benefit, as in the case of maintaining basic standards of civility) of African Americans as a whole. As rapper Tupac Shakur notes, "That's bullshit when a rapper says he don't want to be a role model. You become a role model 'cause what's the biggest role model? The rebel."[32] Here both the gangster as well as the politically oriented conflate the role of gang banger or political fugitive, respectively, with that of rebellious rapper. For example, in the title track from *100 Miles and Runnin'* (1990) NWA boast of being

A nigga wit' nothin' to lose
One of the few who's been accused and abused
With the crime of poisonin' young minds
But you don't know shit 'til you've been in my shoes.

Similarly, in Public Enemy's "Raise the Roof" from *Yo! Bum Rush the Show* (1987), the roles of communist, terrorist, fugitive, entrepreneur, and individual rapper are merged into one:

And for real it's the deal and the actual fact,
Takes a nation of millions to hold me back
Rejected and accepted as a communist
Claimin' fame to my name as a terrorist
Makin' money in corners that you'll never see
Dodgin' judges and the lawyers and the third degree

Nothin' wrong with a song to make the strong survive
Realize gave me five cause I kept 'em alive.

Hardly confined to masculine expressions, the rebel is similarly celebrated in the rhymes of Sister Souljah as well as in the title track of Isis's *Rebel Soul* (1990):

The battle cry for freedom, shout aloud
And it gets sweat drops from the black crowd
The strong with the magic, I am the bearer
The rhythms of my words, my mind is your mirror
Let the war drums on the road
Stand brave and witness rebel soul.

Even more deadly than the police violence waged against African American communities is the internal warfare rooted in drug-related activities. With the rapid growth of inner-city youth gangs and the crack-cocaine trade in the 1980s, the social identities of African American youth in urban areas became increasingly tied to conspicuous commodity consumption: the wearing of expensive jumpsuits, sneakers, watches, rings, thick gold chains (known as "dookie" gold), and the like. Hip hop hairstyles with corporate logos carved in them (Gucci or Dom Perignon, for example) became avenues for youth identification with lifestyles of the rich and powerful. With a cheapening of life wrought by inner-city drug wars, the desire for flashy and costly items led to increasing numbers of murders of black youth by one another, and to the intensification of "black-on-black" crime in general.[33] While rappers tended to emulate and even promote such consumption during an earlier phase, the message rappers of the third wave—including some of the gangstas—have instead emphasized the need to halt internecine black violence and organize for a safer community. In 1990 two major cultural undertakings by rappers to stem the wave of urban violence were registered on the East and West Coasts ("Stop the Violence" and "We're All in the Same Gang," respectively). Out of such efforts gangsta rappers Ren and Dr. Dre of NWA, for their part, invoke a nationalistic appeal in order to curb intracommunity warfare:

Bullets flyin', mothers dyin', brothers dyin'
Lyin' in the streets, that's why we're tryin'
To stop it from fallin' apart and goin' to waste
And keepin' a smile off a white face.[34]

Included in the category of urgent messages are those of gangstas with second thoughts: the Lifer's Group of New Jersey's Rahway Prison.[35] Their basic admonitions to youth are that prison life is pure hell, and that one should lead a life away from any possible interaction with the criminal-justice system. Indeed, a casual hearing of the uncensored versions of "The Real Deal," "Belly of the Beast," and "Nightmare Man" are sufficient to convince most of us. From "Nightmare Man" on the album *Lifer's Group* (1991), a few of the more tranquil lines:

Here in Mr. Gilmore's house
the house of pain, where you can go insane
you'll meet me, your Nightmare Man, Crazy Chris
I'll use you, abuse you, and cause you pain
I'll teach you hate by goya, and plenty of paranoia.

Assessing the high cost of alcoholism on African American communities, not just in terms of alcohol-related diseases but also in incidences of drunken violence and consequent deaths, Public Enemy equates coroners' body bags with "1 Million Bottlebags." In "Night of the Living Baseheads" PE similarly examines the social expense of freebasing and crack smoking. The more specific theme of mothers on crack is carefully explored in Tupac Shakur's "Part Time Mutha" as well as in Yomo and Maulkey's "Mama Don't." And, finally, W.C. and the MAAD Circle pay homage to fathers everywhere in "Fuck My Daddy."[36]

Escape into alcohol or other drugs does not necessarily mark the end of the search for inner peace in the inner city. For example, in a prayer rap called "Tennessee," on the album *3 Years, 5 Months, and 2 Days in the Life of . . .* , lead rapper Speech of Arrested Development expresses a sense of demoralization due to urban strife and searches for a quiet place in the countryside he called his boyhood home:

Lord I've really been real stressed
Down and out, losin' ground
Although I am black & proud
Problems got me pessimistic
Why does it have to be so tuff?
I don't know where I could go
To let these ghosts out of my skull
My grandma passed, my bother's gone
I never at once felt so all alone.

"Take me to another place," he pleads, "Take me to another land / Make me forget all that hurts me / Let me understand your plan."

Invoking "The Evil That Men Do" on *All Hail the Queen* (1989), Queen Latifah wants to know why money spent on personal entertainment cannot be channeled to the needy:

Tell me, don't you think it's a shame
When someone can put a quarter in a video game
But when a homeless person approaches you on the street
You can't treat 'em the same?

In "Language of Violence" from the album *Hypocrisy Is the Greatest Luxury* (1992), on the other hand, the improbable team of Michael Franti (African American) and Rono Tse (Vietnamese), together known as Hiphoprisy, relates the story of a young man presumed to be gay, who was brutally murdered by his schoolmates for that reason:

> He knew the names that they would taunt him with
> faggot, sissy, punk, queen, queer
> although he'd never had sex in his fifteen years
> And when they harassed him
> it was for a reason
> And when they provoked him
> it became open season.

Further demonstrating the wide range of social concerns with which message rap is concerned, Yo-Yo's "Put a Lid on It" warns young women of the consequences of having babies out of wedlock. The more delicate subject of incest is openly explored in De La Soul's "Millie Pulled a Pistol on Santa" as well as in Shakur's "Part Time Mutha."[37] In the latter selection, a female rapper relates the terror of living in an incestuous relationship with her stepfather while her mother, high on crack, remains oblivious to the world around her:

> I grew up in a home where no one liked me
> Mom would hit the pipe and every night she would fight
> Papa was a nasty old man like the rest
> He's feeling on my chest with his hands on my dress. . . .
>
> I want to tell mom, but when she's missed
> She's bound to be bitchin' and she hasn't got a fixin'.

In "Jimmy," on the album *By All Means Necessary* (1988), KRS One takes a positive lead in sounding the alarm against AIDS but stumbles into the ranks of the grossly misinformed when he cautions a need for condoms only in winter!

> 'Cause in winter AIDS attacks
> So run out and get your jimmy hats
> It costs so little for a pack of three
> Get jimmy hats for the winter attack.

"Droppin' science": visions of a more congruous order

Once we are beyond immediate issues of mental or physical survival, reflection at a more profound level kicks in. One of the first questions to arise is, How did we African Americans arrive at the wretched state in which we now find ourselves? Here there is a tendency to rely on the explanatory powers of mythology, as in the case of Islamic rappers discussed earlier; biological determinism, as suggested by Chuck D of Public Enemy,[38] a crude economic-determinist model based upon relations between procurers and prostitutes—more colloquially, "pimps and hos"—as elaborated by BDP's KRS One during his "humanist" phase;[39] or in the moralistic terms of Queen Latifah, the "evil that men do." Once we are satisfied as to the "cause" of the existing state of affairs, the next question concerns how things can once again be made righteous, in mind as well as in societal relations. For the Islamic (male) rappers especially, the issues that swing into play invoke strict orderings of social identity, gender relations, sexuality, and even eating practices, for these are aspects of one's life over which one may more easily exercise direct and immediate control. But other rappers are no less concerned with exercising a revitalized sense of personal order. In "My Philosophy," for example, KRS One extols the virtues of vegetarianism:

> It's about time one of y'all hear it
> First hand, from an intelligent brown man
> A vegetarian, no goat or ham
> Or chicken, or turkey, or hamburger
> 'Cause to me that's suicide, self-murder.[40]

Gender identity / gender roles and relations

The gender roles and relations subscribed to by male rappers are of a highly conservative nature. Within NOI ideology, for example, one of the first steps toward returning to the "original" order resides in "re-establishing" the total subjugation of women to men. Justifying such action by the need to control rampant black female sexuality (and thereby maintain as well the presumed existence of "racial purity"), Elijah Muhammad once advised his followers:

> But, still, go out there today—right now—and you will see every color out there looking at the Black woman. They want her! She's the best walking in the Sun! We're going to take her; we're going to tie her up at home. We know she is the best. We're going to tie her at home an set the bedsteads on her if necessary to keep her there! We're not going to let her run rampant—not like wild animals. She is too good. She is too beautiful![41]

The gender order envisioned by Five Percenters is also highly traditional. Within the Five Percent worldview, the counterpart of male divinity is female fecundity: black men are Gods, black women are Earths. Consequently, "F" in the Supreme Alphabet stands for "Father": "one who is qualified to give life mentally as well as physically. FATHER means to FAT-HER with a true knowledge of herself so that she can show her EQUALITY by rearing the children properly." Assigned to the letter "U," "The UNIVERSE is everything; SUN-MAN, MOON-WOMAN, STARS-BA-BIES."[42] In "Mahogany," from *Let the Rhythm Hit 'Em* (1990), Rakim informs us of changes in the demeanor of his "tenderoni" Moon after exposing her to his self-generated solar activity:

> She's "live-er" and much more wiser
> From the light I shine and her brain cells spark
> Constantly, so she can glow in the dark

Soon you can represent the moon
As long as I keep you in tune
I'll tell you who you are and why you are here.
Take it in stride, 'cause it might take a year.

For the spiritually oriented but non-Islamic rapper Kool Moe Dee, on the other hand, it is "funke wisdom" that guides him to a more complete, if abstract, egalitarianism in male/female relations:

Women—very significant
Power is what she represents
Contrary to what many brothers believe

Learn the metaphysical meaning of Eve
When you get funke wisdom then you'll understand
The woman is the driving force for any powerful man. . . .

Any man without a woman is incomplete
And vice-versa, she's obsolete
So I make sure, then, at the heart of my system
I got funke, funke wisdom.[43]

In general, young black women have been placed on the defensive by the misogynist behavior of men, whether in a "guttering" or "pedastaling" mode.[44] In responding to male-imposed images of women as sluts, "hos," and "skeezers," or as "gold-diggers" or blank minds to be imprinted with a masculine pedagogical stamp, female rappers Queen Latifah and Queen Mother Rage, for example, have found the authoritative garb of the royal black female image far more to their liking. Isis, for her part, is more attracted to the role of black goddess. The best known of the three, Queen Latifah posits salutary moral "laws" for her subjects to follow. And in "Ladies First" on *All Hail the Queen* (1989), Latifah and guest performer Monie Love rap praise rhymes to the "woman standin' up on her own two," whether as rapper or in the wider social context—offering a parallel to the conflation of rapper and rebel described earlier. In an even stronger vein, Sister Souljah in the title cut from *360 Degrees of Power* (1992) steadfastly refuses to accept any secondary role assigned black women:

I'm coming up from the bottom and I'm damn sure rising
You tried to stop me so I guess I'm surprising
I'll never keep quiet, so don't even try it
Sit in the back row, I won't buy it
Necessary but secondary, that's your insecurity
You fear my essence, my soul, my mind, and Black man
          you fear my purity.

Yo-Yo's South Central–style feminism, on the other hand, depicts the "new, intelligent black woman" as one concerned with the general plight of African

American females. But there are some who question the behaviors sanctioned in Yo-Yo's lyrics, such as drinking "Eight-Ball" (Old English 800 malt liquor) or threatening to "smoke" (shoot) any woman who protests Yo-Yo's enticing away her man.[45]

National and civic identity

A profound ambivalence in the national and civic identities of African Americans can be traced back as far as the northern free black community of the early American republic.[46] The nationalist side is represented in a historically evolving Afrocentric cultural identity and an attitude toward the American state that has taken alternative as well as oppositional forms. With respect to cultural identity, an attempt to paint a more positive vision of Africa is what inspired Jungle Brothers to adopt their group's very name. In "Black Is Black" the group invokes the centrality of a pro-black identity for African Americans:

Black is black is black is black
In America today, I have to regret to say
Somethin', somethin' is not right, and it deals with black and white
Tell me my G, is it me? naw, it's just society
Propaganda, huh? why is it we meander, huh?
In a zone with hateful beasts, all of this BS must cease
All I am is one black man in a mighty big white hand
Brother, brother, sister, sister, if you're miss or if you're mister
Listen, please, to this fact: black is black is black is black.[47]

The overriding character of African American identity and interests also motivates the lyrics of Sister Souljah's "Hate That Hate Produced" on *360 Degrees of Power*:

Souljah was not born to make white people feel comfortable
I am African first, I am Black first
I want what's good for me and my people first
And if my survival means your total destruction, then so be it
You built this wicked system
They say two wrongs don't make it right
But it damn sure makes it even.

To hard-core political rappers, the national symbols of U.S. civic identity have become a ready target. For example, the group Juvenile Delinquintz, in a cut by the same name on Terminator X's *In the Valley of the Jeep Beets* (1991), challenges a teacher's request to salute the American flag:

Why pledge allegiance if a nigga ain't patriotic?
So you sent me to the dean, Marcello
She filed a compliant and wrote up a fellow

'Cause I didn't put my right hand on my chest
And fall victim to the next man's progress
I got mad and kicked a crater in the wall
Broke down shit with a stick like Walking Tall
'Cause the African American got offended
I slapped a dean and then got suspended
By a bitch in a red, white, and blue dress
I went home on a parental request.

Similarly, rapping at a time when the U.S. Supreme Court had just upheld flag burning as an expression of First Amendment rights, Yomo and Maulkey in "Glory" on *Are U Experienced?* (1991) tell their listeners:

By the dawn's early light
America's situation is not right
No matter how much they ignore me
They can't, 'cause I can say "burn old glory."

And in response to George Bush's sending troops to the Persian Gulf in January 1991, the Geto Boys responded with "F——— a War" on *We Can't Be Stopped* (1991):

Motherfuck a war, that's how I feel
Send a nigga to the desert to get killed
Cause two suckers can't agree on something
A thousand motherfuckers die for nothing
You can't pay me to join an army camp
Or any other military branch
Of this united goddamned face of that bitch, America.

Before rushing to embrace the Geto Boys, however, pacifists should take note that the group's resistance to war is more an individualistic affair than a principled one. "Y'all lucky I ain't the president," they affirm (and we, no doubt, would agree), "Cause I'd push the motherfucking button and get it over with / Fuck all that waitin' and procastinatin' / And all that goddamn negotiatin'."

Issues of African American national identity are central to two disputes in which message rappers are currently embroiled: the "humanism" of KRS One and Boogie Down Productions, and the market-crossover phenomenon. From the very beginning, KRS One appeared uncomfortable with the black identity label: "I'm not white or red or black, I'm brown," he informed us in his second album, *By All Means Necessary*, in 1988. With his launching of the H.E.A.L. (Human Education Against Lies) Project in 1991, KRS One affirmed his social identity as a human being first:

The H.E.A.L. Project simply says that before you are a race, a religion or an occupation, you are a human being. Once we begin to act human, we can act African correctly. If you're thinking African and not human, you're not a correct African. You've got to think correctly, from the human aspect of yourself. Here I am a human being. I'm not Black, I'm brown, I'm not white, I'm beige. I'm not Jewish, I'm a human being.[48]

This "humanistic" disposition immediately drew flack from more nationalist-oriented rappers such as XCLAN on their 1992 album *XODUS*, after which XCLAN's Professor X attempted to clarify the situation:

Politicians have differences in opinion and philosophies with each other, like Democrats and Republicans. But that does not stop them from having dinner and playing tennis and golf. We differ with KRS-One's philosophy—the humanist view in young Black people does not leave them focused on the real atrocities placed on their existence. Ours is a pro-Black view. We do not have any problem with KRS-One personally. When it comes time to fight I think KRS-One would be a person I would trust at my side. We're not mad at him man.[49]

Unmollified as well as chastened by the low record sales of H.E.A.L.'s *Civilization vs. Technology* album, KRS One recently and angrily reaffirmed his particularity as a black man within a universally defined humanity: "I lecture and rap without rehearsal / I manifest as a black man but I'm universal."

Now what's this all about Chris and humanity?
In my face you're happy but in private you're mad at me
Yo! Pro-blackness is your solution
But I really don't know about the style you're using
Yo! Too many teachers in the class spoil school
After a while, you've got blabberin', fuckin' fools
This person is talking about sex
It ain't enough to study Clarence 13X
The white man ain't the devil, I promise
If you want to see the devil take a look at Clarence Thomas
Now you're sayin' "who?" like you're an owl
Throw in the towel, the devil is Colin Powell.[50]

The highly charged issue surrounding crossover record hits—that is, rap records whose content is deliberately diluted in order to appeal to the pop market, i.e. the white music mainstream—reached a new level of acuteness with the 1992 release of EPMD's deftly executed "Crossover."[51] But the issue is more complex than it might first appear. Increasingly disenchanted with the quality of society pushed upon them by the radical Right over the past decade, white youth, and young white males in particular, are increasingly attracted to the socially rebellious stance of hip hop culture.[52] In this way the crossover phenomenon may be seen, in part, as an unanticipated by-product of a black-oriented cultural activity. But when PE, for example, records "Bring the Noize" on *Apocalypse 91 . . . The Enemy Strikes Back* (1991) with the rock group Anthrax and subsequently tours the country on the white rock circuit, one can be sure that they do so with crossover dollars in their eyes. What makes Public Enemy's approach so ingenious, however, is that the group manages to pull all of this off without any political dilution of its message.[53] For others, however, politics never once entered into the equation. When, for example, Ezy-E on the title cut from NWA's *Niggaz4Life* (1992) unleashes cynical lines like, "Why do I call myself a nigga so quick? / So I can reach in my drawers and pull out a bigger dick," thereby invoking hypersexual, stereotypical images of Bigger Thomas (and his judicial cousin, Clarence), one can rest assured that the marketing target lies squarely outside the African American community. With the release of *Body Count* (1992), Ice-T was added to the crossover ranks. While no one can accuse his album of having reneged on the message side, it nonetheless tilts forcefully toward white audience appeal with its heavy-metal musical backing.[54] In openly and acerbically criticizing the crossover phenomenon, however, rappers and magazine pundits have generally ignored these particular manifestations.

Enmeshed in market relations of the larger society, imprinted with heavy borrowings from the dominant culture, the cultural crossover of rap music remains a fact of life. Black youth of the 1990s appropriate the peace symbol of the 1960s white youth counterculture as their own, and no one blinks an eye. For truly if, by some sleight of hand, the existence of black cultural purity might yet be claimed, it would arrive only at the expense of its own dynamism. Still, the struggle to maintain boundaries, however elusive or illusory, remains a critical issue. Whatever the pitfalls of national consciousness—and they are legion—African American liberation will eventually be won or lost around the question of how, precisely, black national identity is politically harnessed.

Putative solutions: education and community control

From the antebellum era onward, education has remained a major concern for African Americans. If message rap is any indication of the beliefs of contemporary black youth, concern with educational issues has lost little of the vigor of yesteryear.[55] What has changed, and probably for the worse, is how knowledge itself is defined. Most message rappers view *education*—one that specifically teaches one's "true" and "original" social identity—as the solution to the basic social ills of African Americans. For the Armageddon-inclined, the day of judgment marks that juncture where black people, having acquired self-knowledge, shall inherit a social identity and social structure no longer at odds with one another, and a just and lasting peace shall return once more to Planet Earth. For the somewhat more politically astute such as Sister Souljah or Public Enemy, on the other hand, the issue of *community control*—with the formation of powerful and dynamic black business enterprises at the core—constitutes the primary road to self-determination. By no means a reprise of the W.E.B. Du Bois/Booker T. Washington "debate" at the turn of the last century, there is, nonetheless, at least one parallel to be observed: Whether through education or economic entrepreneuralism, the envisioned new "order," as well as the means to that order advanced by the vast majority of rappers, remains distinctly conservative in political terms, notwithstanding frequent contemporary allusions to AK-47 rifles, military formations, or incendiary devices. Militant form, as old-school veterans know too well, should never be confused with revolutionary political content.

On the community-control side, Chuck D notes that "we got to take control of our community and it takes hardcore efforts—being hardcore and positive. We try to show that PE has a strong man and woman point of view, which means if you're over 18, all that fun and games and baby shit got to be tucked away to the side. Business and responsibility has got to be number one and two." But "business is family," and "we ain't got family the way it's supposed to be. So I mean, we've got to go to a school or structure that can teach us family."[56] Hence education and business are indissolubly linked.

In demanding reparations from U.S. corporations, Chuck D advances the argument traditionally used for small neighborhood businesses owned by community outsiders:

> I have a song called "Shut-em Down," about how they got businesses in our community that's just gettin' paid and we're smokin' so much money. I like Nike, but wait a minute—my neighborhood supports them, so they should put some money back in it. The corporations owe us, they got to give up the dough to my crew and my talent, or we got to shut-em down. The best way to boycott a business is not standin' in front of them actin' like monkeys and bangin' on windows, tellin' them to get out! No, you open up your own business and support your own. That's the only way.[57]

And, finally, despite its lack of a credible track record in the economic realm, the post-1975 Nation of Islam's nationalistic quest for economic self-sufficiency appeals strongly to those rappers drawn to the world of petty capitalism—Chuck D and Ice Cube among them.[58] Describing his change in outlook following the birth of his son, Ice Cube recently remarked:

> It opened my eyes. He's not going to have to beg for a job. That's what really made me get involved with the Nation [of Islam], because it's like I don't want him to have to go through the school system and beg for a job at the end. You know, just begging for crumbs from master's table, the thing that Negroes are doing nowadays. I don't want my son to have to fall into that. I want my son to be able to go into a Black business or start his own business, you know, to have something for ourselves.[59]

Concerning the issue of education, in the world of message rap at least three spheres of knowledge are addressed: formal, street, and "scientific." Generally speaking, the body of formal knowledge transmitted at the primary and secondary levels of the public school system is deemed irrelevant to the needs of African American youth. The "lie-bury" (library), moreover, is the place where white folks "bury their lies." Rapper Wise Intelligent of Poor Righteous Teachers describes the situation of sitting in the school all day in history, a must pass class, and they're telling you that George Washington cut down the cherry tree, Christopher Columbus discovered America, Aristotle, Plato, and Socrates are the fathers of philosophy. You're thinking what did black people do? Teach me black history. This school is dominated by black youth, why are we subjected to learning white or caucasian history? So I went outside of school and gained information that wasn't being presented to me.[60]

The process of education consists of the transmission of a certain body of knowledge, values, and skills. Reading into Wise Intelligent's criticism of the formal process, what the curriculum lacks is knowledge about black people—an indication, as well, of the value assigned things Eurocentric. KRS One of Boogie Down Productions observes, moreover, that values transmitted in the classroom often assign greater weight to technological achievement than to the quality of human relations:

> The educational system teaches people to feel that civilization is measured by the tools that a given society creates. In other words, just because we can go to the moon, we have fast cars, boats, planes, etc., etc. that does not make us civilized. The concept "civilization vs. technology" is basically the war of good and evil. Which basically is a war between the civilized and the technological, or should I say the civilized and the barbarian.[61]

Notwithstanding the very real weaknesses of public education, the danger, however, is that knowledge and skills necessary to functioning in a highly technical society will be rejected along with the Eurocentric orientation of the educational system. It is in this vein that Chuck D, in his inimitable way, sends a warning to black youth: "It's true, they're not teaching us our history at school. Those muthafuckas are sayin', 'I ain't supposed to.' They don't give a fuck. But you better get through high school, and whatever they teach, you better do your best to learn it. Spend less time drinkin' them damn 40's [bottles of forty-ounce malt liquor], spend less time on the corner and more time in them books."[62]

Implicitly defined, for the most part, street knowledge is learnedness acquired from one's life experiences in a harsh urban setting, knowledge basically concerned with survival skills: how to avoid being taken advantage of while gaining greatest advantage for oneself.

The highest level of understanding, "scientific" knowledge, lies on the plane of wisdom, which usually denotes a metaphysics influenced in one way or another by astrology or numerology, both often filtered through Masonic teachings. Invoking "Funke Wisdom," the title cut on his 1991 album, *Funke, Funke Wisdom*, Kool Moe Dee believes that those who "live for the money" are worshiping pseudoscience, a "material math":

> Mathematically it all adds up
> All people are equal, but equal to what?
> Once you understand that there's a spirit to math
> Add soul to the science and subtract the riff-raff

24-7-3-65, 'cause 9 to 5 ain't live, we're in no-drive
Take the first power, elevate to the third
Manifest the power of the spoken word
Three hundred and sixty degrees of subliminal
Fortify the book of forty-four minerals
Four elements and four seasons
Four corners of the world, it's all even
Mother nature and father time
Align with the nine planets and combine
To influence the mind and control the whole system
Knowledge ain't enough—you need funke, funke wisdom.

In the case of Five Percent NOI rappers, especially, wisdom resides in a metaphysics that filters the world through a Supreme Alphabet and Supreme Mathematics. The twenty-six categories of the Supreme Alphabet and the additional ten of the Supreme Mathematics furnish overarching guidance for everyday life. For example, in an exposition that might have baffled the Prophet Muhammad himself, the Supreme Alphabet's letter "I" stands for "ISLAM meaning I-SELF-LORD-AND-MASTER [and], in the case of men, I-SELF-LOVE-ALLAH'S-MATHE-MATICS. ISLAM is the Black man, woman and child's true CULTURE meaning way of life." Similarly, the numerals one, two, and three in the Supreme Mathematics stand for KNOWLEDGE ("know the ledge"), WISDOM ("the manifestation of one's knowledge"), and UNDERSTANDING ("the clear picture drawn up in one's mind through knowledge and wisdom"), respectively. The sum of 1 + 2 (knowledge plus wisdom) yields 3 (understanding), thereby placing one's comprehension of the universe on a scientific foundation.[63]

As "poor, righteous teachers," Islamic-oriented rappers are imbued with the duty to proselytize, to spread the truth as they understand it, to every corner of the 85 percent world. In fact, virtually all message rappers seem to consciously regard themselves as teachers with a mission to address the failings of the educational system as regards African American youth. In the opinion of Sister Souljah,

> Hip-hop is a blessing because the [Poor] Righteous Teachers, Brand Nubian and KRS-One have actually been *the* educational system for Black kids, in place of the so-called educational system that is entirely financed by the American government. And in the absence of the voice of young people in hip-hop, we would have even more chaos than we have today.[64]

When not comporting himself in gangsta fashion, KRS One in "My Philosophy" on *By All Means Necessary* (1988) considers his role of teacher in a double way: as an instructor of how "dope" rhymes should be fashioned and as a philosopher contemplating how life should best be lived. "I am a teacher and Scott [La Rock] is a scholar / It ain't about money 'cause we all make dollars." "Teachers teach and do the world good." They also work to counter negative stereotypes:

But I don't walk this way to portray
Or reinforce stereotypes of today
Like all my brothers eatin' chicken and watermelon
Talk broken English and drug sellin'.

The political limits of message rap: defending the king holiday or jeffersonian bumrush?

With respect to the visionary apostles of message rap, Nation of Islam ideology has proved to be the most extensively developed, presenting a cosmology that claims detailed knowledge of the origins of the universe as well as that of black oppression. Offering a transformed social identity—the lost/found "Asiatic black man"—unencumbered by the weight of recorded history, it envisions an ordering of male/female relations founded upon the suppression of women's rights, a belief in millennial salvation, and a rigorous personal discipline reinforced by the vigilance of the Fruit of Islam. Drawing freely upon NOI doctrine, the worldview proffered by Five Percenters, on the other hand, is not much different. But the absence of hierarchical organizational structure and imposed discipline within the Five Percent has allowed for wide-ranging individual interpretations of doctrine, the notion that "all black men are gods" further serving to nullify the authority of male members over one another and thereby preserve individual autonomy.

The political limits of message rap have as much to do with its medium of propagation as with the absence of any current, widespread, grass-roots movement among African Americans for fundamental political change in the United States. Beset by a fragmentation and dilution of its content spurred by powerful market forces, message rap remains a strategic hostage of the audio/video recording industry whose charts it so assiduously rides in tactical terms. And hostage in another sense as well: to the selective and subtle censorship imposed by the corporate owners of the means of record production and distribution, its measures revealed at those precise moments when the political danger posed by African American militancy is deemed of greater consequence than "crazy dollars" to be squeezed from the message itself.[65] Moreover, in the absence of a mass-based social movement, message rap remains enmeshed in a "politics of recognition," a captive of its own naive and youthful subjectivity—thereby (and contrary to all appearances) posing no particular threat to the political status quo. The video version of PE's widely "cussed and discussed" single hit "By the Time I Get to Arizona" on the *Apocalypse 91* album provides a case in point. Rejected by voter referendum, the federal holiday honoring the birthdate of Rev. Martin Luther King, Jr., is not celebrated in Arizona. In PE's "Arizona" video this disrespect to the memory of King, and to African Americans in general, is addressed in the symbolic assassination of Arizona's governor. Although the command "Acknowledge our existence or we'll blow you away symbolically" represents a collective advance over the streetwise "Acknowledge my personal existence or *I'll* blow you away in real life," the overall genre remains trapped in a politics of recognition overdetermined, moreover, by the play of market forces. Substantive economic and political demands, alas, are held subservient to the demands of the collective ego.

With untold power to ignite the political imagination, soundbites and jump cuts seductively play upon our fascination with immediate surface reality, thereby hindering that process of intellectual cohesion that must take place if everyday life is to be grasped in its underlying, historical dimension. The problem appears to be a circular one: The artistic fragmentation of message-rap content provides a good measure of its appeal; paradoxically, a more continuous form and greater cohesiveness of content might well render the message less accessible, less palatable to hard-core listeners.

Growing out of an interpersonal orientation in an effort to "heal the conscience" of American society, the Civil Rights movement of the fifties and sixties matured and passed over into a Black Power phase that began to comprehend that society in terms of social structures, class divisions, and national questions. The collective wisdom of the past generation has not been transmitted to the new one. Where, for example, deconstructionists and other poststructuralists recognize only "objectivities" and structures abstracted from human sentiment, rappers tend to view social reality as subjective, with interpersonal experiences isolated from any consideration of institutional or societal structure. From a generational perspective, contemporary African American youth culture represents a collapse into the world of the personal and intersubjective: where general knowledge is equated with knowledge of self, but also a knowledge ("know the ledge") often governed by mythology; where politics has become a politics of individual recognition; where popular culture is geared toward self-absorption and self-protection; where economics is translated as self-help entrepreneurialism and family business; where the rebel—aside from any consideration of social content—becomes hero; where, for the "hard core," especially, every action, no matter how injurious to others, remains self-justified. The end result is symptomatic not only of the bankruptcy of corporate capitalism vis-à-vis its ability to meet the fundamental needs of basic masses of people, but also of the fundamental shortcomings of solutions and strategies proposed by both the Civil Rights and Black Power movements a generation ago. But while most rappers experience difficulty in seeing beyond the veil of interpersonal relations, a handful, including Speech of Arrested Development, comprehend that the enemy is a

> system that oppresses. You know Thomas Jefferson said way back in his day that if the system doesn't seem to be for the people, then that system needs to be bumrushed. That makes sense. If the system doesn't seem to be for the people, why should the system stay? [66]

And why should it? All in favor of a "Jeffersonian bumrush" signify by saying "Yo!"

Word is bond
Peace-up.
-5000-

Postscript: The original draft of this essay was completed in early 1993. Since that time most of the artists mentioned in this study have disappeared from public view, attesting to the often fragile shelf life of individuals and groups in the music marketplace. Their absence, alas, has also transformed this very article into a colored museum piece of sorts. With message rap pushed off the charts, the rap genre today tends to be dominated by gangsta themes. But the results were predictable: Without an external mass political movement to serve as a guidepost, young message rappers, acting alone, proved incapable of probing deeper into the social content of their art. Moreover, an artistic movement that gave birth to African American political consciousness in the eighties has also served as an obstacle to its further development. Although innovations within rap certainly continue to take place, they have tended to do so on the artistic rather than the political plane.

Notes

Acknowledgments: A most appreciative shout-out to b-girl Zena, and b-boys Antonio and Malik Allen, who provided indispensable research and translations and pointed the way; to Joy James, J. Michael Terry, and Adé Williams for informative insights; to William Eric Perkins for his old-school patience and sagacity; to Janet Francendese for maintaining her sanity; and to the Five College Black Studies Executive Committee for research support.

1. As Angela Davis remarked to Ice Cube: "We need to listen to what you are saying—as hard as it may be to hear it. And believe me, sometimes what I hear in your music thoroughly assaults my ears. It makes me feel as if much of the work we have done over the past decades to change our self-representation as African Americans means little or nothing to so many people in your generation. At the same time, it is exhilarating to hear your appeal to young people to stand up and to be proud of who they are." "Nappy Happy: A Conversation with Ice Cube and Angela Y. Davis," *Transition* 58 (1992):177.

2. See, for example, Clarence Major, comp., *The New Black Poetry* (New York: International Publishers, 1969); LeRoi Jones and Larry Neal, eds., *Black Fire: An Anthology of Afro-American Writing* (New York: Morrow, 1968); and Larry Neal, *Visions of a Liberated Future: Black Arts Movement Writings* (New York: Thunder's Mouth, 1989).

3. William Eric Perkins, "Nation of Islam Ideology in the Rap of Public Enemy," *Black Sacred Music: A Journal of Theomusicology* 5 (Spring 1991): 42.

4. See Todd "Ty" Williams, "Poetically Correct," *The Source* 32 (May 1992): 42–44, 59; Joe Walker, "The 'Last Poets' Explore New Art Form," *Muhammad Speaks*, March 14, 1969, 36; Bill Simmons, "The Last Poets," *Journal of Black Poetry* 1 (Fall 1968): 67–68.

5. Ronald Jemal Stephens, "The Three Waves of Contemporary Rap Music," *Black Sacred Music: A Journal of Theomusicology* 5 (Spring 1991): 25–40. Stephens's essay is insightful in many ways, but I have not found the names he assigned these "waves" to be particularly useful.

6. These are categories of convenience with a considerable overlap between them. For example, some of the more politically "righteous" rappers sometimes behave like gangstas in public, and some of the more gangsta oriented also have been known to invoke religious principles. Those who are nominally secular, on the other hand, may also claim allegiance to the programs of the Five Percenters or the Nation of Islam. And, perhaps even more important, the record albums of many rappers often contain a mix of message, entertainment-oriented, and gangsta-inspired rap in order to appeal to multiple market segments.

7. This section draws, in large part, on informative articles appearing in the *Los Angeles Times:* William Ellet and John Thurber, "Growing Violence in L.A.—A Heritage of Isolation and Hostility," July 23, 1972, G5; and "Modern Gangs Have Roots in Racial Turmoil of '60s," June 26, 1988, 28. See also Léon Bing, *Do or Die* (New York: HarperCollins, 1991), 148–156.

8. "Modern Gangs."

9. On the eve of the May 1992 Los Angeles rebellion, Crip strength was estimated at thirty thousand members, that of the Bloods at ten thousand. Gordon Witkin et al., "The Men Who Created Crack," *U.S. News and World Report*, August 19, 1991, 51.

10. See Jefferson Morley, "Contradictions of Cocaine Capitalism," *The Nation*, October 2, 1989, 341–347; and Witkin et al., "The Men Who Created Crack," 44–53.

11. For documentation of these tendencies, see Ernest Allen, Jr., and John H. Bracey, Jr., eds., *Unite or Perish: The Contours of Black Radical and Black Nationalist Thought, 1954–1975* (in progress).

12. See Richard Brent Turner, "Islam in the United States in the 1920's: The Quest for a New Vision in Afro-American Religion" (Ph.D. diss., Princeton University, 1986); Bernard Lewis, *Race and Color in Islam* (New York: Harper & Row, 1971); and St. Clair Drake, *Black Folk Here and There* (Los Angeles: CAAS and the University of California, 1990), vol. 2, chap. 5 especially.

13. For studies of NOI eschatology, see E. U. Essien-Udom, *Black Nationalism: A Search for an Identity in America* (Chicago: University of Chicago Press, 1962); and C. Eric Lincoln, *The Black Muslims in America*, 2d ed. (Boston: Beacon, 1973). On Moorish Science, see *The Holy Koran of the Moorish Science Temple of America* (Chicago: 1927), chaps. II:18; X:22, 24; XII:8, 9; XLV:1; and XLVIII:8. The Moorish Science Temple was founded by Noble Drew Ali in Newark, New Jersey, in 1913. Contrary to virtually everything written about his so-called mysterious end, Drew Ali died at home on July 20, 1929, following a three-month illness officially ascribed to "tuberculosis broncho-pneumonia." He was buried six days later in Royal Oak Cemetery on Chicago's South Side. Although in the wake of the prophet's death, the Moorish Science Temple of America (MSTA) lost its central authority forever, the organization continued to grow throughout the 1930s in membership as well as in the number of new temples established. See Arna Bontemps and Jack Conroy, *Anyplace But Here* (New York: Hill & Wang, 1966), 205–208, the original written source of misinformation regarding Ali's death; Arthur Huff Fauset, *Black Gods of the Metropolis: Negro Religious Cults in the Urban North* (Philadelphia: University of Pennsylvania Press, 1944), 41–51; Peter Lanborn Wilson, "Shoot-Out at the Circle Seven Koran: Noble Drew Ali and the Moorish Science Temple," *Gnosis* 12 (Summer 1989): 44–49; "Cult Leader Dies; Was in Murder Case," *Chicago Defender*, July 27, 1929, sec. 2, p. 12; "Most Noble Drew Ali Is Laid to Rest," *Chicago Defender*, August 3, 1929, 1; and

Standard Certificate of Death No. 22054, Timothy Drew, issued July 25, 1929, Office of Cook County Clerk, Cook County, Illinois.

14. See Ernest Allen, Jr., "The New Negro: Explorations in Identity and Social Consciousness, 1910–1922," in *1915: The Cultural Moment*, ed. Adele Heller and Lois Rudnick (New Brunswick, N.J.: Rutgers University Press, 1991), 48–68.

15. See John Woodford, "Testing America's Promise of Free Speech: *Muhammad Speaks* in the 1960s, A Memoir," *Voices of the African Diaspora* (CAAS, University of Michigan) 7 (Fall 1991): 3–16; and Ernest Allen, Jr., "Religious Heterodoxy and Nationalist Tradition: The Continuing Evolution of the Nation of Islam," in *New Movements and Trends in the World of Islam*, ed. Peter B. Clarke (London: Curzon, forthcoming).

16. "I am going to shoot dice until I die," claimed Clarence 13X, cited in Prince-A-Cuba, "Black Gods of the Inner City," *Gnosis* 25 (Fall 1992): 60. Born in Danville, Virginia, on February 22, 1928, the former Clarence Edward Smith, a decorated veteran of the Korean War, reportedly joined the NOI in April 1961. Legend has it that he was expelled from Harlem NOI Temple No. 7 by Malcolm X, which would place his departure prior to December 1963. Complicating the story, however, are FBI reports stating that Clarence 13X consistently attended New York City NOI affairs from 1963 through March 1965. See Charlie Ahearn, "The Five Percent Solution," *Spin* 6 (February 1991): 57; Prince-A-Cuba, "Black Gods of the Inner City," 60; Prince-A-Cuba, *Our Mecca Is Harlem: Clarence 13X (Allah) and the Five Percent* (Hampton, Va.: U.B. & U.S. Communications Systems, 1995); Anne Campbell, *The Girls in the Gang*, 2nd ed. (Cambridge, Mass.: Basil Blackwell, 1991), 216–217; Yusuf Nuruddin, "The Five Percenters: A Teenage Nation of Gods and Earths," in *Muslim Communities in North America*, ed. Yvonne Yazbeck Haddad and Jane Idleman Smith (Albany: State University of New York Press, 1994), 109–132; SAC [Special Agent in Charge], New York to Director, FBI, June 1, 1965, FBI New York file 157-1489; SAC, New York to Director, FBI, September 17, 1965; SAC, St. Louis to Director, FBI, September 17, 1965, FBI St. Louis file 100-20019; SAC, St. Louis to Director, FBI, October 22, 1965. These and all subsequent FBI references are taken from the FBI's FOIA file on Clarence 13X and the Five Percenters. I am indebted to Muhammad Abdullah al-Ahari/Bektashi of the Institute of Islamic Information and Education for the Campbell reference and to Prince-A-Cuba for his clarifications of Five Percent history and doctrine.

17. What was worse, Clarence 13X at some point proclaimed *himself* "Allah," thereby implicitly delegating Elijah Muhammad, Messenger of Allah, as his subordinate. The doctrinal relativization of spiritual authority may have contributed to a major MSTA organizational crisis in March 1929, when a recalcitrant official was assassinated by followers loyal to Noble Drew Ali, as well as to the failure of a consolidated leadership to emerge from within the MSTA following the prophet's death some four months later. Similarly, no single leader has been able to claim autonomy over the Five Percenters since the death of founder Clarence 13X in 1969. As rapper Lakim Shabazz noted, "I feel that Father Allah taught us we are all leaders unto ourselves." Cited in Ahearn, "Five Percent Solution," 57.

18. The Five Percenters first came to the attention of the New York City media in 1964, following the murders of a Jewish shopkeeper and his wife in their 125th Street store; Five Percenters were arrested and charged with the slayings. By the summer of 1967,

with the threat of a black urban rebellion hanging in the air, Mayor John Lindsay's Urban Task Force was scrambling to bring African American "militants" under its wing through various activities and programs. The results were peaceful Harlem nights, rapid growth of the Five Percent, and the eventual university matriculation of a handful of its young members. In the early morning hours of June 13, 1969, Clarence 13X Smith was assassinated in the lobby of Martin Luther King Towers, a Harlem housing project, by unknown assailants. [SAC?] New York to Director, FBI, June 1, 1965, FBI file 157-6-34; SAC, New York to Director, FBI, November 16, 1965, FBI file 100-444636; FBI Report, New York City, February 17, 1966; "Black Militant Slain in Harlem," *New York Times*, June 14, 1969, 30; Barry Gottehrer, *The Mayor's Man* (Garden City, N.Y.: Doubleday, 1975), 87–108, 237–40; Campbell, *Girls in the Gang*, 177, 216–224. Campbell reports that in 1978 the Five Percenters accounted for 28 percent of all gang-member arrests in Brooklyn.

19. "Disturbance by Group Called 'Five Percenters,' Harlem, New York City, July 29, 1965, Racial Matters," memorandum, FBI file 157-6-34.

20. Reprinted, in another format and under the title, "English C. Lesson #2 (Lost Found Muslim) (1–40)," in Issa Al Mahdi, *The Book of the Five Percenters* (Monticello, N.Y.: Original Tents of Kedar, 1991), 525–528. See also Campbell, *Girls in the Gang*, 218–219.

21. "Disturbance by Group"; SAC, New York to Director, FBI, October 18, 1965, FBI New York file 157-1489.

22. Lord Jamar of Brand Nubian explains it this way: "When the lessons were written, in 1934, 5% of the population of the Planet Earth had knowledge of self, 85% had no knowledge of themselves at all, and 10% were the preachers, and all of that, who knew that the true and living God was the original Black man, and was teaching Christianity, keeping them in mental slavery. That's where that term 5% comes from. 'Cause we a hundred percent, right and exact." Rakim, of Eric B. and Rakim, asserts that the 5 percent genuinely address the science if Islam; that the 10 percent, who are Muslims, know the science and submit to the will of Allah but are "bloodsuckers of the poor" because they sell, rather than freely distribute, works like the Holy Qur'an; and that the remaining 85 percent practice religions like Christianity and Buddhism—unlike Islam, which involves culture. Harry Allen, "Righteous Indignation," *The Source* 19 (March/April 1991): 52; "Rakim: The Five Percent Science," *Rap Sheet*, October 1992, 16. A creative example of the synthesis between elements of original NOI ideology and enhancements contributed by the Five Percent can be found in Grand Puba's "Soul Controller," *Reel to Reel* (Elektra, 1992) and Brand Nubian's "Allah U Akbar," "Ain't No Mystery," and "Meaning of the 5%" on *In God We Trust* (Elecktra, 1992). See also L-O 7 Self, The Revelator, "Coming Full Circle on a Solo Tip: Grand Puba," *RapPages* 1 (December 1992): 31–35.

23. See Lawrence Mamiya, "From Black Muslim to Bilalian: The Evolution of a Movement," *Journal for the Scientific Study of Religion* 21, 2 (1982): 138–152; Clifton E. Marsh, *From Black Muslims to Muslims: The Transition from Separatism to Islam, 1930–1980* (Metuchen, N.J.: Scarecrow, 1984); and Steven Barboza, "A Divided Legacy," *Emerge* 3 (April 1992): 26–27, 30, 32.

24. Related a Five Percent follower: "We the 5% do not teach Islam as a religion, but as a Divine way of life for the Blackman, but we do not separate ourselves from the Most Honorable Elijah, for we know that he is the last and greatest Messenger of ALLAH." Cited in Campbell, *Girls in the Gang*, 217.

25. See Ahearn, "Five Percent Solution," 55–57, 76, especially p. 57; and H. Allen, "Righteous Indignation," 48–53.

26. See Perkins, "Nation of Islam Ideology," 41–50. Support for Farrakhan can also be found in Professor Griff's *Pawns in the Game* (Skywalker, 1990) and *Kao's II Wiz*7*Dome* (Luke, 1991).

27. Prince Akeem, "Flush the Government," *Coming down Like Babylon* (BRC, 1991). See also James Muhammad, "Prince Akeem Takes Hip-Hop to New Level," *Final Call*, June 17, 1991, 6; and Joseph D. Eure and James G. Spady, eds., *Nation Conscious Rap* (New York: PC International, 1991), 265–305.

28. Gangsta rappers tend to assert that what they describe is "like it is," claiming that they are simply articulating attitudes that already exist within African American communities and therefore have no responsibility themselves for disseminating them. ("I'm not a role model, therefore I have no responsibility to anyone except myself.") The same can be said at times for the reinforcement of antiblack stereotypes ("We're all niggaz because that's what 'society' says we are").

29. See David Mills, "The Gangster Rapper: Violent Hero or Negative Role Model?" *The Source* 16 (December 1990): 30–34, 36, 39–40. Having passed from an Afrocentric orientation in *By All Means Necessary* (Zomba, 1988) and *Ghetto Music: The Blueprint of Hip Hop* (Zomba, 1989) to a more universalist stance in *Edutainment* (Zomba, 1990) and the multiartist H.E.A.L. album *Civilization vs. Technology* (Elektra, 1991), KRS One has more or less reverted to his origins with *Sex and Violence* (Zomba, 1992).

30. Divided into two parts, Ice Cube's recent *Death Certificate* (Priority, 1991) claims to embody a "death side, a mirrored image of where we are today," and a "life side, a vision of where we need to go." But both sides are filled with such pain and abomination that one seriously doubts the ability of most listeners to tell the difference between the two.

31. "Speak Up on It," *Life of a Kid in the Ghetto* (Polygram, 1991).

32. Tupac Amaru Shakur, "I'm Just One Black Man Standing Alone, but I Won't Sell Out," *RapPages* 1 (April 1992): 22. Providing a direct link from the militancy of the sixties to that of the present, Tupac Shakur's godfather, Geronimo Platt (now geronimo ji Jaga), was former minister of defense for the Black Panther Party. See James Bernard, "Doin' the Knowledge," *The Source* 16 (December 1990): 28–29.

33. See, for example, Rick Telander, "Your Sneakers or Your Life," *Sports Illustrated*, May 14, 1990.

34. West Coast Rap All-Stars, "We're All in the Same Gang," *We're All in the Same Gang* (Warner Brothers, 1990). Here recalcitrant fellow–NWA member Ezy-E warns that exposure to violence is one's own responsibility: "Yo, Ezy's no sellout / if you can't hang in the streets then get the hell out."

35. See *The Source* 21 (June 1991): 32–35.

36. Public Enemy, *Apocalypse 91 . . . The Enemy Strikes Black* (Def Jam, 1991); Public Enemy, *It Takes a Nation of Millions to Hold Us Back* (Def Jam, 1988); Tupac Shakur, *2Pacalypse Now* (EastWest, 1991); Yomo and Maulkey, *Are U Experienced?* (Ruthless, 1991); W.C. and the MAAD Circle, "Fuck My Daddy," *Ain't a Damn Thing Changed* (Priority, 1991).

37. Yo-Yo, *Make Way for the Motherlode* (EastWest, 1991); De La Soul, *De La Soul Is Dead* (Tommy Boy, 1991); Tupac Shakur, *2 Pacalypse Now* (EastWest, 1991).

38. "Chuck D All Over the Map: An Interview by Robert Christgau and Greg Tate," *Rock and Roll Quarterly* (Fall 1991): 15. Apparently the NOI's creation mythology

lacks sufficient explanatory power for Chuck D, who has latched onto the equally chimerical musings of one of our more creative, semiskilled intellectuals, Frances Cress Welsing, author of *The Isis Papers* (Chicago: Third World, 1991). The "Cress Theory of Color Confrontation and Racism," which assigns to white racism a biologically determined origin, has been implicitly and historically refuted in the monumental two-volume final work of anthropologist St. Clair Drake, *Black Folk Here and There*.

39. The political economy of pimps and hos is defined thusly: "Capitalism is a 'pimp' and 'hoe' system. It is a system of pimps and hoes. You're either selling, or you're being sold. And if you can buy that means you were selling although you're being sold. Put it this way. The system is so great all of us have the opportunity to become pimps. That should make you feel real good. You usually start out as a hoe and work your way up. . . . In a system like that all men are slaves." KRS One, in Eure and Spady, *Nation Conscious Rap*, 178–179. See also D-Dub's interview with KRS One, "What We Left behind in Africa Was Greater Than What We've Gained Here," *RapPages* 1 (April 1992), 34–35.

40. Boogie Down Productions, "My Philosophy," *By All Means Necessary* (Jive, 1988). Hear also A Tribe Called Quest, "Ham 'n' Eggs," *People's Instinctive Travels and the Paths of Rhythm* (Zomba, 1990).

41. Elijah Muhammad, "The Knowledge of God Himself (Saviour's Day, February 26, 1969)," in *Our Saviour Has Arrived* (Chicago: Muhammad's Temple of Islam No. 2, 1974), 56.

42. Issa Al Mahdi, *Book of the Five Percenters*, 354, 362.

43. "Funke Wisdom," *Funke, Funke Wisdom* (Jive, 1991). For an examination of spirituality in Kool Moe Dee's raps, see Angela Spence, "Theology in the Hip-Hop of Public Enemy and Kool Moe Dee," *Black Sacred Music: A Journal of Theomusicology* 5 (Spring 1991): 51–59.

44. See Michele Wallace, "When Black Feminism Faces the Music, and the Music Is Rap," *New York Times*, July 29, 1990, H20.

45. Yo-Yo, "You Can't Play with My Yo-Yo," *Make Way for the Motherlode* (EastWest, 1991). Hear also the expressive, if not "low-down," female/male exchanges between Yo-Yo and Ice Cube in the latter's "It's a Man's World," *AmeriKKKa's Most Wanted* (Priority, 1990) and continued in Yo-Yo, "What Can I Do?" *Make Way for the Motherlode*.

46. See Ernest Allen, Jr., "Afro-American Identity: Reflections on the Pre–Civil War Era," *Contributions in Black Studies* 7 (1985–1986): 45–93.

47. Jungle Brothers, "Black Is Black," *Straight out the Jungle* (Warlock, 1988). See also J The Sultan, "The Brothers Do the Nature Thing," *The Source* 2 (November/December 1989): 21.

48. D-Dub, "What We Left Behind," 34–35.

49. Louis Romain, "Roots & Boots," *The Source* 32 (May 1992): 36, 39. See also Havelock Nelson, "X-Clan: Four Righteous Messengers from Flatbush," *RapPages* 1 (June 1992): 31–39.

50. Boogie Down Productions, "Build and Destroy," *Sex and Violence* (Zomba, 1992). Interestingly, the number "8" in the Supreme Mathematics stands for "Build or Destroy."

51. EPMD, "Crossover," *Business Never Personal* (Def Jam, 1992). A related issue concerns the role of white rappers within this overwhelmingly African American music idiom; see, for example, Reginald C. Dennis, "The Great White Hoax," *The Source* 25 (October 1991): 52–55.

52. As Chuck D observes, "Heavy metal and rap music are both defiant forms of music. The white kids, they'll go for it, they'll respect you if you come out and say, 'This is

who we are and what we like. Minister Farrakhan is who we support. Fuck it, that's how it is.' Their parents got a problem with it, but they don't." Cited in Ras Baraka, "Return of the Hard," *The Source* 25 (October 1991): 31–32.

53. One of the ways in which PE accomplishes this is through allusion and euphemism—for example, the substitution of "other man" for "white man" in its lyrics. The "other man" is then successfully counterposed to the "brother man," without generating the hostility from potential white fans that a straight nationalist appeal might.

54. Having come under heavy attack for its antipolice lyrics, the album was subsequently re-released with one original selection, "Cop Killer," removed.

55. Preoccupation with the subject of intellect also seems to be an important facet of rap culture. Check out, for example, the very "handles" of individual rappers such as Wise Intelligent, Intelligent Hoodlum, The Genius, or MC Brains; or note the name of Yo-Yo's Los Angeles–based organization, the Intelligent Black Women's Committee; or count the number of times Sister Souljah refers to herself as "intelligent" on the TV talk shows that she frequents.

56. Dane Webb, "Black Is Back, and We're All In," *RapPages* 1 (February 1992): 34; "Chuck D All Over," 14, 16.

57. Webb, "Black Is Back," 38.

58. On NOI economics, see Playthell Benjamin, "The Attitude Is the Message: Louis Farrakhan Pursues the Middle Class," *Village Voice*, August 15, 1989, 23–31. Since the late 1980s Farrakhan family members and the organization itself have substantially increased their economic holdings. See *Chicago Tribune*, March 12, 1995, 1, 16–17.

59. Cited in James Bernard, "Building a Nation," *The Source* 27 (December 1991): 34. Chuck D's business ideals are virtually identical: "So I don't make some statement like, yeah, I hope to make some money to send my daughter to college. I hope to make some businesses that she can run. And that's the fucking thing about capitalism—we as black people keep looking for fucking jobs, we ain't getting no jobs 'cause there's a tight rope on white business, and they definitely ain't giving a black face a fucking job because business is family." "Chuck D All Over," 16.

60. Eure and Spady, *Nation Conscious Rap*, 63.

61. Adario Strange, "Edutaining the Masses," *The Source* 25 (October 1991): 29.

62. Webb, "Black Is Back," 35.

63. Issa Al Mahdi, *Book of the Five Percenters*, 332–334, 356; Erik B. & Rakim make reference to "know the ledge" on "JUICE (Know the Ledge)," in *JUICE* (MCS, 1992).

64. Sister Souljah, interviewed by Gordon Chambers, "Souljah's Mission," *Essence* (December 1991): 108.

65. As Sister Souljah has recently learned, it is "legitimate" to publicly screen music videos with violent scenes, but when the violence depicted is that of African Americans taking the initiative against the state, censors draw a hard line. "For instance, they'll say, 'We can't play your video because there's blood,' but then they'll play Geto Boys, and there's blood. Or they'll say, 'We can't play your video because there's guns,' but then they'll play NWA, and there's guns. Then they'll say, 'Well, you can't show a gun being fired,' then they'll play NWA and you see the smoke coming out of the gun, you know? So, what I'm saying is I think that all of the policies, which these stations say they have, have been ignored in the case of my video because I'm a woman talking about race relations. Sister Souljah, interviewed by Sheena Lester, "Diggin' Deep: RapPages Talks to the Ladies," *RapPages* 1 (October 1992): 32.

66. Cited in Sheena Lester, "Arrested Development Hits Home—And Takes Us There," *RapPages* 1 (December 1992): 51.

who wants to see ten niggers play basketball?

armond white

The title of this essay is taken from *Tougher Than Leather*, the 1987 Run DMC movie written by Rick Menello and directed by former Def Jam Records president Rick Rubin. The film was released around the period Rubin was withdrawing from Def Jam and settling unspecified accounts with his partner Russell Simmons; reacting more to Rubin than to the film, the rap cognoscenti dissed the movie, making it the first victim of "reverse racism" in hip hop. The street vibe dogged Rubin and his movie even though it was and still is the funniest, shrewdest celluloid depiction of the hip hop ethos—the insecurities that make Black American boys aggress, the style that gives them charm, and their inventive derivations from existing pop culture (specifically blaxploitation flicks, booty-begging records, comic books, and mainstream action-and-adventure fantasies) that, through hip hop, gets turned into art.

Rubin admired this ethos from his white, Jewish, suburban, long-haired, metal-head perspective and helped significantly to commercialize it. *Tougher Than Leather* reveals both Rubin's love for b-boy culture and his adept assess-

From Armond White's essay on Marky Mark in *The Resistance: Ten Years of Pop Culture That Shook the World* (New York: Overlook Press, 1995).

ment of its commercial and cultural potential. In contrast, *Krush Groove*, a standard, cheap bio-pic about Rubin's rise to the top produced by *House Party II*, *New Jack City*, and *Disorderlies* shlockmeisters George Jackson and Doug McHenry, trivialized Rubin's entrepreneurial project into make-it-rich dreams of empire. *Tougher Than Leather* got to something stranger and tougher: Rubin presented himself as an exploiter, a bizzer who held no delusions about Presley as a messiah. Acting on the plain knowledge that the American marketplace was no less a stage for class antagonism, racial bias, and sexual orthodoxy than the floor of the Congress, Rubin made Black labor work *for him*. In a venerable tradition (from slavery to sports to rock 'n' roll) Rubin developed this exploitation into symbiotic forms. Workers and beneficiaries traded off each other—the chance to be heard for the chance to control; the chance to be recognized for the chance to be entertained. And everybody gets paid (to varying degrees).

Founding Def Jam and breaking and entering movies via Run DMC were sincere expressions of Rubin's white advantaged condition. His big-screen, film-student wet dream about b-boys-turned-professionals-turned-movie-stars epitomized his deepest feelings about race and culture. Every scene in *Tougher Than Leather* is fascinating; it is Rubin's subconscious, diaristic account of pop as a mirror that reflects desire—for empowerment, for prowess, for fame, for money, for style, for art. Each scene mediates what draws rap listeners and artists together. And there in back of Run DMC's hijinks are Rick Rubin's alter-ego revolutionaries, the Beastie Boys. When a *Tougher Than Leather* character asks him why he's integrating rap with these ill-mannered fuckups, Rubin responds, "Nobody wants to see ten niggers play basketball!"

Those cold words describe American pop as much as they express racism—the phrase conjoins the two phenomena in a perfectly matter-of-fact expression. Rap flourished into corporate-sponsored hip hop *because* of the symbiosis that held whites enthralled to Blacks and kept Blacks indentured. Like sports, the music game needs diversity of playing style and elicits the envy of sideliners, compelling them to step into center court. As Rubin knew when he left hip hop for whiter, more rarefied metal at Def American Records (the label of Slayer and Andrew Dice Clay—also Seattle's Sir Mix-A-Lot), whites don't just want to cheer their own, *they want to play!*

Marky mark and all-american rap

Marky Mark Wahlberg has the best definition of any white rapper—meaning not just that he has better pecs than 3rd Bass or drops his drawers with more style than the Beastie Boys drop science but that he defines hip hop as a *Black* cultural movement. His brashness, as in the song "Just Like the Beastie Boys and 3rd Bass," does not distort the music's essence.

Alright, alright
What an odd sight
Here's another MC whose skin is white
A white kid, a white boy
With a white voice
Just like the Beastie Boys and 3rd Bass
Hmm. This looks like a topic for discussion
To build racial tension
For fussin' and cussin'.

Such honesty makes him the first white rapper to dispel derision. A Marky Mark record and video proudly acknowledge their derivation from Black culture. There's a paradox here: When white artists give Black pop its proper homage, there is still a limit to how far they can take their appreciation. This isn't determined by the artists' ability or the audience's acceptance but by the artists' own imagination. They must be able to borrow without losing sight of themselves as borrowers. The secret is attitude, and the attitude must be shared (as California's Latino rappers Cypress Hill show) before any mannerism can be copied.

From the release of his initial single with the group the Funky Bunch, "Good Vibrations" (featuring vocal excitement by Loleatta Holloway), Marky Mark has shown a genuine understanding of hip hop style and politics. By giving Holloway respect (providing her the visual presence Martha Wash was denied by Black Box and C&C Music Factory), Marky Mark transcended the obvious need for street smarts and hooked up with hip hop's earlier, dance-music influence.

Since it is impossible for any white rapper to achieve originality (the axiom "Too Black, too strong" becomes "Too white, too late"), attempts at combining identification with imitation (such as 3rd Bass's "Steppin' to the A.M.") wind up disingenuous. 3rd Bass's automatic assimilation of street slang and fly rhythm is automatically suspect. But on "Good Vibrations," Holloway's sizzling, piercing growl, which reduces all listeners to stupefaction, made Marky Mark's "difference" a pertinent fact. He seemed justifiably awed yet game—a white rap boy up against the gale force of sensual Black art. Speaking between Holloway's choruses, Marky Mark played out a good-natured cartoon of the racial-sexual envy that makes whites blush.

Call it a secret shame perhaps, because this race-sex thing is rarely gauged properly by the mainstream without shifting the balance of cultural authority. Marky Mark's youth and callowness relative to Holloway's age and power is almost a mythical demonstration of white desire and Black fecundity. The multiethnic, largely Black Funky Bunch (a six-person crew that includes two women) helps maintain Marky Mark's cultural context. That's usually the first thing denied by white crossover acts and counterculture theorists like the Beats and Norman ("The White Negro") Mailer.

This cultural egotism is the main thing Mark learned to avoid from the example of his older brother Donnie Wahlberg of the insufferably derivative New

Kids on the Block—a group that could succeed in pop but never in rap. Donnie Wahlberg produced Marky Mark's debut album, *Music for the People* (Interscope), and co-wrote most of the tracks. This funk-heavy album fulfills the hip hop ambition Wahlberg showed on "Games," the 1990 rap single from the last New Kids album. The other *Music for the People* tracks stay within proven Black pop formulas. (In 1994 the group acronymized its name to NKOTB and released a lame imitation of Snoop Doggy Dogg's sexism called "Dirty Dawg.") For instance, the second and third singles, "Wildside" and "I Need Money," were essentially cover versions of records already marked with strong ethnic referents.

Like many younger siblings, Mark dives into the depth of his older brother's commitment—in this case to Black pop—but the surprise on *Music for the People* is the breadth of the Wahlbergs' pop savvy, from the intense house of "Good Vibrations" to the sex rap "Make Me Say Ooh!" which uses only the revving-up bits of Marvin Gaye's "Let's Get It On." Marky Mark's whispered rap bites L.L. Cool J's loveman pose, yet he gets over, because how many white kids would know the right Gaye parts to use? This show of instinct seems impressively genuine in a third-generation pop addict. It doesn't discredit Marky Mark, but it clarifies the passion for Black pop that one hears in his records.

White communion with Black style is nothing new, but Marky Mark perfects it—politically if no other way. This happens as a benefit of Marky Mark's naiveté, something that a producer as smart as Hank Shocklee can't quite manipulate. Shocklee's white rapper projects, Young Black Teenagers and Kid Panic and the Adventures of Dean Dean, are too "Black," too slick. The amazingly inventive productions for these groups (Young Black Teenagers was a test run for the soundscapes Shocklee perfected with Son of Bazerk) strained the white rappers' plausibility. A similar anxiety affects the musical inventions of writer-producer Sam Sever (3rd Bass and his own duo, Downtown Science), which can't be called innovative without choking on the word. Clunkier funk, like Marky Mark's or the Beastie Boys', would have been a more credible mode for these white rappers.

Shocklee gave his acts more sophistication than the public could recognize—or even wanted to. Such semiadept white rap provokes a tricky debate about cultural authenticity. Rap performance and linguistics connote a particular social, ethnic experience. The use of this idiom is not a right to be earned but a given. For the middle-class, suburban Black kids who assume street manner and philosophy it implies a particular knowledge and empathy that is assiduously maintained by social circumstances if not genetics.

For the moment, rap's codes are inimitable; that's why TV and radio commercials can parody rap without diluting its potency. White rappers who try so hard for Black style confuse the music's communication. Gerardo, JT, and even Falco may know the form but not the essence. And though their tone may get close, their intent is unclear. The issue is not whether there is good music or acceptable rapping on *Radioactive, The Cactus Album, Young Black Teenagers, Licensed to Ill,* or *Music for the People* (there is) but whether these records can give comparable pleasure and enlightenment.

It's difficult to actually *hear* some of this music because its impetus is unknown, its purpose uncommunicated by the halting meter and the white voice (as Marky Mark identified) trying to pass as nothing unusual. Hip hop is such a rich culture that its audience can thrive without paying attention to white rappers. But instead of dismissing this white subgenre, it's best to understand that the audience is not indifferent; its needs (which will determine the shape of hip hop to come) simply preclude records or artists who are shams.

Hip hop has so many styles that it can't be accused of racial exclusivity, but its ethnic specificity is crucial. Rap's seemingly casual expression actually developed as the careful, forceful, personal articulation of social groups without access to America's dominant language and media. Even records as disparate as Young MC's "Bust A Move" and Naughty by Nature's "O.P.P." are informed by this expressive urgency. Both evince an African American yearning to claim, protest, enunciate. The significance of speaking—as an expression of identity and a form of power—gives hip hop endless fascination.

In Ed O.G. & Da Bulldogs' "Speak upon It," the Boston-based group performs the necessary function of interpreting history and recording it for the artists' sanity and the audience's awareness. "Speak upon It" retells the Charles Stuart scandal, in which a white Boston man killed his pregnant wife for an insurance settlement. Stuart's claim that a Black man murdered his wife provoked a police riot in which an innocent Black man, William Bennett, was arrested and charged with the killing. Ed O.G.'s account of this social disgrace is as serious as Scripture; his purpose is to make sense of an unjust world if only by keeping this horrible tale fresh. It is instant folklore made eternal by the rapper's intensity and a blues-righteous backing track.

"Speak upon It" is a classic example of what makes hip hop special; it contains a mythmaking, muckraking imperative about racial and social affronts that white showbizzers cannot be expected to have, an anger they dare not show. Unexpectedly, Marky Mark's "Wildside" makes the grade. Of course "Wildside" can't match the deeply pleasurable nuances of Ed O.G. & Da Bulldogs (their "Gotta Have It" and "Bugaboo" show the rich, humorous foundation for their ethnic identity), yet it is a remarkable display of empathy and a strong polemic.

On "Wildside," Marky Mark narrates several real-life tragedies, but the Stuart case is the song's center; its details are proof of Marky Mark's social consciousness. His voice isn't mature enough to sound bitter, but his sense of outrage gives this Boston Irish kid an undeniable emotional link to Ed O.G. & Da Bulldogs. Marky Mark's hip hop consciousness in "Wildside" is another form of homage, this time to the political status of African Americans that even whites are coming to share. The video begins matter-of-factly with a burning American flag—the kind of inflammatory image Marky Mark was able to get past MTV censors after 2 Black 2 Strong & the MMG's *Burn, Baby Burn* video was stopped.

Marky Mark's racially enlightened social protest is also an advance for white pop, as demonstrated by the "Wildside" bass line from Lou Reed's "Walk on the Wild Side." Bad-boy Marky purposely follows Reed's lawless example, but he stops short of Reed's bohemian white-negro tradition. "Wildside" covers Reed studiously but leaves out his chorus intro, "And the colored girls say . . ." This is intentional and smart for its implicit Afrocentric acknowledgment. There's no exoticism in Marky Mark's crossover; he maintains his own identity without circumscribing an Other. (This healthy approach to pop means he'll never have to cover Reed's masochistic-racist "I Wanna Be Black.")

"Wildside" speaks on a level of social identification that hip hop represents better than any other contemporary art form. (The video for Marky Mark's anti-greed screed "I Need Money" boldly spotlights the era's villains, starting with George Bush, Charles Keating, and Michael Milken and ending with Ronald Reagan.) Marky Mark touches realities that more adept white rappers like Jesse Jaymes or Kid Panic avoid. His empathy allows him to express the tension felt by the new, vocally empowered white working class. Songs like "Wildside" and "I Need Money" provide cross-racial, emotional solidarity; it's hip hop with a purpose, not just radio fodder. Marky Mark isn't simply in it to win it.

■ Young Black Teenagers' best track, "Daddy Kalled Me Niga 'Cause I Likeded to Rhyme," only added to the racial static it attempted to calm. There may be no resolution to the cultural tension provoked by the class and race divisions of rock 'n' roll and hip hop, but the integration happens best when it happens unostentatiously, as in De La Soul's sampling of Wayne Fontana and the Mind Benders on "My Brother's a Basehead" or Marky Mark's "Peace."

Marky Mark relishes that hip hop salutation for more than fun. He poses its ameliorating notion against the "racial tension" and "fussin' and cussin' " he knows he will provoke in some whites and Blacks. His hip hop gregariousness extends to the white b-boy image he cultivates: backwards cap, exposed muscle, peekaboo briefs, and lowriding jeans.

Since whites can't cut it vocally in hip hop, where the texture of African American speech is as musical an element as the samples used, the visual image is all-important. Marky Mark knows that the white assumption of this image is the reason he and Vanilla Ice and Gerardo exist and prosper—they're the non-Black mediators of hip hop aesthetics. But he avoids this racist trap by dint of his boyish, cartoon eroticism. No match for the sexual images of L.L. Cool J, King Sun, Chuck D, Big Daddy Kane, or Treach, Marky Mark simulates their swagger and energy in a way that's as amusing as it is flattering.

Marky Mark delineates how new styles of white fashion result from cultural transference; his hip hop–era innocence presents something new: working-class confidence that proudly maintains the source of witty behavioral innovations without trading it in for middle-class snobbery (cf. his good-sense *Interview* magazine statements on class).

If Public Enemy represents Blackness as (among its many meanings) a metaphorical condition recognizable to any unempowered person, Marky Mark underscores that proposition. He says "Peace" in imitation of hip hop attitude, but it's also fellowship, his communion with homeboys as social and ideological neighbors. Marky Mark takes such honest pleasure in hip hop phrases that when his voice goes surfer-boy flat saying "Wooord!" he still demonstrates the process by which slang moves through culture from Blacks to whites and between generations. Marky Mark himself becomes the site of racial/cultural exchange.

Marky Mark's style may be transparent (the underwear bit suggests that he knows white sexual fear and racial naiveté are inseparable from his success), but his effort is forthright. His manner and delivery capitulate to Black style in ways that those of Vanilla Ice and Tairrie B. don't. It's flattery with intelligence, and on "So What Chu Sayin'?" he defines the entire racial/aesthetic complex of white rappers:

> See, some do hiphop and forget how it started
> They claim their white complexion
> Ain't the reason why their records charted
> Please!
> Man, it's so easy to see
> When a white dude raps
> The public calls it a novelty
> Even me, although I take it seriously
> Some dislike me because of my r-a-c-e
> But I won't quit and I won't stop
> 'Cuz I do hiphop just because I love hiphop
> I never claim to be vanilla
> I'm Irish American
> And never did I claim to be African American . . .
> With respect to the Old School
> That created this art form
> It comes from the heart
> Not from critical acclaim
> 'Cuz that's just the same as the political game.

If hip hop can inspire a white American kid to such cogent cultural analysis that shows respect for others and sees politics even in rock criticism, it surely will outlast all its detractors. Marky Mark makes the prospect of all-American rap a little less frightening.

Whiteface mimicry: dissin' race and culture

Miles Davis asked, "When you say 'pop,' that's white, isn't it?" The answer goes back to Al Jolson singing "Mammy" in blackface—the first Beastie Boy. But an act as meretricious as Vanilla Ice is such a cynically calculated, contemporary example of pop that it destroys any optimistic delusion about shared, democratic culture. Not only does pop put Black art under siege but the natural function of culture and the way it perpetuates itself are all undergoing an obvious, shameless, systematic perversion. (So perverse that even 3rd Bass can make a song and video, "Pop Goes the Weasel," that singles out Vanilla Ice's appropriation of rap as a less noxious act than their own.) The pop forces that conspired to give Vanilla Ice his ascension are disgusting; his rapping is merely rotten.

A conventional critical approach to Vanilla Ice gets us nowhere because it presumes standards of judgment and competence that the whole phenomenon of whites imitating Blacks' music has always obviated. Whether it's Lisa Stansfield, Vanilla Ice, Michael Bolton, or the Beastie Boys, the disgrace of such ethnic/cultural mimicry lies in its political meaning. And that's what is hidden in the unsophisticated, indeed, racist, responses that such work solicits. When "smoothing over" a Black sound occurs, it is a moralizing act, judging the ethnic traits and meanings of a sound inferior, unbeautiful, or bad, somehow in need of white correction.

But listeners responsible for big sales must not be able to hear how awkward some of these imitations look and sound—the strain, the lack of elegance and potency, pass them by or else are received kindly, as fond tics. Despite his dysfunctions, Vanilla Ice is an emblem of usurpation and suppression. The canniest thing about him—his name (replacing the legal Robert Van Winkle)—indicates the issue of taste. Racial preference is central to his existence and explains why he got TV and radio airplay. He is promoted instead of the other Ices—T, Cube, and Just—because of the fiat of marketers. The preference for vanilla sublimates chocolate as it always does in white-run industries that deem Blackness unacceptable or objectionable.

It is a perfect coincidence that what Vanilla Ice has to say—nothing—leaves his representation of whiteness his only point. As mass culture's most prominent exemplar of rap, he helped suppress the music's original African American essence and expression. He even faked reggae rap on "Rostaman" to keep Black ingenuity marginalized. Vanilla Ice's primary cultural achievement is that he lays to rest Norman Mailer's fifties notion of "the white negro" as a white middle-class aspiration. By now the move is past achieving a psychic state of elegance and endurance; it's a move toward omnipotence, the hidden compulsion of white supremacy.

With better, late-eighties whiteface acts like the Beastie Boys and 3rd Bass and Young Black Teenagers, the impulse is also omnivorous. The Beastie Boys' album *Licensed to Ill* offers a set of songs that, heard today, sound less like rap than like a postmodern potpourri of styles from blues-metal to sampled sounds, all borrowed, of course, from Black sources. It is inauthentic as rap because the appropriations lack the effrontery that inspired the first rap artists. The Beastie Boys end up parodying the Black artists' original subversions—and their original celebration—which expressed a special need to achieve some control (some say) over pop-culture influences and to participate in their native musical tradition.

That is why the Beastie Boys' second album, *Paul's Boutique*, sank without a trace: The joke of the group's Black parody came from the novelty of its accomplished white mimicry and not-so-subtle ridicule. (Before the Beastie Boys the best rap record by a white performer was Mel Brooks's aptly titled "It's Good to Be the King.") Like an invading army on its second offensive, the Beasties lost the element of surprise that once startingly announced, "I control what I can deride."

If Black exploitation is the second-oldest profession in the West, there may be significance in it as a neurotic projection of Manifest Destiny. The pop imitation of Black music is less a suggestion of white self-denial than a disguise of tyrant's guilt. And though the envy factor looms large, it's too late to think that white business people appropriate Black art to flatter their powerless dupes—or merely for profit. There is another, less obvious, compulsion to normalize their hegemony.

White appropriation (such as TV's *Murphy Brown* using Aretha Franklin as I.D.) may look like a form of tribute, but it preys more than it praises. And while the political distortion is truly horrible, the traducement of Black aesthetics can be hilariously grosteque: the Beastie Boys' bowdlerized rage, Vanilla Ice's too tense 'tude. Eerily, when I reached to replay *Licensed to Ill* my roughly alphabetical record collection had the Beastie Boys next to Julie Brown's *Trapped in the Body of a White Girl* and the BMOC's twelve-inch single, "Play That Funk."

The latter 1988 curio is a one-record genre of frat rap, made by a pair of white male students from Harvard and Bennington, that I held onto just because it was so gruesome and boasted the prestige of a Nile Rodgers production. These white boys show an almost embarrassing affection for rap, yet they can't help but adulterate its musical and sexual integrity. They steal slang and rhythm that, like the Beasties', say less about how white American males deal with their personal culture than how they condescend to the spontaneous actions of the less advantaged. The air of frivolity reasserts the blithe indifference that came down on rappers in the first place. Carried away, these Big Men on Campus expose themselves:

Sgt. Rock is my middle name
Sucker-punching Nazis is my claim to fame
I'm a Harvard undergrad
A scholarly scholar
And I use rap music
To make me dollar

The ungrammatical choice of "dollar" is an appropriately wack Blackism, portraying BMOC's truest identification with the Black underclass's urge to make money. (Unlike Marky Mark's "I Need Money," BMOC's sentiment is completely unironic.) The song makes a telling move from antifascism to profiteering. When the record flopped, rapper Sultan MC (Jon Shecter) moved on to edit the ad-rich, self-proclaimed "magazine of Hip-hop music, culture & politics," *The Source*—the dollar-making guidebook to rebel music as a simulacrum of white brattiness. *The Source* makes plain the distortion of Black ideas through white mediation. For people who hear Black art only as rhythm or attitude, not as ideas. *The Source*'s editorial bent encourages the artistic vapidity of hip hop culture. Instead of challenging the music to articulate and sustain political ferment—a real affront to the status quo—it emphasizes the tantrum, teen-idol aspect, the infan-tilization. This may be all white rap can ever attain—a parody of Black that, in fact, hides the self-hatred of whites (and the masochism of some Jews, such as Sandra Bernhard brought out in *Without You I'm Nothing*).

These things were more clearly understood before pop-culture machinery be-came so invincible. The 1927 movie *The Jazz Singer* pinpointed the ethics-and-ethnic dilemma that the talented Jewish playwright Samson Raphaelson first out-lined in his original stage play about a rabbi's son who pays the price of fame singing jazz in dives. From Jolson's heartfelt minstrel-show parodies on, some form of darkie mimicking has been the strongest musical tradition in pluralized American culture. It's the love-hate link between the oppressor and the op-pressed—the tension Rick Rubin used to animate *Tougher Than Leather*.

White appropriation attempts to erase the culture it plunders—a metaphor for the submission that dominant groups will upon others. Raphaelson was am-bivalent about this, but he understood that the celebrity and fortune ethnic en-tertainers found through self-abnegation was balanced by a spiritual loss. Almost exactly sixty years later, three New York Jewish boys mimicked the badass atti-tude of rappers (eighties minstrels) and, as the Beastie Boys, broke the barriers of airplay and media promotion that had resisted the efforts of Black rap artists. The advent of Vanilla Ice does not suggest that show-biz politics have improved any.

But the white influence isn't all negative. The Beastie Boys were a watershed for a culture they didn't create because of the social advantages open to those in control of industry and media. The Beastie Boys' *Licensed to Ill* album, like *The Jazz Singer*, Hollywood's first sound film, made history as a technological achieve-ment that revolutionized the art form. That may be only because Hank Shock-lee was burrowing through academe at the time, although a pertinent question nags as to why Rubin, the Beasties' producer, was unable to get an equally rich-sounding mix for Def Jam's Black artists at the time. Rap wasn't waiting for the Beastie Boys to improve its earliest stages—although white listeners and critics may have been in suspense, anticipating rappers whose voices *sounded* like their own—but there's no denying that the form's current prominence partly derives from their boost. As ever, the price of fame is heritage, this time Black heritage, as the music industry paves the way for an onslaught of white artists into Black musical forms—a passing parade from Vanilla Ice to Snow. The Beastie Boys hold the official record for the first number-one rap album and single. These racial anomalies are cultural facts, but they shouldn't be swallowed whole.

Me-too acts: an empathic top ten

America disseminates Black culture much more readily than Black politics, so thank God for the particular genius of life that turns Black culture's influence into political fact. I want to comment on ten acts that would have been unthinkable without the inspiration the artists (good and bad) got from hip hop. Listening to a bunch of white rappers is as remote from the pleasure of listening to indigenous rap as reading is from dancing, but it is the particular genius of rap to bring out some intellectual spark, some musical pleasure, in almost anyone who attempts it. Among these "me-too, me-too" acts are some expected abominations but also some surprising, legitimate pop wonder. Like their Black counterparts, these white acts capture a moment in America's social-cultural-political development revealing the empathy that occurs between social groups despite the official divisions of race.

The goats, *tricks of the shade* (ruffhouse/columbia)

Trying too hard to copy the uncanny political fantasia of a De La Soul skit, The Goats conceived their debut album around the idea of capitalist America as a racist carnival in which spectators and performers all are "freaks." The word is a faulty imitation of the surreal hatred/affection in the term *nigger*, which no white group should feel right about using. Yet, The Goats' choice for a substitute proves them imaginatively stunted, witless. The satire here is more like a collegiate revue than Black rappers' street-rooted colloquial humor: British carny barkers . . . ("This is the Shoot-the-Black-Guy Gallery"); suburban naifs ("Scam's our uncle, he's gonna take care of us"); and fatuous ironists ("I'll be dreaming of a Black Christmas") make up The Goats' menagerie.

White critics celebrated The Goats, perhaps after relating to the prospect of cultural scavenging in the name but also—no doubt—approving the group's "correct" political sentiments, which are stated as dully but more straightforwardly than the implicit liberalism of most white rock criticism. The Goats' masochism (referring to their own dreaded selves as Hangerheads in several of the album's lamely enunciated pro-choice abortion songs) syncs with the way white rock critics like to identify Black victimhood. It's hard to tell if, in a song about the vengeance African Americans are entitled to, the lines "Rodney King would love [to take] a swing / if Yusuf Hawkins was walkin' he'd say the same thing" are cruel or just stupid. But by concentrating on this position, The Goats willingly indulge pity rather than actual acts of Black defiance as in the great (but critically despised) Willie D song "Rodney K."

Snow, *12 inches of snow* (eastwest records america)

The most successful white rap act since Vanilla Ice, Snow has a better monicker (which occasions the best line on the album: "Snow's getting deeper"). Plus, he benefits from the rootsy credibility of his reggae imitations. "Informer," the spring 1993 number-one single, cashed in on hip hop's borrowing from dance hall, a historically distorted certification of cultural trends that the market insists have a white signifier. (Snow gets the credit for Shabba Ranks's foregone artistic impact.) While Snow is more vocally adept than your average white rap wannabe—his tongue breezily twists the raggamuffin-style fast talk—there is a sameness and lapsing intensity, despite the more musical sense of rhythm that reggae confers on anyone. (Snow's attempts at singing "Uhh in You" and "Can't Get Enough" recall the sweet-voiced, reggae-intoxicated ballads of Scritti Politti's Green Gartside.) "Informer" is actually the first hit record by New York rapper MC Shan, who produced Snow's smash and vocalizes the rap break. Shan's own savvy business maneuvering is disguised in the song's story about Snow being set up to the police by a "friend." It's classic folk-art subterfuge, an updated Uncle Remus tale portraying a pretentious white's fear of being caught out.

In colonial countries struggling for independence Shan would be called a native informant. He plays the almost indispensible role of Black teacher/trainer who helps the white star successfully translate Black culture to the mass audience. There's poetic justice of a kind in Shan's biggest record's belonging to someone else while confessing, "See, this is what I had to do to get paid in the overcrowded rap field."

Kid rock, *the polyfuze method* (continuum/top dog records)

This completes the rock-to-rap metamorphosis that started with *Licensed to Ill* and surpasses the Beastie Boys through the absence of a single snide line or sample. Kid Rock's recipe is rudeness + metal. Instead of imitating rap rhythms and melodies, he proceeds on its liberation of subject matter and attitude, its legitimizing of youthful disaffection that *acknowledges* racial politics.

The subtext of this album is the typical dissatisfaction of white youth in the hip hop era: Kid Rock confronts the shibboleths of his white working-class (Detroit suburban) upbringing; each brazen guitar riff and profane rhyme announces the revolution that has already happened in his mind. The centerpiece, "My Oedipus Complex," tells a better story than Body Count's "Momma's Gotta Die Tonight"—trouncing parental limitations, agonizing over their distance like primal-scream John Lennon, then recognizing the pathetic humanity of misguided parents and topping that off with a leap of faith, recalling the parents' past reckless youth. It's a coup that outdoes Springsteen's family epics.

Kid Rock's emotional range includes Slick Rick's folky raunch ("Fuck U Blind") and the cogent alienation of seventies punk rock ("In So Deep," a worthy match for any seventies punk classic). Playing his own guitar on most of the tracks, Kid Rock is a more accomplished and expressive artist than the Beastie Boys on their single release *Check Your Head*; each form he uses has a meaning and purpose, it's not for showing off. Skeptical of this white-rock tendency, Kid Rock disses House of Pain as an example of faking the punk.

This is intricate business. Attitude—as seen in ex-3rd Basser Minister Pete Nice's "Rat Bastard"—isn't enough to make a rapper. Kid Rock shows an authentic feel for hip hop impudence on "Balls in Your Mouth" when he loops a macho obscenity for the dirty thrill of it, yes, but the art of it comes from exposing boyish ego. (The difference is what makes 2 Live Crew's "Me So Horny" sexist and this cut . . . well, fair.)

Instead of meanness, Kid Rock raps brattiness, spite rather than arrogance. When "Back from the Dead" reveals samples from both The Smiths and Public Enemy, it's plain that this is not a work of rockist privilege but of true, wide, and deep hip hop sophistication.

Young black teenagers (soul)

The name is the only art here. Public Enemy producer Hank Shocklee's business determination obscures what truth and affection he knows about the white youth who admire rap. Except for the intensity of "My TV Went Black and White on Me"—a veritable instrumental—little truth or affection are apparent here. (YBT raps too fast; their imitator's eagerness gives the game away, just as whites, unsure of the rhythm, sometimes dance too fast to a slow groove.) The second album, *Dead Enz Kidz Doin' Lifetime Bidz,* has even less impact, except when it bites House of Pain on "Tap the Bottle" and "Outta My Head." But the group's name is the important cultural footnote: It's meant to confuse pop's racist precepts and signify the common rock 'n' rap identity. The name can be read cynically or hopefully, but, until Shocklee, Kamron, and Skribble can come up with raps that convey the complications of the white-to-Black crossover compulsion, the name conceit will just seem unfortunate.

Consolidated, *friendly fascism* (nettwerk)

Consolidated's explosive aural environments are truly alarming. The group spews out leftist doctrine so fast that it gains crazy lyricism of a kind. The band uses a violent artifice—smart talk and rampaging sonic energy—to combat musical inanity. This is the group the Disposable Heroes of Hiphoprisy are mistaken for. The straight-on approach to political pop music is solidly in the tradition legitimized in America by rap, even though the band's industrial sound is recognizable only as hip hop's extreme. That means Public Enemy and the powerful opening riff that explodes throughout "Informodities '92" (from the second album, *Play More Music*) is worthy of Shocklee's loudest, most undeniable aural dream. Consolidated go right for the political issue—homophobia, vegetarianism, abortion—without the insulting placation of cute, dumb rhymes like the Disposables use. This approach respects its audience's intelligence—the most direct method to moving the mind and butt by white people since Gang of Four. Consolidated's impact is unrelenting except for the vox pop tracks recorded at the band's gigs, where fans get to give a piece of their mind or just criticize the band; it's as beautifully democratic as the neighborhood shout-outs on the New York cable-TV rap show *Video Music Box.*

who wants to see ten niggers play basketball? ■

House of pain (tommy boy)

A B-side remix of "Put on Your Shit Kickers" is a live performance (superior to the LP version) where the lead rapper begins another good-natured litany of things Irish: "I got the corned beef." His partner Danny Boy responds in a stoned, happily incredulous voice, "I got the matzoh?!" wonderfully summing up white rap's ethnic confusion. House of Pain's many Irish American boasts (from shillelaghs to cladagh rings) recognize that rap's specificity isn't simply about race but about ethnicity. The form gives America's ethnic groups a new way to celebrate themselves, asserting the pride necessary to maintain self-esteem in a society that otherwise oppresses and diminishes them. Even the specific forms of loutishness that House of Pain brag on—carousing, fighting, drinking—are more about legitimizing oneself through subcultural habit than about defying middle-class conformity. This is the basis of House of Pain's ethnocentric hip hop—it's a complex, irresistable act of white emulation by the group's leader, Erik Schrody, who, as a solo artist in Ice-T's Rhyme Syndicate, first became known as Everlast (a reference to boxing as a way out of poverty for Irish as well as African Americans). It also derives from the social circumstances implicit in the Latino rap of the Los Angeles group Cypress Hill, who also produced this LP.

"Jump Around," House of Pain's establishing single, is a triumph of ethnic illing—the very thing the Beastie Boys were slick enough to gainsay but that Cypress Hill, with significantly more ethnic fortitude, used to energize their own superb eponymous debut album that mixed funk and Latin rhythms, Black and Hispanic sensibilities. (It's also indicative of the class confines that the Jewish Beastie Boys have escaped.) The song's rubbery piano melody accommodates Irish step dancing, but DJ Muggs's arrangement also distorts the rhythm, first into Public Enemy–style caginess and then into a purely blunted high. And Everlast keeps up (the record debuts his sharpened rapping style), spitting out words menacingly, raising drunken barroom spiel to hip hop lyricism.

House of Pain's superiority over the Beastie Boys comes out of this intrinsic sense of fun in class attitude and behavior. Identity's the central element, and the depth of this cross-cultural Irish-Latino-African-American commiseration and comradeship can be found in one tiny but telling detail: the way House of Pain use the word *punk*—not in the British sense or the usual (white) rock-crit or Establishment sense, but as a sexist (originally homophobic) street epithet. This macho identification is a rap commonplace that House of Pain does not transcend; in fact, the group's startling command of nonwhite lingo and delinquent's attitude is disturbingly similar to the subcult toughness of white hate groups. Everlast's skinhead, tattooed image is additionally disorienting—another complication of pop semiotics that typifies the harsher, more strained political climate than what produced the Beastie Boys' mideighties appropriations. As America's poor increasingly are divided against each other, their isolation, frustration, and fury blurs. The dispossessed begin to look alike.

It turns out that the response on that live exchange is actually "I got the Motts"—the rapper's delirious consternation is, of course, applesauce. Like any good rap group, House of Pain—an excellent name for personal paranoia, as well as the general state of things (taken from the movie *The Island of Lost Souls*)—offers reasons to be cheerful and uneasy.

The beastie boys, *licensed to ill* (def jam/columbia)

Their only good album, despite the rock-crit acclaim that mounts with each later release (the uneven hodge-podge *Paul's Boutique*, the execrable *Check Your Head*, and the unlistenable *Ill Communication*). Some of this record's impudence influenced later white artists' releases, but even those albums (by House of Pain, Kid Rock) transcended the Beastie Boys' dilettantish slumming in rap style. This first album was full of humor, making the group hip hop comedians, their posturing on a par with the Fat Boys. But subsequent records confirm the suspicion that much of the Beastie Boys' agenda was a condescending parody of rap. Their style is to do rap vocalizing over a silly mélange of metal, soul, salsa, R & B, whatever, but with decreasing vigor and wit. The 1992 track "The Biz vs. the Nuge," a Beasties-sponsored collision between Biz Markie and Ted Nugent (Black rap and white rock reduced to its inanities), was pointless except to imply that all pop is travesty. And that's what it means to those who don't care about it.

Jesse jaymes, *thirty footer in your face* (delicious vinyl)

Matt Dike and Michael Ross, the "chefs" at Delicious Vinyl, have committed the recipe for commercial hip hop to their memories and bank vault. After their big successes signing and producing Tone Loc and Young MC, they finally cooked up a white rapper. Jesse Jaymes is lo-cal rap from SoCal, with fun, not decadent, beats.

J.J. has a sunny disposition, like all Delicious Vinyl acts, but the suspicion builds throughout this album that Dike and Ross add sweetness only to make up for the lack of grit. The spiciest part of "Wild Thing" and "Bust a Move" was the taste of life lived hard (Blackness). J.J.'s only crisis is a cartoon escapade called "Dave the Bookie." It shows that white youth see life as fun (while Black youth see it as survival). Bleaching rap—even this well—means neutering it. Compare J.J.'s "$55 Motel" (in which he raps, "I was rocking those bells just like L.L.") to L.L. Cool J's "Bristol Hotel," and note the effort to whitewash an art form almost beyond recognition. Mission accomplished.

The disposable heroes of hiphoprisy, *hypocrisy is the greatest luxury* (4th & broadway)

If you dismiss this group, you must be cruel—or else about to have a party. This is the least fun hip hop band I can think of. Not only are rapper Michael Franti and partner Rono Tse groove stingy, but their messages are presumptuous to the point of boredom.

The pretentious, cumbersome monicker is a tip-off to their literal-minded seriousness. "Hiphoprisy" is not a witty coinage; it lacks the free-and-easy disregard of linguistic rules that often is evident when rappers flip meanings and tweak homonyms. (Try Chuck D's "The women make the men all pause" to describe a situation of sexual dysfunction.)

Franti is straining, sweating to be clever. When this kind of guy hits the books you can feel the pages cringe—just like your neck muscles. But when a rapper displays this kind of nerdy solemnity, it makes white critics all cough up their most pandering tributes. The Disposables have been called "smart" and important—the kind of assessment that most often means that the reviewer approves of what is being said. Certainly the Disposables are not musically important; they are "important" the way *Time* and *Newsweek* are considered more important than *X-Men* or *The Punisher*.

But reading newsmagazines doesn't make one smart, it doesn't make one a poet, and it doesn't mean one's regurgitation of "facts" matters. The Disposables have not transformed anything they read; their lyrics are cold, dull, obvious. Their slogans lie inert atop even the few bumptious rhythm tracks. But in the game of pop-music politics, the Disposables are being hailed as hip hop intellectuals. The Disposables have been horribly misused by reviewers anxious to find "acceptable," "proper," "polite" rappers. In a most pathetic (and foolish) divide-and-conquer tactic, these San Francisco hip hoppers have been propped up as ideals against the unruly, disputatious Public Enemy, Ice Cube, and Sister Souljah.

Their elevation starts with the basic inability to appreciate rap as a genuine intellectual, rhythmic vocal-art form. The Disposables exemplify a made-up, bourgeois "smartness" instead of giving off the sense of a newly discovered, freshly felt idea or experience—and even when Slick Rick, DJ Quick, or Roxanne Shanté achieves that, it is the art of hard thought transformed into an *act*. Those street rappers only seem nonintellectual, while the Disposables practically wave *The Economist* in your face, hoping you'll notice everything they say has been processed from some official middlebrow source and wasn't merely felt.

This group lacks precisely the thing that is so fundamentally charming and thrilling about Sister Souljah, that unbeatable ability to convey passion. Franti is a withering, dry vocalist. He doesn't rap; he talks. And the only time he summons creative energy is to do an imitation of Chuck D that is, arguably, a dis. It's on the title track, which predictably has been praised as a brave confrontation with the "hypocrisy" of rap artists. Franti's list of career errors targets those performers with the bad taste to grow up in public. Worst of all, this gets interpreted as a defense of the moral standards that rappers ought not offend (you know, white capitalist politics). Funny thing is, the Disposables didn't do this album for charity. Sad thing is, this album isn't funny.

Only a churl could get a kick out of Chuck D vocal inflections chained to rhymes as awful as this one from "Television, the Drug of the Nation" (catchy title): "The bass, the treble / Don't make a rebel / Having your life together does."

On this song, the Disposables' first single, they come up with observations such as "breeding ignorance and feeding radiation" that weren't even news thirty years ago. These are traditional gripes, easy to take because they are not revolutionary. In fact, it *is* TV—a homogenization of what we already know.

That also goes for the words-music counterpoint. The Disposables (Franti and Tse used to be members of the West Coast thrash band The Beatnuts) use dissonance and rhythm in obvious, dull ways—as sonic effect and background noise. This is weak stuff compared to San Francisco thrash rappers Consolidated, and though the group is acknowledged on The Disposables' liner notes, there's no evidence that Consolidated's talent rubbed off.

Even the most Consolidated-like song, "Language of Violence," is an utter failure. It's a supposed attack on homophobia but done in the idiotic, essentially homophobic manner of Terence Trent D'Arby's "Billy Don't Fall." In Franti's scenario, a gay basher goes to prison and gets raped: "The young bully felt fear / He'd never been on this side of the name calling." By Franti's effed-up logic, homo sex remains a crime. But that's just the second offense in a song with these lines:

> But dehumanizing the victim makes things simpler
> It's like breathing with a respirator
> It eases the conscience of even the most conscious
> And calculating violator.

The best thing about the Disposables is the appropriateness of the name they gave themselves.

Marky mark, "you gotta believe" (interscope)

At the moment Marky Mark disgraced his rap credibility by selling it out to a racist Calvin Klein ad, he released his best record. This single (again produced by brother Donnie) confirms Marky's naive rap faith, but it doesn't take off until female vocalist Darcelle Wilson wails encouragement and Marky delivers his most urgent, rhythmic rap. It makes a good farewell disc, insisting on Marky's good intentions in the face of the media's backlash exposé of his juvenile court rap sheet for ethnic and gay bashing. It's a pitiful end for what should have been a happy American story, but this disc shows it's still a classic tale.

Marky's growth out of white Boston's racist, insular environment into being a frontman for an integrated rap group and a gay icon is the bildungsroman that American fiction celebrated before hip hop. Now, with new nonwhite examples of Horatio Alger (superficial) success, Marky seems to be doing penance for nothing more than reminding the larger society of its hypocrisies—the race baiting and gay bashing that white males indulge in as a right of passage and big business's noxious exploitation of sexuality. Now the insincerity includes appropriating Marky's rap bona fides (and show-biz gimmickry) and attempting to convert it into images of white erotic supremacy. A Black rapper's sexuality would upset the balance of trade, whereas the nasty look of a white thug rapper like Everlast is equally threatening. Marky conveys the innocent dumbness of probably most white rap aficionados. His very innocuousness has been turned against him. And still he insists, for the best reasons you can imagine, "You gotta believe!"

■ **flavas**

■

■

■

■

■

■

part **III**

■ hip hop 101

■ robert farris thompson

■

■

■

■

■

■ **8** Hip hop ain't no Hula-Hoop, no matter what the trend spotters say. In 1984, of course, hip hop was hot news. Everywhere you looked, you could see hip hop in one or more of its manifestations: break and electric-boogie dancing, rap music and graffiti. Then the media moved on, leaving the impression that hip hop was a fad. Here today, gone later today. Over and out.

But traditions just don't work that way. Hip hop is still with us in all its sainted sassiness, and its impact is likely to reverberate for years and years. Rappers in concert crisscross the nation. During his last tour, Prince shared the limelight with Tony Draughon, a break dancer known as Mr. Wave. Michael Jackson's 3-D Disney project, *Captain Eo,* will feature one of the main innovators of electric boogaloo, Pop'in Pete (Timothy Solomon) of Fresno, California. And this summer, Mr. Wave, along with the New York City Breakers, will bring his inimitable body lightning to sixty American cities.

All of this is simply part of an enduring cultural evolution. And the roots go back, baby. *Way* back.

Consider Charles Dickens in 1842. He's in New York, digging the action at the Cotton Club of that era, Almack's, in a tough but vibrant Manhattan district known as Five Points. The scene, which he wrote about at length in a travel book, *American Notes*, really blows his mind. He describes the manager of Almack's, an elegant black woman in a multicolored African-style head tie. Then he zeroes in on the work of a master black dancer, of that city and of that time, performing what the landlord of the bar actually calls "a regular break-down":

> Single shuffle, double shuffle, cut and cross-cut: snapping his fingers, rolling his eyes, turning in his knees, presenting the backs of his legs in front, spinning about on his toes and heels . . . dancing with two left legs, two right legs, two wooden legs, two wire legs, two spring legs.

What does this have to do with hip hop and its roots? A lot. For example, in 1986, as part of his New York electric boogie, Tony Draughon turns in his knees, then spins around to present the backs of his legs. African American dance history is evident in other moves that Dickens witnessed. There were intimations of Kongo, an ancient and distinguished black civilization in central Africa, in the shuffle and double shuffle (in the Kongo language, these contrasting modes of perambulation are called *ta masamba* and *ta masamba n'swalu*). And the Kongo people, apparently since the Middle Ages, have poked fun at a knock-kneed bird in a dance they call *ta minswele* and have patted their thighs and chests and snapped their fingers for extra percussion in a dance called *mbele*, which was described by a French priest in May 1698.

Back to the future. It's 1969. James Brown, Soul Brother Number One, needing no further praise or introduction, is performing onstage at Madison Square Garden. *Newsweek* is there, taking down the moves: "dazzling double shuffles, knock-kneed camel-walks and high-tailed, chicken-pecking atavisms." The imperative was clear: get loose and let loose. A cultural threshold had been reached. Moves Dickens had seen, and some he hadn't, were coming into play again. And all creative hell was breaking loose. James Brown begat soul. And soul begat George Clinton and the funk movement. And James Brown and George Clinton and others, in combination with cultural forces including jazz, salsa, and reggae (dub and the sound-system style of record playing more than the music itself), begat Afrika Bambaataa and the Zulu Nation—in short, the hip hop revolution.

Watching James Brown and listening to George Clinton from afar were young black dancers like the Solomon brothers in Fresno and Afrika Bambaataa and his followers along 174th Street in the Bronx. Out of the Bronx emerged breakdancing, turntable percussion, the beat-box sound, and rap. And out of Fresno and black Los Angeles emerged electric boogaloo, which New York renamed electric boogie. All of which takes us up to where we are today.

Of course, it's easier to savor the influence of tropical Africa in the DUN-tuh-PAH, DUN-DUN-tuh-PAH, DUN-tuh-PAH, DUN-DUN-tuh-PAH now resounding from a thousand beat boxes than to comprehend that sound as an aspect of a serious historical tradition. But in the effort to do just that, we might discover why 12.2 percent of our population, black Americans, are consistently responsible for more than 50 percent of our popular music.

Hip hop is a tale of three cities. As I've said, breakdancing and the hip hop sound emerged in the Bronx, electric-boogaloo poppin' and tickin' moves arose in Fresno and Los Angeles (Watts, Long Beach, Crenshaw Heights). Naturally, the outsider might wonder how the devastated lots of the South Bronx and the suburban sprawl of Fresno and Los Angeles could have sustained the energy and the beauty of the hip hop arts. Well, in the Bronx at least, it seems the young men and women of that much-misunderstood borough *had* to invent hip hop to regain the voice that had been denied them through media indifference or manipulation. By manipulation I mean filmmakers' exploitation of what they took to be prototypical ruins, along the southernmost edges of the South Bronx, as backdrops for the social apocalypse—witness the film *1990: The Bronx Warriors*.

Michael Ventura, in the fascinating chapter "We All Live in the South Bronx," from his *Shadow Dancing in the USA*, describes how the cameramen in the streets would seek negative local color and apparently little else: "In roughly six hours of footage—*Fort Apache, Wolfen*, and *Koyaamsqatsi*—we haven't been introduced to one soul who actually lives in the South Bronx. We haven't heard one voice speaking its own language. We've merely watched a symbol of ruin: the South Bronx [as] last act before the end of the world."

How wonderful, then, when the Bronx started to talk back. In the late spring of 1981, there was a panel at a Bronx-based conference on the folk culture of that borough with the title "This Is Not Fort Apache, This Is Our Home: Students Document Their South Bronx." Tony Draughon, who grew up on 169th Street near Yankee Stadium, maintains: "That performing-in-the-ruins stuff is all a crock. There are no abandoned buildings where I live, and breakdancing didn't start where all those broken buildings were—we danced at Bronx River, where Bambaataa and the Zulu Nation was, and Poe Park and the schoolyards and even the back of classrooms when the bell would ring." It also happens that Bambaataa grew up in a comfortable apartment in the Bronx River Project, on East 174th Street, with his mother, a nurse. The bottom line is that Bambaataa, Grandmaster Flash, DJ Kool Herc, and the other South Bronx hip hop performers transcended and transmuted violence with music and peacemaking.

Nor were the original hip hoppers confined, as some outsiders imagined, to a single, monolithic black culture. If lesson one is that a living, creative, ebullient people live in the Bronx, then lesson two in hip hop history is the appreciation that these creative people can be divided into at least five distinct African-influenced cultures:

First, English-speaking blacks from Barbados live in the Bronx. Afrika Bambaataa's mother and her two sisters were from Barbados, as was the family of that other prominent Bronx DJ, Grandmaster Flash.

Second, black Jamaicans live in the Bronx. Among them figures most famously DJ Kool Herc (Clive Campbell), originally from Kingston, who was immortalized in the 1984 film *Beat Street*.

Third, thousands of blacks from Cuba live in the Bronx. The smell of Cuban coffee and the sound of Cuban mambos enliven the streets. (As early as 1954, a blind black Cuban guitarist, Arsenio Rodríguez, had extolled in song the talents of a legendary "guy from the Bronx," or "el elemento del Bronx," according to the original Spanish lyric. In line after swinging line, Rodríguez praised him because he could dance mambo and *danzón* like a Cuban, right in the middle of the Bronx.) It was only natural for Afro-Cuban conga drums to become one of the favored percussive springboards for early breakdance improvisation. "Afro-Cuban bongos gave power to our dance," says Draughon.

Fourth, there are thousands and thousands more of *boricuas*—Puerto Ricans—and they not only augmented the Afro-Cuban impact, in the timbales of Tito Puente and the salsa of Eddie Palmieri and Willie Colón, but eventually provided an able-bodied army of knowing dancers who were to take breakdancing to its second, efflorescent phase between 1979 and 1982, after its invention in the South Bronx by black dancers, circa 1975.

Fifth and finally, there are the North American blacks, whose music was jazz and soul and funk. And the Bronx also loved rock. In the sixties and seventies, James Brown, Sly and the Family Stone, and George Clinton were the main men. Bambaataa elaborates: "I loved their *funk*—hard-hitting bass and heavy percussion. Before James Brown, funk meant the smell of sweat. But James Brown turned it into a sign of life. And George Clinton changed it into a *way* of life, with funk adverbs, the funk sign [pointer and little finger up, other digits and thumb tucked behind the palm], funky costumes, funky glasses—all that came in with him. And Sly took rock and crossed it with funk, and had 500,000 people rising to their feet at Woodstock."

In short, to live in the Bronx was to live in a multicultural happening. The Bronx blacks had the cultural depth and confidence to talk back, when challenged by the media, staying loose, creative, different. "They stayed fresh, they maintained that certain volatility that hip hop craves," recalls Michael Holman, a young black hip hop impresario, student filmmaker, and author. No fear of the end of the world, just fear of being stuck: "If you became classifiable," Holman says, "you became all the things that kept you in check."

In 1975, the lines of cultural brilliance, North American black, Afro-Cuban, et al., were beginning to crisscross. Many of these musics, however different, shared Kongo qualities of sound and motion. The wheel of creative creole interaction was turning again, as it had once in New Orleans, Havana, and Rio de Janeiro when Kongo rhythmic impulses collided with Western dance and music. One reason for the Kongo tinge in New World dancing is the sheer number of Kongo and Angolan peoples brought to our shores in the Atlantic slave trade—a miracle of cultural resistance, demographically reinforced. The historian Joseph C. Miller tells us that some 40 percent of the ten million or so Africans brought to the New World between 1500 and 1870 in the slave trade came from the ports of Kongo and neighboring Angola.

These powerful numbers, in combination with the spiritual and artistic gifts of the Kongo people, changed the course of the popular music of the world. In New Orleans, the city of jazz, the Kongo people were so numerous and their Kongo dance was so famous (in Mississippi, too) that the place where everyone hung out to hear the latest sounds and check out the newest moves, a vast dancing plaza called Congo Square, was named after them. Dena J. Epstein, an expert in the history of black folk music, has discovered a letter from New Orleans, dated 1819, that includes this telling sentence: "On sabbath evening the African slaves meet on the green . . . and rock the city with their Congo dances."

They also took creole Kongo beats and rocked Havana with rumba and Rio de Janeiro with samba. (Both *rumba* and *samba* are Kongo words for certain dance moves.) The upshot?

First, black Rio taught us how to samba, to dance to the sound of tambourines and Angolan friction drums.

Second, from Cuba came rumba and the conga line, the circling line of dancers moving one-two-three-*kick*. This style has returned to the spotlight in 1986 with the Miami Sound Machine's "Conga," the first Latin song since the sixties to become a major U.S. hit.

Third, from the Kongo dance of Congo Square, from jazz dance, and from rumba came "the Congo grind" (*tienga*), the hip-rotating sign of life that kept missionaries to Kongo muttering for centuries, that gave American Puritans cardiac arrest, that ultimately inspired Elvis Presley's famous suite of moves. Some of these motions have become part of the dance code of American people, white and black.

Fourth, wherever the Kongo people came in significant numbers, you frequently found their concept of the dance performance break: in Haiti, where *cassé* ("break") stands for the deliberate disruption of the beat of the drums, which throws the dancers into ecstasy, or in Cuba, where *rumba abierta* refers to the dropping out of melodic instrumentation and the taking over of the conga drums.

Must we know this to pass what music critic Robert Christgau calls raptitude tests? Bet. Because a fusion of break musics in the Bronx sparked the rise of hip hop. Afrika Bambaataa explains what happened in *The Beginning of Break Beat (Hip-Hop) Music:*

> Break music has been around for a long time, but not until the early '70s
> . . . brought to popularity. Break music is that certain part of the record
> that you just be waiting for to come up and when that certain part comes,
> that percussion part with all those drums, congas, it makes you dance
> real wild. . . . That break is so short in the record, you get mad, because
> the break was not long enough for you to really get down to do your
> thing.

How to restore the delicious length of live music breaks in a mechanical, turntable situation? The answer was found around 1973. The Jamaican DJ Kool Herc armed himself with gigantic speakers and thundering frequency ranges and defined a world where, as one hip hopper put it, "the loudest noises were the newest." Herc took a conga drum break and extended it across two copies of the same record on two turntables. As soon as one break ended, he switched to its beginning on the second record, and the beat went on. This was the birth of Bronx-style break music.

In response, no later than 1975, young black dancers in the Bronx were improvising moves to match the new length and intensity of the music. They danced to break music, so they called themselves breakdancers. Or b-boys, for short.

In neighborhood gyms and in the parks and playgrounds, they would break to the percussion portion of a tune. I remember running full tilt into one of these scenes while driving in the Bronx in the late seventies. There was a park filled with fifty or more radios, *all playing the same thing*. It left me thrilled and reeling. This was the musical background for the earliest forms of breakdancing as seen in 1976 on the schoolyard of P.S. 110 in the Bronx by G.L.O.B.E. and Pow Wow, two prominent rappers now working with Afrika Bambaataa: "Like, it'd be two guys, both doing uprock, stand-up moves, side to side, profile, and then one of them would fall back and the other guy would catch him."

Uprock was martial posing. Uprock meant battle mime. It was danced combat, a fight with steps instead of fists. One basic sequence: hop, step, *lunge*. Or the hands were used as if they were a knife in a form of uprock known as zipping, witnessed by a historian of breakdancing, Sally Sommer. Uprock is not unlike *nsunsa*, a fast-moving Kongo battle dance—a sport, really—that's also one-on-one and also very popular with men. Can this also be the black social amusement called *soesa*, which J. G. Stedman observed in Suriname in South America and described in a book published in 1796: "[It] consists in footing opposite to each other and clapping with their hands upon their sides to keep in time."

The Bronx fall-back-and-be-caught moves recall another Kongo dance game, *lukaya lweto*, "our leaf that never falls." In this game, the child who is "it" leans back precariously and is spun around in the hands of children seated in a circle on the ground around him. They spin him roughly, quickly, but never let him fall.

Then the b-boys brought breakdancing down to the level of the ground. G.L.O.B.E. and Pow Wow elaborate:

> We got tired of just stand up and catch. We started kicking side to side and hitting the ground. Jump down, bend, crouch and take a set, all down, doing whatever moves we could, spinning top, sweep, back spin. There were guys who danced [these moves] so much they said every week they had to get a new pair of sneakers. Anyhow, you'd fall, touch your hand on the ground, improvise something, bounce right up, and freeze.

Tony Draughon participated in the creation of these early moves. He says these strokes of prowess deliberately set up a contrast between the spin and the freeze: "Imagine, man, you're *spinning*, as fast as you can, and then you *stop*, in a beautiful position, in the twinkling of an eye."

Tradition built this tone of confidence, this arsenal of instant moves and creative options. What kinds of tradition? Why, freeze and swipes and spins, of course.

Move-and-freeze sequences were legendary in the history of jazz dance. From the fifties, I remember the New York mambo picture step, in which William Pittman and Teresita Pérez, two well-known mambo dancers at the Palladium on Broadway, turned and froze, becoming momentary sculpture. I also remember the legend of a rock & rolling freeze dancer in Dallas in the fifties. It is told that he'd show up with an alarm clock concealed within his britches. He'd sweat and dance and freeze, then shake and shimmy and freeze. The ladies loved him. And then an alarm clock would go off in his pants, signaling departure time for an amorous rendezvous, and he'd disappear, mysteriously.

But there is nothing mysterious about the origins of the sweeps and swipes of early breakdancing. They clearly represent an ingenious adaptation of the pommel-horse exercises of Western gymnastics to the Africanizing "get down" level of the ground. Keep the muscle, get rid of the horse, and get on down.

The spin also recalls, in part, the virtuosic whirls of Kongo dances. In the summer of 1985, I saw a dancer spin on his right hand in the middle of a revolving, chanting circle of children in Kiluango, a hilltop village near Luozi not far from the river Congo. In other villages, I saw standing children link arms with horizontal children, spinning them close to the ground. In another town, a youngster spun on his back.

What are we to make of all this? Simply that it's no more surprising to find spin dancing in the black Bronx than it is to find "London Bridge Is Falling Down" on the playgrounds of Anglo-Saxon America. In fact, some intervening links between Kongo and the Bronx can be found:

First, a marvelously detailed nineteenth-century Cuban engraving shows a black dancer, bare chested and with a belt of bells, spinning on his left palm in the streets of Havana on Epiphany, the Day of the Kings. His pose is like a stop frame from a film of today's New York breaking step, the four corners.

Second, hand spins came from Angola to Brazil, where they turn up as one of the moves of *capoeira de Angola*, the black martial art of the city of Salvador, in the state of Bahia.

Third, as we learn in Lydia Parrish's classic *Slave Songs of the Georgia Sea Islands*, a ring shout in black Georgia includes a sequence in which one member "gets down on his knees and, with head touching the floor, rotates with the group as it moves around the circle."

Fourth, powerfully illustrative is a silent, very early kinescope, *Three-Man Dance*, probably from the period between 1890 and 1910. This film bears an extraordinary relation both to ancient Kongo and to the modern Bronx. While one black man plays a harmonica and another beats time with his hands, a third comes in and choreographically introduces himself with a time step. (One of the other men has just danced a rudimentary version of today's moonwalk.) Then he turns his back to the camera, and he *breaks*. Suddenly, he's dropping on the ground, touching the floor with his hand, flipping his body upside down, then resuming, in a twinkling, verticality.

Spin-pattern vocabulary, coming down the body line from Kongo culture, was very likely reinforced by other sources. Blues historian Samuel Charters saw a West African Fula dancer fling himself down on the ground, land on one hand and begin spinning wildly, and I have seen similar stunts among the Gelede dancers of Ketu, an ancient town in what is now the Republic of Benin. But however blended and recombined, the spins in the Bronx were far from fixed or static. Indeed, the special intensity of the breakdance revolution split the atom of the spins and released more creative energy than had probably ever before been seen in this particular suite of moves.

Enter the Puerto Ricans. They took breakdancing to another level in the late seventies and early eighties. They built tough, athletic structures around the original spins, mirroring an age of joggers, Adidas outfits, and Nautilus-trained bodies. For one thing, as suggested by hip hop scholar David Sternbach, they added a fast-stepping entry pattern that strongly recalled the flash and celerity of some of the steps of the Puerto Rican dance known as the *bomba*. The Puerto Ricans added new spins to the lexicon: head spins, windmills (a variation on the back spin, with flaring legs), and helicopters (one person spins two other dancers like human blades), plus a superathletic bit of virtuosity, a whirling one-arm handstand called the 1990.

By April 1981, when Sally Banes published the first article on breakdancing, the original black and subsequent Puerto Rican improvisations had fused to form the full-blown, breakdance sequence: entry (rapid-fire stepping), break (down to the hands), swipes (the ground gymnastics imparting momentum and special flair), spins (on the hands, the back, the shoulders, the head, and other body parts), finishing with a freeze and then an exit (returning the performer to verticality).

Some dancers pushed these moves to the limits of human anatomy. One dancer, for example, who dreamed that he had spun on his chin, tried it in real life and damn near broke his jaw. But the way some spins dissolved into the freeze could be truly magical. In the end there was no way of confusing the daredevil baroque of breakdancing with the straightforward spin games of ancient Kongo. For one was early and the other was late, and enormous amounts of time and creativity had intervened.

Meanwhile, drum machines were coming in: DUN tuh-PAH, DUN-DUN tuh-PAH, DUN tuh-PAH, DUN-DUN tuh-PAH. "These beats," reports Doug Wimbish, a musician who has worked with Bambaataa, "build the total tack-head experience—the tack head is young, formative, black, out for whatever, and the safest way to keep that tack head listening is to keep that beat."

The hard, relentless beat-box pulse—"total tack"—called for a correspondingly hard and relentless motion. Once again, the Afro-American vernacular was more than equal to the challenge.

For more had come from Kongo than horizontal play spins. Most remarkable were ecstatic healers, dancing in trance, famed for "sending waves" (*fila minika*). Kongo healers in trance make sharp, sudden pulsations with their shoulder blades as a sign that the spirit of God is with them.

Cut to the Solomon brothers (their stage names are Boogaloo Sam, Pop 'in Pete, and Tickin' Deck), who were to invent electric boogaloo. While attending services at the First Corinthians Baptist Church on Thorn Street in West Fresno in the sixties and early seventies, they saw women in the front row "jerking and trembling" with the Spirit. This may not have been a direct inspiration, but the fact remains that several years later they came up with poppin' and tickin', rhythmic angulations of the torso and the limbs executed at a moderate tempo if one is poppin' or very fast if one is tickin'. With electric boogaloo, dancers could scintillate as if strobe-lit.

Boogaloo was a Fresno term of honor. It meant that a dancer could master anything. It meant he could even mime electricity, pass it through his body and put his own stamp on it. These brilliant moves reached New York via Los Angeles, Cleveland, South Carolina, and other mediating points in the late seventies. New York turned the style slightly around and called it electric boogie.

Dancers of California electric boogaloo or South Bronx electric boogie, "popping hard, hard waves," perfectly captured the hard and driving sound of hip hop drum-machine percussion. In addition, according to hip hop tradition, some of the flashier moves were copied off jerky, badly synced Saturday-morning television cartoons. By this theory, wave dancing, in collision with "found motions" borrowed from television animation, helped build the corporeal cubism of the finest masters. Dancing like pneumatic drills given life and spirit, or shattering into fragments of deliberate oscillation, their cultural engine, fueled by the past and driven toward a high-tech future, matches exactly the rationale behind the work of New York painter Keith Haring. "I'm attracted by the [past], but at the same time I feel driven toward the future," says Haring. "Primordial [styles] help you to be new."

Being ancient and being new explains the contrasts in Haring's drawings: silhouetted pyramids irradiated by flying saucers and ancient-looking jars vitalized by boogie friezes. You might say that Haring is the Degas of the b-boys. In murals on Manhattan's Avenue D near Houston Street, on the FDR Drive at Ninety-first Street and in fugitive chalk drawings in subway stations all over town, he has captured some of the basic moves of breakdancing. He also captures the volatility and the camaraderie of the hip hop world, which I have experienced firsthand.

I remember sitting with friends in a New York restaurant one night after a breaking contest. A dancer who had seen us at the contest passed by on the street. Immediately he started a wave with his left hand, passed this current through his shoulders, down his right arm and into his hand, and aimed the energy at me. It shot like a laser from the street through the plate glass, stopping my pointless conversation with this message: We saw you digging us. Come back. 'Cause hip hop is here to stay.

■ dance in hip hop culture

■ katrina hazzard-donald

■

■

■

■

■

9 A cyclical quality distinguishes African American dance from dance elsewhere in the African diaspora. That is, an African American dance appears, then goes underground or seems to die out, only to emerge twenty or so years later as a "new" dance.[1] Consider Cuban rumba, Brazilian samba, Jamaican skank, or any number of dances that have originated in black Atlantic cultures; these dances, which have become familiar nationally and internationally, seem to have continuous rather than cyclical histories.

Rumba, the national dance and rhythm of Cuba, more than any other dance genre reflects the aesthetic sentiments and historical self-characterizations of the Cuban people. As in many New World African dances, including those appearing in the United States, rumba uses derision, polymeter, mimetic characterization, and, often, biting commentary. Cuba is rumba; its daily rhythms at work and play contribute to the rumba consciousness. In rumba various aspects of life are expressed and overlaid with a strong mimetic mating dialogue between male and female.[2]

In Brazil the throbbing syncopations of samba have inspired samba schools and competitions in which large numbers of Brazilians actively participate. Like

Cuban rumba, Brazilian samba is a genre that expresses the national character and is familiar to old and young alike.

Like many popular dances in the United States, both samba and rumba originated among working-class and lower-class members of black communities only to be adopted and often modified by the "white" and upper-strata segments of society. The dances survive, largely intact, despite the contestation and class conflict that accompany their dissemination.

In contrast the cyclical nature of African American secular dance may reflect unique social forces; the rapidity with which the dance vocabulary is recycled and renamed in African American dance appears to be a by-product of the ever changing U.S. commodity market, which continually demands new dance material. The popular-culture market and industry are also international in scope, so that African American vernacular/popular dance eventually shows up in places such as Cuba or Sri Lanka.[3]

As influential as the external demands are, however, African American popular cultural creation is also driven by a desire for uniqueness and a tendency toward embellishment referred to as "the will to adorn" by anthropologist Zora Neale Hurston, which provide African American youth with wide parameters for unique expressiveness. Popular creation appears to change, even if only slightly, from one generation to the next.[4]

Shifting circumstances of class stratification and work, particularly as they impact on the changing African American national identity and character, also shaped the general movement of African American popular dance as a primarily agricultural labor force changed to one engaged in proletarian and other forms of urban labor. Immediately after Emancipation and the mass migration of rural freedmen into the cities and industries of both the South and North, African American secular social dance began to lose its rural character and take on more urban characteristics. The rural dances were marked by flat-footedness, bent or crouched postures, and group dancing rather than partnered couples. In the approximately sixty years of peak migration north, dances such as shuckin' corn, pitchin' hay, and milkin' the cow gave way to dances with more upright postures, less flat-footedness, and names that reflected a new urban reality.[5] But even today, after more than three-quarters of a century of proletarianization, African Americans still include agrarian references in their dance and in their music, particularly the blues.

Urbanization and proletarianization also transformed partnering relationships; the group and community-oriented dancing typical of rural dancing gave way to the single couple, with emphasis on sexual coupling. Subjected to less community scrutiny and participation, partners on the urban dance floor were alone with each other and required no contact with others. This isolation of the couple was a significant departure from the traditional circle and line dances familiar in both West African culture and in the dances of the rural bondsman and freedman. Traditional West African dances and even the Euro-American forms could not proceed without the participation of a sizeable community. Even so, the rural, community-oriented character of African American social dance was not completely obliterated. Evidence of this rural and community orientation surfaces in any group dance that does not emphasize sexual coupling. Think of dances such as the Madison, the continental, the birdland, the surplus, the bus stop, and the most recent, the electric slide—group dances with little or no partnering relationships—these are all single-line dances. Double-line dances such as the stroll and the soul train line require two lines, formed according to gender, and facing each other in a potential partnering arrangement. In both the stroll and the soul train line, dancers commonly featured a movement in which the partners move down the center between the lines; this limited partnering offered an opportunity for cooperation, but it was by no means required. Other evidence of rural influence can be observed in the mimetic character of African American dances. Dances such as the chicken (and its variation, the funky chicken), the horse, the snakehips, the pony, and milking the cow refer directly to the rural environment.

At any given moment in African American cultural history the working classes have had (and today have) a working repertoire of about half a dozen up-to-date dances from which to choose, and a general repertoire of around thirty.[6] There is no shortage of creative recycling. Each generation of African American youth, it seems, recalls demonstrating what they think is a new dance step, only to be told that their elders did that same dance twenty, thirty, forty, or more years ago. I had that experience many times as a young street dancer in Cleveland, Ohio. Like a language, the basic vocabulary of African American dance is passed along.[7] As did many of my peers, I learned it both in my home and "in the street" with my peer group. Former Cotton Club performer Howard "Stretch" Johnson and I once compared historical and regional variations on a number of dances. I asked him if he had ever heard of a dance called the twine. Yes, he had, and as we each demonstrated the versions we had learned, we agreed that his 1920s New York version, imported from "down South," was far more flat-footed and rooted into the earth than mine. My 1960s urban, midwestern version was more upright, lighter, with less weight in the arm strokes and freer movement in the legs and feet. After comparing a number of dances and making similar observations on all of them, we jointly concluded that his bent, flat-footed version of the dances might reflect a time when upright postures in African American dance were not well tolerated by white audiences. Many whites who attended the minstrel theater in particular were not ready to see Africans in postures that suggested anything but the bent, flat-footed, crouched, lowered head of the old "buck-dancing" styles. Since there was a widespread and influential exchange of dance material between the vernacular-popular-folk dances and the black professional performance tradition, many early versions of recycled popular dances bore that stamp of theatrical and plantation subservience, particularly when performed before a white audience. This was probably true as well on the southern plantation, since slaves were often called upon to entertain their master and his guests. The cakewalk, a dance that utilized exaggerated upright postures, was the notable exception.

The cakewalk is believed to have originally ridiculed the arrogant, upright, erect postures of the slaveholding class; it was a dance of derision.[8] The widespread change from the old Uncle Tom postures, bent and cowardly, to the more upright dancing styles appears simultaneously with the return of African American GIs from World War I and the heaviest recruitment of black male workers by northern industry.[9] African Americans had a new national pride and self-consciousness, reflected in the phrase "the new Negro," in the theater dance style of the "class acts," and in the slogan "All tap, no Tom." Performers like Eddie Rector purged the old postures from their routines.[10] Later in the popular-dance arena the lindy hop struck a new cord of defiance, public self-redefinition, and cultural pride.

Supporting these new dance trends in both the popular theater and in the rent parties, dance halls, honky-tonks, after-hours joints, and jooks were the significant numbers of black men who were increasingly being employed in industry or jobs related to or dependent upon industrial production: in factories, steel mills, auto plants, and the post office, and on the construction crews laying the nation's roads and later the new interstate highways. Both the economy and the community offered support for forming and maintaining African American families. Black men's lives were considerably less stressful and economically insecure than they would later become. This trend toward a positive environment for marriage and family was clearly expressed in the urban song and dance styles emerging and dominating African American popular culture between 1920 and the mid-1970s.

The themes of security, marriage, mating, sexual coupling, heartbreak, and cheating became more popular and well developed in the music and dance era of rhythm and blues. Blacks, like many other Americans, enjoyed the postwar prosperity and security of the forties, fifties, and sixties. For those who remained marginally employed, the thriving alternative economy—particularly "the numbers"—provided supplemental and, for some, occasional full-time employment.[11] But even the alternative economy had at its foundation African American male breadwinners, for without the wealth generated by African American male labor and the income of working black men, and to a lesser extent women, "the numbers" would not have thrived. The labor of many African American women was an important supplement to that of the men. All this would change.

In the 1960s a number of economic and social changes began to transform the culture-creating environment of African American life. First, the state-sponsored educational, social, and economic programs in black communities, many of them born of the sixties, suffered large funding cuts and were phased out. The remaining jobs were privately funded for relatively short periods, affording workers little job security. Nevertheless, some of these programs served as centers of community activism as well as providing employment and economic services such as job training. The Job Corps, street academies, Model Cities, drug education and abuse treatment, Opportunities Industrialization Center, and black-culture community centers and programs became focal points for those on the bottom of society who wanted to make it, thus providing an additional buffer to economic deprivation and instilling hope and societal concern. Many of these programs had youth orientations; most focused at least some of their energies on young people. At these focal points culture was generated, reworked, challenged, and disseminated.

Second, while racial integration brought about many positive changes, it also resulted in the demise or weakening of some traditional black economic networks and institutions. For example, the old "numbers" or "policy" games were converted into state-controlled lotteries, and specialized "race" products and services, such as those related to hair and beauty, were drawn into the mainstream. The third, and by no means least, important change was the uprooting of U.S. industry, marked by corporate flight and the move to a service-based economy. The loss of manufacturing jobs disproportionately affected black men who headed households; as the percentage of black male unemployment began a steady rise, the percentage of female-headed households began to increase dramatically.

By the late 1960s and early 1970s popular music and dance had become increasingly political as the industrial base that supported much black cultural creation eroded; the politicized forms of popular music and dance were successfully challenged by the apolitical, slick dance and music called disco. Disco gave voice to a newly empowered economic strata, the yuppie, and the midlevel service worker.[12] Despite the social, political, and economic accomplishments that their grandparents and parents had struggled for, African American youth inherited economically unstable and eroded ground for their hopes and dreams. Vicious attacks on all phases of the black movement deprived this generation of a viable social movement through which to work against their frustrations and for their economic needs. Where would this generation of African American youth find employment? Where would they find the working, productive male role models so necessary to the health of any community? With what material would they create their dreams? In the midst of rapidly worsening social conditions, how could this generation find meaning in their community's traditional music and dance forms as their predecessors had? Would they create utterly new dance and music forms that spoke more directly to their unique experiences in a world without its former industrial base? In this era of African American male economic insecurity, of popular conspicuous consumption (e.g., the brazen display of designer labels and brand names), of widening gaps between rich and poor, and of a moribund social movement for black and minority inclusion, hip hop emerged.

Why hip hop?

Hip hop is an expressive cultural genre originating among lower- and often marginalized working-class African American youth; it has West Indian influences, particularly dance hall, dub, and DJ style.[13] The genre includes rapping and rap music, graffiti writing, particular dance styles (including breakdancing), specific attire, and a specialized language and vocabulary. Hip hop appears at the crucial juncture of postindustrial stagnation, increased family dissolution, and a weakened struggle for black economic and political rights. Might one expect the pressures of mutually antagonistic social forces such as high unemployment, heightened job competition, and expectations of conspicuous consumption to influence both the popular expressive culture and the culture-creating apparatus of a community? I say yes. It is no coincidence that many youth of the hip hop generation have never known the relative security that some of their parents and even grandparents knew.

Hip hop dance is clearly masculine in style, with postures assertive in their own right as well as in relation to a female partner. In its early stages, hip hop rejected the partnering ritual between men and women; at a party or dance, hip hop dance was performed between men or by a lone man. About 1973 or 1974 I attended a dance given by African American students at Cornell University. I took the initiative and asked a young man to dance; on refusing my invitation, he explained that he couldn't dance with women, that the way he danced was unsuitable for dancing with women. He proceeded to give me a demonstration of how that was so, running through several dance steps that I had seen performed by Fred "Rerun" Berry and the Lockers. Correctly performed, the dance did not allow for female partnering; it was a purely male expression and rarely performed by females. Particularly in early hip hop the male does not assume the easygoing, cool, confident polish characteristic of earlier popular-dance expression. Even in its early stages hip hop dancing aggressively asserted male dominance.

Waack and breakin'

Hip hop dance can be characterized in three stages; waack, breakdancing, and rap dance. Waack dancing appears about 1972. Dance moves such as locking (later known on the East Coast as pop-locking), the robot, and the spank, along with splits and rapidly revolving spins combined with unexpected freezes, were part of waack's outrageous style.[14] Here the fusion of theatrical expectation and outrageous showmanship occurs that would mark later hip hop styles known as breakdancing.

A staple in the vocabularies of waack, breaking, and, to a lesser degree, rap dance was the pop and lock, a movement technique that was part of the jerk in the late 1950s before that dance left black communities and crossed over to mainstream America in the mid- to late 1960s. (The mainstream version is almost unrecognizable to the dancers who performed the original.) The pop and lock is both a way of handling the body and a movement quality in which a jerking and freezing of movement takes place. In this particular style a segmented body part such as the foot or hand initiates a free-flowing, undulating movement that flows up the leg or arm and ends with a jerking and freezing in place. It can be done with almost any combination of body parts but is most often performed with the torso, arms, and legs. The pop-and-lock technique could also be observed in the snakehips, as that dance was performed by the Cotton Club's Earl "Snakehips" Tucker in the 1920s.[15] Going farther back, a dance called the snakehips was popular in the Georgia Sea Islands and throughout the antebellum plantation South, and I have no reason to doubt that it resembled the version I learned in a 1950s midwestern African American community.[16]

As with later stages of development, clothing was an essential part of hip hop style. Big apple hats (an oversized style cap popularized by the late Donny Hathaway and soon to be replaced by Kangol caps, then by baseball caps); knickers, or suspenders with baggy pants, or pants tucked into striped knee socks; open-laced combat boots (soon to be replaced by open-laced sneakers); sun visors—all were part of waack's style of dress. Through mass-media exposure, particularly on the TV dance show *Soul Train*, the dance group the Lockers and the Outrageous Waack Dancers popularized the early hip hop dancing styles, helped along by TV sitcoms such as *What's Happening*, featuring Fred "Rerun" Berry. Rerun was often allowed short solos to demonstrate the early hip hop dance and clothing style. Both the Waacks' and Lockers' dancing was full of jerks and staccato movement, with up-and-down motion providing the center from which flashy embellishments such as high kicks and sudden unexpected turns emanated.

Breakdancing, the second stage of hip hop dancing, draws on a traditional and familiar concept in African American music, dance, and verbal arts: competitive one-upmanship. In music, breaking appears in the cutting contests of Harlem rent-party musicians, or in the competitive dialogue between musician and dancer. Look for it in the verbal arts of toasting, signifying, burnin', or "cutting his mouth out," usually performed with rhyming dexterity, articulation, and style; this verbal skill is highly valued in certain contexts. The principle of competitive dialogue shows up in African American street rhyme (e.g., the Signifying Monkey, Stackolee, and Shine rhymes), in the ritual of insult known as "the dozens," in contemporary rap music, and in a sacred context in the African American sermon.[17] It is not surprising that the competitive acrobatics involved in breakdancing were labeled *breaking* or that this traditional principle provides the form through which rappers and DJs would express themselves.

It is generally agreed that breaking as a dance style emerged around 1973 or 1974, concurrent with disco but confined to the African American youth subculture of male street associations known as crews. Breakdancing involved acrobatics that used headspins, backspins, moonwalking (a recycled version of the late 1950s, early 1960s dance the creep), waving, and the robot; it was mediated by a preparatory step known as top rockin' and pressed into competitive virtuosity. By 1976 the Zulus, a group of African American teenagers from the Bronx (the Zulu Nation formed as an alternative to the gangs in that community), had perfected the top rockin' footwork, backspins, and headspins. By 1978 many black youth had given up breaking and moved on to DJing, but the dance form would be rejuvenated among Puerto Rican youth, who took it up later than blacks and extended its longevity.[18]

Breaking's introduction to the general public by the mass media in April

1981 surely marked the beginning of its decline as a functional apparatus for competitive challenge among rival groups or individuals. Breakdancers began rehearsing in order to be discovered and appear in movies or for competitive street exhibition rather than practicing to compete with a rival. Far more acrobatic than either preceding or subsequent hip hop dance forms, without competition, breaking loses its thrust, its raison d'être. Movement into the mainstream negated its status as countercultural by redefining it from a subcultural form to one widely accepted and imitated, a move that inadvertently linked breakers with the society that had previously excluded them. Breaking became so popular that it was featured as entertainment in the opening extravaganza of the 1984 Olympics.

Rap dancing

The third stage of hip-hop dance, which I will label rap dance, developed as a response to the popularity and athletic requirements of breaking. Combining aspects of both breaking and waack, it is influenced and cross-fertilized by a less athletic form of popular dance, house dancing, which uses much of the traditional African American vocabulary. Further influenced by the older rhythm-and-blues dances of the 1950s and 1960s, rap dance is male oriented, even male dominated, but unlike breakdancing not exclusively male. Its movements suit male-female partnering better than those of either waack or breaking, but less well than older popular dance forms such as the lindy hop or the rhythm-and-blues dances.

Like the lindy hop, hip hop dance is often athletic, youth oriented, and competitive, but rap dancing, and hip hop dance generally, require considerably less cooperation between partners. In the era of both rhythm and blues and the lindy hop, the contingencies of African American life required and fostered a firmer cooperation and interdependence from the racial group and the extended family to an extent virtually unknown to most of today's young hip hoppers. The lindy demonstrates a celebratory exuberance foreign to the breakdancing phase of hip hop dance and largely absent from the other two phases as well. This exuberance was fed by the celebration of the individual bound by in-group solidarity, community accountability, and cooperation.

Though I would not categorize rap dance as a dance of celebration, it does appear to celebrate male solidarity, strength, and competitiveness, themes that might be expected to emerge via the social dance in an era of high black male unemployment and of scarce jobs for which men are increasingly forced to compete with women. At the same time, the lack of commitment to the traditional partnering ritual also breaks with at least one function found in earlier African American social dancing: selecting a romantic partner. Dancers who want to couple off romantically must return to the dance styles of a previous era. Hip hop shows no trace of the male-leadership themes expressed in the lindy and its 1950s and 1960s variants (the strand, offtime, jitterbug, and hand dancing), although they are still observable in the slow drag variations of what is now called slow dancing.

I was ambivalent about the hip hop phenomenon until I noticed the dancing that accompanied the rapping; it was energetic, athletic, and noticeably male dominated, using a very African movement vocabulary. It revived movements that had been out of popular use for thirty years, like splits and rapidly revolving turns (movements still employed by performers). "Splits have made a comeback," I thought. Over time I observed more of this "new" dancing and spoke with African American youth about where they got their dance steps. Many had learned them from friends, but most of the young people I spoke with in West Philadelphia also identified several dance steps with a popular hip hop artist or said that they learned the step from watching a particular performer. This indicated to me that the interplay between the popular/vernacular dance and the black commercial performer is still very strong. In observing rap dance I have seen the following traditional African American dances or dance fragments recycled and recontextualized: the black bottom, roach, Watusi, splits, boogaloo, mashed potatoes, funky butt (funky bottom, boodie green, 'da butt), chicken, four corners, worm, snakehips, and horse (old and new versions). I have also observed the use of traditional opposition or counterpoint as well as traditional characteristics such as percussive phrasing, polyrhythm, derision, mimetic play, and competition.

The rappers whose dance movements best encompass and personify the extremes in the genre of hip hop movement are Flavor Flav, of the group Public Enemy, and M.C. Hammer. Flavor Flav resembles the contemporary urban Esu-Elegba, or deity (principle) of uncertainty and unpredictability, also known as the trickster deity.[19] M.C. Hammer's well-choreographed movements draw directly from a strong rhythm-and-blues tradition. Hammer credits James Brown, a rhythm-and-blues artist, as the most powerful influence on his dance-performance style.

Contemporary rap dances such as the pump, running man, and Roger Rabbit, as well as the dance styles from a concurrent genre, house dancing, all exhibit structural and functional continuity with previous dances. House dancing and rap dance are cross-fertilizing each other. Like most African dance styles, these exhibit angularity, asymmetry, polyrhythmic sensitivity, derision themes, segmentation and delineation of body parts, earth-centeredness, and percussive performance.[20] To this list we can add apart dancing.

Apart dancing describes dancing in which the partners do not touch each other during the dance, yet the commitment to the partnering ritual is clear; this quality helps characterize both the traditional West African dance styles and many dance styles in African communities in the Americas. In the old rhythm-and-blues forms, apart dancing was a dominant theme, and little competition between partners emerged. Individual virtuosity often took the form of display rather than challenge as a dominant governing principle. Themes of challenge pervade both breakdancing and rap dance to a greater degree than occurs in either waack dancing or the older rhythm-and-blues dances such as the twist, the slop, or the horse. Challenge could and did emerge in these older dances, however, particularly when there was a dispute to be settled.

What hip hop dance says

The richness of gesture and motion in hip hop dance, as in numerous other forms of popular American dance styles that develop among marginalized African American, West Indian, and Puerto Rican youth, reflects the effect of social and economic marginalization on their lives.

Competitiveness in hip hop dance occurs not only against these backdrops but also with strained gender relations thrown into the mix. Since U.S. society regards young African American males as threatening, attitudes of fear and suspicion restrict their entry into the mainstream service economy as well as other areas of mainstream life. That economy thus more easily absorbs African American female workers than males; add the effects of the feminist movement on black women's attitudes toward traditional female roles, and you have raised the potential for cultural expression of rivalry and self-assertion between black men and women.

Hip hop dance permits and encourages a public (and private) male bonding that simultaneously protects the participants from and presents a challenge to the racist society that marginalized them. This dance is not necessarily observer friendly; its movements establish immediate external boundaries while enacting an aggressive self-definition. Hip hop's outwardly aggressive postures and gestures seem to contain and channel the dancer's rage.

The whole of African American dance reflects the postures and gestures that African Americans esteem. Observe today's popular dancing and note how important unpredictability is; reflected in the term "fresh" and emphasized in the new movement styles, this unpredictability has a certain logic that calls forth praise and admiration.

Hip hop dance reflects an alienation not only of young African American males from mainstream society and of African American males from females but also of one African American generation from another. Despite the many continuities and similarities to earlier dances, hip hop represents a clear demarcation between generations in ways previously unknown in African American dance culture. Because of its athletic nature, its performance in popular arenas is largely confined to those under about twenty-five years of age. This might reflect the commodity market's emphasis on youth; it certainly coincides with current marketing strategies that appeal to the "cult of youth," strategies that do not exclude African American cultural commodities. Or it might simply reflect the cultural leadership of young black men in creating African American dances.

Although hip hop dance possesses an air of defiance of authority and mainstream society that reflects a critical vision observable in earlier dances of derision, it lacks the dominant or strongly stated derision that one finds in dances such as the PeeWee Herman or the Patty Duke of the 1970s, or even the cakewalk. True, hip hop's critical vision comes out of a marginalized youth culture with its own language, its own values and symbols, its own dance and style, yet unlike a true counterculture, hip hop does not reject the mainstream materialism of designer leisure wear, brand-name kicks, expensive cars, and (until recently) dookie gold.[21] Perhaps this embracing or materialism by the later hip hop stylists modifies or otherwise influences the emergence of derision themes, but this connection is by no means clear-cut.

Still, as dance has done for youth in other times, hip hop dance does more than express the view of the social and economic outsider, or even of the wanna-be insider. It encompasses a highly functional system of symbols that affect individual identity development, peer-group status, and intergroup dynamics and conflict.[22] For example, youth in New York City used the breaking form of hip hop to settle lower-level gang disputes and assert territorial dominance. A similar function for dancing was observed among gang members in Chicago in the late 1950s and early 1960s: "Dancing is even more important in Vice Lord life. Almost all Vice Lords take intense pride in their dancing ability and lose few opportunities to demonstrate it."[23]

Malcolm X describes the importance of dancing ability in facilitating peer-group inclusion for him: "Like hundreds of thousands of country-bred Negroes who had come to the Northern black ghetto before me, and have come since, I'd also acquired all the other fashionable ghetto adornments—the zoot suits and conk that I have described, liquor, cigarettes, then reefers—all to erase my embarrassing background. But I harbored one secret humiliation: I couldn't dance."[24]

I have understood the significance of dance in negotiating peer-group inclusion since childhood. As in many African American communities, dancing was important among the young people I knew for peer-group status and acceptance. In the mid-1950s a dance known as the slop was extremely popular.[25] I heard my peers joyfully discussing this dance that I knew nothing about, and I felt excluded. One day I asked an older girl (about twelve or thirteen years old), Thelmari Workman, who lived downstairs from me, to demonstrate the dance for me. She teased me, taunted me, told me that I was "too little to learn the slop." She had me crying. I begged her, "Thelmari, please, please teach me how to do the slop." I knew that dance could help me to belong with my peers and garner admiration from within my community, and it could open an entire new realm of being, self-definition, and socialization.[26]

Just as the jookers and jitterbugs of another era were given their monikers, African American working- and lower-class youth who participate in the hip hop genre, who adopt its persona as their personal presentation style, are sometimes called b-boys, b-girls, or hip hop people.[27] Like their forerunners, they are the product of a specific sociohistoric backdrop and time-bound cultural experience. And like the *rumbista* with Cuban rumba and the *sambista* with Brazilian samba, hip hop people identify with, embrace, and live the genre completely, however short-lived it may be.

The hip hop persona emphasizes converting postures that in another context would indicate alienation and defeat into postures of self-assurance in the face of unbeatable odds. For instance, holding one's arms crossed high on the chest might be interpreted as an insecure and withdrawing posture; in hip hop dance I interpret this posture as affirming African American maleness, strength, and readiness for physical and sexual competition. It also indicates the vision of an inside observer who is simultaneously on the outside. "Laying in the cut," this observer sees something invisible to most people; his bobbing head and crossed arms reaffirm this secretly observed universal truth.

Though hip hop music and dance are today enjoyed by virtually every socioecnomic segment of American society, hip hop postures and presentation of self are born of the African-derived core culture of the street, and they are still used to negotiate a place there. Fear was among the general white public's initial reaction to the latter-day hip hop genre. I have observed young men with hip hop carriage and in hip hop attire—sneaker laces open, baseball cap, sweatsuit—listening to and carrying their beat boxes blasting rap music in the public space of the street, and I have observed whites threatened and intimidated by their presence.

Talkin' the talk and walkin' the walk in the mainstream

But the image of hip hop dance and music is changing, influenced by women's entry into the genre, by the media, and by the adoption of hip hop by the popular-music and advertising industries. The recent entry of females into the rap recording and video industry has challenged the hard, male-dominated, often misogynist hip hop identity reflected in the themes of some rap songs. Women are talkin' the talk of hip hop; they are dancing and creating new dance materials, as well as recycling older dances and crosscultural black dances such as the butterfly in ways that voice the moral, romantic, and political concerns, the aesthetic preferences, the needs and desires of this generation.[28]

Since the popular market has recently embraced hip hop as a marketing strategy, movement and music once identified with African American, West Indian, and Latino male street associations are being used to sell everything from pastry to autos, and they are being incorporated into aerobics classes and exercise videos.

At the same time, widespread acceptance of hip hop music has led to modifications in the masculine, confrontive nature of the dance, resulting in less athletic new dances that can be performed to hip hop music. Hip hop songs are increasingly danceable, even using the movement of a previous era. For television and movies, in dance competitions, and in commercials, professional choreographers have adopted hip hop energy and style.

Although the wide acceptance and exploitation of hip hop in the advertising and popular-music industries has on one level robbed the dance of its original significance, hip hop still functions in the places of its origin. Most mainstream Americans will never see the subtle codes, gestures, and meanings of hip hop as they are displayed in African American communities, and that is true of much dance originating in African American culture.

Meanwhile, the aspects of hip hop that can be commercialized will affect the daily rhythms of mainstream American life, but even watered down, hip hop's influence will have profound and enduring effects on American culture.

Notes

1. Chadwick Hansen, "Jenny's Toe: Negro Shaking Dances in America," *American Quarterly* 19 (1967): 554–563.

2. For accounts and analyses of rumba, see Yvonne Daniel, *Rumba: Dance and Social Change in Contemporary Cuba* (Bloomington: Indiana University Press, 1995). See also Janheinz Jahn, *Muntu: The New African Culture* (New York: Grove, 1961).

3. In July 1990 I observed breakdancing in a cabaret in Havana. The crew, attired in open-laced sneakers, baseball caps, and baggy trousers or jeans, performed popping and locking, headspins, backspins, and moonwalking that rivaled any I have observed in the United States. Television, videotape, and returning relatives were sources for cultural transference from the United States to Cuba. As far back as 1983 I was informed by Sri Lankan students at Cornell University in Ithaca, New York, that breakdancing was being attempted in Sri Lanka. One male student in particular was avidly learning the new moves in order to carry them back to his homeland. For accounts of the international impact of hip hop, see "A Newcomer Abroad, Rap Speaks Up," *New York Times*, Arts and Leisure section, August 23, 1992, which discusses the emergence of hip hop in Russia, China, India, West Africa, Eastern Europe, Britain, France, and Mexico.

4. Zora Neale Hurston, "Characteristics of Negro Expression," in *Negro Anthology*, ed. Nancy Cunard (New York: Negro Universities Press, 1969), 44.

5. Renamed the toilet stool, the dance milkin' the cow appears in the urban Midwest, Cleveland, Detroit, and Gary, Indiana, in the late 1940s and early 1950s; the footwork and lateral pelvic isolation goes on to become part of a popular 1960s dance, the Watusi, and later reappears once more in the late 1970s as the rock.

6. Regional variation in this repertoire becomes less pronounced when dances have popular media exposure, and it is even less apparent generally than it was in the past. Today regional variation is short lived.

7. For a discussion of dance's languagelike properties, see Judith Lynn Hanna, *To Dance Is Human: A Theory of Non-Verbal Communication* (Chicago: University of Chicago Press, 1988).

8. For accounts of the cakewalk, see Tom Fletcher, *The Tom Fletcher Story—100 Years of the Negro in Show Business* (New York: Burdge, 1954); see also "Cakewalk King: 81-Year-Old Charles E. Johnson Still Dreams of New Comeback with Dance Step of Gay 90s," *Ebony*, February 1953, 99–102, and Lynne Fauley Emery, *Black Dance from 1619 to Today*, 2d ed. (Princeton, N.J.: Princeton Book Co., 1988). It is interesting to note that waack, a 1970s hip hop style of dance, used high kicks similar to those used in the cakewalk. My current research leads me to question the interpretation of the cakewalk as purely imitative of exaggerated Euro-American postures. There are numerous dances in West Africa that use the leg in high kicks or extensions. Dances such as sabar, in Senegal, use high leg raises and arched erect spines.

9. Florette Henri, *Black Migration: Movement North, 1900–1920* (Garden City, N.Y.: Anchor, 1976).

10. Marshall Stearns and Jean Stearns, *Jazz Dance* (New York: Macmillan, 1966), 285–297. African American performers who worked the TOBA (Theater Owners Booking Association) circuit responded to the demand for subservient postures with the phrase "All tap, no Tom," indicating that they were not willing to perform Uncle Tom postures in their dance routines. Interview with Howard "Stretch" Johnson,

former Cotton Club and TOBA performer and brother-in-law of Lincoln Perry, whose stage name was Step 'n Fetchit, New Paltz, New York, December 1979.

11. "The numbers" was an illegal lottery played in black communities. See St. Clair Drake and Horace Cayton, *Black Metropolis* (New York: Harper & Row, 1962). See also Harold Gosnell, *Negro Politicians* (Chicago: University of Chicago Press, 1935); J. Saunders Redding, "Playing the Numbers," *North American Review* 238 (December 1934); and George J. McCall, "Symbiosis: The Case of Hoodoo and the Numbers Racket," *Social Problems* 10 (Spring 1963): 361–371.

12. That the famous Motown sound came out of Detroit, Michigan, is no coincidence. The Motor City was a midwestern industrial center that employed thousands of African American men and women in auto production. This economic base provided a sociocultural and economic backdrop for a particular type of popular-culture creation. The Motown sound found a ready market in the black communities of Detroit, Cleveland, Gary, Pittsburgh, and other centers of heavy industry with large southern first- and second-generation migrant populations.

13. The vainglorious boasting, sexual innuendo (recently labeled sexist), and mocking commentary on a wide range of topics including social issues, racism, economics, and politics have existed in Trinidadian calypso for at least sixty years. Trinidadian calypso, with its high level of improvisation and verbal dexterity requirements, was the most influential musical form in the English-speaking Caribbean until the early 1970s commercial emergence of Jamaican reggae. In the mid-1970s Jamaican bands began experimenting with and integrating calypso's verbal improvisation into their music. Jamaican DJs scatted over reggae records, intersecting with traditional African American scatting heard over transistor radios in the Caribbean. Known as "toasting" (not to be confused with the African American toast rhyme, though culturally similar), this technique was mastered, recorded, and popularized by artists like U Roy and Big Youth and can be heard today in the running rap style of Shabba Ranks. Jamaican and other West Indian immigrants to the United States brought their musical styles with them, and in the 1970s toasters could be heard on the streets of South Bronx, an economically marginalized community with significant West Indian, African American, and Puerto Rican populations. Many of the early rappers and DJs like Afrika Bambaataa had West Indian parents at home and absorbed the strong West Indian influences. See "The Forgotten Caribbean Connection," *New York Times*, August 23, 1992, Pop Music section.

14. "The 'Outrageous' Waack Dancers," *Ebony*, August 1978, 64. I observed similar popping and locking in a sacred ceremony to the deity Shango in Cuba in July 1990, and the movement can be observed in dances to Shango in Nigeria. Interviews with Abiodune Adekunle, Nigerian Yoruba devotee of Shango, Philadelphia, March 1991 and with Unoboje Aisiku, Nigerian Yoruba, May 1992.

15. Interview with Charles "Honi" Coles, Ithaca, New York, March 1980. During an after-dinner chat at a mutual friend's home, Honi performed the old snakehips dance the way he had seen Earl Tucker perform it. Watching Coles perform it made me realize that the 1950s dance move known as poppin' the hips, which I learned around 1957, was an updated version of the 1920s snakehips.

16. Georgia Writers Project, *Drums and Shadows* (Athens: University of Georgia Press, 1940), 115; Stearns, *Jazz Dance*, 235–238.

17. For an excellent commentary on the importance of verbal dexterity among African Americans, both on the mainland and in the Caribbean, see Roger D. Abrahams, *The*

Man of Words in the West Indies (Baltimore: Johns Hopkins University Press, 1983); see also Abrahams, "Playing the Dozens," *Journal of American Folklore* 75: 209–220, and *Deep Down in the Jungle: Negro Narrative Folklore from the Streets of Philadelphia* (Hatboro, Pa.: Folklore Associates, 1964); Lawrence W. Levine, *Black Culture and Black Consciousness* (New York: Oxford University Press, 1977), 298–366.

18. Steven Hager, *Hip Hop* (New York: St. Martin's, 1984), 81–90. I learned the moonwalk in the late 1950s or early 1960s in Cleveland, Ohio, as a dance named the creep. Michael Jackson, who popularized it as the moonwalk, was born in 1958 just as the creep was emerging and gaining popularity; he could have seen it performed or learned it in the midwestern community of Gary, Indiana, where he grew up the child of a steel-mill employee.

19. During performance, Flavor Flav bears a striking resemblance to other New World African performers—King Warrin of the John Canoe celebrations, Haiti's Baron Samedi, and even the Uruguayan "el Gramillero." All exhibit aspects of Esu-Elegba. See Ira De A. Reid, "The John Canoe Festival," *Phylon* 3 (4): 350, 356; Dougald MacMillan, "John Kuners," *Journal of American Folklore* 39 (January–March 1926): 53–57; Margaret Shedd, "Carib Dance Patterns," *Theater Arts Monthly* 17 (January 1933): 65–77; Paulo deCarvalho Neto, "The Candombe, a Dramatic Dance from Afro-Uruguayan Folklore," *Journal of the Society for Ethnomusicology* 5 (1962): 164–174; and Katrina Hazzard-Gordon, "Dancing to Rebalance the Universe: African-American Secular Dance," *Journal of Physical Education, Recreation & Dance* 62 (February 1991): 36. Flavor Flav and other rappers pronounce the word "boy" as "bwoy," drawing out the "wo" and giving it an "oi" sound. Melville J. Herskovits comments on Africanized speech patterns in Jamaica and Suriname: "In addition we found correspondences in such pronunciations as 'bwoy' for 'boy.' " See *The Myth of the Negro Past* (Boston: Beacon, 1990), 282.

20. John Szwed, "Musical Adaptation among Afro-Americans," *Journal of American Folklore* 82 (April–June 1969); Hurston, "Characteristics of Negro Expression."

21. *Kicks*, the name given to the designer sneakers worn by the youth, is a term at least forty years old in many African American communities. *Dookie gold* refers to the large gold chains admired and desired by some youth.

22. Katrina Hazzard-Gordon, "Afro-American Core Culture Social Dance: An Examination of Four Aspects of Meaning," in *Perspectives of Black Popular Culture*, ed. Harry Shaw (Bowling Green, Ohio: Bowling Green State University Popular Press), 46; see also Roy Milton Clark, "Dance Party as a Socialization Mechanism," *Sociology and Sociological Research* 58 (1974).

23. R. Lincoln Keiser, *The Vice Lords* (New York: Holt, Rinehart & Winston, 1969), 52. The dance–martial arts form known as *capoeira* also serves this purpose. See Bira Almeida, *Capoeira, a Brazilian Art Form* (Richmond, Calif.: North Atlantic, 1981).

24. Alex Haley with Malcolm X, *The Autobiography of Malcolm X* (New York: Grove, 1966), 56.

25. The slop today is known as the George Jefferson, named for the main character in a TV sitcom, who performed it on a number of occasions.

26. For further discussion of the function of dance in African American culture, see Hazzard-Gordon, "Afro-American Core Culture Social Dance," 46.

27. Interview with North Philadelphia youth who participate in the hip hop genre, Philadelphia, December 1990. I found the label "hip hop people" used when no other term fit. It is used in North Philadelphia among lower- and working-class black youth

only to describe those who wear the appropriate clothes, listen to rap, and immerse themselves in the genre through the verbal and nonverbal language. The appropriate terms to describe hip hop participants, formerly "b-boy" or "b-girl," seem to have changed as hip hop becomes widely accepted.

28. For a discussion of female rappers, see "Female Rappers Invade the Male Rap Industry," *Donahue Transcripts*, show #0529-91, transcript #3216, May 29, 1991; Tricia Rose, "Never Trust a Big Butt and a Smile," *Camera Obscura*, no. 23 (May 1990): 108–130; "The Women of Rap," *Rappin Magazine*, July 1990; Jill Pearlman, "Rap's Gender Gap," *Option*, Fall 1988, 32–36; and Nancy Guevara, "Women, Writin', Rappin', Breakin'," in *The Year Left 2*, ed. Mike Davis et al. (New York: Verso, 1987), 160–175. The butterfly is a dance imported to East Coast cities from Jamaican dance-hall style.

hidden politics: discursive and institutional policing
of rap music

tricia rose

The sometimes-hostile approach to rap clubs has been evident in the Alameda police scandal. Five officers have been disciplined for transmitting racist remarks over their patrol car computers. Some of the messages referred to black patrons of two rap clubs ... officers had joked about dressing up in Ku Klux Klan attire and about barbequing and killing black people.

The *San Francisco Chronicle*, January 10, 1992

10 Confining the discussion of politics in rap to lyrical analysis addresses only the most explicit dimension of the politics of contemporary black cultural expression. Rap's cultural politics lie in its lyrical expression, its articulation of communal knowledge, and in the context for its public reception. As is the case for cultural production in general, the politics of rap music involves the contestation over public space, the meanings, interpretations, and value of the lyrics and music, and the investment of cultural capital. In short, it is not just what you say, it is where you can say it, how others react to it, and whether you have the power to command access to public space. To dismiss rappers who do not choose "political" subjects as having no politically resistive role ignores the complex web of institutional policing to which all rappers are subjected, especially in large public-space contexts. The struggle over context, meaning, and access to public space is critical to contemporary cultural politics. Power and resistance are exercised through signs, language, and institutions. Consequently, popular pleasure involves physical, ideological, and territorial struggles. Black popular pleasure involves a particularly thorny struggle.

Tricia Rose, "Hidden Politics," pp. 124–145, from *Black Noise*, © 1994 by Tricia Rose, Wesleyan University Press, by permission of University Press of New England.

My central concern here is the exercise of institutional and ideological power over rap music and the manner in which rap fans and artists relate and respond to ideological and institutional constraints. More specifically, I try to untangle the complex relationships between the political economy of rap and the sociologically based crime discourse that frames it. This involves a close examination of the resistance to rap in large venues, media interpretations of rap concerts, and incidents of "violence" that have occurred.[1] In addition, venue security reaction to a predominantly black rap audience is an important facet of this process of institutional policing. It sets the tone of the audience's relationship to public space and is a manifestation of the arena owners' ideological position on black youths.

> Voice 1: The Economy, Phuhh!
> Voice 2: Yeah, I know.
>> Voice 1: Politics, Phuffh!
>> Voice 2: Yeah, say that also.
>>> Voice 1: The Police . . .
>>> Voice 2: Guilty, guilty . . .
>>>> Voice 1: Everything!
>>>> Voice 2: Uhuh. Wait a, wait wait wait . . .
>>>>> Voice 1: Except for the youth,
>>>>> Voice 2: Yeah, yeah, wait wait.
>
> Voice 1: It's about to come back!
> Voice 2: Yeah I know . . . Here it comes, ALRIGHT OKAY!
> "Youthful Expressions," A Tribe Called Quest[2]

The way rap and rap-related violence are discussed in the popular media is fundamentally linked to the larger social discourse on the spacial control of black people. Formal policies that explicitly circumscribe housing, school, and job options for black people have been outlawed; however, informal yet trenchant forms of institutional discrimination still exist in full force. Underwriting these de facto forms of social containment is the understanding that black people are a threat to social order. Inside of this, black urban teenagers are the most profound symbolic referent for internal threats to social order. Not surprisingly, then, young African Americans are in fundamentally antagonistic relationships to the institutions that most prominently frame and constrain their lives. The public school system, the police, and the popular media perceive and construct young African Americans as a dangerous internal element in urban America; an element that, if allowed to roam freely, will threaten the social order; an element that must be policed. Since rap music is understood as the predominant symbolic voice of black urban males, it heightens this sense of threat and reinforces dominant white middle-class objections to urban black youths who do not aspire to (but are haunted by) white middle-class standards.

My experiences and observations while attending several large-venue rap concerts in major urban centers serve as disturbingly obvious cases of how black urban youth are stigmatized, vilified, and approached with hostility and suspicion by authority figures. I offer a description of my confrontation and related observations not simply to prove that such racially and class-motivated hostility exists but, instead, to use it as a case from which to tease out how the public-space policing of black youth and rap music feeds into and interacts with other media, municipal, and corporate policies that determine who can publicly gather and how.

■ Thousands of young black people milled around waiting to get into the large arena. The big rap summer tour was in town, and it was a prime night to see and be seen. The "preshow show" was in full effect. Folks were dressed in the latest fly-gear: bicycle shorts, high-top sneakers, chunk jewelry, baggie pants, and polka-dotted tops. Hair style was a fashion show in itself: high-top fade designs, dreads, corkscrews, and braids with gold-and-purple sparkles. Crews of young women were checking out the brothers; posses of brothers were scoping out the sisters, each comparing styles among themselves. Some wide-eyed preteenyboppers were soaking in the teenage energy, thrilled to be out with the older kids.

As the lines for entering the arena began to form, dozens of mostly white private security guards hired by the arena management (many of whom are off-duty cops making extra money), dressed in red polyester V-neck sweaters and grey work pants, began corralling the crowd through security checkpoints. The free-floating spirit began to sour, and in its place began to crystallize a sense of hostility mixed with humiliation. Men and women were lined up separately in preparation for the weapon search. Each of the concertgoers would go through a body pat down, pocketbook, knapsack, and soul search. Co-ed groups dispersed, people moved toward their respective search lines. The search process was conducted in such a way that each person being searched was separated from the rest of the line. Those searched could not function as a group, and subtle interactions between the guard and person being searched could not be easily observed. As the concertgoers approached the guards. I noticed a distinct change in posture and attitude. From a distance, it seemed that the men were being treated with more hostility than the women in line. In the men's area, there was an almost palpable sense of hostility on behalf of the guards as well as the male patrons. Laughing and joking among men and women, which had been loud and buoyant up until this point, turned into virtual silence.

As I approached the female security guards, my own anxiety increased. What if they found something I was not allowed to bring inside? What was prohibited, anyway? I stopped and thought: All I have in my small purse is my wallet, eyeglasses, keys, and a notepad—nothing "dangerous." The security woman patted me down, scanned my body with an electronic scanner while she anxiously kept an eye on the other black women in line to make sure that no one slipped past her. She opened my purse and fumbled through it pulling out a nail file. She stared at me provocatively, as if to say "Why did you bring this in here?" I didn't answer her right away and hoped that she would drop it back into my purse and

let me go through. She continued to stare at me, sizing me up to see if I was "there
to cause trouble." By now, my attitude had turned foul; my childlike enthusiasm
to see my favorite rappers had all but fizzled out. I didn't know the file was in my
purse, but the guard's accusatory posture rendered such excuses moot. I finally
replied tensely, "It's a nail file, what's the problem?" She handed it back to me,
satisfied, I suppose, that I was not intending to use it as a weapon, and I went to
the arena. As I passed her, I thought to myself, "This arena is a public place, and
I am entitled to come here and bring a nail file if I want to." But these words rang
empty in my head; the language of entitlement couldn't erase my sense of alienation. I felt harassed and unwanted. This arena wasn't mine; it was hostile, alien
territory. The unspoken message hung in the air: "You're not wanted here. Let's
get this over with and send you all back to where you came from."

I recount this incident for two reasons. First, a hostile tenor, if not actual verbal abuse, is a regular part of rap-fan contact with arena security and police. This
is not an isolated or rare example; incidents similar to it continue to take place
at many rap concerts.[3] Rap concertgoers were barely tolerated and regarded with
heightened suspicion. Second, arena security forces, a critical facet in the political economy of rap and its related sociologically based crime discourse, contribute
to the high level of anxiety and antagonism that confront young African Americans. Their military posture is a surface manifestation of a complex network of
ideological and economic processes that "justify" the policing of rap music, black
youths, and black people in general. Although my immediate sense of indignation in response to public humiliation may be related to a sense of entitlement
that comes from my status as a cultural critic, thus separating me from many of
the concertgoers, my status as a young African American woman is a critical factor in the way I was *treated* in this instance, as well as many others.[4]

Rap artists articulate a range of reactions to the scope of institutional policing faced by many young African Americans. However, the lyrics that address the
police directly—what Ice Cube has called "revenge fantasies"—have caused the
most extreme and unconstitutional reaction from law-enforcement officials in
metropolitan concert arena venues. The precedent-setting example took place in
1989 and involved Compton-based rap group NWA (Niggas with Attitude) that
at that time featured Ice Cube as a lead rapper. Their album *Straight outta Compton* contained a cinematic, well-crafted, gritty, and Vulgar rap entitled "———
the Police," which in the rap itself filled in the f-u-c-k at every appropriate opportunity. This song and its apparent social resonance among rap fans and black
youths in general provoked an unprecedented official FBI letter from Milt
Ahlerich, an FBI assistant director, which expressed the FBI's concern over increasing violence (indirectly linking music to this increase) and stated that, as
law-enforcement officials "dedicate their lives to the protection of our citizens
. . . recordings such as the one from NWA are both discouraging and degrading
to the brave, dedicated officers." He justifies this targeting of NWA by suggesting that the song allegedly advocates violence against police officers. As far as
Ahlerich knows, the FBI has never adopted an official position on a record, book,

or artwork in the history of the agency.[5] NWA's "——— the Police" is what finally smoked them out. This official statement would be extraordinary enough, given its tenuous constitutionality, but what follows is even worse. According to Dave Marsh and Phyllis Pollack, nobody at the agency purchased the record, nor could Ahlerich explain how he had received these lyrics other than from "responsible fellow officers." Furthermore, Ahlerich's letter fueled an informal fax network among police agencies that urged cops to help cancel NWA's concerts. Marsh and Pollack summarize the effects of this campaign:

> Since late spring (of 1989), their shows have been jeopardized or aborted in Detroit (where the group was briefly detained by cops), Washington, D.C., Chattanooga, Milwaukee, and Tyler, Texas. NWA played Cincinnati only after Bengal lineback[er] and City Councilman Reggie Williams and several of his teammates spoke up for them. During the summer's tour, NWA prudently chose not to perform "——— the Police" (its best song), and just singing a few lines of it at Detroit's Joe Louis arena caused the Motor City police to rush the stage. While the cops scuffled with the security staff, NWA escaped to their hotel. Dozens of policemen were waiting for them there, and they detained the group for 15 minutes. "We just wanted to show the kids," an officer told the Hollywood Reporter, "that you can't say 'fuck the police' in Detroit."[6]

Unless, of course, you're a cop. Clearly, police forces have almost unchallengeable entree in these arenas. If the police break through security to rush the stage, whom do security call to contain the police? Or as KRS One might say, "Who Protects Us from You?" These large arenas are not only surveilled, but also they are, with the transmission of a police fax, subject to immediate occupation. What "justifies" this occupation? A symbolic challenge to the police in a song that, as March and Pollack observe, "tells of a young man who loses his temper over brutal police sweeps based on appearance, not actions, like the ones frequently performed by the LAPD. In the end the young man threatens to smoke the next flatfoot who fucks with him." It is clearly not in the interests of business owners to challenge the police on these matters—they cannot afford to jeopardize their access to future police services—so that the artists, in this case, find themselves fleeing the stage after attempting to perform a song that is supposed to be constitutionally protected. NWA's lyrics have even more resonance after the FBI's response:

> Fuck the police, comin' straight from the underground
> A young nigga got it bad 'cause I'm brown
> And not the other color, so police think
> They have the authority to kill a minority.[7]

It is this ideological position on black youth that frames the media and institutional attacks on rap and separates resistance to rap from attack sustained by rock 'n' roll artists. Rap music is by no means the only form of expression under attack.

Popular white forms of expression, especially heavy metal, have recently been the target of increased sanctions and assaults by politically and economically powerful organizations, such as the Parent's Music Resource Center, the American Family Association, and Focus on the Family. These organizations are not fringe groups; they are supported by major corporations, national-level politicians, school associations, and local police and municipal officials.[8]

However, there are critical differences between the attacks made against black youth expression and white youth expression. The terms of the assault on rap music, for example, are part of a long-standing sociologically based discourse that considers black influences a cultural threat to American society.[9] Consequently, rappers, their fans, and black youths in general are constructed as co-conspirators in the spread of black cultural influence. For the antirock organizations, heavy metal is a "threat to the fiber of American society," but the fans (e.g., "our children") are *victims* of its influence. Unlike heavy metal's victims, rap fans are the youngest representatives of a black presence whose cultural difference is perceived as an internal threat to America's cultural development. *They* victimize *us*. These differences in the ideological nature of the sanctions against rap and heavy metal are of critical importance, because they illuminate the ways in which racial discourses deeply inform public transcripts and social-control efforts. This racial discourse is so profound that when Ice-T's speed metal band (*not rap group*) Body Count was forced to remove "Cop Killer" from their debut album because of attacks from politicians, these attacks consistently referred to it as a rap song (even though it in no way can be mistaken for rap) to build a negative head of steam in the public. As Ice-T describes it, "There is absolutely no way to listen to the song Cop Killer and call it a rap record. It's so far from rap. But, politically, they know by saying the word *rap* they can get a lot of people who think, 'Rap-black-rap-black-ghetto,' and don't like it. You say the word *rock,* people say, 'Oh, but I like Jefferson Airplane, I like Fleetwood Mac—that's rock.' They don't want to use the word rock & roll to describe this song."[10]

According to a December 16, 1989, *Billboard* magazine article on rap tours, "venue availability is down 33% because buildings are limiting rap shows." One apparent genesis of this "growing concern" is the September 10, 1988, Nassau Coliseum rap show, where the stabbing death of nineteen-year-old Julio Fuentes prompted national attention on rap concert-related "violence": "In the wake of that incident, TransAmerica cancelled blanket insurance coverage for shows produced by G Street Express in Washington, D.C., the show's promoter. Although G Street has since obtained coverage, the fallout of that cancellation has cast a pall over rap shows, resulting in many venues imposing stringent conditions or refusing to host the shows at all."[11]

I do not contest that the experience was frightening and dangerous for those involved. What I am concerned with here is the underlying racial and class motivation for the responses to the episode. This incident was not the first to result in an arena death nor was it the largest or most threatening. During the same weekend of the Fuentes stabbing, 1,500 people were hurt during Michael Jackson's performance in Liverpool, England. At Jackson's concert a crowd of youths without tickets tried to pull down a fence to get a view of the show. Yet, in an Associated Press article on the Jackson incident entitled "1500 Hurt at Jackson Concert," I found no mention of Jackson-related insurance-company cancellations, no pall was cast over his music or the genre, and no particular group was held accountable for the incident.[12] What sparked the venue owners' panic in the Coliseum event was a preexisting anxiety regarding rap's core audience— black working-class youths—the growing popularity of rap music, and the media's interpretation of the incident, which fed directly into those preexisting anxieties. The Coliseum incident and the social-control discourse that framed it provided a justification for a wide range of efforts to contain and control black teen presence while shielding, behind concerns over public safety, Coliseum policies aimed at black-dominated events.

The pall cast over rap shows was primarily facilitated by the New York media coverage of the incident. A *New York Post* headline, "Rampaging Teen Gang Slays 'Rap' Fan," fed easily into white fears that black teens need only a spark to start an uncontrollable urban forest fire.[13] Fear of black anger, lawlessness, and amorality was affirmed by the media's interpretation and description of this incident. Venue owners all over the country were waiting to see what happened that night in Nassau County, and press interpretations were a critical aid in constructing a memory of the event. According to Bruce Haring, Norm Smith, assistant general manager for the San Diego Sports Arena, "attributes the venue's caution to the influence of discussions building management has had with other arenas regarding problems at rap shows."[14] These "discussions" between venue managers and owners are framed by incident reports (which are documented by venue security staff and local police) as well as by next-day media coverage. These self-referential reports are woven together into a hegemonic interpretation of "what took place." According to the *New York Times* coverage of the incident, the stabbing was a by-product of a "robbery spree" conducted by a dozen or so young men. Fuentes was stabbed while attempting to retrieve his girlfriend's stolen jewelry. Staff writer Michel Marriott noted that out of the 10,000 concertgoers, this dirty dozen were solely responsible for the incident. Although the race of the perpetrators was not mentioned in the text, a photo of a handcuffed black male (sporting a Beverly Hills Polo Club sweatshirt!) and mention of their Bedford Stuyvesant residences stereotypically positioned them as members of the inner-city black poor. The portrait of black male aggression was framed by an enlarged inset quote that read: "a detective said the thieves 'were in a frenzy, like sharks feeding.' "[15] The vast majority of poor youths who commit street crimes do so to get money and consumer goods. In a society in which the quality and quantity of amassed consumer goods are equated with status and prowess, it should not be surprising that some of these teenagers who have accurately assessed their unlikely chances for economic mobility steal from other people.[16] Described as black predators who seek blood for sustenance, these twelve black boys were viciously dehumanized. Marriott not only mischaracterized their motives but also set a tone of uncontrolled widespread violence for the entire concert. There were no quotes from other patrons or anyone other than Police Commissioner Rozzi and detective Nolan. The event was framed exclusively by the perspective of the police. However, in my own conversations with people who attended the event, I learned that many concertgoers had no idea the incident took place until they read about it in the newspapers the next day.

In Haring's article on venue resistance, Hilary Hartung, director of marketing for the Nassau Coliseum, reports that there have been no rap shows since the September 1988 stabbing incident and that she "suspects it's by mutual choice": "The venue looks at every concert individually. We check with all arenas before a concert comes here to check incident reports for damage or unruly crowds. It could be [a] heavy metal concert or [a] rap concert."[17] In the Nassau Coliseum case, the police reports and the media coverage work in tandem, producing a unified narrative that binds racist depictions of blacks as animals to the ostensibly objective, statistically based police documentation, rendering any other interpretation of the "rampage" irrelevant. They provide perfect justification for venue owners to significantly curtail or ban rap performances from performing in their arenas.

The social construction of "violence," that is, when and how particular acts are defined as violent, is part of a larger process of labeling social phenomena.[18] Rap-related violence is one facet of the contemporary "urban crisis" that consists of a "rampant drug culture" and "wilding gangs" of black and Hispanic youths. When the *Daily News* headline reads, "L.I. Rap-Slayers Sought" or a *Newsweek* story is dubbed "The Rap Attitude," these labels are important, because they assign a particular meaning to an event and locate that event in a larger context.[19] Labels are critical to the process of interpretation, because they provide a context and frame for social behavior. As Stuart Hall et al. point out in *Policing the Crisis*, once a label is assigned, "the use of the label is likely to mobilize this whole referential context, with all its associated meaning and connotations."[20] The question then, is not Is there really violence at rap concerts, but How are these crimes contextualized, labeled? In what already existing categories was this pivotal Nassau Coliseum incident framed? Whose interests do these interpretive strategies serve? What are the repercussions?

Venue owners have the final word on booking decisions, but they are not the only group of institutional gatekeepers. The other major power broker, the insurance industry, can refuse to insure an act approved by venue management. In order for any tour to gain access to a venue, the band or group hires a booking agent who negotiates the act's fee. The booking agent hires a concert promoter who "purchases" the band and then presents the band to both the insurance company and the venue managers. If an insurance company will not insure the act, because they decide it represents an unprofitable risk, then the venue owner will not book the act. Furthermore, the insurance company and the venue owner reserve the right to charge whatever insurance or permit fees they deem reasonable on a case-by-case basis. So, for example, Three Rivers Stadium in Pittsburgh,

Pennsylvania, tripled its normal $20,000 permit fee for the Grateful Dead. The insurance companies who still insure rap concerts have raised their minimum coverage from about $500,000 to between $4 and $5 million worth of coverage per show.[21] Several major arenas make it almost impossible to book a rap show, and others have refused outright to book rap acts at all.

These responses to rap music bear a striking resemblance to the New York City cabaret laws instituted in the 1920s in response to jazz music. A wide range of licensing and zoning laws, many of which remained in effect until the late 1980s, restricted the places where jazz could be played and how it could be played. These laws were attached to moral anxieties regarding black cultural effects and were in part intended to protect white patrons from jazz's "immoral influences." They defined and contained the kind of jazz that could be played by restricting the use of certain licensing policies that favored more established and mainstream jazz-club owners and prevented a number of prominent musicians with minor criminal records from obtaining cabaret cards.[22]

During an interview with "Richard" from a major talent agency that books many prominent rap acts, I asked him if booking agents had responded to venue bans on rap music by leveling charges of racial discrimination against venue owners. His answer clearly illustrates the significance of the institutional power at stake:

> These facilities are privately owned, they can do anything they want. You say to them: "You won't let us in because you're discriminating against black kids." They say to you, "Fuck you, who cares. Do whatever you got to do, but you're not coming in here. You, I don't need you, I don't want you. Don't come, don't bother me. I will book hockey, ice shows, basketball, country music and graduations. I will do all kinds of things 360 days out of the year. But I don't need you. I don't need fighting, shootings and stabbings." Why do they care? They have their image to maintain.[23]

Richard's imaginary conversation with a venue owner is a pointed description of the scope of power these owners have over access to large public urban spaces and the racially exclusionary silent policy that governs booking policies. It is also an explicit articulation of the aura created by the ideological soldiers: the red-and-grey arena security force described earlier. Given this scenario, the death of Julio Fuentes was not cause for regret over an unnecessary loss of life, it was the source of an image problem for venue owners, a sign of invasion by an unwanted element.

Because rap has an especially strong urban metropolitan following, freezing it out of these major metropolitan arenas has a dramatic impact on rappers' ability to reach their fan base in live performance. Public Enemy, Queen Latifah, and other rap groups use live-performance settings to address current social issues, media miscoverage, and other problems that especially concern black America. For example, during a December 1988 concert in Providence, Rhode Island, Chuck D from Public Enemy explained that the Boston arena refused to book the show and read from a *Boston Herald* article that depicted rap fans as a problematic element and that gave its approval of the banning of the show. To make up for this rejection, Chuck D called out to the "Roxbury crowd in the house," to make them feel at home in Providence. Each time Chuck mentioned Roxbury, sections of the arena erupted in especially exuberant shouts and screams.[24] Because black youths are constructed as a permanent threat to social order, large public gatherings will always be viewed as dangerous events. The larger arenas possess greater potential for mass access and unsanctioned behavior. And black youths, who are highly conscious of their alienated and marginalized lives, will continue to be hostile toward those institutions and environments that reaffirm this aspect of their reality.

The presence of a predominantly black audience in a 15,000 capacity arena, communicating with major black cultural icons whose music, lyrics, and attitude illuminate and affirm black fears and grievances, provokes a fear of the consolidation of black rage. Venue-owner and insurance-company anxiety over broken chairs, insurance claims, or fatalities are not important in and of themselves; they are important because they symbolize a loss of control that might involve challenges to the current social configuration. They suggest the possibility that black rage can be directed at the people and institutions that support the containment and oppression of black people. As West Coast rapper Ice Cube points out in *The Nigga Ya Love to Hate*, "Just think if niggas decided to retaliate?"[25]

Venue resistance to rap music is driven by both economic calculations and the hegemonic media interpretation of rap fans, music, and violence. The relationship between real acts of violence, police incident reports, economic calculations, and media accounts is complex and interactive and has most often worked to reproduce readings of rap concert violence as examples of black cultural disorder and sickness. This matrix masks the source of institutional power by directing attention away from blatant acts of discrimination and racially motivated control efforts by the police and discriminatory insurance and booking policies. Media accounts of these rap-related incidents solidify these hegemonic interpretations of black criminality. Paul Gilroy's study of race and class in Britain, *There Ain't No Black in the Union Jack,* devotes considerable attention to deconstructing dominant images of black criminality. Gilroy's study reveals several ideological similarities between dominant media and police interpretations of race and crime in the United States and Britain. His interpretation of the construction of black criminality in Britain is appropriate here:

> Distinctions between the actual crimes which blacks commit and the symbolism with which the representation of these crimes has become endowed is highly significant. . . . The manner in which anxiety about black crime has provided hubs for the wheels of popular racism is an extraordinary process which is connected with the day to day struggle of police to maintain order and control at street level, and at a different point, to the political conflicts which mark Britain's move towards more authoritarian modes of government intervention and social regulation.[26]

Deconstructing the media's ideological perspective on black crime does not suggest that real acts of violence by and against black youths do not take place. However, real acts are not accessible to us without critical mediation by hegemonic discourses. Consequently, this "real" violence is always/already positioned as a part of images of black violence and within the larger discourse on the urban black threat. Although violence at rap concerts can be understood as a visible instance of crimes by and against blacks, because it takes place in a white safety zone, it is interpreted as a loss of control on home territory. The fact that rap-related concert violence takes place outside the invisible fence that surrounds black poor communities raises the threat factor. Rappers have rearticulated a long-standing awareness among African Americans that crimes against blacks (especially black-on-black crimes) do not carry equal moral weight or political imperative.

The two exceptions to the rule remain within the logic of social-control discourse: black-on-black crimes that occur *outside* designated black areas (blacks can kill each other as long as they do it in "their" neighborhoods) and the undeniably racist attacks against blacks (as in the Howard Beach incident) that result in social outcry. (These unwarranted attacks might result in race wars that could seriously disrupt the current social configuration.) Each of these exceptions is circumscribed by the logic of social control and carries with it hefty institutional scrutiny.[27] The rap community is aware that the label "violence at rap concerts" is being used to contain black mobility and rap music, not to diminish violence against blacks. Ice Cube captures a familiar reading of state-sanctioned violence against young black males:

> Every cop killer ignored
> They just send another nigger to the morgue
> A point scored
> They could give a fuck about us
> They'd rather find us with guns and white powder
>
> . . .
>
> Now kill ten of me to get the job correct.
> To serve, protect and break a nigga's neck[28]

Cognizant of the fact that violence is a selectively employed term, KRS One points out the historical links between music, social protest, and social control:

> When some get together and think of rap,
> They tend to think of violence
> But when they are challenged on some rock group
> The result is always silence.
> Even before the rock 'n' roll era, violence played a big part in music
> It's all according to your meaning of violence
> And how or in which way you use it.
> By all means necessary, it is time to end the hypocrisy,
> What I call violence I can't do,
> But your kind of violence is stopping me.[29]

Since the Nassau Coliseum incident, "violence" at rap concerts has continued to take place, and the media's assumption of links between rap and disorder has grown more facile. On more than a dozen occasions I have been called by various media outlets around the country to comment on the violence that is expected or has taken place at a given rap concert. The violence angle is the reason for the article, even in cases where incidents have not taken place. When I have challenged the writers or radio hosts about their presumptions, they have almost always returned to their own coverage as evidence of the reality of violence and usually ignored my comments. In one striking case I was told that without the violence angle they would kill the story. In effect, they were saying that there was no way around it. The media's repetition of rap-related violence and the urban problematic that it conjures are not limited to the crime blotters, they also inform live-performance critiques. In both contexts, the assumption is that what makes rap newsworthy is its spatial and cultural disruption, not its musical innovation and expressive capacity.[30] Consequently, dominant media critiques of rap's sounds and styles are necessarily conditioned by the omnipresent fears of black influence, fears of a black-aesthetic planet.

In a particularly hostile *Los Angeles Times* review of the Public Enemy 1990 summer tour at the San Diego Sports Arena, John D'Agostino articulates a complex microcosm of social anxieties concerning black youths, black aesthetics, and rap music. D'Agostino's extended next-day rock review column entitled "Rap Concert Fails to Sizzle in San Diego" features a prominent sidebar that reads: "Although it included a brawl, the Sports Arena concert seemed to lack steam and could not keep the under-sized capacity audience energized." In the opening sentence, he confesses that "rap is not a critics' music; it is a disciples' music," a confession that hints at his cultural illiteracy and should be enough to render his subsequent critique irrelevant. What music *is* for critics? To which critics is he referring? Evidently, critical reviews of rap music in *The Source* and the *Village Voice* are written by disciples. D'Agostino's opening paragraph presents the concert audience as mindless and dangerous religious followers, mesmerized by rap's rhythms:

> For almost five hours, devotees of the Afros, Queen Latifah, Kid 'N Play, Digital Underground, Big Daddy Kane and headliners Public Enemy were jerked into spasmodic movement by what seemed little more than intermittent segments of a single rhythmic continuum. It was hypnotic in the way of sensory deprivation, a mind- and body-numbing marathon of monotony whose deafening, prerecorded drum and bass tracks and roving klieg lights frequently turned the audience of 6,500 into a single-minded moveable beast. Funk meets Nuremberg Rally.[31]

Apparently, the music is completely unintelligible to him, and his inability to interpret the sounds frightens him. His reading, which makes explicit his fear and ignorance, condemns rap precisely on the grounds that make it compelling. For example, because he cannot explain why a series of bass or drum lines moves the crowd, the audience seems "jerked into spasmodic movement," clearly suggesting an "automatic" or "involuntary" response to the music. The coded familiarity of the rhythms and hooks that rap samples from other black music, especially funk and soul music, carries with it the power of black collective memory. These sounds are cultural markers, and responses to them are not involuntary at all but in fact densely and actively intertextual; they immediately conjure collective black experience, past and present.[32] He senses the rhythmic continuum but interprets it as "monotonous and mind- and body-numbing." The very pulse that fortified the audience in San Diego left him feeling "sensory deprived." The rhythms that empowered and stimulated the crowd numbed his body and mind.

His description of the music as "numbing" and yet capable of moving the crowd as a "single-minded, moveable beast" captures his confusion and anxiety regarding the power and meaning of the drums. What appeared "monotonous" frightened him precisely because that same pulse energized and empowered the audience. Unable to negotiate the relationship between his fear of the audience and the wall of sound that supported black pleasure while it pushed him to the margins, D'Agostino interprets black pleasure as dangerous and automatic. As his representation of the concert aura regressed, mindless religious rap disciples no longer provided a sufficient metaphor. The hegemonic ideology to which D'Agostino's article subscribes was displaced by the sense of community facilitated by rap music as well as the black aesthetics the music privileged.[33] He ends his introduction by linking funk music to an actual Nazi rally to produce the ultimate depiction of black youths as an aggressive, dangerous, racist element whose behavior is sick, inexplicable, and orchestrated by rappers (that is, rally organizers). Rap, he ultimately suggests, is a disciples' sound track for the celebration of black fascist domination. The concert that "failed to sizzle" was in fact too hot to handle.

Once his construction of black fascism is in place, D'Agostino devotes the bulk of his review to the performances, describing them as "juvenile," "puerile," and, in the case of Public Enemy, one that "relies on controversy to maintain interest." Halfway through the review, he describes the "brawl" that followed Digital Underground's performance:

> After the house lights were brought up following DU's exit, a fight broke out in front of the stage. Security guards, members of various rappers' entourages, and fans joined in the fray that grew to mob size and then pushed into a corner of the floor at one side of the stage. People rushed the area from all parts of the arena, but the scrappers were so tightly balled together that few serious punches could be thrown, and, in a few minutes, a tussle that threatened to become a small scale riot instead lost steam.[34]

From my mezzanine-level stageside seat, which had a clear view of the stage, this "brawl" looked like nothing more than a small-scale scuffle. Fans did not rush from all areas to participate in the fight, which was easily contained, as he himself points out, in a few minutes. In fact, few people responded to the fight except by watching silently until the fracas fizzled out. He neglects to consider that the twenty-plus minute waiting periods *between each act* and the overarching sense of disrespect with which young black fans are treated might have contributed to the frustration. Out of 6,500 people, a group of no more than 20, who were quickly surrounded by security guards, falls significantly short of a "mob" and "threatened to become a small scale riot" only in D'Agostino's colonial imagination.

D'Agostino's review closes by suggesting that rap is fizzling out, that juvenile antics and staged controversy no longer hold the audience's attention and therefore signify the death of rap music. What happened to the "single-minded moveable beast" that reared its ugly head in the introduction? How did black fascism dissolve into harmless puerility in less than five hours? D'Agostino had to make that move; his distaste for rap music, coupled with his fear of black youths, left him little alternative but to slay the single-minded beast by disconnecting its power source. His review sustains a fear of black energy and passion and at the same time allays these fears by suggesting that rap is dying. The imminent death of rap music is a dominant myth that deliberately misconstructs black rage as juvenile rebellion and at the same time retains the necessary specter of black violence, justifying the social repression of rap music and black youths.

Mass-media representations and institutional policing have necessarily leavened rap's expressive potential. "Rap-related violence" media coverage has had a significant impact on rappers' musical and lyrical content and presentation. The most explicit response to rap-related violence and media coverage has been the music industry–based Stop the Violence movement (STV). Organized in direct response to the pivotal Nassau Coliseum incident in September 1988, "it was," in the words of STV's primary organizer, writer and music critic Nelson George, "time for rappers to define the problem and defend themselves." STV was an attempt to redefine the interpretation and meaning of rap-related violence and discourage black-on-black crime: "The goals of the STV [were] for the rappers to raise public awareness of black on black crime and point out its real causes and social costs; to raise funds for a charitable organization already dealing with the problems of illiteracy and crime in the inner city; [and] to show that rap music is a viable tool for stimulating reading and writing skills among inner-city kids."[35] In January of 1990, STV released a twelve-inch single entitled "Self-Destruction" featuring several prominent rappers "dropping science" on the cost of black-on-black crime for African Americans, on crime and drugs as dead-end professions, and on the media's stereotypical depiction of rap fans as criminals. The lyrics for "Self-Destruction" focused on the need to crush the stereotype of the violent rap fan. They separated rap fans from the "one or two ignorant brothers" who commit crime and they called for unity in the community. At one point, rapper Heavy D pointed out that blacks are often considered animals and although he doesn't agree with these depictions he thinks rap fans are proving them right by exhibiting violent, self-destructive behavior.[36] In addition to producing the all-star single music video and organizing several public marches, STV published a book in photo-essay style on the STV movement. *Stop the Violence: Overcoming Self-Destruction* offered a history of STV, pages of black-crime statistics, and teen testimonials about black-on-black violence. STV targeted young, urban African Americans with the hope to "educate and reform" them, to help them to "overcome" self-destruction. The book and the overall project were cosponsored by the National Urban League, which also served as the beneficiary for all donations raised as a result of STV's efforts.

Unfortunately, STV's reform-oriented response did not redefine the problem; it accepted the sociologically based terms laid out in the media's coverage. STV responded within the parameters already in place regarding black youth behavior. Uncritically employing the labels "black-on-black crime" and "self-destruction," STV's self-help agenda fit comfortably into the social pathology discourse that explained rap-related violence in the first place. STV's minimal attempts to position these acts of violence and crimes as symptoms of economic inequality were not sufficient to compensate for the logic of cultural pathology that dominated their statements. Pages of statistics documenting the number of blacks killed by other blacks reinforced the dominant construction of black pathology, while the economic, social, and institutional violence to which blacks are subjected remained unexplored.

The media's systematic avoidance of the destructive elements in urban renewal, deindustrialization, corporate crime, and the woefully flawed public education system were left undiscussed, effectively severing the mass media and government from their critical role in perpetuating the conditions that foster violent street crime. As Michael Parenti's study on the politics of the mass media, *Inventing Reality*, makes clear, minimal coverage of these larger social crimes, coupled with maximum coverage of street crimes, are directly related and illuminate the significance of class and race in defining the public transcript:

> Press coverage focuses public attention on crime in the streets with scarcely a mention of "crime in the suites," downplaying such corporate crimes as briberies, embezzlements, kickbacks, monopolistic restraints of trade, illegal uses of public funds by private interests, occupational safety violations . . . and environmental poisonings which can cost the public dearly in money and lives. . . . How the press defines and reports on crime, then, is largely determined by the class and racial background of the victim and victimizer . . . blacks, Latinos and other minorities are more likely to be publicized as criminals than the corporate leaders whose crimes may even be more serious and of wider scope and repercussion than the street criminal's.[37]

Economically oppressed black communities face scarce and substandard housing and health services, minimal municipal services (911, as Public Enemy says, *is* a joke), constant police harassment and brutality, and economic, racial, and sexual discrimination; these conditions are fundamentally linked to "black-on-black crime" and constructions of social violence. The label *black-on-black* crime, Congressman John Conyers points out, "gives the erroneous impression of a strange, aberrant, or exotic activity, when it is taken out of the context of the social and economic roots of crime."[38] Furthermore, as Bernard Headley argues, the violence experienced by black and working-class people as a result of poor medical services, police use of deadly force, and industrial negligence far exceeds the threat of black-on-black crime." Black-on-black crime is a concept that necessarily severs crime from the conditions that create it: "Crime is not the result of blackness (which is what the notion of 'black on black' crime implies), but rather of a complex of social and economic conditions—a negative 'situational matrix'—brought on by the capitalist mode of production, in which both the black victim and the black victimizer are inextricably locked in a deadly game of survival."[39]

These missed connections were critical flaws in the STV movement. The STV agenda should have retained a dialectical tension between black self-destructive behavior *and* the immense institutional forces that foster such behaviors. Cries in the lyrics of "Self-Destruction" to avoid walking the (destructive) path that has been laid, to "keep ourselves in check," and to "love your brother, treat him as an equal," overemphasized the autonomy of black agency in the face of massive structural counterforces. There is an inherent tension between a desire to preserve personal agency and free will (e.g., fight the power, *self-destruction*) and a necessary acknowledgment of structural forces that constrain agency (e.g., institutional racism, white supremacy, class oppression). The illusion that exercising black agency can be undertaken outside of the racist and discriminatory context within which such action takes place ignores the tension between individual agency and structural oppression. Once severed from social context, agency is easily translated into theories of cultural pathology that blame the victim for his or her behavior and, therefore, circumstances. This discursive tension is a critical element in contemporary black cultural politics; the forces that constrain black agency must be acknowledged while the spirit and reality of black free will must be preserved. Agency and oppression must be joined at the hip, otherwise an incapacity to "overcome" self-destructive behavior is no longer connected to structures of oppression and is easily equated with cultural pathology. Unfortunately, STV did not successfully negotiate this tension. Instead, they garnered significant financial resources and mobilized a critical mass of rap music representatives to speak on behalf of social control in the name of black free will.

The greatest irony of the STV movement is that it borrowed its name and spirit from a 1988 KRS One rap that sustained the tensions and contextualizations that remained unrealized in the STV movement. KRS One's "Stop the Violence" draws direct links between the media, the educational system, the government, and the frustrations that contribute to street crime, especially as it relates to hip hop. His portrait of the relationships between class, race, institutional power, and crime is subtle and complex and contrasts sharply with the lyrics from the STV project:

> Time and time again, as I pick up the pen,
> As my thoughts emerge, these are those words
> I glance at the paper to know what's going on,
> Someone's doing wrong, the story goes on
> Mari Lou had a baby, some one else decapitated

The drama of the world shouldn't keep us so frustrated
I look, but it doesn't coincide with my books
Social studies will not speak upon political crooks
It's just the presidents and all the money they spent
All the things they invent and how the house is so immaculate
They create missiles, my family's eating gristle
Then they get upset when the press blows the whistle

. . .

What's the solution to stop all this confusion?
Re-write the constitution, change the drug which you're using?
Re-write the constitution, or the emancipation proclamation
We're fighting inflation, yet the president is still on vacation

. . .

This might sound a little strange to you
But here's the reason I came to you
We got to put our heads together and stop the violence
'Cause real bad boys move in silence
When you're in a club you come to chill out
Not watch someone's blood just spill out
That's what these other people want to see
Another race fight endlessly[40]

KRS One's narrative weaves social conditions and violence together, illustrating the links between them. He calls on hip hop fans to stop killing one another, to avoid turning their rage against society on one another, but he refuses to identify their behavior as the source of the problem. He captures the essence of the illusions created in the "dangerous street criminal" narrative in one critical line: "We've got to put our heads together and stop the violence / 'Cause real bad boys move in silence." For KRS One, young black teenage males killing each other and their neighbors are acts of violence, but they are not any more violent than the federal government's abandonment of black and Hispanic Vietnam veterans and billion-dollar expenditures for weapons while "his family eats gristle"; no more violent than the educational system's historical narratives that "will not speak upon political crooks," giving the green light to tomorrow's generation of powerful criminals.

The first stanza in KRS One's "Stop the Violence" is organized as a series of news fragments punctuated by his interpretations. At first, the fragments seem self-contained, but his comments begin to tie them together, weaving a narrative that illustrates contradictions in dominant transcripts and suggesting the existence of a common enemy. In the second main stanza, KRS One addresses the hip hop community directly, suggesting that the first stanza was necessary background for his real agenda: violent crimes among poor black teenagers. Unfortunately, KRS

One does not have a "solution to stop this confusion"; his suggestion to rewrite the Constitution reads like rhetorical sarcasm, not a solution. What he does quite effectively, however, is to illustrate the self-destructive nature of crime among black teenagers without identifying black teenagers as the problem. KRS One's "Stop the Violence" contextualizes these crimes as an outgrowth of the immense institutional forces that foster such behaviors. In this version, individual agency and structural oppression are in tension. Finally, unlike many social scientists, he bypasses the culture-of-poverty trap as an explanation for contemporary inequality and the conditions it fosters.[41]

▪ The institutional policing of rap music is a complex and interactive process that has had a significant impact on rap's content, image, and reception. The Nassau Coliseum incident, which necessarily includes the social construction of the incident, the already existing discourse on black urban crime and fears of rap's political and social power, served as a catalyst for the explicit and sanctioned containment of rap's influence and public presence. This pivotal incident allowed an already suspicious public to "blame rap for encouraging urban violence," placed the rap community on the defensive, and effectively refocused attention away from the systemic reasons for street crime.

Rap music is fundamentally linked to larger social constructions of black culture as an internal threat to dominant American culture and social order. Rap's capacity as a form of testimony, as an articulation of a young black urban critical voice of social protest, has profound potential as a basis for a language of liberation.[42] Contestation over the meaning and significance of rap music and its ability to occupy public space and retain expressive freedom constitutes a central aspect of contemporary black cultural politics.

During the centuries-long period of Western slavery, there were elaborate rules and laws designed to control slave populations. Constraining the mobility of slaves, especially at night and in groups, was of special concern; slave masters reasoned that revolts could be organized by blacks who moved too freely and without surveillance.[43] Slave masters were rightfully confident that blacks had good reason to escape, revolt, and retaliate. Contemporary laws and practices curtailing and constraining black mobility in urban America function in much the same way and for similar reasons. Large groups of African Americans, especially teenagers, represent a threat to the social order of oppression. Albeit more sophisticated and more difficult to trace, contemporary policing of African Americans resonates with the legacy of slavery.

Rap's poetic voice is deeply political in content and spirit, but rap's hidden struggle, the struggle over access to public space, community resources, and the interpretation of black expression constitutes rap's hidden politics; hegemonic discourses have rendered these institutional aspects of black cultural politics invisible. Political interpretations of rap's explosive and resistive lyrics are critical to understanding contemporary black cultural politics, but they reflect only a part of the battle. Rap's hidden politics must also be revealed and contested; otherwise, whether we believe the hype or not won't make a difference.

Notes

1. Venues are clubs, theaters, and other performance spaces. I am concerned specifically with large venues, such as the Capital Center, Nassau Coliseum, and Madison Square Garden. Larger venues constitute the most significant public-arena contestations, because they are located in urban-development zones, outside black areas, and because they can house the largest numbers of people. I am particularly interested in accounts of rap music in major newspapers. Music periodicals are not the focus here.
2. A Tribe Called Quest, "Youthful Expressions," *People's Instinctive Travels and the Paths of Rhythm* (Jive, 1989/1990).
3. At a 1988 rap concert in New Haven, Connecticut, a young African American male protested the weapon search shouting, "Fuck it! I'm not going through the search." But after a short protest, realizing that he would have to forfeit his ticket, he entered the lines and proceeded through the search station. In the summer of 1990, outside the San Diego Sports Arena, a young woman wanted to go inside to see if her friend had already arrived and was waiting inside, but she said that she would rather wait outside a bit longer instead of having to go through the search twice if it turned out that her friend was not in fact inside.
4. Public-space discrimination and the public injury to dignity it creates is not limited to black teenagers. Feagin's "Continuing Significance of Race" illustrates that in post–Civil Rights America, discriminatory practices against blacks of all ages and classes remain a significant part of public-space interaction with whites. He points out a number of critical public spaces in which black men and women are likely to be humiliated and discriminated against. His findings are in keeping with my experiences and observations and the context within which they took place. See Joe R. Feagin, "The Continuing Significance of Race: Antiblack Discrimination in Public Places," *ASR* 56 (1991): 101–116.
5. Dave Marsh and Phyllis Pollack, "Wanted for Attitude," *Village Voice*, October 10, 1989, 33–37.
6. Ibid., 33–37.
7. NWA, "——— the Police," *Straight outta Compton* (Priority, 1988).
8. See Robert Walser, *Running with the Devil: Power, Gender, and Madness in Heavy Metal Music* (Hanover, N.H.: University Press of New England, 1993). See also Marsh and Pollack, "Wanted," and *Rock and Roll Confidential (RRC)*, especially their special pamphlet "You've Got a Right to Rock: Don't Let Them Take It Away." This pamphlet is a detailed documentation of the censorship movements and their institutional bases and attacks. The *RRC* is edited by David Marsh and can be subscribed to by writing to *RRC*, Dept. 7, Box 341305, Los Angeles, CA 90034. See also Linda Martin and Kerry Seagrave, *Anti-Rock: The Opposition to Rock n Roll* (Hamden, Conn.: Archon, 1988).
9. In fact, the attacks on earlier popular black expressions, such as jazz and rock 'n' roll, were grounded in fears that white youths were deriving too much pleasure from black expressions and that these primitive, alien expressions were dangerous to their moral development. See Steve Chapple and Reebee Garofalo, *Rock 'n' Roll Is Here to Pay* (Chicago: Nelson, 1979); Lewis A. Erenberg, *Steppin' Out: New York Night Life and*

the Transformation of American Culture, 1890–1930 (Chicago: University of Chicago Press, 1981); LeRoi Jones, *Blues People: The Negro Experience in White America and the Music That Developed from It* (New York: Morrow Quill, 1963); Kathy J. Ogren, *The Jazz Revolution: Twenties America and the Meaning of Jazz* (New York: Oxford University Press, 1989); George Lipsitz, *Time Passages: Collective Memory and American Popular Culture* (Minneapolis: University of Minnesota Press, 1990).

10. Cited in Alan Light, "Ice-T," *Rolling Stone*, August 20, 1992.

11. Bruce Haring, "Many Doors Still Closed to Rap Tours," *Billboard*, December 16, 1989, 1. Obviously, Haring means building *owners*. Writers and venue representatives consistently refer to the buildings, not their owners, as the point of power. This language renders invisible the powerful people who control public-space access and make discriminatory bureaucratic decisions.

12. "1500 Hurt at Jackson Concert," *New York Post*, September 12, 1988, 9.

13. Carl J. Pelleck and Charles Sussman, "Rampaging Teen Gang Slays 'Rap' Fan," *New York Post*, September 12, 1988, 9. See the January 1991 issue of *The Source*, p. 24, for a discussion on bans on rap concerts and on rap-related violence.

14. Haring, "Many Doors Still Closed."

15. Michel Marriott, "9 Charged, 4 with Murder, in Robbery Spree at L.I. Rap Concert," *New York Times*, September 19, 1988, B3. It is deliberate and significant that the race of the suspects was not actually mentioned. As Timothy Maliqualim Simone points out: "In the aftermath of the civil rights movement of the sixties and seventies, American culture has discovered that racial effects are more efficiently achieved in a language cleansed of overt racial reference. . . . Instead they employ more subtle signifiers: 'Street youths,' 'welfare mothers,' 'inner-city residents.' " Timothy Maliqualim Simone, *About Face: Race in Postmodern America* (New York: Autonomedia, 1989), 17. Given this astute observation, the picture that accompanied the text was unnecessary and might be considered gratuitous overkill.

16. James W. Messerschmidt, *Capitalism, Patriarchy, and Crime: Toward a Socialist Feminist Criminology* (Savage, Md.: Rowman & Littlefield, 1986). See especially pp. 54–58.

17. Haring, "Many Doors Still Closed," p. 80.

18. See Messerschmidt, *Capitalism*, especially Chapter 3, "Powerless Men and Street Crime." Messerschmidt notes, "Public perception of what serious violent crime is— and who the violent criminals are—is determined first by what the state defines as violent and the types of violence it overlooks. . . . The criminal law defines only certain kinds of violence as criminal—namely, one-on-one forms of murder, assault, and robbery, which are the types of violence young marginalized minority males primarily engage in. The criminal law excludes certain types of avoidable killings, injuries and thefts engaged in by powerful white males, such as maintaining hazardous working conditions or producing unsafe products" (52).

19. Mark Kruggel and Jerry Roga, "L.I. Rap Slayer Sought," New York *Daily News*, September 12, 1988, 3; David Gates et al., "The Rap Attitude," *Newsweek*, March 19, 1990, 56–63.

20. Stuart Hall et al., *Policing the Crisis* (London: Macmillan, 1977), 19.

21. Interview with "Richard," a talent-agency representative from a major agency that represents dozens of major rap groups, October 1990.

22. Paul Chevigny, *Gigs: Jazz and the Cabaret Laws in New York City* (London: Routledge, 1991). See also Ogren, *Jazz Revolution*.

23. Rose interview with "Richard." I have decided not to reveal the identity of this talent-agency representative, because it serves no particular purpose here and may have a detrimental effect on his employment.

24. Roxbury is a poor, predominantly black area in Boston.

25. Ice Cube, "The Nigga You Love to Hate," *AmeriKKKa's Most Wanted* (Priority, 1990).

26. Paul Gilroy, *There Ain't No Black in the Union Jack* (London: Hutchinson, 1987), 110. See also, Gilroy, "Police and Thieves," in *The Empire Strikes Back*, ed., Center for Contemporary Cultural Studies (London: CCCS Hutchinson University Library, 1982).

27. In the Howard Beach case, vicious racism was the only reasonable explanation for the brutal attack against three black men (one of whom was murdered) whose car had broken down. Yet, a question that preoccupied the defense was whether they had a "good reason" to be in the solidly white neighborhood. This question was established by pointing out that they had passed a number of gas stations and pizza parlors before stopping to call for help with their automobile. (Of course, they might have passed by establishments that seemed hostile, hoping the next might seem less threatening, or have some patrons of color in them.) My point here is that if they hadn't had a disabled car as an excuse, they would have had significantly less moral leverage with white New Yorkers. As it was, the press was counting phone booths and open restaurants in the area to "explain" why they walked as far as they did. These three black men had transgressed across the boundaries that circumscribe black mobility, a transgression that makes sense within the social-control discourse, explains white fear, and renders violence against blacks logical and understandable. See Patricia J. Williams, *The Alchemy of Race and Rights* (Cambridge: Harvard University Press, 1991) for an extended and important reading of the Howard Beach case and of several other recent racially motivated crimes.

28. Ice Cube, "Endangered Species," *AmeriKKKa's Most Wanted* (Priority, 1990).

29. Boogie Down Productions, "Necessary," *By All Means Necessary* (Jive, 1988).

30. See especially David Samuel, "The Real Face of Rap," *The New Republic*, November 11, 1991, and Gates et al., "The Rap Attitude." In contrast, Jon Pareles and Peter Watrous, the primary popular music critics for the *New York Times*, have made noteworthy attempts to offer complex and interesting critiques of rap music. In many cases, a significant number of letters to the editor appeared in following weeks complaining about the appearance and content of their reviews and articles.

31. John D'Agostino, "Rap Concert Fails to Sizzle in San Diego," *Los Angeles Times* (San Diego edition), August 28, 1990, F1, F5. This review is accompanied by subsequent short articles about charges brought against rappers for "obscene conduct" while on stage—fully clothed—during this concert and the massive coverage of the 2 Live Crew controversy regarding obscene lyrics. For example, Michael Granberry, "Digital Underground May Face Prosecution," *Los Angeles Times*, November 17, 1990, F9; "2 Rap Beat, Must Beat Rap," *New York Daily News*, August 4, 1990, 3. It is also quite important to point out how much D'Agostino's description of rap music is modeled after arguments made by T. W. Adorno regarding jazz music in the 1940s. In "On Popular Music," Adorno refers to rhythms in jazz as a sign of obedience to domination of the machine age: "The cult of the machine which is represented by unabating jazz beats involves a self-renunciation that cannot but take root in the form of a fluctuating uneasiness somewhere in the personality of the obedient." See *On Record: Rock, Pop and the Written Word*, ed. Simon Frith and Andrew Goodwin (New York: Pantheon, 1990), 313.

32. See Lipsitz, *Time Passages*, for an extended analysis of this process.

33. See Ray Pratt, "Popular Music, Free Space, and the Quest for Community," *Popular Music and Society* 13, 4 (1989): 59–76, on the question of public-space moments of community experiences, and see James A. Snead, "On Repetition in Black Culture," in *"Race" Writing and Difference*, ed. Henry L. Gates, Jr. (Chicago: University of Chicago Press, 1986).

34. D'Agostino, "Rap Concert," F5.

35. Nelson George, ed., *Stop the Violence: Overcoming Self-Destruction* (New York: Pantheon, 1990), 12.

36. "Self-Destruction," *Stop the Violence* (Jive, 1990).

37. Michael Parenti, *Inventing Reality: The Politics of the Mass Media* (New York: St. Martin's, 1986), 12.

38. Congressman John Conyers, "Main Solution Is National Plan Correcting Economic Injustice," *Ebony*, August 1979.

39. Bernard D. Headley, " 'Black on Black' Crime: The Myth and the Reality," *Crime and Social Justice* 20 (1983): 52.

40. Boogie Down Productions, "Stop the Violence," *By All Means Necessary* (Jive, 1988).

41. For a critique of the discourse on the underclass, its relationship to the culture-of-poverty literature, and the rightward political shift over the 1980s, see Adolph L. Reed, Jr., "The 'Underclass' as Myth and Symbol: The Poverty of Discourse about Poverty," *Radical America* 24, 1(1991): 20–40; Michael Katz, *The Undeserving Poor* (New York: Pantheon, 1989); and Raymond S. Franklin, *Shadows of Race and Class* (Minneapolis: University of Minnesota Press, 1991).

42. bell hooks, *Yearning: Race, Gender and Cultural Politics* (Boston: South End, 1990).

43. David Brion Davis, *The Problem of Slavery in Western Culture* (Ithaca, N.Y.: Cornell University Press, 1966).

youth's global village: an epilogue

william eric perkins

By no stretch of the imagination have we identified and examined all of the schools, trends, and personalities of hip hop's global push. The hip hop revolution is just that, an uprooting of the old way in style and culture, and the introduction of a taste of black and Latino urban authenticity to every corner of the globe. Some examples: in 1989, I was attending a conference in Santa Fe, New Mexico. Driving from Albuquerque to Santa Fe, I came across a baffling array of rap lyrics in the distinct idiom of southwestern Spanish on a local barrio radio station. When I asked my Chicano friends who was rapping, they told me that these were local high-school kids who had made their first demo tapes. In 1990, in Havana, Cuba, I was with a group of Hunter College colleagues involved in making a video documentary on the plight of Cuban artists and intellectuals in the wake of the ongoing U.S. embargo and the collapse of the Soviet Union. On a sultry night in May, we attended a concert of Los Van Van, one of Cuba's most popular groups. The show opened with a young woman who was not singing a conventional bolero but was rapping to the uniquely Cuban beat of horns and congas; she was surrounded by a wave of Cuban-style "fly boys," breakin' and moonwalkin' in one of the uniforms of hip hop—loose-fitting jeans and untied leather boots (no doubt a gift of the Cuban armed forces). In

Philadelphia in 1991, I spoke with five Polish rappers who proclaimed their spiritual affinity for black rap (especially the Fresh Prince and DJ Jazzy Jeff, whom they
had seen on the television sitcom "The Fresh Prince of Bel-Air") and their wish to
express Polish reality in rap. In Japan, the bastion of an anachronistic traditional-
ism, youth rush to consume such products of the hip hop revolution as eight-ball
leather jackets and designer sneakers, and even cut shapes and patterns into their
hair, openly admiring the rebellion that rap presents. These recollections are a reminder of the role that one segment of African American culture plays in the global
interdependence shaping the postindustrial, post-Soviet world. As the lead editorial in the August 1991 issue of *Ebony* announced: "From be-bop to hip-hop, from
cornrows to the fade, from zoot suits to harem pants, and from the high-five to the
Arsenio "bark," Blacks have been the pacesetters for American style, defining
what's 'cool,' 'fresh,' and who's got it going on."[1] Rap has led this global charge.

Self-innovation is what keeps rap music and hip hop alive. Old-school flavor has given birth to new-school flavor and alternative rap. There's rap-and-jazz
fusion, rap and R and B, playground and popsicle rap, rap comedy, rap films or
films where rap is the backdrop, gospel rap and preachers who rap, rap fashion,
rap jewelry, and even hip hop haircuts.

More flavors than ever

Heavy D, of Mount Vernon, New York, is one of the major forces in rap who defies classification. I would call his style fun rap, mixing bits of the lover's style,
party flavor, and an occasional message. Frequently his raps play on his large size,
with hits such as "Mr. Big Stuff," "The Overweight Lover's in the House," and
"Swingin' with the Hevster." Heavy D's projected naiveté and innocence were
shattered in 1992 when a concert and basketball game ended in disaster after a
crowd of two thousand stampeded in the City College of New York gymnasium.
Nine people died, and the public staging of rap events came under greater
scrutiny.[2] Heavy D absented himself from the rap scene temporarily and is now
doing more television and commercials. He has returned larger than ever in the
"95" with a "phat" hit, "I Got Nuthin' but Love for You, Baby."

Oakland's Digital Underground, whose comic persona combines eccentric-
ity and idiosyncracy, is led by Shock G and MC Clever (Humpty), whose trademark Groucho Marx mock-up elicits a lot of laughter. DU's comic style of rap has
expanded hip hop parameters. As Humpty said in MTV's 1991 *Rapumentary*,
"The most important thing in my music is to come up with the craziest, sickest,
berserk idea I could but still stay loyal to hip hop." DU's most famous son, though,
is 2Pac Shakur, whose ascendancy in 1993 has been marred by controversies over
gun toting, assault, and abuse against women.

Popsicle rap is represented by Illegal, Da Youngstas, and Kris-Kros, whose
1992 release, *Totally Crossed Out*, contained the hit single "Jump" and catapulted
the group into the national limelight with their clothes worn backwards. Though

these two adolescents may appear to be innocent naifs, Kris-Kros is constantly experimenting with their rap style, able to incorporate powerful messages, as in the meditation on inner-city violence, "Shame," or to wickedly dis fellow popsicle rappers Another Bad Creation in "Freak Da Funk," from the 1993 release *DA Bomb*, where Mack Daddy proclaims: "That alphabet crew to make my day / so I can drop and chop and drop them little punk quick / and teach 'em to never mess with this Krossed-out kid." Daddy Mack counters, "I'm a nappy, happy bad little son of a gun." They continue to engage in recorded disses against fellow teenage rappers Da Youngstas and Chi-Ali, revealing that they have a commitment to remain true to the original intention of old-school fun and verbal combat. In contrast, Illegal, produced by Erick Sermon (formerly of the group EPMD), adapted the gangsta style to popsicle in a 1993 single, "Head or Gut," a mean dis of seventeen-year-old rapper Chi-Ali. The video shows them in typical gangsta fashion—denim suits, carrying machetes and clubs. Da Youngstas, who began as typical kid rappers (waxing on curfews, bullies, and Mom), have also taken on the hard-core look, sporting bald heads and gold teeth, along with their machetes and clubs. Their second release, *The Aftermath*, contains the hit single "Crewz Pop," another violent expression of youthful rage. The transformation of popsicle rap is yet another indication of the appeal and the recording industry's mass marketing of its hard-core gangsta style.

An intellectual dimension in rap music also defies categorization. Its most prominent practitioners, De La Soul, represent a distinct middle-class, high-brow style of rap that rejects the props of the gangstas or the Afrocentrists. The first wave of their music, which the group called the D.A.I.S.Y. ("da inner self y'all"), rhymed in a lyrical style that borrowed heavily from the imagery and symbolism of the psychedelic era, as here from "Me, Myself, and I":

> Mirror, mirror on the wall
> Tell me, mirror, what is wrong
> Can it be my De La clothes
> Or is it just my De La Song
> What I do ain't make believe
> People say I sit and try
> But when it comes to being De La
> It's just me, myself, and I

After a 1991 release, *De La Soul Is Dead*, the group was resurrected in 1993 with *Buhllone Mind State*, which continues their original and slightly egomaniacal style of rap.[3]

The titleholder for eclectic rap is Cypress Hill, whose 1991 *Cypress Hill* and 1993 *Black Sunday* reveal one obsession—marijuana. Hip hop's priests of the blunt invoke the Book of Genesis in "Legalize It": "I have given you all of the seeds and herbs of the land." Led by MC B-Real, whose nasal twang speaks of the blessing of cannabis, they have, more than any other force, revived "reefer madness" and introduced it to a new generation as an alternative to alcohol, particularly malt liquor. We can be on the lookout for a message that poses new challenges to a nation bent on linking all drug consumption with violent crime.[4]

The alternative future of rap music lies in the style of music made by two groups, the now disbanded Arrested Development and Digable Planets. *Billboard* labeled AD "alternative rap." In their first release, *Three Years, Five Months, and Two Days in the Life of . . .* (1992), fronted by spokesperson and lead MC Speech, the Atlanta-based group celebrates the rural South and the kind of virtuous life that has disappeared from urban black America, as on their hit single and video "Tennessee." Against the backdrop of a farm, it recounts the history of slavery, lynching, and hardship and suggests that the values of rural southern African Americans allowed them to weather adversity.

Speech became noticeably upset when the group was chided for pushing a diluted form of rap:

> We're as much hip-hop as Eric B. and Rakim. . . . I mean we use the same techniques of turntables and sampling. We just wanted to broaden the scope of how rap is perceived. . . . Arrested Development wants to show [black youth] how you can channel that anger. We never wanted to eclipse what Public Enemy or Ice Cube were saying. We wanted to give another side.

Defining "life music," as the group calls its hip hop style, Speech went on: "Everything was death, death, death. . . . I wanted people to appreciate life, not in a passive way, but as a way to fight for your rights as a person." The group was featured in a 1992 front-page profile in the *Wall Street Journal* that contrasted its laid-back style to the hard-core gangsta formula. Arrested Development captured several Grammys and MTV music awards, but their 1994 album, *Zigalamundi*, was a marketing flop, selling fewer than 250,000 units.[5]

The second group that anticipates rap's alternative future, Digable Planets, is fulfilling a prophecy by jazz organist Shirley Scott, who told me in early 1993 that the future of jazz begins with hip hop and that as rappers matured and sought wider sources for samples, they would inevitably be forced to explore and experiment with jazz. DP's first album, *Reachin' (A New Refutation of Time and Space)* and their single "Rebirth of Slick ('Cool like Dat')" mix a startling array of jazz samples with lyrical sophistication, tossing in a generous helping of metaphorical messages, historical allusions, and literary heavies. They sample from jazz iconoclasts like Charlie Mingus, the be-bop riffs of Charlie Parker and Dizzy Gillespie, and the cool of Miles Davis and Lee Morgan, as well as old-school rappers like Doug E. Fresh and the Sugar Hill Gang. Ishmael Butler, the group's leader, commented on their intellectual style:

> The references, allusions, are all things that are important in our lives. . . . References to personalities, musicians, or authors are there because we've read or listened to this stuff, or experienced it, and we think it's important information to spread around. We try to bring in all sorts of information,

because pop songs today don't have anything substantial to say, except the same old monotonous drone about love triangles.[6]

Rap music and the hip hop style have also managed to cross linguistic and cultural boundaries, testimony to their widespread appeal to youth. There is a burgeoning Asian American rap scene on the West Coast, led by groups like Asiatic Apostles, Bubula Tribe, Undercover, Brotherhood from Another Hood, the Seoul Brothers, Lani Luv, and the Boo-Yaa Tribe. These Asian American rappers represent a wide variety of styles, and their messages range from the murder of Vincent Chin in Detroit to the black and Korean tension in every major American city. The Asiatic Apostles wrote a response rap to Ice Cube's "Black Korea," which received wide support from the Oakland black youth community. Lani Luv is the first Asian American female rapper, starting out in the Philippines; she remarked that her party-oriented style changed when she hooked up with D-Yee at the University of California, Davis, where they have taken up the Asian American agenda. Luv also brings a new feminist orientation to her rap style "to break down the stereotype of Asian women as being passive and submissive," a mighty challenge to the ultra-traditional Asian American community. DJ D-Bert, a Filipino Hawaiian who has been spinning raps in the Bay Area for more than seven years with his group FM 2.0, maintains the old-school style with basic beats and the extensive use of turntables for scratching.[7]

The cross-cultural trend has been most extensive among Latinos. From the Puerto Rican, Cuban, and Chicano communities comes a rap style that makes extensive use of Latin rhythms, including the horn sections of the Cuban son, the flutes of the charanga and pachanga, conga drums, Mexican country music, and the Latin/rock fusion of Santana. Latin Empire signals the maturing of Latino rap, incorporating the best of Nuyorican rap (Spanglish lyrics and salsa-based beats), Chicano gangsta style, and the dance-based beats of Miami. Composed of Puerto Ricans MC Puerto Rock, KT and DJ Corchado of New York, Kid Frost of East Los Angeles, and Mellow Man Ace of Miami, the group's goal is to unite all Latin rappers. In essays included in this volume, Juan Flores provides an extensive analysis of the group and Mandalit del Barco charts the Puerto Rican influence on early hip hop. In an interview with Juan Flores, MC Puerto Rock and KT and DJ Corchado converse comfortably about the alternating use of Spanish and English in their rap style:

> 'Cause like in Puerto Rico, they use their own slang. And we got slang, we even use slang from Puerto Rico, like "*Nitido*," "Right through." We go over there, we learn the slang from Puerto Rico and pure Puerto Ricans, and we bring it into our little raps, too. And they be, "Oh, that's Puerto Rican slang," like Mellow Man Ace used Cuban slang. Ah man, Jalaboa, Salo, whatever, and these guys like Kid Frost have their slang from Chicanos, and all that, *vatos, cholos*. It's good. I like it. I consider it an art the whole thing of hip hop, consider it crazy art. Like graffiti, breakin', dancin', the fashion trends, everything. The music of rap and everything, music by itself helps bring all different types of cultures together.[8]

Mellow Man Ace is considered the prince of Latino rap. Although the first Spanish verses in rap were sung in 1985 by the Mean Machine in their single "Disco Dream," Ace's 1989 single, "Mentirosa" (Lying Woman), was Latino rap's first big hit. Latino rap even has a crossover artist, Gerardo, whose 1991 release *Mo' Ritmo* made him a superstar. He starred in Dennis Hopper's pro-police look at Los Angeles gang life, *Colors*, but prefers the slick Motown style of the Latin-lover image he has created.

The other dominant trend in Latino rap is the politicized gangsta style led by Kid Frost of East Los Angeles—El Jefe, "the Hispanic causin' panic"—who makes extensive use of Mexican traditional music and whose lyrics are quintessential Spanglish. In a recent interview he defended Chicano rappers: "Now there's this big race issue in rap and it shouldn't be a big issue. People should not be amazed at Latin rappers because it's a sound of the streets, it's in our culture. And rap is the sound of the street."[9] From Kid Frost's 1989 release *Hispanic Causin' Panic*, "La Raza" vividly portrays Chicano identity and culture, set against the barrio background of East Los Angeles. Unlike black gangsta rappers (and they should take note), Frost has used rap to promote Chicano nationalism, the restoration of Aztlán, and the memory of the pachuco aesthetic and sensibility.

Frost has been joined by a host of Chicano rappers: Aztlán Underground, who marches to the slogan: "We didn't cross the border, the border crossed us"; Down for Brown, from Santa Cruz; Aztlán Nation, a sort of Chicano Public Enemy, who sample Malcolm X and invoke Che Guevara as an inspirational source; Machete and the Chicano Squad, who proclaim: "All my heroes are crooks in your books"; A Lighter Shade of Brown, with two releases, 1990's *Brown and Proud*, with the single "Latin Active," and 1993's *Hip-Hop Locos*; and Of Mexican Descent, whose mission is the restoration of California to Mexico.[10]

The Chicano influence has spilled across geographical borders as hip hop goes global. From Mexico to Asia, from Brazil to Zimbabwe, the rap attack is on. The Mexican rap group Calo won Mexico's biggest award as musical newcomers in 1991. DJ Claudio Yarto of Calo acknowledged Kid Frost as his major influence; he secretly recorded a mid-eighties concert of El Jefe and taught himself the techniques and technology of rap. Calo's 1992 hit "Get Wise" was played all over Mexico. A Russian brand of rap is led by Raketa (the Rocket), who has adapted the rap beat "to make it a bit more technobeat, more house music, a bit more European, because after all, we're white." Bambaataa's Planet Rock has come full circle. Chinese rap is led by Dou Wei, who raps in Chinese freestyle. There's rap from India, led by Baba Schgal, who raps in Hindi, "Thanda Thanda Pani Thanda Thanda Pani" (Cold Cold Water Cold Cold Water) and acknowledges that MTV introduced him to Vanilla Ice, whose style he mimics. Japanese rap has a uniquely American flavor because the language can accommodate rap's rapid-fire staccato. Rap in Japan and France are the two most promising and important trends in hip hop's globalization. There's South African rap coming straight out of the youth movement and with an uncompromising political message. From Brazil, even the pop genius Sergio Mendez has recorded a series of raps. Finally, I can only mention the existence of rap's b-side—the Jamaican dance-hall idiom and Afro-British "raggamuffin," a fusion of rap and reggae; analyzing these forms of music would require a separate essay.[11]

Rap wraps and props

The rap attitude thrives on fashion, and corporate America, while attacking rap's lyrical style, has elevated the "street look" to fashion prominence. The b-boy and b-girl look of rap's first wave, with its designer sweatsuits and sneakers, dookie gold, and leather jackets, yielded to the political fashion craze of "X" wear when Public Enemy and KRS One popularized Malcolm's philosophy and speeches, and is now dominated by athletic fashion. A "Back to Africa" trend, reflecting the industry's ongoing fascination with anything "ethnic," made Kinte cloth, African waxed fabrics, and harem pants permanent features of contemporary fashion, a look still popular among the African-oriented rappers and followers of that school. In 1991 novelty leather coats arrived on the fashion scene, with designs that included the "eight-ball" and traffic signals. Once Arsenio Hall legitimized the style on his talk show, every kid had to have one.

Here are some of the style elements of rap, according to Diane Cardwell, who did a report for the now-defunct Styles of the Times section of the *New York Times*: "Survivalist b-boy" began with the athletic wear of hip hop's first wave but has now been taken over by Timberland and combat boots (along with the hundreds of imitations), tucked-in jeans and camouflage, ski jackets, and hunting vests; gangsta females wear bandannas, colors, plaid flannel shirts, army field jackets, and boots, frequently accompanied by the ubiquitous blunt and a forty, as seen in Apache's "Gangsta' Bitch" and Boss's "Progress of Elimination." There's a distinctly middle-class tinge to the aspiring, carefully tailored suits for men and, for women, slinky dresses (never too tight), heels or loafers, and never too much gold. There's a hip hop Western look, mirroring the recycling of the West in American popular culture (a trend initiated by Ralph Lauren), with fringed suede jackets as its hallmark, revealing an obsession with the city as a kind of final frontier. There's the TLC look, loose-fitting layered clothing that repudiates the "video ho" image: I don't have to wear tight clothes, Daisy Duks, or bare my body to be sexy. As Ruth La Ferla suggests, the hip hop look is as popular in the salons as on the street:

> A black-inspired style has asserted itself in schools, at malls and at concerts, as an urge to merge clashing patterns and vibrant colors—mixes are unruly as a ticking-striped shirt worn with batik harem pants, an extravagant gold chain mingled with chunky trading beads or a Bart Simpson slipped under a seersucker suit. This brand of artful incongruity . . . has found favor not just on the airwaves, where rap and reggae stars are its most ardent proponents, and on the streets, but in fashion's most rarefied precincts.[12]

And headwear: sports-team caps (favorites are the Florida Marlins, Colorado Rockies, Chicago White Sox, and the old Negro leagues); caps emblazoned with the marijuana leaf, popularized by Dr. Dre in his 1993 release *The Chronic*; and the tube-shaped head covering that was a "cross between the classic stocking cap and African head wrapping," which appeared in 1992 as winter wear. The Kris-Kros craze initiated a style that continues to enjoy fashion dominance; Woody Hochswender locates the source of the craze for the "backwards" look:

> The look is also an extension of the backward-caps phenomenon and the gravity-defying trousers popularized by rap performers in general. The low-slung, beltless pants, typically worn several sizes too large, were originally inspired by the enforced style of prison, where inmates are not allowed to wear belts.[13]

And hair: Fades, cut patterns, stripes, logos, and names; close-shaven sides with a box on top; dreadlocks in a variety of styles from the "mop top" (short locks above close-shaven sides) to "roots rasta" (long untended locks, a "rasta natural"). The Afro is making a return, as the retro-gimmickry of popular culture recycles the seventies for a new audience. For women, African-inspired braids and weaves are now essential fashion, but we can expect the short-Afro and near bald heads popularized by the new group Zhane to compete with braids.[14]

Rap fashion, always true to its urban origins, will not be controlled by Madison Avenue or the garment industry; what post-b-boys and b-girls wear will remain "true to the game."

Check itself or wreck itself

As hip hop continues to grow and prosper as the defining culture and style expression for this generation, corporate capitalism's appetite for new styles and trends will inevitably influence its course. The marketing legions will continue to search for new ways to absorb hip hop, which in turn will generate innovative responses to resist becoming a commodity. As early as 1987, the merits of rap were being observed by Wall Street:

> More marketeers recognize rap music's powerful influence with teenagers. Rap—which is characterized by rhyming lyric and a driving, monotonous beat—appeals most strongly to inner-city black youths. But its popularity transcends boundaries or class and color. A lot of advertisers were afraid at first to use rap because it came from the street culture, says Lyor Cohen, who manages several artists at Rush management. "Now these white, suburban, establishment types see that their own kids are into rap."[15]

And in 1990 Kim Foltz reported in the *New York Times* that corporate giants like Coca-Cola, British Knights, and Pepsi were using rappers to promote their products. Peter Fould, director of marketing at Pepsi, called rap "perfectly suited to the television commercial's short form. . . . It's an easy way to tell a story."[16] In 1991 the *Wall Street Journal* profiled *The Source*, the leading magazine on hip hop culture, which cofounder and publisher David Mays said could be "the *Rolling Stone* for the next generation. . . . We see the potential market as half a million to a million."[17] From malt liquor to sneakers, the "rap attack" is proving to be a marketing bonanza. To compete with *The Source*, Time-Warner has bankrolled Quincy Jones's *VIBE*, a slick, high-profile magazine of what he calls "urban culture." Its premier 144-page issue in the fall of 1992 contained 54 pages of advertising. Jones told the *New York Times*, "all of a sudden you look up and see a whole new culture that has become the culture."[18] Resisting this corporate onslaught has been one of hip hop's major virtues, honoring the "no sellout" ethic, but only the future will reveal if there will be corporate rap, in the vein of corporate rock.

On the other hand, hip hop experienced a major crisis in 1993 that augurs internal change. In November 1993, 2Pac Shakur, formerly of Digital Underground and now a successful solo performer (including starring roles in the films *Juice* and John Singleton's *Poetic Justice* with Janet Jackson) was arrested in Atlanta for allegedly firing a gun at two off-duty policemen. A month later he was charged with assault for allegedly holding a woman down while three of his crew members raped and sodomized her. He was released on probation in November 1995. Dr. Dre's protégé Snoop Doggy Dogg was charged as an accessory to murder for being in the car in which his bodyguard executed a rival accused of threatening them. At this writing he faces trial on conspiracy to murder. This incident occurred at the time of Snoop Doggy Dogg's first release, which in the last weeks of 1993 sold 1.2 million units, making this record not only the most anticipated but also the largest-selling debut album in rap history. Public Enemy's Flavor Flav, accused of threatening a neighbor with a gun for attempting to sleep with his girlfriend, was immediately forced to check into the Betty Ford Clinic for addiction to crack cocaine. And even Lisa Lopes of TLC was arrested for pulling a gun on boyfriend Andre Rison in September 1993.[19] This series of incidents has led to countless editorials by the ruling establishment and calls for a get-tough attitude with rappers. Reverend Calvin Butts has spearheaded a move to banish rap recordings with "vulgar and sexist" lyrics and led a major demonstration in the summer of 1993 calling for censorship.[20] In December 1993 Inner City Broadcasting took the lead in refusing to play recordings with "negative and misogynistic" lyrics. And there has been a major debate initiated in the black community over hard-core lyrics and even the use of the word "nigger."[21]

This debate has moved to the forefront of the 1996 presidential election campaign as GOP front-runner Senator Bob Dole has launched an attack on popular culture, singling out rap music and Hollywood movies as threatening "our character as a nation." Dole's mention of the Geto Boys and 2 Live Crew was especially forceful for their celebration of "nightmares of depravity," and he singled out Time-Warner for its support of rap music. Dole's attack was just one more salvo initiated by the right wing. Former Reagan war-on-drugs head William

Bennett and C. DeLores Tucker, architect of the boycott of SONY music and a supporter of the Reverend Calvin Butts, are currently engaged in a major campaign to censor rap music. In June 1995 they wrote:

> Time Warner Inc. recently increased its investment in gangsta rap and now owns 50 percent of Interscope Records, the record label behind such "artists" as Snoop Doggy Dog, Dr. Dre, Nine Inch Nails and TuPac Shakur—whose songs of violence are notorious. We are in the process of identifying other corporations we regard as culprits.[22]

Prior to this editorial, Bennett and Tucker, representing Empower America and the National Political Congress of Black Women, raised the rap-lyrics issue at the annual meeting of Time-Warner's shareholders. This political grandstanding forced Time-Warner's chairman, Gerald Levin, to begin investigating the development of labeling standards for rap music. What lies behind this latest assault on the hip hop nation? There can be no doubt that gangsta rap's growing penetration of the white youth market has raised the ire of cultural conservatives. One reporter commented on this trend:

> When rap first began 20 years ago its audience was almost exclusively an inner-city one. Today, its audience has spread out. Of the 1.7 million copies sold of the soundtrack to "Friday", a top-10 album featuring some of gangsta rap's best-known names, 31.7 percent were sold in suburbs and 29.4 percent in rural areas, said Soundscan, a company in Hartsdale, N.Y. that monitors retail sales. Though *Billboard*, the industry trade magazine, has suggested that gangsta rap is losing its white audience, record store employees do not agree.[23]

The cultural Right has merged forces with the religious Right to rescue white youth from the rap infection and has summoned major politicians to join this battle for the minds and ears of white youth. Hip hop's claim of ghetto authenticity is what carries its appeal far outside its inner-city boundaries; it represents a clear and present danger, and despite the claims of hip hop artists that their music is art and is about "getting paid," rappers are seen as thugs, hoodlums, and misogynists rather than as quintessential entrepreneurs.

Hip hop had taken a decidedly interesting turn by mid-1995. First the hip hop nation was stunned by the death of Ezy-E from AIDS in February. One of the pioneers of gangsta rap, his legacy cannot be measured. The year also saw the resurgence of East Coast rap, led by a band of nine eclectic MCs from Staten Island: the Wu-Tang Clan and Brooklyn's Notorious B.I.G. Ezy-E's death, Snoop Doggy Dogg's impending murder trial, Ice Cube's continuing ascent into the pantheon of black Hollywood, and Dr. Dre's reclusiveness have allowed the East Coast rappers to begin redefining hip hop, lyrically and aesthetically.

Rap has come a long way from the lyrical innocent charm of the Sugar Hill Gang or the party flavor of Afrika Bambaataa, but the critics and pundits are too quick to impose this "blackwork orange" scenario on youth. They ignore the music's and the culture's ability to engage in self-regulation and self-critique, opting for paternalism, repression, and censorship instead. Rap can "check itself before it wrecks itself," in Ice Cube's felicitous phrase. We would do well to heed Ralph Ellison's warning that American society has "failed to provide rites of passage adequate to the wide variety and broad freedom of experience available to the young."[24] Ellison's words also reflect the role hip hop plays as a form of initiation in the cosmological philosophy of the Bakongo, in whose society achieving one's individuality within the context of the group is intimately related to commanding the power of the word. We may view hip hop, then, as a structured set of rituals, filled with pain and promise; like an adolescent, it serves as a mirror of what our society has become and can become. Hip hop has endured its growing pains. As it moves toward adulthood, its voice will continue to be heard, on its own terms.

Notes

1. "The High-Five Revolution," *Ebony*, August 1991, 28. For conservative *Ebony* to editorialize on matters of style itself testifies to hip hop's significance.
2. This was the first serious incident that called for state intervention within the public arena of rap music; see Robert McFadden, "No Liability Insurance at Game Led to Deaths of 9," *New York Times*, January 3, 1992, B1, 4, and Veronica Webster, "Hangin' with the Hevster," *The Source*, August 1991, 48–51.
3. Armond White, "De La Soul: Living in Metaphor," *City Sun*, September 20–26, 1989, 17; and on their comeback, Greg Tate, "They Go Where Few Rappers Dare to Follow," *New York Times*, October 17, 1993, Arts & Leisure section, 34, and Colson Whitehead, "Up Up and Away," *Village Voice*, October 19, 1993, 71.
4. Dmitri Erlich, "Cypress Hill Turns Menace into a Gleeful Mess," *New York Times*, September 5, 1993, 22; Isaac Fergusson, "Blunt Posse: Why the Hip Hop Nation Is Getting High on 'The Chronic,' " *Village Voice*, June 22, 1993, 34, 36; and Sonya Senkowsky, "Marijuana Blunts: A Youth Craze," *Philadelphia Inquirer*, April 20, 1995, A1, 17.
5. Scott Poulson-Bryant, "Arrested Development Travels Its Own Road," *New York Times*, March 28, 1993, Arts & Leisure section, 29; Meg Cox, "Rap Music Is Taking a Positive Turn and Winning Fans," *Wall Street Journal*, October 8, 1992, A1, 7. AD's leader, Speech, responded to critics in Daryl James, "Arrested Development: Still Fighting the Revolution of Everyday People," *Rap Sheet*, November 1994, 26, 41. The group disbanded in December 1994.
6. Peter Watrous, "Digable Planets' Jazz Raps," *New York Times*, March 7, 1993, Arts & Leisure section, 31. Todd Boyd has critically reviewed the jazz–hip hop trend as follows: "In order to effectively fuse jazz with hip-hop, the people behind the fusion must sit down and study the music they want to reinterpret." The Digable Planets meet Boyd's criterion as serious students of jazz. Martin Johnson has highlighted the jazz–hip hop club scene and the new hip hop poetry in "Black & Blue: Hip-Hop Jazz, African Culture Summit or Nu-lite Soul Habit?" *PULSE*, May 1994, 50.
7. Darow Han, "Asian-American Rap," *The Bomb* (Seattle) 12 (October 1992): 13–14.
8. Juan Flores, "Latin Empire: Puerto Raps," *Bulletin of El Centro*, Fall 1992.
9. Lynette Jones, "Latin Hip-Hop's Veterano: Kid Frost," *Rap Sheet*, December 1993, 025; see also Ronin Ro, "Riding Shotgun," *The Source*, September 1992, 32–36.

10. Raegan Kelly, "Down for the Brown: Rap Por La Raza," *RapPages*, April 1993, 44–46, an essential survey of Chicano rap in California.

11. This survey of the global rap attack is based on James Bernard, "A Newcomer Abroad, Rap Speaks Up," *New York Times*, August 23, 1992, Arts & Leisure section, 1, 22–23, with contributions on Mexico by William Schomberg, on Russia by Steven Erlanger, on China by Nicholas Kristof, on Japan by Steven Weisman (the Japanese rap explosion is worthy of extensive investigation), on India by Edward Gargan; France, with its extensive Antillean, Arab, and African populations, leads the way in the production of rap music. The DJ MC Solaar has even recorded with Guru (of the jazz-rap group Jazzmatazz), and rap in France has been the subject of an extraordinary film, *Rime et Raison*, by Francis Guibert, which surveys the French rap scene in Paris, Marseilles, and even as far north as Alsace-Lorraine. There has even been a major French crossover hit by five-year-old Jordy, *"Dur, d'Etre Bébé"* (It's Hard to Be a Baby) (Christopher Burns, "Five-Year-Old Jordy Is Truly Rap's Enfant Terrible," *Philadelphia Inquirer*, February 13, 1993, D8). France's cultural history has always had an attachment to African and African American culture, and the country's growing interest in rap magnifies that concern. William Grimes, "Traveling from France to Harlem to Study Rap Culture at Its Roots," *New York Times*, November 18, 1991, C11, 12, documents an extraordinary meeting of French officials, police, academics, and "rappeurs" with African American rappers, academics, and radio personalities. India's Apache Indian has taken the bhangra music of southern India and fused it with the Afro–West Indian ragga idiom (rapping to the bass beat of reggae) to create a new hip hop sound, "bhangramuffin." His three singles, "Movie over India," "Chok There," and "Don Raja," are major sellers in India, and his hit "Arranged Marriage" has challenged that tradition, provoking a major attack against him by the Indian right wing. His first album, *No Reservations*, outsold Michael Jackson and Whitney Houston. Andy Pemberton, "The World According to Apache Indian," *Hip-Hop Connection 55* (September 1993): 20–21, and Brooke Wentz, "Apache Home," *VIBE*, November 1993, 84–87. Zimbabwe Legit pioneers hip hop in Zimbabwe, where they fuse the Shona language with English in their first single, "Doin' Damage in my Native Language," Zimbabwe Legit, "Short Interview," *Art Form* 18 (1992): 18–22. Rap in the Cape of South Africa is covered nicely in Janet Anderson, "Rap in the Cape," *Hip Hop Connection* 34 (November 1991): 16–17. I am currently investigating the dance-hall/raggamuffin craze. A starting point is Ben Mapp, "First Reggae. Then Rap. Now Dancehall," *New York Times*, June 21, 1992, Arts & Leisure section. This article contains suggestions of the best dance-hall releases. Simrette Selassie, "Reggae Dancehall for the 90s," *The Beat* 10, 4 (1991): 42–43, is an essential discography. In that same issue, Scott Greer profiles Shabba Ranks, who almost singlehandedly has made dance hall a worldwide phenomenon ("Shabba Ranks: Raggamuffin Revolutionary," 43–45, 50. *The Beat* is an absolutely essential reference. Robert J. Stewart, "Linton Kwesi Johnson: Poetry down a Regge Wire," *New West Indian Guide/Nieuwe West Indische Gids* 67, 1, 2 (1993): 69–89, is an important analysis of the dub poetry of Johnson, who has been a major influence on the raggamuffin style. Finally, the whole idiom of "slackness" (Jamaican creole for *sex*) and its dominant influence on dance hall is magnificently covered in Frank Owen, "In Praise of Slackness," *Village Voice*, June 23, 1995, 63, 70.

12. Ruth La Ferla, "Street-Smart: Dressing Our Own Way," *New York Times Magazine*, June 24, 1990, 46; see also Roy Campbell, "Hip-Hop Couture," *Philadelphia Inquirer*,

April 24, 1991, 1C, 5C. The African-oriented look, with its overburdening commodification of African and Afro–West Indian style, is covered in Lena Williams, "In Leather Medallions and Hats, Symbol of Renewed Black Pride," *New York Times*, July 30, 1989, Lifestyle section, 46; see also Roy Campbell, "Accentuating the Positive," *Philadelphia Inquirer*, August 22, 1990, 1C, 8C. On the "reggae style," see the mini–photo essay in the column On the Street, "Reflecting Reggae and Rap," September 16, 1990, 61. Hair style is one of the biggest statements made by inner-city youth, from the chrome-domed look (initially made fashionable and sexy by the late Telly Savalas, Yul Brynner, and African American actors Woody Strode [Spartacus] and Lou Gossett, Jr.) to the nineties look donned by the most prominent athletes (led by Michael Jordan, Charles Barkley, and new sensation Shaquille O'Neill). The bald head is not the only head fashion, however. Haircut artistry in the form of the carved fade dominated in the late eighties and early nineties, with its assortment of patterns, logos, and eclectic symbols (it was common for slaves during the Middle Passage to carve elaborate hair sculptures to create a shipmate bond to replace the bonds of language and ethnicity) (On the Street, "To Take on an Artful Look, Use Your Head," *New York Times*, June 25, 1989); see also "The Artistry of African-Inspired Braids," *New York Times*, September 8, 1991, Fashion section. Lisa Jones's wicked piece, "Planet Hair," *Village Voice*, February 6, 1990, 42, examines a wig shop frequented by African American women searching for the right color and texture of hair to have woven into those elaborate braided do's, and she brilliantly analyzes the fade in, "Fade to Black," *Village Voice*, August 1, 1989, 40–41; this is also covered in Ruth M. Bond, "New Status for Stylish Art of Braiding," *New York Times*, July 7, 1993, C10. Anita Samuels examines the fashion of dreadlocks, now featured on models in *Vogue* and *Elle*, in "Just Locks," Styles of the Times, *New York Times*, January 23, 1994, 4. This whole pattern of crossover fashion is examined in Lena Williams, "In Looks, a Sense of Racial Unity," *New York Times*, May 9, 1990, C1, 8. She quotes Professor Charles Thomas, who calls the phenomenon "the darkening of white America. . . . What we are seeing is white people being totally engulfed in black life style and behavior patterns." The obverse of this trend is covered in Degen Pener's column Egos & Ids, "Black Skin, Blond Hair," Styles of the Times, *New York Times*, September 12, 1993, 4. Singer Lonnie Gordon commented, "Black hair is sexy, but it's just normal. If you are an entertainer, blond hair totally stands out." The entire issue of hair is given a magnificent analysis in Kobena Mercer, "Black Hair/Style Politics," *New Formations* 3 (Winter 1987): 33–54. Despite this essay's deconstructionist density, it is well worth reading for its analysis of African American and Afro–West Indian hair fashion. Ayoka Chenzira's early eighties animated short, *Hairpiece*, does much to set the context of African American women's hair politics. The fashion subgenres are covered in Diane Cardwell, "Rapwear. Soulwear. Hipwear," Styles of the Times, *New York Times*, February 14, 1993, 5. The donning of football's Oakland Raiders garb as a hip hop fashion statement (it leads in sales in the sports-apparel market) is covered in Tim Golden, "Raiders Chic: A Style, and Sinister Overtones," *New York Times*, February 4, 1991. Philadelphia pioneered one of hip hop's greatest fashion crazes: the eight-ball and traffic-light leather jackets (Roy Campbell, "Hide and Chic," *Philadelphia Inquirer*, January 20, 1991, 1F, 4F). The Carhartt jacket, one of the essential garments of the nineties, is documented in Michel Marriott, "The Carhartt Jacket," Styles of the Times, *New York Times*, November 29, 1992. The explosion of Timberland boots (which I wore in the 1960s) is dissected in Michel Mariott, "Out of the

Woods," Styles of the Times, *New York Times*, November 7, 1993, 1, 11, which stated
that hip hop fashion had the "highest quarterly revenues in its twenty-year history."
The tube hat is given a neat photo-montage in the On the Street column, "Cat in
the Hat Comes Back," *New York Times*, September 27, 1992, 3. The women's side of
hip hop fashion is explored in Martin Kihn, "Tommy Boy Is a Girl," Styles of the
Times, *New York Times*, July 5, 1992, 5. Lisa Jones, "Blaxploitation: Supermamas Re-
visited," *Village Voice*, June 5, 1990, 40–41, discusses the featured look of the scantily clad dancers frequently dubbed "video hos." Roy Campbell, "Dazzy Dukes Generate a Whole Lot of Heat," *Philadelphia Inquirer*, July 18, 1993, G3, is the first critical
look at this fashion revival and its implications for youth culture, particularly sexual
assault and harassment. The earring craze is covered in the On the Street column
"No, You Don't Need Ear Lobes of Steel," Fashion, *New York Times*, July 23, 1989,
43, while body piercing is explored in Suzy Menkes, "Fashion or Fetish," Styles of the
Times, *New York Times*, November 21, 1993, 1, 9. The neo-nationalist style of Arrested Development is covered in Randi Gollin, "The Mix as Message," Styles of the
Times, *New York Times*, December 6, 1992, 14. Gollin describes the group's look as
"funky, gospely, Southern, rural hip-hop." Youth fashion has been one of the major
sources of violent crime, as thugs threaten kids over their sneakers, leather jackets,
earrings, and the like. This has been the cause of great concern to the business establishment (Krystal Miller, "School Dress Codes Aim to Discourage Clothing Robberies," *Wall Street Journal*, April 5, 1990, A1, 13).

13. Woody Hochswender, "Is It Retro?" Styles of the Times, *New York Times*, May 17,
1992. Inmate chic is covered in an extraordinary article by Patricia McLaughlin,
"Prisoners of Fashion," *Philadelphia Inquirer Sunday Magazine*, April 17, 1994, 27. She
notes, "Even as former L.A. gang members are designing clothes to cash in on crime,
one longtime jeans maker is exploiting it to 'reinvent prisons.'" The "joint" is no
longer sacred.

14. Zhane was prominently featured on the cover of *Essence* magazine in January 1994.

15. "Advertisers Tap the Popularity of Rap," *Wall Street Journal*, editorial, November 19,
1987. This line follows Theodor Adorno's observation, "the *qualitas occulta* of hits is
a borderline value of advertising, in which they are embedded and which the greatest of them have turned into their own substance. People are ceaselessly wooed in behalf of what they crave anyway." Theodor Adorno, *Introduction to the Sociology of Music*, translated by E. B. Ashton (New York: Seabury, 1976), 37.

16. Kim Foltz, "Madison Ave. Turns an Ear to Rap Music," *New York Times*, July 6,
1990, D16.

17. Meg Cox, "Little Rap-Music Magazine Has Big Aims," *Wall Street Journal*, September 25, 1991, B2.

18. Deidre Carmody, "Hip-Hop Dances to the Newsstands," *New York Times*, September 14, 1992, D8.

19. The 2Pac incidents and Flavor Flav's arrest are documented in Ronald Smothers,
"Rapper Charged in Shootings of Off-Duty Officers," *New York Times*, November 2,
1993, A16; on the general media hype on 2Pac and Snoop Dogg, see Tom Moon's
commentary, "In Gangsta, Violence Pummels Art," *Philadelphia Inquirer*, November
14, 1993; Calvin Sims's Week in Review piece, "Gangster Rappers: The Lives, the
Lyrics," *New York Times*, November 28, 1993, 3. At least this editorial piece provides
balance by observing the "recent troubles of some rappers as reflecting the problems
of poor young black and Hispanic men." Richard Lacayo, "Shootin' Up the Charts,"

Time,. November 15, 1993, 81–82. If there ever was an icon created by the media, Snoop Doggy Dogg is just that, turned from a back-up rapper in Dr. Dre's posse into an overnight sensation. The profile by Toure, "Snoop Dogg's Gentle Hip-Hop Growl," *New York Times*, November 21, 1993, Arts & Leisure section, 32, is magnificent. It is Snoop's low-key, quiet rap style that accounts for his popularity. Dream Hampton's stunning portrayal of the Death Row posse (Dr. Dre's record label) and the Dogg Pound is required reading for those who want to understand the fascination of rap for lower-middle-class African Americans: Dream Hampton, "G-Down," *The Source*, September 1993, 64–70. The role of record companies in creating the style and personalities of hip hop remains to be investigated. An indication of this trend was dissected in "Big Record Labels Making Big Investments in Rap Music," *New York Times*, August 10, 1990, D11. This marketing strategy has spurred the ongoing protest and calls for censorship led by Calvin Butts and others and the congressional hearings held in February 1994 by Senator Carol Moseley-Braun and Representative Cardiss Collins. Doug Simmons rips the hearings and their political motivation apart in "Gangsta Was the Case," *Village Voice*, March 8, 1994, 63, 66C. Delores Tucker of the National Political Congress of Black Women has launched pickets against major record-store chains like the Wiz and Sam Goody; see Michael Farquhar, "Rap Ripped by Feminist Protestors," *Washington Post*, November 22, 1993, F1, 2. The impetus for these protests was a series of remarks made by the Geto Boys' Bushwick Bill, who told a panel at the annual meeting of the National Association of Black Journalists, "I call women bitches and 'hos because all the women I've met since I've been out here are bitches and 'hos." This was reported and editorialized on by William Raspberry, "Foulmouthed Trash," *Washington Post*, July 30, 1993, A21. Paul Delaney has parodied the hard-core segment of rappers in "Amos 'n' Andy in Nikes," a scurrilous editorial on stereotypical aspects of gangstas in comparison with the comic buffoonery and malapropisms of the "Kingfish" (*New York Times*, op-ed, October 11, 1993, A17). A nice counterpart to that editorial is Michael Eric Dyson, "Bum Rap," op-ed, *New York Times*, February 3, 1994, A20. Annette Leslie Williams, former director of the National Political Congress of Black Women (Delores Tucker's organization), has written an important editorial, which in turn is testimony to hip hop's ability to criticize itself; see "Is Violence Killing Hip-Hop," *RapPages*, March 1994, 20–21.
20. See Clifford Levy, "Harlem Protest of Rap Lyrics Draws Debate and Steamroller," *New York Times*, June 6, 1993, 39, and Peter Noel, "Butts on Tha Brain," *Village Voice*, June 15, 1993, 12. The debate flowers in Michel Marriott, "Hard-Core Lyrics Stir Black Backlash," *New York Times*, August 15, 1993, 1, 42.
21. On the debate surrounding the use of the word "nigger" ("nigga" in hip hop parlance), Michel Marriott, "Rap's Embrace of 'Nigger' Fires Bitter Debate," *New York Times*, January 24, 1993.
22. On the Dole attack, see Bernard Weinraub, "Dole Attacks Hollywood Wares as Undermining Social Values," *New York Times*, June 1, 1995, B1, 10. The quote from Bennett and Tucker is from an op-ed piece, "Lyrics from the Gutter," *New York Times*, June 2, 1995, A29. In response to this onslaught, Time-Warner dismissed Doug Morris, chief executive of Time-Warner's U.S. music operation. Morris was instrumental in mainstreaming gangsta rap; see Mark Landler, "A Defender of Gangsta Rap Is Dismissed at Warner Music," *New York Times*, June 22, 1995, D1, 6, and Jeffrey Trachtenberg and Eben Shapiro, "Warner Music's Doug Morris Is Fired," *Wall*

Street Journal, June 22, 1995, B8. The philistines of the GOP seem to have short memories, forgetting their courtship of Ezy-E during the 1992 election, as Frank Rich reminds us in "G.O.P. Gangsta Rap," op-ed, *New York Times*, June 11, 1995, 15. Time-Warner's economic position might be one reason it is kowtowing to the GOP; see Thomas Goetz's Rockbeat column, "Back in the Day (Again)," *Village Voice*, June 20, 1995, 64. The changing demographics of rap's consumption are covered in Neil Strauss, "Rap's a Ten Percent Slice of the Recording Industry Pie," *New York Times*, June 5, 1995, D8, while David Samuels, "The Rap on Rap: The 'Black Music' That Isn't Either," in *Rap on Rap*, ed. Adam Sexton (New York: Dell, 1995), 241–252, carefully examines the corporate takeover of rap recording to appease the white market. He overlooks hip hop's ability to go back underground to prevent that takeover. One of hip hop's most perceptive observers commented that hip hop is at a critical juncture because many of the old school are near the end of their careers, while new-school members are playing for "higher stakes" (Brian Lassiter, "Who Makes the Loot: Hiphop and Money," *Beatdown* 7 [1995]: 10). Finally, I have examined the whole ideology of "gettin' paid," in " 'It All Comes Down to Money': The Political Economy of Hiphop," unpublished manuscript.

23. Neil Strauss, "Rap's a Ten Percent Slice of the Recording Industry Pie," *New York Times*, June 5, 1995, D8.

24. In an altogether remarkable essay, Ralph Ellison, "On Initiation Rites: Ralph Ellison Speaks at West Point," in *Going to the Territory* (New York: Random House, 1986), 51, echoes the philosophical underpinnings of Kongo cosmology. Nganga K. Kia Bunseki Fu-Kiau has been instrumental in shaping my understanding of rites of passage and initiation.

■ about the contributors

■

■

■

■

■

■

■ **ernest allen, jr.,** associate professor of Afro-American studies at the University of Massachusetts, is one of the leading authorities on Black Nationalism in the United States.

■ **mandalit del barco** is a reporter for National Public Radio in Los Angeles.

■ **juan flores** is director of the Center for Puerto Rican Studies at the City University of New York and author of numerous works on Puerto Rican culture.

■ **nancy guevara** did graduate work in sociology at the City University of New York graduate center and became one of the pioneering interpreters of hip hop culture, particularly the role of women in both the music and the (graffiti) writing.

■ **katrina hazzard-donald**, associate professor of sociology at Rutgers University and author of *Jookin'* (Temple University Press, 1990), also teaches African American, African, and Afro-Cuban dance.

■ **robin d. g. kelley** is professor of history at New York University and author of *Hammer and Hoe: Alabama Communists during the Great Depression* and *Race Rebels: Culture, Politics, and the Black Working Class*, a book of essays.

■ **ernie paniccioli** has been documenting hip hop through photography since the early 1980s. His photographs have appeared in *The Source*, *RapPages*, *Rap Sheet*, *VIBE*, and numerous other publications. He is also active in the American Movement.

■ **william eric perkins**, a faculty fellow at the University of Pennsylvania and adjunct professor of communications at Hunter College, City University of New York, is the author of numerous articles on popular culture.

■ **tricia rose** is assistant professor of history and Africana studies at New York University and author of *Black Noise: Rap Music and Black Culture in Contemporary America* and of numerous articles on rap music and contemporary popular culture.

■ **robert farris thompson** is professor of African and African American art history and master of Timothy Dwight College at Yale University. He is the author of *Flash of the Spirit: African and Afro-American Art and Philosophy* and numerous other works on the African diaspora.

■ **armond white** is an award-winning pop journalist and author of *The Resistance: Ten Years of Pop Culture That Shook the World*. He has also curated *Change the Style*, *West of MTV*, and *Romanek Fiction* music video programs at the New York Film Festival. White was 1994 chairman of the New York Film Critics Circle and is a member of the National Society of Film Critics. He has written about popular music for numerous publications.